TRANSITION SERVICES IN SPECIAL EDUCATION

A Practical Approach

ROGER PIERANGELO
Long Island University

GEORGE A. GIULIANI
Hofstra University

PEARSON

Boston ■ New York ■ San Francisco ■ Mexico City
Montreal ■ Toronto ■ London ■ Madrid ■ Munich ■ Paris
Hong Kong ■ Singapore ■ Tokyo ■ Cape Town ■ Sydney

Executive Editor: *Virginia Lanigan*
Editorial Assistant: *Robert Champagne*
Executive Marketing Manager: *Amy Cronin Jordan*
Editorial-Production Service: *Omegatype Typography, Inc.*
Manufacturing Buyer: *Andrew Turso*
Composition and Prepress Buyer: *Linda Cox*
Cover Administrator: *Kristina Mose-Libon*
Electronic Composition: *Omegatype Typography, Inc.*

For related titles and support materials, visit our online catalog at
www.ablongman.com

Between the time Website information is gathered and published, some sites may have
closed. Also, the transcription of URLs can result in typographical errors. The publishers
would appreciate notification where these errors occur so that they may be corrected in
subsequent editions.

Library of Congress Cataloging-in-Publication Data

Pierangelo, Roger.
    Transition services in special education : a practical approach / Roger Pierangelo, George
A. Giuliani.
        p. cm.
    Includes bibliographical references and index.
    ISBN 0-205-34569-7 (alk. paper)
    1. Students with disabilities—Services for—United States. 2. Life skills—Study and
teaching (Secondary)—United States. 3. School-to-work transition—United States. 4.
Special education—United States. I. Giuliani, George A. II. Title.

LC4019.P534 2004
371.9—dc21
                                                                    2003048043

Printed in the United States of America
10 9 8 7 6 5 4 3 2 1   08 07 06 05 04 03

This book is dedicated to my wife, Jackie, and my two children, Jacqueline and Scott, who provide me with the love and the purpose for undertaking projects that will hopefully enhance the lives of others. The fact that they are such a loving presence in my life is the reason why my life has been so blessed. I also dedicate this book to my parents, who provided me with the secure and loving foundation from which to grow; my sister Carol, who has always made me smile and laugh; and my brother-in-law George, who has always been a very positive guiding light in my professional journey.

—*Roger Pierangelo*

This book is dedicated to my wife Anita, who has emotionally supported me throughout my entire professional career. Her love and guidance have made writing this book a very rewarding experience. Also, I dedicate this book to my children, Collin and Brittany, who have truly taught me about how wonderful life is as a father. I could not have asked for a more special and loving family. I also dedicate this book to my parents, who provided me with the confidence and love in life to show me that anything is possible with hard work, dedication, and effort.

—*George Giuliani*

CONTENTS

CHAPTER FOUR

Transition Services in the IEP   49

CHAPTER FIVE

Vocational Assessment   77

CHAPTER SIX

Employment Planning   93

CHAPTER SEVEN

Social and Sexual Issues   105

CHAPTER EIGHT

Transportation Education   117

CHAPTER NINE

Recreational and Leisure Options   137

CHAPTER THIRTEEN

Financial and Health Insurance Issues   187

CHAPTER FOURTEEN

Estate Planning   205

There are two common "crises" in the lives of children with disabilities and their families. The first turning point is when they enter the special education system. The second is when they leave it. This book is geared toward helping this population as they prepare to leave the world of special education. In order for students with disabilities to make a successful transition from the context of secondary school to the next phase—either further schooling or work—educators and teachers need to help families and others prepare for issues that should be addressed well in advance. Teachers need to become knowledgeable about resources at the local, state, and federal levels that are available during the transition phase of special education to assist students and families.

In the transition process there are issues that are common to all. However, there is also a great variety of specific personal needs that depend on the personality, interests, and nature and severity of the disability of the individual.

Transition Services in Special Education: A Practical Approach has been developed to help teachers through the difficult and confusing process of transitioning students from school to adulthood. The process of transition and the services that are available have only recently been developed and utilized by school districts. The federal and state laws governing this phase are also new and continually changing. Schools and institutions must now provide transitional IEPs and services for these students and their families. However, many teachers in special education and regular education are unaware of or uninformed about procedures, rights, school responsibilities, organizations, present laws, parents' responsibilities, and available support services within the school, community, and city, state, and federal agencies.

Although many local school districts offer some pamphlets or short manuals on transition, they focus only on local responsibilities and services. The purpose of this textbook is to provide teachers, administrators, parents, and students with a valuable reference source that will include procedures, laws, school responsibilities, organizations, forms, legal requirements, parents' responsibilities, state and government agencies, and anything else that they would ever need to help ease them through this process.

Teachers and parents of students with disabilities face a difficult task trying to maneuver through all the red tape, options, forms, and so on that are involved in the special education process. Nowhere is that procedure more intense and important than in the transition to adulthood. Confronted with a lack of information and responsibilities that they did not have to face for 18–21 years, teachers and parents sometimes become anxious about what will occur when their students with disabilities leave the safety of their local schools. The transition process first begins when the student with a disability reaches 13 or 14 years of age and continues through 21 if necessary. Parents need the assistance of special education teachers who are aware of transition needs for students every step of the way, and teachers need to be ready to help students and parents with the most up-to-date options possible. This text will fill that void.

STATE OF THE FIELD

The last two decades have witnessed significant changes for people with disabilities, in large part due to the disability rights movement, which in many ways paralleled the civil rights movement. People with disabilities used to be thought of as the invisible minority. They were overlooked and "hidden away." They were often considered embarrassments and treated as objects of pity and shame. Now these individuals are taking their place in an inclusive society. Individuals with disabilities are a presence in many forms of public life. Changes in the laws and progress and technology have helped make these advances possible. Despite these gains, the barriers to acceptance remain society's myths, fears, and stereotypes about people with disabilities. Consequently, the efforts for change need to be viewed as an ongoing process. The implementation of transition services is a significant component of this pathway to acceptance.

As most adults know from their own experience, adolescence is probably the most difficult and unsettling period of adjustment in one's development. It is a time filled with physical, emotional, and social upheavals. Until a child leaves secondary school, parents experience a sense of protective control over their child's life. This protective guidance normally involves educational, medical, financial, and social support to assist their child's growth. When the child leaves this setting, there is a personal struggle on the part of parents in letting go. There is always a normal amount of apprehension associated with the child's entrance into the adult world. It is a period when the greater responsibility for adjustment shifts to the child, and the parents' role diminishes.

However, for the child with a disability, this developmental period can be fraught with even greater apprehension for a variety of reasons. Depending on the nature and severity of the disability, parents may play more of an ongoing role in their child's life even after he or she leaves secondary education. Historically parents and their children have spent years actively involved in transitional IEP development and CSE meetings concerning educational and developmental welfare. Depending on the mental competence (the capability to make reasoned decisions) of the child with disabilities, some parents may have to continue to make vital decisions affecting all aspects of their child's life. On the other hand, the parents of such children not affected by diminished mental competence should use all their energies to encourage their child's steps toward independence. Consequently, parents need not shy away thinking that they are being overprotective if they are involved in their child's life after he or she leaves school.

Because planning for the future of a student with disabilities can arouse fear of the unknown, there may be a tendency for parents to delay addressing these issues and instead focus only on the present. However, it is our belief that working through these fears and thinking about the child's best future interest will ensure a meaningful outcome. Regardless of the nature and severity of a disability, parents will be exposed to a transitional process during their child's school years that will provide a foundation for life in the adult world. This transitional process will include many facets of planning for the future and should be fully understood by everyone concerned at every step of the way. Planning for the future is an investment in a child's well-being, and we hope this book helps you understand all the aspects of this important time.

ACKNOWLEDGMENTS

In the course of writing this book, we have encountered many professional and outstanding sites. It has been our experience that those resources contribute enormous amounts of information, support, guidance, and education to parents, students, and professionals in the area of special education. Although we have accessed many worthwhile sites, we would especially like to thank and acknowledge the National Information Center for Children and Youths with Disabilities

(NICHCY) for the use of their research pertaining to transition services in special education. NICHCY's fact sheets on specific disabilities, state resource sheets, parent guides, and resource lists were a tremendous asset in writing this book. Furthermore, the research and writing in NICHCY News Digests 12 through 18 and Transition Summaries 6 through 10 were invaluable resources in the course of writing this text. NICHCY's dedication to and mission of helping children with special needs, as well as parents and educators, are highly evident. We thank NICHCY for the copyright free information provided, and credit them here and in the Reference section of this text.

Dr. Roger Pierangelo extends thanks to the following: Ollie Simmons, for her friendship, loyalty, and great personality, and for her extraordinary friendship with the students and parents of the Herricks Public Schools she has worked with and known for the past 30 years; the late Bill Smyth, a truly gifted and extraordinary man; Helen Firestone, for her influence on his career and tireless support of him; and editor Virginia Lanigan, who believed in this project and made the journey very enjoyable.

Dr. George Giuliani would like to thank the following: my brother and sister, Roger and Claudia; mother-in-law, Ursula Jenkeleit; and grandfather, all of whom have provided me with the encouragement and reinforcement in all of my personal and professional endeavors.

We would like to thank Robert Champagne, our Editorial Assistant, for always helping us attain any materials or information necessary to complete this textbook. We would also like to thank the reviewers of this book: Mary Ellen Bargerhuff, Wright State University; Mark Brown, Eastern Illinois University; Billie L. Friedland, Eastern Illinois University; Carol Kochhar-Bryant, George Washington University; Teresa A. Taber, Purdue University; and Sue Anne Thorson, University of Maine, Farmington.

Dr. Roger Pierangelo has over 30 years of experience as a regular classroom teacher, school psychologist in the Herricks Public School system in New Hyde Park, New York; administrator of special education programs; associate professor in the Department of Special Education and Literacy at Long Island University; licensed clinical psychologist; member of Committees on Special Education; evaluator for the New York State Education Department; director of a private clinic; Diplomate Fellow in Forensic Psychology; and consultant to numerous private and public schools, PTA and SEPTA groups.

Dr. Pierangelo earned his B.S. from St. John's University, M.S. from Queens College, Professional Diploma from Queens College, Ph.D. from Yeshiva University, and Diplomate Fellow in Forensic Psychology from the International College of Professional Psychology.

Dr. Pierangelo is a member of the American Psychological Association, New York State Psychological Association, Nassau County Psychological Association, New York State Union of Teachers, and Phi Delta Kappa.

Dr. Pierangelo is the author of *Survival Kit for the Special Education Teacher* and *The Special Education Teacher's Book of Lists* and coauthor of the *Parent's Complete Guide to Special Education, The Special Educator's Complete Guide to Transition Services, The Special Educator's Guide to 109 Diagnostic Tests*, the coauthor of *The Special Education Yellow Pages, Assessment in Special Education: A Practical Approach*, published by Allyn and Bacon, *The Special Educator's Book of Lists*, coauthor of *Why Your Students Do What They Do—and What to Do When They Do It—Grades K–5, Why Your Students Do What They Do—and What to Do When They Do It—Grades 6–12, Creating Confident Children in the Classroom: The Use of Positive Restructuring*, and *What Every Teacher Should Know about Students with Special Needs*, and *301 Ways to Be a Loving Parent*.

Dr. George A. Giuliani earned his B.A. from the College of the Holy Cross, M.S. from St. John's University, J.D. from City University Law School, and Psy.D. from Rutgers University, The Graduate School of Applied and Professional Psychology, and is a Diplomate Fellow in Forensic Psychology. Dr. Giuliani is also a New York state–licensed psychologist with an extensive private practice focusing on marital counseling, individual psychotherapy, and children with special needs. He is a member of the New York Association of School Psychologists, New York Psychological Association, and the National Association of School Psychologists.

Dr. Giuliani is involved in early intervention for children with special needs and is a consultant for school districts and early childhood agencies. Dr. Giuliani has provided numerous workshops for parents and teachers on a variety of psychological and educational topics.

Dr. Giuliani is also the coauthor of *The Special Educator's Guide to 109 Diagnostic Tests*, and coauthor of *Why Your Students Do What They Do—and What to Do When They Do It—Grades K–5, Why Your Students Do What They Do—and What to Do When They Do It—Grades 6–12, Creating Confident Children in the Classroom: The Use of Positive Restructuring*, and *What Every Teacher Should Know about Students with Special Needs*, and *Assessment in Special Education: A Practical Approach*, published by Allyn and Bacon.

CHAPTER ONE

OVERVIEW OF
TRANSITION SERVICES

OVERVIEW

The last two decades have witnessed significant changes for people with disabilities, in large part because of the disability rights movement, which in many ways paralleled the civil rights movement. People with disabilities used to be thought of as "the invisible minority." They were overlooked and "hidden away." They were embarrassments—treated as objects of pity and shame. Now these individuals are taking their place in an inclusive society. Individuals with disabilities are now a presence in all the media, commercial advertising, and many forms of public life. Changes in the laws and progress and technology have helped make these advances possible. Despite these gains, the barriers to acceptance remain society's myths, fears, and stereotypes about people with disabilites. Consequently, the efforts for change must be viewed as an ongoing process. The implementation of *transition services* is a significant component of this pathway to acceptance.

This chapter will present a broad overview of transition services in special education. After reading this chapter, you should understand the following:

THE WORLD OF TRANSITION SERVICES

DEFINING TRANSITION

INTENT OF TRANSITION SERVICES

SCHOOL TO WORK OPPORTUNITIES ACT OF 1994 (P.L. 103-239)

CLASSIFICATIONS UNDER IDEA

SPECIFIC TRANSITION SERVICES

SELF-DETERMINATION: MAKING THEIR OWN CHOICES AND DECISIONS

THE DEVELOPMENT OF SELF-DETERMINATION SKILLS

IMPORTANCE OF KEEPING RECORDS

TRANSITION PLANNING TIME LINE

THE WORLD OF TRANSITION SERVICES

As most adults know from their own experience, the period known as adolescence is probably the most difficult and unsettling period of adjustment in one's development. It is a time filled with physical, emotional, and social upheavals. Until a child leaves secondary school, a parent experiences a sense of protective control over the child's life. This protective guidance normally involves educational, medical, financial, and social input to assist the child's growth. When the child leaves this setting, a parent undergoes a personal struggle in "letting go." There is always a certain amount of apprehension associated with the child's entrance into the adult world, as the greater responsibility for adjustment now falls on the child and the parent's role diminishes.

For the child with a disability, this developmental period can be fraught with even greater apprehension for a variety of reasons. Depending on the nature and severity of the disability, parents may play more of an ongoing role in their child's life even after he or she leaves secondary education. Historically, parents and the children have spent years actively involved in individual educational plan (IEP) development and meetings, transitional IEP (ITEP) development, and Committee on Special Education (CSE) meetings concerning educational and developmental welfare (see Chapters 2 and 4 for a complete discussion on IEPs, ITEPs, and CSE meetings). Depending on the mental competence (the capability to make reasoned decisions) of the child with disabilities, some parents may have to continue to make vital decisions affecting all aspects of their children's lives; they need not shy away, thinking that they are being overprotective if they are involved in the child's life after the child leaves school. On the other hand, the parents of children not affected by diminished mental competence should use all their energies to encourage the child's steps toward independence.

Because planning for the future of a student with disabilities can arouse fear of the unknown, a parent may tend to delay addressing these issues and instead focus only on the present. It is our belief, however, that working through these fears and thinking about the child's best future interest will ensure a meaningful outcome. Regardless of the nature and severity of a disability, parents will be exposed to a transitional process during the child's school years that will provide a foundation for the adult world. This transitional process will include many facets of planning for the future and should be fully understood by everyone concerned each step of the way. Planning for the future is an investment in a child's well-being, and the purpose of this book is to help you understand all the aspects of this important time.

DEFINING TRANSITION

For many years, educators have been concerned about the lack of success in adult life for students with disabilities. Research has shown that a large proportion of special education students did not go for further training and often did not receive post-school support and services. As these children "aged out" (at age 21 students were no longer eligible for a free and appropriate education including services and support) of the educational system, the families felt that they were being dropped into a void. Although there were many services out in the community, parents were left to their own devices and would find out about such services and supports by chance. Parents and students were confronted with a complex array of service options and resources, each with unique roles, services, funding sources, forms, and eligibility requirements. The need for a collaborative, readily accessible system was obvious.

What seemed to be missing was the bridge between a student's school system and services for post–secondary school life. As a result, the concept of transitional services was developed to provide students who have special needs with a more structured path to adulthood.

Numerous definitions of what constitutes transition exist in the literature. According to Levinson (1998), the term *transition* has been used to refer to different processes within the educational environment (e.g., it has been used to describe movement from preschool to kindergarten and from elementary school to junior high school to high school). He defines transition as the process of facilitating the postschool adjustment of students, particularly students with disabilities. Postschool adjustment is broadly defined to include adjustment to work, leisure, and independent functioning in the community. Furthermore, deFur and Patton (1999, p. 15) state that "transition refers to a change in status from behaving primarily as a student to assuming emergent adult roles." These roles include employment, participating in post-secondary education, maintaining a home, becoming appropriately involved in the community, and experiencing satisfactory personal and social relationships (the DCDT Position on Transition, Halpern, 1994).

Simply put, transition is helping students and families think about their lives after high school and identify long-range goals, designing the high school experience to ensure that students gain the skills and connections they need to achieve these goals, and providing funds and services to local school districts to assist in the transition process.

INTENT OF TRANSITION SERVICES

In 1992, the laws governing the education of children with disabilities took a major step forward with the introduction of transition services. The rules and regulations for IDEA (Individuals with Disabilities Education Act; see Chapter 2 for a detailed explanation of IDEA) released in 1992 define *transition* services as:

> A coordinated set of activities for a student, designed within an outcome-oriented process that promotes movement from school to post school activities, including post secondary education, vocational training, integrated employment (including supported employment), continuing and adult education, adult services, independent living, or community participation.
>
> The coordinated set of activities must be based on the individual student's needs, taking into account the student's preferences and interests including instruction, community experience, the development of employment and other post school adult living objectives and, if appropriate, acquisition of daily living skills and functional evaluation. (IDEA P.L. 101-476, 34 C.F.R. 300.18)

In 1997 IDEA was amended to P.L. 105-17. In Section 1401 (22) of the IDEA reauthorization in 1997, related services were expanded to include speech and language pathology and audiology services, psychological services, physical and occupational therapy, recreation, including therapeutic recreation, social work services, counseling services (including rehabilitation counseling), orientation and mobility services, and medical services, except that such medical services shall be used for diagnostic and evaluation purposes only.

SCHOOL TO WORK OPPORTUNITIES
ACT OF 1994 (P.L. 103-239)

In May 1994, President Clinton signed the School to Work Opportunities Act. This act is the blueprint to empower all individuals, including those with disabilities, to acquire the skills and experiences they need to compete. This landmark bill demonstrates that transition is clearly now a national priority, important to ensure our economic viability as well as offer every young person a chance at a productive life. (See Chapter 2 for a detailed discussion of P.L. 103-239.)

CLASSIFICATIONS UNDER IDEA

The Individuals with Disabilities Education Act (IDEA), Public Law 105-17, is the federal law that protects the right to a free and appropriate education of those in special education. This law will be discussed at length in Chapter 2. IDEA lists separate categories of disabilities under which children may be eligible for special education and related services. Children are eligible to receive special education services and supports if they meet the eligibility requirements for at least one of the disabling conditions listed in P.L. 105-17 and if it is determined that they are in need of special education services (Bigge & Stump, 1999).

According to federal law [IDEA Amendments of 1997, Sec. 602(3)(A)], a child with a disability is a child:

(1) with mental retardation, hearing impairments (including deafness), speech or language impairments, visual impairments, serious emotional disturbance, ortho-pedic impairments, autism, traumatic brain injury, other health impairments, or specific learning disability; and

(2) who, by reason thereof, needs special education and related services.

The definitions of disabling conditions under federal law [34 C.F.R. 300.7(a) (1–13) pp. 55069–55070, October 1997] are listed next (cited in Bigge & Stump, 1999, p. 8). Each of these will be discussed in detail in Chapter 3:

Autism. A developmental disability significantly affecting verbal and nonver-bal communication and social interaction, generally evident before age 3 that adversely affects a child's educational performance. Other characteristics often associated with autism are engagement in repetitive activities and stereotyped movements, resistance to environmental change or change in daily routines, and unusual responses to sensory experiences. The term does not apply if a child's educational performance is adversely affected because the child has an emotional disturbance.

Deaf-blindness. Concomitant hearing and visual impairments, the combi-nation of which causes such severe communication and other developmental and educational problems that they cannot be accommodated in special edu-cation programs solely for children with deafness or children with blindness.

Deafness. A hearing impairment that is so severe that the child's processing linguistic information through hearing is impaired, with or without amplifi-cation, that adversely affects a child's educational performance.

Emotional disturbance. A condition exhibiting one or more of the follow-ing characteristics over a long period of time and to a marked degree that ad-versely affects a child's educational performance: (A) An inability to learn that cannot be explained by intellectual, sensory or health factors. (B) An in-ability to build or maintain satisfactory interpersonal relationships with peers and teachers. (C) Inappropriate types of behaviors or feelings under normal circumstances. (D) A general pervasive mood of unhappiness or depression. (E) A tendency to develop physical symptoms or fears associated with per-sonal or school problems. (ii) The term includes schizophrenia. The term does not apply to children who are socially maladjusted, unless it is deter-mined that they have an emotional disturbance.

Hearing impairment. An impairment in hearing, whether permanent or fluctuating, that adversely affects a child's performance but that is not included under the definition of deafness in this section.

Mental retardation. Significantly sub-average general intellectual function-ing existing concurrently with deficits in adaptive behavior and manifested during the developmental period that adversely affects a child's performance.

Multiple disabilities. Concomitant impairments (such as mental retardation-blindness, mental retardation-orthopedic impairment, etc.) the combination of which causes such severe educational problems that the problems cannot be accommodated in special education programs solely for one of the impair-ments. The term does not include deaf-blindness.

Orthopedic impairment. A severe orthopedic impairment that adversely affects a child's educational performance. The term includes impairments caused by congenital anomaly (e.g., club foot, absence of some member, etc.), impairments caused by disease (e.g., poliomyelitis, bone tuberculosis, etc.), and impairments from other causes (e.g., cerebral palsy, amputations, and fractures or burns that cause contractures).

Other health impairment. Having limited strength, vitality or alertness due to chronic or acute health problems such as a heart condition, tuberculosis, rheumatic fever, nephritis, asthma, sickle cell anemia, hemophilia, epilepsy, lead poisoning, leukemia, or diabetes, which adversely affect a child's educational performance.

Specific learning disability. A disorder in one or more of the basic psychological processes involved in understanding or in using language, spoken or written, which may manifest itself in an imperfect ability to listen, think, speak, read, write, spell, or do mathematical calculations, also including such conditions as perceptual disabilities, brain injury, minimal brain dysfunction, dyslexia, and developmental aphasia. The term does not include learning problems that are primarily due to the result of visual, hearing, or motor disabilities, mental retardation, of emotional disturbance, or of environmental, cultural or economic disadvantage.

Speech or language impairment. A communication disorder such as stuttering, impaired articulation, a language impairment or a voice impairment that adversely affects a child's educational performance.

Traumatic brain injury. An acquired injury to the brain caused by an external physical force, resulting in total or partial functional disability or psychosocial impairment or both, and that adversely affects a child's educational performance. The term applies to open or closed head injuries resulting in impairments in one or more areas, such as cognition; language; memory; attention; reasoning; abstract thinking; judgment; problem solving; sensory, perceptual, and motor abilities; psychosocial behavior; physical functions; information processing; and speech. The term does not apply to brain injuries that are congenital or degenerative or to brain injuries induced by birth trauma.

Visual impairment. An impairment in vision that, even with correction, adversely affects a child's educational performance. The term includes both partial and sight blindness.

SPECIFIC TRANSITION SERVICES

Transition services are aimed at providing students and their families with the practical and experiential skills and knowledge that will assist in a successful transition to adult life. Although transition services are provided in each of the following areas, it is important to understand that not every student with disabilities will need to receive all of these services. The available services included in the transition process are:

- instruction
- employment
- postschool activities
- community experiences
- activities of daily living
- functional vocational evaluations

More specifically, the intent of transition services is to explore and plan a variety of areas that will allow the student with disabilities to construct a useful and practical bridge to the adult world. This planning is a process that can begin by age 14 or younger (if necessary). The suggested areas to be considered when beginning transition planning follow:

1. **Occupational/vocational education.** Participation in occupational education programs can provide important experiences and specific vocational training. Specific areas include the following:
   - vocational assessment and training
   - academic skills
   - individualized curriculum to meet transition needs

2. **Postsecondary/continuing education.** Starting in junior high school, the student's IEP should include educational goals that prepare the student for further education or vocational training. Specific areas include the following:
   - application assistance
   - college fairs
   - financial aid
   - investigation of Plan for Achieving Self-Support (PASS) to save for postsecondary expenses
   - study skills
   - transportation
   - discussion of academic supports
   - assistance with contacting on-campus supports

3. **Legal/advocacy.** Advocacy is speaking up for oneself and working with others to make systems work for the individual. People with disabilities have the right to an opportunity for working, living, and socializing in the community. Specific areas include the following:
   - learning to advocate for oneself
   - understanding accommodations
   - understanding one's rights
   - program accessibility
   - participation in team planning

4. **Transportation.** The ability to use transportation options is crucial for independence. Inability to use transportation or the lack of accessible transportation can seriously limit social and work opportunities. Specific areas include the following:
   - mobility training
   - transportation to work or school
   - investigation of PASS plan to save for transportation
   - use of public transportation
   - driver evaluation/training

5. **Financial/income.** Planning in advance is the best way to avoid difficulty later. The school district may be able to provide information on how to get assistance pertaining to financial matters. Specific areas include the following:
   - money management/budgeting
   - Supplemental Security Income (SSI)
   - Social Security Disability Income (SSDI)
   - work incentives
   - wills, trusts, and estates

6. **Personal independence/residential.** Independence is about self-determination. An individual with disabilities can be independent while living with

family or friends. He or she may even choose to live alone and have support staff to assist him or her. Specific areas include the following:

- personal care
- meal preparation
- household chores
- sexuality
- living options
- shopping
- time management
- banking skills
- telephone skills
- decision-making skills

7. **Medical/health.** Maintaining good health allows one to focus on life activities and goals that have been set. Specific areas include the following:
- medication
- ongoing medical care
- fitness and nutrition
- insurance
- Medicaid/Medicare
- management of personal assistance

8. **Employment.** It is important for one to consider all the work experience options when selecting a career. Specific areas include the following:
- competitive employment
- enclave
- job-seeking skills
- job coach
- job-related social skills
- supported employment
- sheltered work
- employer support
- volunteering

9. **Recreation/leisure.** Everyone needs a break from work and school. Having fun is an important way to get mental and physical exercise. It is also a good way to meet people and to make new friends. Specific areas include the following:
- community recreation activities
- leisure time activities
- special interest areas
- hobbies

10. **Other support needs.** An individual with disabilities may need to develop a resource list of supports that will help him or her make the transition to the adult world. Specific areas include the following:
- support groups
- psychological services
- social work services
- respite
- social peer groups
- case management
- assistive technology
- speech and language pathology
- audiology services
- rehabilitation counseling
- physical and occupational therapy
- orientation and mobility services

Some students with severe disabilities will need more extensive intervention for transition to adult life. Students with less involved disabilities may require only limited services in one or two of the preceding areas, with specific attention given to how the disability affects a particular aspect of transition.

Transition service regulations have to do with communication, collaboration, and coordination of plans, programs, services, supports, and resources. This communication, collaboration, and coordination must occur among students, families, schools, agencies, and communities. Together, they make decisions as well as share responsibilities and resources. All this is based on what is needed by and in the best interest of each student.

SELF-DETERMINATION: MAKING THEIR OWN CHOICES AND DECISIONS

One of the most significant concepts to emerge in the last few decades is the awareness of the importance of self-determination in the life of an individual with a disability. For too long, professionals made decisions for people with disabilities with little input from the individuals or parents. Although these decisions were motivated by good intentions, they may have overlooked the desires, hopes, and aspirations that remained hidden within the person with disabilities. As our society has become more sensitive to the needs and rights of people with disabilities, we have moved to the concept of self-determination as a crucial element in the design of a life plan.

Self-determination is a person's ability to control his or her own destiny. A crucial part of the concept of self-determination involves the combination of attitudes and abilities that will lead children or individuals to set goals for themselves and to take the initiative to reach these goals. To do this individuals must be in charge, which is not necessarily the same thing as self-sufficiency or independence, make their own choices, learn to solve problems effectively, take control and responsibility for their lives, and learn to experience and cope with the consequences of making decisions on their own.

Martin and Marshall (1995, cited in Wehmeyer et al., 1998) summarize the evolving definition of self-determination in the special education literature as describing individuals who:

> . . . know how to choose—they know what they want and how to get it. From an awareness of personal needs, self-determined individuals choose goals and then doggedly pursue them. This involves asserting an individual's presence, making his or her needs known, evaluating progress toward meeting goals, adjusting performance and creating unique approaches to solve problems. (p. 147)

THE DEVELOPMENT OF SELF-DETERMINATION SKILLS

The development of self-determination skills is a process that begins in childhood and continues throughout one's life. It must be fully understood by parents when a child is still in school. This process begins early, so that the child learns how to grow up as a self-advocate and not be afraid to voice his or her needs, concerns, and opinions.

Parents of children with adequate mental competence sometimes "protect" them by making all their decisions. Parents interested in developing self-determination skills for their children must help them learn to:

- set goals
- evaluate options
- make choices
- work to achieve goals
- practice self-determination experiences by offering opportunities for decision making, socialization, leisure activities, and more
- explore employment and housing options
- explore community recreation programs in their community by utilizing their own network of relatives and friends, as well as formal service systems
- take an active role in the decisions that will determine their future—even if it means allowing them to make mistakes.

IMPORTANCE OF KEEPING RECORDS

During the transition process, it is extremely important that parents and students develop a recordkeeping system. This system should encompass three specific categories: official documents (as well as medical and psychological reports), financial documents, and a chronicle of information.

The first category, official documents, involves maintaining a file of a student's written official documents. Examples include all high school transcripts, evaluation test results, medical records, letters of recommendation, job coach reports, on-the-job training reports, teacher comments, schedules, therapist reports, IEPs, transitional IEPs, and end-of-the-year reports.

The second category, financial documents, includes sources of income and assets (pension funds, interest income, etc.), Social Security and Medicare information, investment income, insurance information with policy numbers, bank accounts, location of safe deposit boxes, copies of recent income tax returns, liabilities (what is owed to whom and when payments are due), credit card and charge account names and numbers, property taxes, and location of personal items. Refer to the chapters on financial concerns, insurance issues, and estate planning for additional information on this important subject.

The third category involves an ongoing chronicle of information gathered as the result of phone conversations with school or agency officials, summary of meeting, copies of letters written by parents, copies of letters received, and brochures handed out by organizations.

TRANSITION PLANNING TIME LINE

Any transition process must take into account all of the necessary procedures and issues that will facilitate the student's transition to adulthood. Although this may vary from state to state, a practical time line will assist you in helping both the student and the parents be as prepared as possible. You should help families consider the following checklist of transition activities when preparing transition plans with the IEP team. The student's skills and interests will determine which items on the checklist are relevant and whether these transition issues should be addressed at IEP transition meetings. The checklist can also help identify who should be part of the IEP transition team. Responsibility for carrying out the specific transition activities should be determined at the IEP transition meetings.

The following chapters of the text will take you through this transition time line process in an organized manner. All of the major transition concepts will be discussed in this text so refer to the specific chapter to gain further information.

The following list is provided to serve as an optional planning tool and only as a guideline:

FOUR TO FIVE YEARS BEFORE LEAVING THE SCHOOL DISTRICT

- Introduce and discuss transition services with parents and student (Chapter 4).
- Notify parents that transition services will be incorporated into the IEP, beginning at age 15 (Chapter 4).
- Initiate vocational assessment (Chapter 5).
- Develop and implement strategies to increase responsibilities and independence at home (Chapter 1).
- Identify personal learning styles and the necessary accommodations if the child is to be a successful learner and worker (Chapter 5).
- Identify career interests and skills, complete interest and career inventories, and identify additional education or training requirements (Chapters 5 and 6).
- Explore options for postsecondary education and admission criteria (Chapter 12).
- Consider the need for residential opportunities, including completing applications, as appropriate (Chapter 11).
- Identify interests and options for future living arrangements, including supports (Chapter 11).
- Learn to help the child communicate his or her interests, preferences, and needs effectively (Chapters 1 and 7).
- Teach the student how to explain his or her disability and the necessary accommodations (Chapter 7).
- Learn and practice informed decision-making skills (Chapter 7).
- Investigate assistive technology tools that can increase community involvement and employment opportunities (Chapter 10).
- Broaden the child's experiences with community activities and help him or her form friendships (Chapters 7).
- Pursue and use transportation options (Chapter 8).
- Investigate money management and identify necessary skills (Chapter 13).
- Acquire identification card and the ability to communicate personal information (Chapter 7).
- Identify and begin learning skills necessary for independent living (Chapters 7, 11, and 14).
- Learn and practice personal health care (Chapters 7 and 14).

TWO TO THREE YEARS BEFORE LEAVING THE SCHOOL DISTRICT

- Identify community support services and programs (vocational rehabilitation, county services, centers for independent living, etc.) (Chapters 5–14).
- Invite adult service providers, peers, and others to the IEP transition meeting (Chapter 4).
- Begin exploring recreation/community leisure activities—Chapter 9).
- Match career interests and skills with vocational course work and community work experiences (Chapters 5 and 6).
- Involve state vocational rehabilitation agencies, as appropriate within two years of school exit (Chapters 5 and 6).
- Gather more information on postsecondary programs and the support services offered and make arrangements for accommodations to take college entrance exams (Chapter 12).
- Assure that copies of work-related documents are available (Chapter 6).
  - Social Security card
  - Birth certificate
  - Working papers (if appropriate)

- Identify health care providers and become informed about sexuality and family planning issues (Chapters 7 and 13).
- Consider summer employment or volunteer experience (Chapters 9).
- Determine the need for financial support (Supplemental Security Income, state financial supplemental programs, Medicare) (Chapters 13 and 14).
- Learn and practice appropriate interpersonal, communication, and social skills for different settings (employment, school, recreation, with peers, etc.) (Chapter 7).
- Explore legal status with regard to decision making prior to age of majority—wills, guardianship, special needs trust (Chapters 2 and 14).
- Practice independent living skills—budgeting, shopping, cooking, and housekeeping (Chapters 5–14).
- Identify needed personal assistance or enabling supports and, if appropriate, learn to direct and manage these services (Chapters 5–14).

ONE YEAR BEFORE LEAVING THE SCHOOL DISTRICT (FOR THE CHILD)
- Apply for financial support programs (Supplemental Security Income, vocational rehabilitation, and personal assistant services) (Chapters 13 and 14).
- Identify the post–secondary school plan and arrange for accommodations (Chapter 12).
- Practice effective communication by developing interview skills, asking for help, and identifying necessary accommodations at postsecondary and work environments (Chapter 12).
- Obtain driver's training and license (Chapter 8).
- Develop transportation/mobility strategies
  - Independent travel skills training (Chapter 8).
  - Public or paratransit transportation (Chapter 8).
  - Needs for travel attendant (Chapter 8).
- Specify desired job and obtain paid employment with supports as needed (Chapters 5 and 6).
- Investigate SSDI/SSI/Medicaid programs (Chapter 13).
- Consider and seek guardianship or emancipation (Chapters 11 and 14).
- Develop and update employment plans (Chapters 5 and 6).
- Investigate and apply for postschool opportunities (further educational vocational training, college, military, etc.) (Chapter 12).
- Develop a résumé (Chapter 6).
- Take responsibility for arriving on time to work, appointments, and social activities (Chapters 6 and 9).
- Assume responsibility for health care needs (making appointments, filling and taking prescriptions, etc.) (Chapters 7 and 14).
- Register to vote (Chapter 7).
- Male students register for the draft (no exceptions) (Chapter 7).
- Review health insurance coverage. Inform insurance company of child's disability and investigate rider of continued eligibility (Chapter 13).

PRIOR TO GRADUATION OR AGING OUT OF SCHOOL
- Complete transition to employment, further education or training, and community living, affirming that arrangements are in place for the following:
  - Postsecondary/continuing education (Chapter 12).
  - Employment (Chapters 5 and 6).
  - Legal/advocacy (Chapters 2 and 14).
  - Personal independence/residential (Chapters 11 and 14).
  - Recreation/leisure (Chapter 9).
  - Medical/health (Chapter 13).

- Counseling (Chapters 7 and 13).
- Financial/income (Chapters 13 and 14).
- Transportation/independent travel skills (Chapter 8).

CONCLUSION

The chapters that follow alert parents, students, and professionals to the variety of important issues that they will face in the coming years. During this process, it is important to remain proactive, informed, involved, and hopeful.

When what you need doesn't exist, form bonds and join groups with others in the same situation. It has only been through personal struggles and efforts of parents, professionals, and individuals with disabilities that laws and attitudes have changed. Initially, the collaborative efforts of parents and professionals best meet the needs of young children with disabilities. As these children enter the adult world, however, they should become partners in this collaborative team to promote their own well-being.

CHAPTER TWO

LEGAL ISSUES IN THE EDUCATION OF CHILDREN AND YOUTH WITH SPECIAL NEEDS

OVERVIEW

If students are to mature into independent, productive adults and become increasingly responsible for their actions and accomplishments, they need to acquire the skills that are of value in the adult world. The Individuals with Disabilities Education Act (IDEA) acknowledges this and contains provisions mandating student involvement and shared decision making.

Since 1990, transition services have been a requirement of law for students who are age 16 or younger if deemed appropriate by the IEP team. The services are planned at the IEP meeting to which students must be invited. Thus, the 1990 IDEA legislation provided students with an enormous new opportunity to be involved in planning their own education, to look into the future, to voice their strengths, needs, and interests, to be heard, to share in making decisions that so directly affect them.

Now, under the latest reauthorization of the Individuals with Disabilities Education Act in 1997 (IDEA '97), this involvement has been expanded. In addition to transition services beginning at age 16, a statement of transition service needs is required at age 14. At this time and updated annually thereafter, the IEP team looks at the child's courses of study (such as advanced placement courses or vocational education programs) and determines whether those courses of study are leading the student to where the student needs to be at graduation. What other courses might be indicated, given the student's goals for life after secondary school? Beginning to plan at age 14, with an eye to necessary course work, is expected to help students plan and prepare educationally. Then, at age 16 or younger if appropriate, transition services are delivered in a wide range of areas.

Understanding legal issues in special education is critical as a future educator. Legislation plays a very important role in transition services. In order to fully understand transition services in special education, you must have a strong working knowledge of the various federal laws that are relevant to it. This chapter will discuss legal issues in the education of children and youth with special needs. After reading this chapter, you should understand the following:

HISTORY OF LEGAL ISSUES IN THE EDUCATION OF CHILDREN AND YOUTH WITH SPECIAL NEEDS

HOW FEDERAL LAWS AND REGULATIONS ARE DETERMINED

EARLY FEDERAL EDUCATION LAWS AND COURT CASES

OTHER FEDERAL LAWS AFFECTING CHILDREN AND YOUTH WITH DISABILITIES

STATE LAWS RELATING TO CHILDREN AND YOUTH WITH DISABILITIES

HISTORY OF LEGAL ISSUES IN THE EDUCATION
OF CHILDREN AND YOUTH WITH SPECIAL NEEDS

The first federal laws designed to assist individuals with disabilities date back to the early days of the nation. In 1798, the Fifth Congress passed the first federal law concerned with the care of persons with disabilities (Braddock, 1987). This law authorized a Marine Hospital Service to provide medical services to sick and disabled seamen. By 1912, this service became known as the Public Health Service. However, prior to World War II, there were relatively few federal laws authorizing special benefits for persons with disabilities. Those that did exist were intended to address the needs of war veterans with service-connected disabilities. This meant that, for most of our nation's history, schools were allowed to exclude—and often did exclude—certain children, especially those with disabilities. Since the 1960s, however, there has been a virtual avalanche of federal legislation that relates directly or indirectly to individuals with disabilities, particularly children and youth. The numerous court decisions rendered, and state and federal laws passed since the 1960s, now protect the rights of those with disabilities and guarantee that they receive a free and appropriate, publicly supported education.

There have been many heroes and heroines in this effort, most certainly the families of children with disabilities. The positive changes in the laws and the attitudes of the public toward those with disabilities would not have occurred without the active and persistent involvement of many dedicated people over the years. Today, people with disabilities have accomplished more than ever dreamed possible, due to increases in the number and quality of programs, better trained professionals, continuous research in education, information dissemination and technical assistance, and the collaboration between parents and professionals to obtain the best education possible for the nation's children and youth with disabilities.

As evidence of these changes, in 1994, over 5 million children and youth with disabilities received special education and related services under the Individuals with Disabilities Education Act (IDEA) (U.S. Department of Education, 1995). Federal efforts have also extended this right to the youngest of children—infants and toddlers. A survey conducted by Louis Harris and Associates (1989) for the International Center for the Disabled suggests that more children with disabilities appear to be receiving a far better education today than they were 10 to 12 years ago, and that parents are reasonably satisfied with their children's education. However, many families and professionals have little knowledge about the laws. According to this report, 61 percent of the parents surveyed knew little or nothing about their rights under both the Education of the Handicapped Act (EHA), P.L. 94-142 (the predecessor to the IDEA), and Section 504 of the Rehabilitation Act of 1973, P.L. 93-112. Even a greater number of these parents—85 percent—were not aware of the vocational education law, the Carl D. Perkins Vocational Education Act of 1984, P.L. 98-524. Finally, a majority of both principals and teachers surveyed felt they had not had adequate training in special education.

Awareness of the laws that ensure equal opportunities to individuals with disabilities is vitally important for the following reasons:

- Knowledge of the language and intention of the laws empowers families to advocate more effectively for their children and strengthens their ability to participate fully as partners in their children's educational teams.
- As independence and self-sufficiency for individuals become increasingly important outcomes of special education, it is important that individuals with disabilities understand the laws and their implications for making decisions.

- Knowledge of the laws can assist professionals in understanding the entire service delivery system, ensure protection of civil rights, and improve collaboration with other agencies and families.
- Knowledge of the laws can help parents and professionals work together on behalf of children to make the equal education opportunity guaranteed by law a reality.

HOW FEDERAL LAWS AND REGULATIONS ARE DETERMINED

It is helpful to know how laws are named or referred to in understanding legal issues. Whenever an act is passed by Congress and signed into law by the president, it is given a number, such as P.L. 94-142. *P.L.* stands for Public Law. The first set of numbers means the session of Congress during which the law was passed. For example, the 94 means the 94th session of the U.S. Congress. The second set of numbers identifies what number the law was in the sequence of passage and enactment during that session. Thus, the 142 means that this was the 142nd law that Congress passed and the president signed during the 94th session of Congress.

It is also important to understand that federal laws are often changed, or amended, regularly. Public Law 94-142, the Education for All Handicapped Children Act, has had several amendments since its passage in 1975. Therefore, it is important to keep up to date on these changes, as they often affect the delivery of special education, related services, and other programs in your state.

Laws passed by Congress provide a general framework of policy related to a particular issue. Once a law is passed, Congress delegates the task of developing detailed regulations to guide the law's implementation to an administrative agency within the executive branch. Federal regulations are detailed in the *Code of Federal Regulations* (C.F.R.). The C.F.R. interprets the law, discusses each point of a law, and further explains it. Copies of most federal regulations are available in the public library. The C.F.R. is helpful in understanding the laws. State agencies must comply with federal laws and regulations. At the federal level, special education is an area in which elaborate sets of regulations exist. The regulations for the Individuals with Disabilities Education Act, for example, spell out the procedures and programming that must be provided to children and youth with disabilities in order for states to receive federal funds. States may go beyond what is required in the regulations. For example, some states have broader definitions of which children are entitled to special education and, thus, may include gifted children in their special education programming.

EARLY FEDERAL EDUCATION LAWS AND COURT CASES

Looking back over the last 25 years, it is clear that federal protection and guarantees of the educational rights of individuals with disabilities have been an evolving story. Direct federal support for the education of children with disabilities has its roots in the Elementary and Secondary Education Act of 1965 (ESEA), P.L. 89-10. The purpose of this law was to strengthen and improve educational quality and opportunity in the nation's elementary and secondary schools (DeStefano & Snauwaert, 1989). Eight months later, P.L. 89-10 was amended with the enactment of P.L. 89-313. Public Law 89-313, the Elementary and Secondary Education Act Amendments of 1965, authorized the first federal grant program specifically targeted for children and youth with disabilities. This law authorized grants to state agencies to educate children with disabilities in state-operated or state-supported schools and institutions.

In 1966, P.L. 89-750, the Elementary and Secondary Education Act Amendments of 1966, established the first federal grant program for the education of children with disabilities at the local school level rather than state-operated schools and institutions. This section of the law became known as Title VI. In addition, P.L. 89-750 established the Bureau of Education for the Handicapped (BEH) to administer all Office of Education programs for children and youth with disabilities. BEH was charged with helping states to implement and monitor programs; support demonstration programs; conduct research and evaluate federally funded programs; provide financial support for training special educators, other teachers, support personnel, and parents; and support research, training, production, and distribution of educational media. Public Law 89-750 also established the National Advisory Council (NAC), which today is called the National Council on Disability.

In 1968, P.L. 90-247, the Elementary and Secondary Education Act Amendments of 1968, became the final special education legislation enacted at the federal level in the 1960s. Public Law 90-247 established a set of programs that supplemented and supported the expansion and improvement of special education services. These programs later become known as "discretionary." These programs included funding for regional resource centers, centers and services for children with deaf-blindness, the expansion of instructional media programs, continued research in special education, and funds to establish a center to help improve the recruitment of education personnel and to disseminate information concerning education opportunities for children and youth with disabilities.

Two years later, Congress passed the Elementary and Secondary Education Amendments of 1970, P.L. 91-230. Public Law 91-230 consolidated into one act a number of previously separate federal grant programs related to the education of children with disabilities, including Title VI of ESEA under P.L. 89-750. This new authorization, which became known as Part B, was titled the Education of the Handicapped Act (EHA) and was the precursor to the 1975 act that would significantly expand the educational rights of children and youth with disabilities.

By the mid-1970s, several right-to-education cases were brought to court in states all over the country. Two precedent-setting cases involving the education of children with disabilities took place in Pennsylvania and the District of Columbia. In Pennsylvania, the Pennsylvania Association for Retarded Citizens (PARC) and 13 school-aged children with mental retardation brought a class action suit against the Commonwealth of Pennsylvania for its alleged failure to provide all of its school-aged children with mental retardation with a publicly supported education (*Pennsylvania Association for Retarded Citizens v. Commonwealth of Pennsylvania,* 1972). The *PARC* suit was resolved by a consent agreement that specified that the state could not apply any law that would postpone, end, or deny children with mental retardation access to a publicly supported education. Furthermore, the agreement required the state to identify all school-aged children with mental retardation who were excluded from the public schools and to place them in a "free public program of education and training appropriate to their capacity." Finally, the agreement claimed that it was highly desirable to educate these children in programs most like those for nondisabled children.

In 1972, the parents and guardians of seven District of Columbia children brought a class action suit against the District of Columbia Board of Education on behalf of all out-of-school children with disabilities (*Mills v. Board of Education,* 1972). Unlike *PARC, Mills* was resolved by a judgment against the district school board. The result was a court order that the District of Columbia must provide all children with disabilities, regardless of the severity of their disabilities, with a publicly supported education.

In 1974, P.L. 93-380, the Education Amendments of 1974, was passed. These amendments contained a variety of changes to existing federal education programs of the ESEA. One of the most important amendments was to Title VI of the ESEA, which was renamed as the Education of the Handicapped Act Amendments of 1974. This law required states to establish a timetable toward achieving full educational opportunity for all children with disabilities. The act provided procedural safeguards for use in the identification, evaluation, and placement of children with disabilities; mandated that such children be integrated into regular classes when possible; and required assurances that testing and evaluation materials be selected and administered on a nondiscriminatory basis. Even with P.L. 94-142 on the horizon, P.L. 93-380 was important because it began the focus, through a major federal program to the states, on fully educating all children with disabilities. Public Law 94-142, the Education for All Handicapped Children Act, was passed by Congress and signed into law by President Ford in 1975.

The rights of individuals with disabilities were significantly strengthened with the passage of three federal laws and their periodic amendments. These laws were P.L. 93-112, the Rehabilitation Act of 1973, P.L. 94-142, the Education of All Handicapped Children Act of 1975, and P.L. 98-524, the Carl Perkins Vocational Education Act of 1984.

These three laws, and their subsequent amendments, form the core of current protection against discrimination and current guarantees of equal educational opportunity that individuals with disabilities have in our nation. Because these laws are so important to ensuring the rights of those with disabilities, you should become familiar with both the laws and their regulations. Each law is described in some detail next.

P.L. 93-112: The Rehabilitation Act of 1973

The Rehabilitation Act of 1973 is critical because it addresses discrimination against persons with disabilities. The law has different sections, which refer to different areas of discrimination, as follows:

Section 501: Employment of Individuals with Disabilities

Section 502: Architectural and Transportation Barriers Compliance

Section 503: Employment under Federal Contracts

Section 504: Non-Discrimination in Programs or Activities Receiving Federal Financial Assistance

Section 505: Non-Discrimination in Programs or Activities Conducted by Federal Agencies (In 1978, this provision was added by Public Law 95-602.)

To this day, Section 504 provides qualified individuals with disabilities with basic civil rights protection in programs and activities that receive federal financial assistance. The law states that "no otherwise qualified disabled individual in the United States . . . shall, solely by reason of a disability, be excluded from the participation in, be denied the benefits of, or be subjected to discrimination under any program or activity receiving federal financial assistance."

To be eligible for the protections under Section 504, an individual must meet the definition of a person with a disability. This definition is "any person who (i) has a physical or mental impairment which substantially limits one or more of such person's major life activities, (ii) has a record of such an impairment, or (iii) is regarded as having such an impairment." Major life activities include self-care, performing manual tasks, seeing, hearing, speaking, breathing, learning, and walking. Section 504 covers only those persons with a disability who would otherwise be qualified to participate and benefit from the programs or other activities receiving federal financial assistance.

The U.S. Department of Education's regulation implementing Section 504 applies to preschool, elementary, secondary, postsecondary, vocational, and other programs and activities that receive or benefit from federal financial assistance. This regulation is found at 34 *Code of Federal Regulations* (C.F.R.), Part 104. The U.S. Department of Education's Section 504 regulation prohibits discrimination against children and youth with disabilities in educational institutions receiving federal funds. Agencies that persist in acts of discrimination face the loss of federal funds.

Public Law 93-112 has been amended several times. In 1983, P.L. 98-221, the Rehabilitation Act Amendments of 1983, authorized several demonstration projects regarding the transition of youth with disabilities from school to work. In 1986, P.L. 99-506, the Rehabilitation Act Amendments of 1986, provided for programs in supported employment services for individuals with disabilities. The two most recent amendments are P.L. 102-569, the Rehabilitation Act Amendments of 1992, and P.L. 103-73, the Rehabilitation Act Amendments of 1993.

In order to receive technical assistance regarding the requirements of the U.S. Department of Education's Section 504 regulation, contact the U.S. Department of Education's Office for Civil Rights (OCR). OCR consists of administrative offices that are located at the U.S. Department of Education's headquarters in Washington, D.C., and 10 regional offices around the country.

P.L. 94-142: The Education for All Handicapped Children Act of 1975

This law was passed in 1975 and went into effect in October 1977 when the regulations were finalized. This law grew out of and strengthened earlier acts of a similar name, including P.L. 91-230 and P.L. 93-380. Ballard, Ramirez, and Zantal-Weiner (1987) and DeStefano and Snauwaert (1989) summarize the major purposes of P.L. 94-142 as:

- To guarantee that a "free and appropriate education," including special education and related service programming, is available to all children and youth with disabilities who require it.
- To ensure that the rights of children and youth with disabilities and their parents or guardians are protected (e.g., fairness, appropriateness, and due process in decision making about providing special education and related services to children and youth with disabilities).
- To assess and ensure the effectiveness of special education at all levels of government.
- To financially assist the efforts of state and local governments in providing full educational opportunities to all children and youth with disabilities through the use of federal funds.

In 1983, through the Education of the Handicapped Act Amendments of 1983 (P.L. 98-199), Congress amended, or changed, the law to expand incentives for preschool special education programs, early intervention, and transition programs. All programs under EHA became the responsibility of the Office of Special Education Programs (OSEP), which by this time had replaced the Bureau of Education for the Handicapped (BEH).

In 1986, EHA was again amended through P.L. 99-457, the Education of the Handicapped Act Amendments of 1986. One of the important outcomes of these amendments was that the age of eligibility for special education and related services for all children with disabilities was lowered to age 3, a change to be implemented by school year 1991–1992. The law also established the Handicapped Infants and Toddlers Program (Part H). As specified by law, this program is directed to the needs of children, from birth to their third birthday, who need early intervention services. In addition, under this program the infant or toddler's family may receive services that are needed to help them assist in the development of their child. State definitions of eligibility under this program vary.

P.L. 101-476: Individuals with Disabilities Education Act (IDEA)

In 1990, Congress passed the Education of the Handicapped Act Amendments of 1990 (P.L. 101-476). The new amendments resulted in some significant changes. For example, the name of the law, the Education of the Handicapped Act (EHA), was changed to the Individuals with Disabilities Education Act (IDEA). Many of the discretionary programs authorized under the law were expanded. Some new discretionary programs, including special programs on transition, a new program to improve services for children and youth with serious emotional disturbance, and a research and information dissemination program on attention deficit disorder, were created. In addition, the law added transition services and assistive technology services as new definitions of special education services that must be included in a child's or youth's IEP. Also, rehabilitation counseling and social work services were included as related services under the law. Finally, the services and rights under this law were expanded to more fully include children with autism and traumatic brain injury.

IDEA has been amended since the amendment passed in 1990. The following amendment, P.L. 102-119, primarily addressed the Part H program, now known as the Early Intervention Program for Infants and Toddlers with Disabilities.

IDEA makes it possible for states and localities to receive federal funds to assist in the education of infants, toddlers, preschoolers, children, and youth with disabilities. Basically, in order to remain eligible for federal funds under the law, states must ensure that:

- All children and youth with disabilities, regardless of the severity of their disability, will receive a free and appropriate public education (FAPE) at public expense.
- Education of children and youth with disabilities will be based on a complete and individual evaluation and assessment of the specific, unique needs of each child.
- An individualized education plan (IEP) or an individualized family services plan (IFSP) will be drawn up for every child or youth found eligible for special education or early intervention services, stating precisely what kinds of special education and related services or the types of early intervention services each infant, toddler, preschooler, child, or youth will receive.
- To the maximum extent appropriate, all children and youth with disabilities will be educated in the regular education environment.
- Children and youth receiving special education have the right to receive the related services necessary to benefit from special education instruction. Related services include "transportation and such developmental, corrective, and other supportive services as are required to assist a child with a disability to benefit from special education, and includes speech pathology and audiology,

psychological services, physical and occupational therapy, recreation, including therapeutic recreation, early identification and assessment of disabilities in children, counseling services, including rehabilitation counseling, and medical services for diagnostic or evaluation purposes. The term also includes school health services, social work services in schools, and parent counseling and training" (C.F.R.: Title 34; Education; Part 300.16, 1993).

- Parents have the right to participate in every decision related to the identification, evaluation, and placement of their child or youth with a disability.
- Parents must give consent for any initial evaluation, assessment, or placement; be notified of any change in placement that may occur; be included, along with teachers, in conferences and meetings held to draw up individualized programs; and must approve these plans before they go into effect for the first time.
- The right of parents to challenge and appeal any decision related to the identification, evaluation, and placement, or any issue concerning the provision of Free and Appropriate Public Education (FAPE), of their child is fully protected by clearly spelled-out due process procedures.
- Parents have the right to confidentiality of information. No one may see a child's records unless the parents give their written permission. (The exception to this is school personnel with legitimate educational interests.)

As they currently stand, the Individuals with Disabilities Education Act and Section 504 of the Rehabilitation Act of 1973 strengthen each other in important areas. For example, they both call for school systems to carry out a systematic search for every child with a disability in need of a public education, mandate a free and appropriate public education (FAPE) regardless of the nature and severity of an individual's disability, make it clear that education and related services must be provided at no cost to parents, have similar requirements to ensure that testing and evaluation of a child's needs are not based on a single testing instrument, and emphasize the importance of educating children and youth with disabilities with their nondisabled peers to the maximum extent appropriate.

Under IDEA, most of the mandates under P.L. 94-142 remained intact. However, some of the most important revisions and additions included:

- IDEA added significantly to the provisions for very young children with disabilities and for students preparing to leave secondary school.
- IDEA added two new categories in special education: Autism and Traumatic Brain Injury.
- Under IDEA, the term *handicapped* was removed from the law and the preferred term, *disability*, was substituted.
- IDEA mandated transition services no later than age 16.
- IDEA required further public commenting on defining attention deficit disorder in the law.
- IDEA provided that states can be sued in federal courts for violating the laws.

The Education of the Handicapped Act, P.L. 94-142, and its amendments, P.L. 98-199, P.L. 99-457, and now the Individuals with Disabilities Education Act, P.L. 105-17 and P.L. 102-119, represent the most important pieces of educational legislation in the history of educating children and youth with disabilities. As noted earlier, parents and professionals should make every effort to familiarize themselves with these laws. The regulations that cover the Individuals with Disabilities Education Act are also to be found in the *Code of Federal Regulations* (C.F.R.: Title 34; Education; Parts 300 to 399).

P.L. 105-17: The Individuals with Disabilities Education Act of 1997 (IDEA '97)

IDEA was amended to P.L. 105-17 on June 4, 1997. It is now often referred to as IDEA '97. Some of the changes made were substantial whereas others fine-tune processes already in place for schools and parents to follow in planning and providing special education and related services for children with special needs (Venn, 1994).

Besides the guidelines and procedures set forth from P. L. 94-142 and IDEA of 1990, IDEA '97 strengthened the least restrictive environment (LRE) mandate. IDEA '97 fosters increased efforts to educate students with disabilities in the LRE. For example, if a child is to be placed in special education, it must be considered whether and how the child can participate in the general curriculum, and the IEP is to indicate the extent to which the student will not be with nondisabled peers [20 U.S.C. 1414(d)(1)(A)(i)–(iv)]. Prior to IDEA '97, the IEP was to indicate the opposite, that is, the extent to which the student would be educated with nondisabled peers.

IDEA '97 strengthened parents' roles further. Perhaps only making it explicit what should already have been obvious, schools must now consider the results of evaluations, the strengths of the child, and the concerns of the parents for enhancing the child's education when developing the IEP [20 U.S.C. 1414(d)(3)(A)]. Under IDEA '97, parents are to be a part of the group that determines their child's eligibility [Section 300.534.535(a)(1)]. IDEA '97 also stated that parents should have the opportunity to examine all records pertaining to their child, not just "relevant" records as stated in the former law.

IDEA '97 added related services to the types of services to be provided for transition. Services are to be based on the individual student's needs taking into account the student's preferences and interests. IDEA '97 enlarged the scope of an appropriate education by requiring that not only should it meet students' unique needs, but it should also "prepare them for employment and independent living" [20 U.S.C. 1400(d)(1)(A)].

IDEA '97 strengthened the obligations of other agencies to provide services to students while they are still in school. All states must now have interagency agreements to ensure that all public agencies that are responsible for providing services that are also considered special education services fulfill their responsibilities. The agreement must also specify how the various agencies will cooperate to ensure the timely and appropriate delivery of services to students [20 U.S.C. 1412(a)(12)].

IDEA '97 emphasized assistive technology. The need for assistive technology must now be considered for all students when developing the individualized education plan. IDEA '97 further expands the number of members of the IEP team. In addition to parents, the team must include at least one special education teacher, and at least one teacher from the regular education classroom, if the child participates in regular education.

IDEA '97 gives school authorities several options in disciplining a student with a disability. Schools can suspend a child for up to 10 days or order a change in the child's education setting for up to 10 days, if they discipline students without disabilities in the same way.

IDEA '97 changed Part H, serving young children, to Part C. In doing so, IDEA '97 expanded provisions to "at-risk" children from birth to 5 years old, in addition to children already being served. This will be explained in detail in Chapter 13.

Finally, under IDEA '97, children and youth receiving special education have the right to receive the related services necessary to benefit from special education instruction. Related services include "transportation and such developmental, corrective, and other supportive services as are required to assist a child with a disability to benefit from special education, and includes speech pathology and audiology, psychological services, physical and occupational therapy, recreation, including therapeutic recreation, early identification and assessment of disabilities in children, counseling services, including rehabilitation counseling, and medical services for diagnostic or evaluation purposes. The term also includes school health services, social work services in schools, and parent counseling and training" (C.F.R.: Title 34; Education; Part 300.16, 1993).

P.L. 98-524: The Vocational Education Act of 1984

The Vocational Education Act of 1984 is often referred to as the Carl D. Perkins Act, or the Perkins Act, and authorizes federal funds to support vocational education programs. One of the goals of the Perkins Act is to improve the access of those who either have been underserved in the past or who have greater than average educational needs. Under the act, "special populations" include those who have a disability, are disadvantaged, or have limited English proficiency. This law is particularly important because it requires that vocational education be provided for students with disabilities. The regulations that cover this law are called C.F.R.: Title 34; Education; Parts 400–499.

The law states that individuals who are members of special populations (including individuals with disabilities) must be provided with equal access to recruitment, enrollment, and placement activities in vocational education. In addition, these individuals must be provided with equal access to the full range of vocational education programs available to others, including occupationally specific courses of study, cooperative education, apprenticeship programs, and, to the extent practical, comprehensive guidance and counseling services. Under the law, vocational education planning should be coordinated among public agencies, including vocational education, special education, and the state vocational rehabilitation agencies. The provision of vocational education to youth with disabilities should be monitored to ensure that such education is consistent with objectives stated in the youth's IEP.

In 1990 and 1991, Congress amended this law by passing P.L. 101-392 and P.L. 102-103, respectively. The name of the law was changed to the Carl D. Perkins Vocational and Applied Technology Education Act. The purpose of this law is to make the United States more competitive in the world economy by developing more fully the academic and occupational skills of all segments of the population. This law concentrates resources on improving educational programs leading to the academic and occupational skill competencies needed to work in a technologically advanced society. The new law expands the term *special populations* to include individuals with disabilities, individuals who are economically and educationally disadvantaged (including foster children), individuals with limited English proficiency, individuals who participate in programs to eliminate sex bias, and those in correctional institutions. Public Law 102-103 is closely interwoven with the IDEA (P.L. 101-476) to guarantee full vocational education opportunities for youth with disabilities.

OTHER FEDERAL LAWS AFFECTING CHILDREN AND YOUTH WITH DISABILITIES

In addition to the Individuals with Disabilities Education Act, Section 504 of the Rehabilitation Act, and the Perkins Act, other federal laws provide civil rights and service programs for children and youth with disabilities. The following is a general overview of some of these important laws.

P.L. 93-380: The Family Education Rights and Privacy Act (FERPA)

P.L. 93-380, The Family Education Rights and Privacy Act (FERPA), often called the Buckley Amendment, gives parents of students under age 18, and students age 18 and over, the right to examine records kept in the student's personal file. The FERPA was passed in 1974 to cover all students, including those in postsecondary education. The major provisions of the act are:

- Parents and eligible students have the right to inspect and review students' educational records.
- Schools must have written permission from the parent or eligible student before releasing any information from a student's records. Although a school may disclose education records without consent to others, such as other school officials, schools to which a student is transferring, certain government officials, and state and local authorities, the school must keep track, within the student's files, of the requests for these records. This information can be inspected by the parent or eligible student.
- Parents and eligible students have the right to have the records explained and interpreted by school officials.
- School officials may not destroy any education records if there is an outstanding request to inspect and review them.
- Parents and eligible students who believe that information in the education records is inaccurate or misleading may request that the records be amended. The parent or eligible student must be advised if the school decides that the records should not be amended. The parent or eligible student has the right to a hearing.
- Finally, each school district must give parents of students in attendance, or students age 18 or over, an annual notice to inform them of their rights under this law and the right of parents or eligible students to file a complaint with the U.S. Department of Education.

P.L. 99-372: The Handicapped Children's Protection Act of 1986

This law was enacted in 1986 "to amend the Education of the Handicapped Act to authorize the award of reasonable attorneys' fees to certain prevailing parties, to clarify the effect of the Education of the Handicapped Act on rights, procedures, and remedies under the other laws relating to the prohibition of discrimination, and for other purposes." Public Law 99-372 provides for reasonable attorneys' fees and costs to parents and guardians who prevail in administrative hearings or court when there is a dispute with a school system concerning their child's right to a free appropriate special education and related services; applies to all cases initiated after July 3, 1984 . . . and requests the General Accounting Office to study the impact of the law and submit findings to Congress concerning the number of complaints, prevailing parties, amounts of attorneys' fees, and other data.

P.L. 99-401: The Temporary Child Care for Handicapped Children and Crisis Nurseries Act of 1986

The Temporary Child Care for Handicapped Children and Crisis Nurseries Act was first introduced in 1985 as part of an omnibus child care bill and enacted by the

99th Congress in 1986. The act was later incorporated into the Children's Justice and Assistance Act of 1986 (P.L. 99-401). The act was most recently reauthorized and otherwise amended by the Child Abuse, Domestic Violence, Adoption and Family Services Act of 1992 (P.L. 102-295).

This law provides funding through competitive grants to states and U.S. territories to develop nonmedical respite services (specialized temporary child care) for children with disabilities or chronic or terminal illnesses and to develop crisis nursery services for children at risk of abuse and neglect. In addition to temporary child care, the programs created also offer an array of family support services or referral to such services.

In 1988, the U.S. Department of Health and Human Services awarded approximately $2 million to 16 states to develop and implement respite care services. In 1989, this law was amended by P.L. 101-127, the Children with Disabilities Temporary Care Reauthorization Act of 1989.

Since federal funding became available in 1988, a total of 175 crisis nursery and respite grants and two resource center grants (177 total) have been awarded to 47 states and one U.S. territory.

P.L. 100-146: The Developmental Disabilities and Bill of Rights Act Amendments of 1987

The original law was the Mental Retardation Facilities and Community Mental Health Centers Construction Act of 1963 (P.L. 88-164). A bill of rights section for people with developmental disabilities was included in the 1987 amendments. Persons covered under these amendments included those with mental retardation, autism, cerebral palsy, and epilepsy. Formula grants (noncompetitive, basic yearly allotments) were provided to states to establish Developmental Disabilities Councils to support the planning, coordination, and delivery of specialized services to persons with developmental disabilities. The law also authorized formula awards to support the establishment and operation of state protection and advocacy systems. Discretionary grants were awarded to support university-affiliated programs to provide interdisciplinary training in the field of developmental disabilities and to projects of national significance aimed at increasing the independence, productivity, and community integration of persons with developmental disabilities. The 1987 amendments also established a federal interagency committee to plan for and coordinate activities related to persons with developmental disabilities.

The act was amended in 1990 (P.L. 101-496) and in 1994 (P.L. 103-230) by the Developmental Disabilities Assistance and Bill of Rights Act of 1994. The formula grants to support councils in the states are for promoting, through systemic change, capacity building, and advocacy activities, the development of a consumer and family-centered, comprehensive system and a coordinated array of culturally competent services, supports, and other assistance designed to achieve independence, productivity, and integration and inclusion into the community. Another key provision of these amendments was the definition of "developmental disability," which means:

> a severe, chronic disability of an individual 5 years of age or older that: (a) is attributable to a mental or physical impairment or combination of mental and physical impairments; (b) is manifested before the person attains age 22; (c) is likely to continue indefinitely; (d) results in substantial functional limitations in three or more of the following areas of major life activity: (i) self-care; (ii) receptive and expressive language; (iii) learning; (iv) mobility; (v) self-direction; (vi) capacity for independent living; and (vii) economic sufficiency; and (e) reflects the individual's need for a combination and sequence of special, interdisciplinary, or generic ser-

vices, supports, or other assistance that is of lifelong or extended duration and is individually planned and coordinated. (p. 1)

The 1994 amendments make a specific exception to the age limitation for developmental disabilities, to include individuals from birth through age 5 who have substantial developmental delays or specific congenital or acquired conditions with a high probability of resulting in developmental disabilities if services are not provided.

Furthermore, all programs, projects, and activities receiving assistance under the act must be carried out in a manner consistent with a number of principles, including (1) that individuals with developmental disabilities, including those with the most severe developmental disabilities, are capable of achieving independence, productivity, and integration and inclusion into the community, given appropriate support; (2) that these individuals and their families are the primary decision makers regarding the services and supports to be received; and (3) that services, supports, and other assistance need to be provided in a manner that demonstrates respect for individual dignity, personal preference, and cultural differences.

P.L. 100-407: The Technology-Related Assistance for Individuals with Disabilities Act of 1988

The primary purpose of this act is to assist states in developing comprehensive, consumer-oriented programs of technology-related assistance and to increase the availability of assistive technology to individuals with disabilities and their families. The act was reauthorized in 1994 by P.L. 103-218. The reauthorization requires the development of a national classification system for assistive technology devices and services.

"Assistive technology device" is defined by the act as "any item, piece of equipment, or product system whether acquired off the shelf, modified or customized that is used to increase, maintain, or improve functional capabilities of individuals with disabilities."

"Assistive technology services" are any services that directly assist an individual with a disability to select, acquire, or use an assistive technology device. This entails evaluating the needs of the child, including a functional evaluation in the child's customary environment.

Title I of P.L. 100-407 provides states with funds to develop a consumer-responsive state system of assistive technology services. States receiving funds may develop or carry out any of the following: (1) model delivery systems; (2) statewide needs assessment; (3) support groups; (4) public awareness programs; (5) training and technical assistance; (6) access to related information; (7) interagency agreements; and (8) other activities necessary for developing, implementing, or evaluating a statewide service delivery system. This range of optional activities gives states flexibility in how to focus efforts and spend funds.

P.L. 101-336: The Americans with Disabilities Act of 1990

To be protected by the Americans with Disabilities Act of 1990 (ADA), one must have a disability or have a relationship or association with an individual with a disability. An individual with a disability is defined by the ADA as a person who has a physical or mental impairment that substantially limits one or more major life activities, a person who has a history or record of such impairment, or a person who is perceived by others as having such impairment. The ADA does not specifically name all of the impairments that are covered.

ADA Title I: Employment.   Title I requires employers with 15 or more employees to provide qualified individuals with disabilities an equal opportunity to benefit from the full range of employment-related opportunities available to others. For example, it prohibits discrimination in recruitment, hiring, promotions, training, pay, social activities, and other privileges of employment. It restricts questions that can be asked about an applicant's disability before a job offer is made, and it requires that employers make reasonable accommodation to the known physical or mental limitations of otherwise qualified individuals with disabilities, unless it results in undue hardship. Religious entities with 15 or more employees are covered under Title I.

Title I complaints must be filed with the U.S. Equal Employment Opportunity Commission (EEOC) within 180 days of the date of discrimination, or 300 days if the charge is filed with a designated state or local fair employment practice agency. Individuals may file a lawsuit in federal court only after they receive a "right-to-sue" letter from the EEOC.

Charges of employment discrimination on the basis of disability may be filed at any U.S. Equal Employment Opportunity Commission field office. Field offices are located in 50 cities throughout the United States and are listed in most telephone directories under "U.S. Government."

ADA Title II: State and Local Government Activities.   Title II covers all activities of state and local governments regardless of the government entity's size or receipt of federal funding. Title II requires that state and local governments give people with disabilities an equal opportunity to benefit from all of their programs, services, and activities (e.g., public education, employment, transportation, recreation, health care, social services, courts, voting, and town meetings).

State and local governments are required to follow specific architectural standards in the new construction and alteration of their buildings. They also must relocate programs or otherwise provide access in inaccessible older buildings and communicate effectively with people who have hearing, vision, or speech disabilities. Public entities are not required to take actions that would result in undue financial and administrative burdens. They are required to make reasonable modifications to policies, practices, and procedures where necessary to avoid discrimination, unless they can demonstrate that doing so would fundamentally alter the nature of the service, program, or activity being provided.

Complaints of Title II violations may be filed with the Department of Justice (DOJ) within 180 days of the date of discrimination. In certain situations, cases may be referred to a mediation program sponsored by the DOJ. The Department of Justice may bring a lawsuit where it has investigated a matter and has been unable to resolve violations.

Title II may also be enforced through private lawsuits in federal court. It is not necessary to file a complaint with the DOJ or any other federal agency, or to receive a "right-to-sue" letter, before going to court.

ADA Title II: Public Transportation.   The transportation provisions of Title II cover public transportation services, such as city buses and public rail transit (e.g., subways, commuter rails, Amtrak). Public transportation authorities may not discriminate against people with disabilities in the provision of their services. They must comply with requirements for accessibility in newly purchased vehicles, make good faith efforts to purchase or lease accessible used buses, remanufacture buses in an accessible manner, and, unless it would result in an undue burden, provide paratransit where they operate fixed-route bus or rail systems. Paratransit is a service where individuals who are unable to use the regular transit system independently (because of a physical or mental impairment) are picked up and dropped off at their destinations.

ADA Title III: Public Accommodations.   Title III covers businesses and non-profit service providers that are public accommodations, privately operated entities offering certain types of courses and examinations, privately operated transportation, and commercial facilities. Public accommodations are private entities that own, lease, or operate facilities such as restaurants, retail stores, hotels, movie theaters, private schools, convention centers, doctors' offices, homeless shelters, transportation depots, zoos, funeral homes, day care centers, and recreation facilities including sports stadiums and fitness clubs. Transportation services provided by private entities are also covered by Title III.

Public accommodations must comply with basic nondiscrimination requirements that prohibit exclusion, segregation, and unequal treatment. They also must comply with specific requirements related to architectural standards for new and altered buildings; reasonable modifications to policies, practices, and procedures; effective communication with people with hearing, vision, or speech disabilities; and other access requirements. Additionally, public accommodations must remove barriers in existing buildings where it is possible to do so without much difficulty or expense, given the public accommodation's resources.

Courses and examinations related to professional, educational, or trade-related applications, licensing, certifications, or credentialing must be provided in a place and manner accessible to people with disabilities, or alternative accessible arrangements must be offered.

Commercial facilities, such as factories and warehouses, must comply with the ADA's architectural standards for new construction and alterations.

Complaints of Title III violations may be filed with the Department of Justice. In certain situations, cases may be referred to a mediation program sponsored by the Department. The DOJ is authorized to bring a lawsuit where there is a pattern or practice of discrimination in violation of Title III, or where an act of discrimination raises an issue of general public importance. Title III may also be enforced through private lawsuits. It is not necessary to file a complaint with the Department of Justice (or any federal agency), or to receive a "right-to-sue" letter, before going to court.

ADA Title IV: Telecommunications Relay Services.   Title IV addresses telephone and television access for people with hearing and speech disabilities. It requires common carriers (telephone companies) to establish interstate and intrastate telecommunications relay services (TRS) 24 hours a day, 7 days a week. TRS enables callers with hearing and speech disabilities who use telecommunications devices for the deaf (TDDs), which are also known as teletypewriters (TTYs), and callers who use voice telephones to communicate with each other through a third-party communications assistant. The Federal Communications Commission (FCC) has set minimum standards for TRS services. Title IV also requires closed captioning of federally funded public service announcements.

P.L. 103-239: School to Work Opportunities Act of 1994

In May 1994, President Clinton signed the School to Work Opportunities Act. This act has the blueprint to empower all individuals, including those with disabilities, to acquire the skills and experiences they need to compete. This landmark bill demonstrates that transition is clearly now a national priority, important to ensure our economic viability as well as offer every young person a chance at a productive life. (See Chapter 2 for a detailed discussion of P.L. 103-239.)

Every state receives federal special education monies through Part B of IDEA, and in turn, most of these funds "flow through" to local school districts and other state-supported programs providing special education services. As a requirement of receiving these funds, state education agencies monitor the programs for which the funds are made available.

The following sections of the School to Work Opportunities Act of 1994 describe the school-based learning component, the work-based learning component, and the connecting activities component (North Central Regional Educational Laboratory, 2003):

SECT. 102. SCHOOL-BASED LEARNING COMPONENT

The school-based learning component of a School-to-Work Opportunities program shall include:

1. Career awareness and career exploration and counseling (beginning at the earliest possible age, but not later than the 7th grade) in order to help students who may be interested to identify, and select or reconsider, their interests, goals, and career majors, including those options that may not be traditional for their gender, race, or ethnicity.
2. Initial selection by interested students of a career major not later than the beginning of the 11th grade.
3. A program of study designed to meet the same academic content standards the State has established for all students, including, where applicable, standards established under the Goals 2000: Educate America Act, and to meet the requirements necessary to prepare a student for postsecondary education and the requirements necessary for a student to earn a skill certificate.
4. A program of instruction and curriculum that integrates academic and vocational learning (including applied methodologies and team-teaching strategies), and incorporates instruction, to the extent practicable, in all aspects of an industry, appropriately tied to the career major of a participant.
5. Regularly scheduled evaluations involving ongoing consultation and problem solving with students and school dropouts to identify their academic strengths and weaknesses, academic progress, workplace knowledge, goals, and the need for additional learning opportunities to master core academic and vocational skills.
6. Procedures to facilitate the entry of students participating in a School-to-Work Opportunities program into additional training or postsecondary education programs, as well as to facilitate the transfer of the students between education and training programs.

SEC. 103. WORK-BASED LEARNING COMPONENT

(a) Mandatory Activities: The work-based learning component of a School-to-Work Opportunities program shall include:
1. Work experience
2. A planned program of job training and work experiences (including training related to preemployment and employment skills to be mastered at progressively higher levels) that are coordinated with learning in the school-based learning component described in section 102 and are relevant to the career majors of students and lead to the award of skill certificates.
3. Workplace mentoring
4. Instruction in general workplace competencies, including instruction and activities related to developing positive work attitudes, and employability and participative skills.
5. Broad instruction, to the extent practicable, in all aspects of the industry.
(b) Permissible Activities: Such component may include such activities as paid work experience, job shadowing, school-sponsored enterprises, or on-the-job training.

SEC. 104. CONNECTING ACTIVITIES COMPONENT

The connecting component of a School-to-Work Opportunities program shall include:
1. Matching students with the work-based learning opportunities of employers.
2. Providing, with respect to each student, a school site mentor to act as a liaison among the student and the employer, school, teacher, school administrator, and parent of the student, and, if appropriate, other community partners.

3. Providing technical assistance and services to employers, including small- and medium-sized businesses, and other parties in:
    (A) Designing school-based learning components described in section 102, work-based learning components described in section 103, and counseling and case management services.
    (B) Training teachers, workplace mentors, school site mentors and counselors.
4. Providing assistance to schools and employers to integrate school-based and work-based learning and integrate academic and occupational learning into the program.
5. Encouraging the active participation of employers, in cooperation with local education officials, in the implementation of local activities described in section 102, section 103, or this section.
6. (A) Providing assistance to participants who have completed the program in finding an appropriate job, continuing their education, or entering into an additional training program.
    (B) Linking the participants with other community services that may be necessary to assure a successful transition from school to work.
7. Collecting and analyzing information regarding post-program outcomes of participants in the School-to-Work Opportunities program, to the extent practicable, on the basis of socioeconomic status, race, gender, ethnicity, culture, and disability, and on the basis of whether the participants are students with limited-English proficiency, school dropouts, disadvantaged students, or academically talented students.
8. Linking youth development activities under this Act with employer and industry strategies for upgrading the skills of their workers.

P.L. 105-220: The Workforce Investment Act of 1998

From 1983 until June 30, 2000, the Job Training Partnership Act (JTPA), Public Law 97-300, directed and funded the largest federal employment training program in the nation, serving dislocated workers, homeless individuals, and economically disadvantaged adults, youths, and older workers. On July 1, 2000, the Workforce Investment Act (WIA) of 1998 replaced JTPA. WIA affects many other federally funded employment and training, literacy and vocational rehabilitation programs, coordinating a vast range of federally funded jobs programs offered by many U.S. government departments and agencies.

The Workforce Investment Act of 1998 rewrites federal laws governing workforce preparation programs including job training, adult education and literacy, and vocational rehabilitation, replacing them with streamlined and more flexible systems. The act directs these programs to provide the system's customers with universal access to a broad range of services and to streamline all the services the system provides. This new system emphasizes the role that labor market information (or "employment statistics" as it is called in the act) plays in workforce preparation to provide timely, accurate, and accessible information about the world of work to support informed decision making.

STATE LAWS RELATING TO CHILDREN AND YOUTH WITH DISABILITIES

How states implement the requirements of federal laws is covered by the primary and basic source of law for the nation—the United States Constitution. Federal laws passed by Congress must be based on the provisions of the Constitution. State constitutions and laws may go beyond what is provided in the federal law, as long as there is no conflict between them, and as long as state laws do not address areas reserved to the federal government, such as providing for the nation's defense. The major constitutional provisions that are of importance to children and youth with disabilities are (a) those that provide for the spending of money to protect the general welfare, and (b) the Fourteenth Amendment, which provides that no states shall "deprive any person of life, liberty, or property, without the due process of law . . . nor deny . . . equal protection of the laws." It is important to remember that there is no constitutional provision requiring that the federal government provide education. The Tenth Amendment to the Constitution states, "Powers not delegated to the United States by the Constitution, nor prohibited to the States, are reserved to the States. . . ." Therefore, all states have provided for public education, either by state constitution or state law or both. States are required under the due process and equal protection clauses of the Fourteenth Amendment to provide education on an equal basis and to provide due process before denying equal educational programming.

As you can see, most laws providing for public education are generally state and local rather than federal. Although some educational programs, such as Head Start and special education, are highly regulated by the federal government, education is, for the most part, a state function. It is important to remember that most federal laws and regulations that provide for educational programming establish minimum standards that states must follow for the delivery of services and programs in order to receive federal funds. Quite often, federal laws give flexibility to the states in implementing the programs or services established with federal funds. Laws and regulations regarding civil rights, on the other hand, are much more firm and concrete.

CONCLUSION

Finally, it is important to remember that laws provide a framework for policy and that regulations provide the specific requirements for implementing the policy. Where there are differences, inconsistencies, or ambiguities in interpretation or in implementation, the judicial system is responsible for resolving these disputes. Often court decisions lead to changes in the law or in regulations. It is interesting to note that laws are not made by various branches of the system (legislative, executive, and judicial) in a vacuum. Often laws are made by one branch in response to developments in other arenas. State and federal laws are frequently interactive in this process. The development of special education law is an excellent example. It is likely that interaction among the various branches of government at both the federal and state levels in the development of special education law and the civil rights of individuals with disabilities will continue for some time.

CHAPTER THREE

DISABILITY POPULATION RECEIVING TRANSITION SERVICES

OVERVIEW

The completion of high school is the beginning of adult life. Entitlement to public education ends, and young people and their families are faced with many options and decisions about the future. The most common choices for the future are pursuing vocational training or further academic education, getting a job, and living independently.

For students with disabilities, these choices may be more complex and may require a great deal of planning. Planning the transition from school to adult life begins, at the latest, during high school. In fact, transition planning is required, by law, to start once a student reaches 14 years of age, or younger, if appropriate. This transition planning becomes formalized as part of the student's individualized education program (IEP).

Transition services are provided for students with disabilities to help make the transition from the world of school to the world of adulthood. The population that is eligible under IDEA to receive such services includes students classified as disabled under 13 separate categories. This chapter will focus on those 13 categories and provide the reader with an overview of each specific disability. After reading this chapter, the reader should be familiar with the following areas:

ELIGIBILITY FOR TRANSITION SERVICES	ORTHOPEDIC IMPAIRMENT
AUTISM	OTHER HEALTH IMPAIRMENT
DEAFNESS	SERIOUS EMOTIONAL DISTURBANCE
DEAF-BLINDNESS	SPECIFIC LEARNING DISABILITY
HEARING IMPAIRMENT	SPEECH OR LANGUAGE IMPAIRMENT
MENTAL RETARDATION	TRAUMATIC BRAIN INJURY
MULTIPLE DISABILITIES	VISUAL IMPAIRMENT

ELIGIBILITY FOR TRANSITION SERVICES

The Education of the Handicapped Act, Public Law (P.L.) 94-142, was passed by Congress in 1975 and amended by P.L. 99-457 in 1986 to ensure that all children with disabilities would have a free and appropriate public education available to them that would meet their unique needs. It was again amended in 1990 and the name was changed to Individuals with Disabilities Education Act (IDEA).

IDEA defines **"children with disabilities"** as having any of the following types of disabilities: autism, deaf, deaf-blindness, hearing impairments (including deafness), mental retardation, multiple disabilities, orthopedic impairments, other health impairments, serious emotional disturbance, specific learning disabilities, speech or language impairments, traumatic brain injury, and visual impairments (including blindness). These terms are defined in the regulations for IDEA, as described next.

AUTISM

Definition

Autism and Pervasive Developmental Disorder-NOS (not otherwise specified) are developmental disabilities that share many of the same characteristics. Usually evident by age 3, autism and PDD-NOS are neurological disorders that affect a child's ability to communicate, understand language, play, and relate to others.

In the diagnostic manual used to classify disabilities, the *DSM-IV* (American Psychiatric Association, 1994), "autistic disorder" is listed as a category under the heading of "Pervasive Developmental Disorders." A diagnosis of autistic disorder is made when an individual displays six or more of 12 symptoms listed across three major areas: social interaction, communication, and behavior. When children display similar behaviors but do not meet the criteria for autistic disorder, they may receive a diagnosis of Pervasive Developmental Disorder-NOS (PDD not otherwise specified). Although the diagnosis is referred to as PDD-NOS, throughout the remainder of this fact sheet, we will refer to the diagnosis as PDD, as it is more commonly known.

Autistic disorder is one of the disabilities specifically defined in the Individuals with Disabilities Education Act (IDEA), the federal legislation under which children and youth with disabilities receive special education and related services. IDEA, which uses the term *autism,* defines the disorder as "a developmental disability significantly affecting verbal and nonverbal communication and social interaction, usually evident before age 3, that adversely affects a child's educational performance. Other characteristics often associated with autism are engagement in repetitive activities and stereotyped movements, resistance to environmental change or change in daily routines, and unusual responses to sensory experiences."

Due to the similarity of behaviors associated with autism and PDD, use of the term *pervasive developmental disorder* has caused some confusion among parents and professionals. However, the treatment and educational needs are similar for both diagnoses.

Incidence

Autism and PDD occur in approximately 5 to 15 per 10,000 births. These disorders are four times more common in boys than girls. The causes of autism and PDD are unknown. Currently, researchers are investigating areas such as neurological damage and biochemical imbalance in the brain. These disorders are not caused by psychological factors.

Characteristics

Some or all of the following characteristics may be observed in mild to severe forms:

- communication problems (e.g., using and understanding language)
- difficulty in relating to people, objects, and events

- unusual play with toys and other objects
- difficulty with changes in routine or familiar surroundings
- repetitive body movements or behavior patterns

Children with autism or PDD vary widely in abilities, intelligence, and behaviors. Some children do not speak; others have limited language that often includes repeated phrases or conversations. People with more advanced language skills tend to use a small range of topics and have difficulty with abstract concepts. Repetitive play skills, a limited range of interests, and impaired social skills are generally evident as well. Unusual responses to sensory information—for example, loud noises, lights, and certain textures of food or fabrics—are also common.

Educational Implications

Early diagnosis and appropriate educational programs are very important to children with autism or PDD. Public Law 105-17, the Individuals with Disabilities Education Act (IDEA), formerly the Education of the Handicapped Children's Act, includes autism as a disability category. From age 3, children with autism and PDD are eligible for an educational program appropriate to their individual needs. Educational programs for students with autism or PDD focus on improving communication, social, academic, behavioral, and daily living skills. Behavior and communication problems that interfere with learning sometimes require the assistance of a knowledgeable professional in the autism field who develops and helps to implement a plan that can be carried out at home and school.

The classroom environment should be structured so that the program is consistent and predictable. Students with autism or PDD learn better and are less confused when information is presented visually as well as verbally. Interaction with peers without disabilities is also important, for these students provide models of appropriate language, social, and behavior skills. To overcome frequent problems in generalizing skills learned at school, it is very important to develop programs with parents, so that learning activities, experiences, and approaches can be carried over into the home and community.

With educational programs designed to meet a student's individual needs and specialized adult support services in employment and living arrangements, children and adults with autism or PDD can live and work in the community.

DEAFNESS

Definition

The Individuals with Disabilities Education Act (IDEA) includes "hearing impairment" and "deafness" as two of the categories under which children with disabilities may be eligible for special education and related service programming. Although the term *hearing impairment* is often used generically to describe a wide range of hearing losses, including deafness, the regulations for IDEA define hearing loss and deafness separately.

Hearing impairment is defined by IDEA as "an impairment in hearing, whether permanent or fluctuating, that adversely affects a child's educational performance." Deafness is defined as "a hearing impairment that is so severe that the child is impaired in processing linguistic information through hearing, with or without amplification." Thus, deafness may be viewed as a condition that prevents an individual from receiving sound in all or most of its forms. In contrast, a child with a hearing loss can generally respond to auditory stimuli, including speech.

Incidence

Hearing loss and deafness affect individuals of all ages and may occur at any time from infancy through old age. The U.S. Department of Education (2000) reports that, during the 1998–99 school year, 70,813 students ages 6 to 21 (or 1.3 percent of all students with disabilities) received special education services under the category of "hearing impairment." However, the number of children with hearing loss and deafness is undoubtedly higher, since many of these students may have other disabilities as well and may be served under other categories.

Characteristics

It is useful to know that sound is measured by its loudness or intensity (measured in units called decibels, dB) and its frequency or pitch (measured in units called hertz, Hz). Impairments in hearing can occur in either or both areas and may exist in only one ear or in both ears. Hearing loss is generally described as slight, mild, moderate, severe, or profound, depending on how well a person can hear the intensities or frequencies most greatly associated with speech. Generally, only children whose hearing loss is greater than 90 decibels (dB) are considered deaf for the purposes of educational placement.

There are four types of hearing loss:

- *Conductive hearing losses* are caused by diseases or obstructions in the outer or middle ear (the conduction pathways for sound to reach the inner ear). Conductive hearing losses usually affect all frequencies of hearing evenly and do not result in severe losses. A person with a conductive hearing loss usually is able to use a hearing aid well or can be helped medically or surgically.
- *Sensorineural hearing losses* result from damage to the delicate sensory hair cells of the inner ear or the nerves that supply it. These hearing losses can range from mild to profound. They often affect the person's ability to hear certain frequencies more than others. Thus, even with amplification to increase the sound level, a person with a sensorineural hearing loss may perceive distorted sounds, sometimes making the successful use of a hearing aid impossible.
- *Mixed hearing loss* refers to a combination of conductive and sensorineural loss and means that a problem occurs in both the outer or middle and the inner ear.
- *Central hearing loss* results from damage or impairment to the nerves or nuclei of the central nervous system, either in the pathways to the brain or in the brain itself.

Educational Implications

Hearing loss or deafness does not affect a person's intellectual capacity or ability to learn. However, children who are either hard of hearing or deaf generally require some form of special education services in order to receive an adequate education. Such services may include regular speech, language, and auditory training from a specialist; amplification systems; services of an interpreter for those students who use manual communication; favorable seating in the class to facilitate speech reading; captioned films/videos; assistance of a note taker, who takes notes for the student with a hearing loss, so that the student can fully attend to instruction; instruction for the teacher and peers in alternate communication methods, such as sign language; and counseling.

Children who are hard of hearing will find it much more difficult than children who have normal hearing to learn vocabulary, grammar, word order, idiomatic expressions, and other aspects of verbal communication. For children who are deaf or have severe hearing losses, early, consistent, and conscious use of visible communication modes (such as sign language, finger spelling, and Cued Speech) and/or amplification and aural/oral training can help reduce this language delay. By age 4 or 5, most children who are deaf are enrolled in school on a full-day basis and do special work on communication and language development. It is important for teachers and audiologists to work together to teach the child to use his or her residual hearing to the maximum extent possible, even if the preferred means of communication is manual. Because the great majority of deaf children (over 90 percent) are born to hearing parents, programs should provide instruction for parents on implications of deafness within the family.

People with hearing loss use oral or manual means of communication or a combination of the two. *Oral communication* includes speech, speech reading, and the use of residual hearing. *Manual communication* involves signs and finger spelling. Total Communication, as a method of instruction, is a combination of the oral method plus signs and finger spelling.

Individuals with hearing loss, including those who are deaf, now have many helpful devices available to them. Text telephones (known as TTs, TTYs, or TDDs) enable persons to type phone messages over the telephone network. The Telecommunications Relay Service (TRS), now required by law, makes it possible for text telephone users to communicate with virtually anyone (and vice versa) via telephone.

DEAF-BLINDNESS

Deaf-blindness involves simultaneous hearing and visual impairments, the combination of which causes such severe communication and other developmental and educational problems that a child cannot be accommodated in special education programs solely for children with deafness or children with blindness.

HEARING IMPAIRMENT

A hearing impairment, whether permanent or fluctuating, adversely affects a child's educational performance but is not included under the definition of "deafness."

MENTAL RETARDATION

Definition

People with mental retardation are those who develop at a below average rate and experience difficulty in learning and social adjustment. The regulations for the Individuals with Disabilities Education Act (IDEA) provide the following technical definition for mental retardation: "Mental retardation means significantly subaverage general intellectual functioning existing concurrently with deficits in adaptive behavior and manifested during the developmental period, that adversely affects a child's educational performance."

"General intellectual functioning" is typically measured by an intelligence test. Persons with mental retardation usually score 70 or below on such tests. "Adaptive behavior" refers to a person's adjustment to everyday life. Difficulties may occur in learning, communication, social, academic, vocational, and independent living skills.

Mental retardation is not a disease, nor should it be confused with mental illness. Children with mental retardation become adults; they do not remain "eternal children." They do learn, but slowly, and with difficulty.

Probably the greatest number of children with mental retardation have chromosome abnormalities. Other biological factors include (but are not limited to) asphyxia (lack of oxygen); blood incompatibilities between the mother and fetus; and maternal infections, such as rubella or herpes. Certain drugs have also been linked to problems in fetal development.

Incidence

Some studies suggest that approximately 1 percent of the general population has mental retardation (when both intelligence and adaptive behavior measures are used). According to data reported to the U.S. Department of Education by the states, in the 1998–99 school year, 610,445 students ages 6 to 21 were classified as having mental retardation and were provided special education and related services by the public schools. This figure does not include students reported as having multiple disabilities or those in noncategorical special education preschool programs who may also have mental retardation.

Characteristics

Many authorities agree that people with mental retardation develop in the same way as people without mental retardation but at a slower rate. Others suggest that persons with mental retardation have difficulties in particular areas of basic thinking and learning such as attention, perception, or memory. Depending on the extent of the impairment—mild, moderate, severe, or profound—individuals with mental retardation will develop differently in academic, social, and vocational skills.

Educational Implications

Persons with mental retardation have the capacity to learn, to develop, and to grow. The great majority of these citizens can become productive and full participants in society.

Appropriate educational services that begin in infancy and continue throughout the developmental period and beyond will enable children with mental retardation to develop to their fullest potential.

As with all education, modifying instruction to meet individual needs is the starting point for successful learning. Throughout their child's education, parents should be an integral part of the planning and teaching team.

In teaching persons with mental retardation, it is important to:

- Use concrete materials that are interesting, age appropriate, and relevant to the students.
- Present information and instructions in small, sequential steps and review each step frequently.
- Provide prompt and consistent feedback.
- Teach these children, whenever possible, in the same school they would attend if they did not have mental retardation.
- Teach tasks or skills that students will use frequently in such a way that students can apply the tasks or skills in settings outside of school.

- Remember that tasks that many people learn without instruction may need to be structured, or broken down into small steps or segments, with each step being carefully taught.

Children and adults with mental retardation need the same basic services that all people need for normal development. These include education, vocational preparation, health services, recreational opportunities, and many more. In addition, many persons with mental retardation need specialized services for special needs. Such services include diagnostic and evaluation centers; special early education opportunities, beginning with infant stimulation programs and continuing through preschool; and educational programs that include age-appropriate activities, functional academics, transition training, and opportunities for independent living and competitive employment to the maximum extent possible.

MULTIPLE DISABILITIES

Definition

People with severe and/or multiple disabilities are those who traditionally have been labeled as having severe to profound mental retardation. These people require ongoing, extensive support in more than one major life activity in order to participate in integrated community settings and enjoy the quality of life available to people with fewer or no disabilities. They frequently have additional disabilities, including movement difficulties, sensory losses, and behavior problems.

Incidence

In the 1998–99 school year, the states reported to the U.S. Department of Education that they were providing services to 107,591 students with multiple disabilities (U.S. Dept. of Education, 2000).

Characteristics

Children and youth with severe or multiple disabilities may exhibit a wide range of characteristics, depending on the combination and severity of disabilities and the person's age. Some of these characteristics may include limited speech or communication, difficulty in basic physical mobility, tendency to forget skills through disuse, trouble generalizing skills from one situation to another, and/or a need for support in major life activities (e.g., domestic, leisure, community use, vocational).

Medical Implications

A variety of medical problems may accompany severe disabilities. Examples include seizures, sensory loss, hydrocephalus, and scoliosis. These conditions should be considered when establishing school services. A multidisciplinary team consisting of the student's parents, educational specialists, and medical specialists in the areas in which the individual demonstrates problems should work together to plan and coordinate necessary services.

Educational Implications

Early intervention programs and preschool and educational programs with the appropriate support services are important to children with severe disabilities.

Educators, physical therapists, occupational therapists, and speech-language pathologists are all members of the team that may provide services, along with others, as needed for each individual. Assistive technology, such as computers and augmentative/alternative communication devices and techniques, may provide valuable instructional assistance in the educational programs for students with severe or multiple disabilities.

In order to effectively address the considerable needs of individuals with severe or multiple disabilities, educational programs need to incorporate a variety of components, including language development, social skill development, functional skill development (i.e., self-help skills), and vocational skill development. Related services are of great importance, and the appropriate therapists (such as speech and language, occupational, physical, behavioral, and recreational therapists) need to work closely with classroom teachers and parents. Best practices indicate that related services are best offered during the natural routine of the school and community rather than by removing the student from class for isolated therapy.

Classroom arrangements must take into consideration students' needs for medications, special diets, or special equipment. Adaptive aids and equipment enable students to increase their range of functioning. The use of computers, augmentative/alternative communication systems, communication boards, head sticks, and adaptive switches are some of the technological advances that enable students with severe disabilities to participate more fully in integrated settings.

Integration/inclusion with peers without disabilities is another important component of the educational setting. Research is showing that attending the same school and participating in the same activities as their peers without disabilities are crucial to the development of social skills and friendships for children and youth with severe disabilities. Traditionally, children with severe disabilities have been educated in center-based, segregated schools. However, recently many schools are effectively and successfully educating children with severe disabilities in their neighborhood school within the regular classroom, making sure that appropriate support services and curriculum modifications are available. The benefits to inclusion are being seen to benefit not only those with disabilities but also their peers without disabilities and the professionals who work with them.

Schools are addressing the needs of students in several ways, generally involving a team approach. Modifications to the regular curriculum require collaboration on the part of the special educator, the regular educator, and other specialists involved in the student's program. Community-based instruction is also an important characteristic of educational programming, particularly as students grow older and where increasing time is spent in the community. School to work transition planning and working toward job placement in integrated, competitive settings are important to a student's success and the long-range quality of his or her life.

In light of the current Vocational Rehabilitation Act and the practice of supported employment, schools are now using school-to-work transition planning and working toward job placement in integrated, competitive settings rather than sheltered employment and day activity centers.

ORTHOPEDIC IMPAIRMENT

A severe orthopedic impairment adversely affects a child's educational performance. The term includes impairments caused by a congenital anomaly (e.g., clubfoot, absence of some member, etc.), impairments caused by disease (e.g., poliomyelitis, bone tuberculosis, etc.), and impairments from other causes (e.g., cerebral palsy, amputations, and fractures or burns that cause contractures).

OTHER HEALTH IMPAIRMENT

Other health impairment includes having limited strength, vitality, or alertness due to chronic or acute health problems, such as a heart condition, tuberculosis, rheumatic fever, nephritis, asthma, sickle cell anemia, hemophilia, seizure disorders, lead poisoning, leukemia, or diabetes, which adversely affects a child's educational performance. According to the Office of Special Education and Rehabilitative Services' clarification statement of September 16, 1991, eligible children with ADD may also be classified under "other health impairment."

SERIOUS EMOTIONAL DISTURBANCE

Definition

Many terms are used to describe emotional, behavioral or mental disorders. Currently, students with such disorders are categorized as having a serious emotional disturbance, which is defined under the Individuals with Disabilities Education Act as follows:

> a condition exhibiting one or more of the following characteristics over a long period of time and to a marked degree that adversely affects educational performance—
> (A) An inability to learn that cannot be explained by intellectual, sensory, or health factors;
> (B) An inability to build or maintain satisfactory interpersonal relationships with peers and teachers;
> (C) Inappropriate types of behavior or feelings under normal circumstances;
> (D) A general pervasive mood of unhappiness or depression; or
> (E) A tendency to develop physical symptoms or fears associated with personal or school problems." [C.F.R., Title 34, Section 300.7(b)(9)] As defined by the IDEA, serious emotional disturbance includes schizophrenia but does not apply to children who are socially maladjusted, unless it is determined that they have a serious emotional disturbance. [C.F.R., Title 34, Section 300.7(b)(9)]

It is important to know that the federal government is currently reviewing the way in which serious emotional disturbance is defined and that the definition may be revised.

Incidence

For the 1998–99 school year, 463,172 children and youth with a serious emotional disturbance were provided services in the public schools (Twenty-Second Annual Report to Congress, U.S. Department of Education, 2000).

Characteristics

The causes of emotional disturbance have not been adequately determined. Although various factors such as heredity, brain disorder, diet, stress, and family functioning have been suggested as possible causes, research has not shown any of these factors to be the direct cause of behavior problems. Some of the characteristics and behaviors seen in children who have emotional disturbances include:

- hyperactivity (short attention span, impulsiveness)
- aggression/self-injurious behavior (acting out, fighting)

- withdrawal (failure to initiate interaction with others; retreat from exchanges of social interaction, excessive fear or anxiety)
- immaturity (inappropriate crying, temper tantrums, poor coping skills)
- learning difficulties (academically performing below grade level)

Children with the most serious emotional disturbances may exhibit distorted thinking, excessive anxiety, bizarre motor acts, and abnormal mood swings and are sometimes identified as children who have a severe psychosis or schizophrenia.

Many children who do not have emotional disturbances may display some of these same behaviors at various times during their development. However, when children have serious emotional disturbances, these behaviors continue over long periods of time. Their behavior, thus, signals that they are not coping with their environment or peers.

Educational Implications

The educational programs for students with a serious emotional disturbance need to include attention to mastering academics, developing social skills, and increasing self-awareness, self-esteem, and self-control. Career education (both academic and vocational programs) is also a major part of secondary education and should be a part of every adolescent's transition plan in his or her individualized education program (IEP).

Behavior intervention planning and implementation are the most widely used approaches to helping children with a serious emotional disturbance. However, there are many other techniques that are also successful and may be used in combination with behavior modification.

Students eligible for special education services under the category of serious emotional disturbance may have IEPs that include psychological or counseling services as a related service. This is an important related service that is available under the law and is to be provided by a qualified social worker, psychologist, guidance counselor, or other qualified personnel.

There is growing recognition that families, as well as their children, need support, respite care, intensive case management services, and a multi-agency treatment plan. Many communities are working toward providing these wraparound services, and there are a growing number of agencies and organizations actively involved in establishing support services in the community. Parent support groups are also important, and organizations such as the Federation of Families for Children's Mental Health and the National Alliance for the Mentally Ill (NAMI) have parent representatives and groups in every state.

Other Considerations

Families of children with emotional disturbances may need help in understanding their children's condition and in learning how to work effectively with them. Help is available from psychiatrists, psychologists, or other mental health professionals in public or private mental health settings. Children should be provided services based on their individual needs, and all persons who are involved with these children should be aware of the care they are receiving. It is important to coordinate all services between home, school, and therapeutic community with open communication.

SPECIFIC LEARNING DISABILITY

Definition

The regulations for Public Law (P.L.) 101-476, the Individuals with Disabilities Education Act (IDEA), define a learning disability as a "disorder in one or more of the basic psychological processes involved in understanding or in using spoken or written language, which may manifest itself in an imperfect ability to listen, think, speak, read, write, spell or to do mathematical calculations."

The federal definition further states that learning disabilities include "such conditions as perceptual disabilities, brain injury, minimal brain dysfunction, dyslexia, and developmental aphasia." According to the law, learning disabilities do not include learning problems that are primarily the result of visual, hearing, or motor disabilities; mental retardation; or environmental, cultural, or economic disadvantage. Definitions of learning disabilities also vary among states.

Having a single term to describe this category of children with disabilities reduces some of the confusion, but there are many conflicting theories about what causes learning disabilities and how many there are. The label *learning disabilities* is all-embracing; it describes a syndrome, not a specific child with specific problems. The definition assists in classifying children, not teaching them. Parents and teachers need to concentrate on the individual child. They need to observe both how and how well the child performs, to assess strengths and weaknesses, and develop ways to help each child learn. It is important to remember that there is a high degree of interrelationship and overlapping among the areas of learning. Therefore, children with learning disabilities may exhibit a combination of characteristics. These problems may mildly, moderately, or severely impair the learning process.

Incidence

Many different estimates of the number of children with learning disabilities have appeared in the literature (ranging from 1 percent to 30 percent of the general population). Differences in estimates perhaps reflect variations in the definition. In 1987, the Interagency Committee on Learning Disabilities concluded that 5 percent to 10 percent is a reasonable estimate of the percentage of persons affected by learning disabilities. The U.S. Department of Education (2000) reported that, in the 1998–99 school year, over 2.8 million children with learning disabilities received special education and related services.

Characteristics

Learning disabilities are characterized by a significant difference in the child's achievement in some areas, as compared to his or her overall intelligence.

Students who have learning disabilities may exhibit a wide range of traits, including problems with reading comprehension, spoken language, writing, or reasoning ability. Hyperactivity, inattention, and perceptual coordination problems may also be associated with learning disabilities. Other traits that may be present include a variety of symptoms, such as uneven and unpredictable test performance, perceptual impairments, motor disorders, and behaviors such as impulsiveness, low tolerance for frustration, and problems in handling day-to-day social interactions and situations.

Learning disabilities may occur in the following academic areas:

- spoken language: delays, disorders, or discrepancies in listening and speaking
- written language: difficulties with reading, writing, and spelling
- arithmetic: difficulty in performing arithmetic functions or in comprehending basic concepts
- reasoning: difficulty in organizing and integrating thoughts
- organization skills: difficulty in organizing all facets of learning

Educational Implications

Because learning disabilities are manifested in a variety of behavior patterns, the individual education program (IEP) must be designed carefully. A team approach is important for educating the child with a learning disability, beginning with the assessment process and continuing through the development of the IEP. Close collaboration among special class teachers, parents, resource room teachers, regular class teachers, and others will facilitate the overall development of a child with learning disabilities.

Some teachers report that the following strategies have been effective with some students who have learning disabilities:

- Capitalize on the student's strengths.
- Provide high structure and clear expectations.
- Use short sentences and a simple vocabulary.
- Provide opportunities for success in a supportive atmosphere to help build self-esteem.
- Allow flexibility in classroom procedures (e.g., allowing the use of tape recorders for note taking and test taking when students have trouble with written language).
- Make use of self-correcting materials, which provide immediate feedback without embarrassment.
- Use computers for drill and practice and teaching word processing.
- Provide positive reinforcement of appropriate social skills at school and home.
- Recognize that students with learning disabilities can greatly benefit from the gift of time to grow and mature.

SPEECH OR LANGUAGE IMPAIRMENT

Definition

Speech and language disorders refer to problems in communication and related areas such as oral motor function. These delays and disorders range from simple sound substitutions to the inability to understand or use language or use the oral-motor mechanism for functional speech and feeding. Some causes of speech and language disorders include hearing loss, neurological disorders, brain injury, mental retardation, drug abuse, physical impairments such as cleft lip or palate, and vocal abuse or misuse. Frequently, however, the cause is unknown.

Incidence

More than 1 million of the students served in the public schools' special education programs in the 1998–99 school year were categorized as having a speech or language impairment. This estimate does not include children who have speech/language problems secondary to other conditions such as deafness. Language disorders may be related to other disabilities such as mental retardation, autism, or cerebral palsy. It is estimated that communication disorders (including speech, language, and hearing disorders) affect one of every 10 people in the United States.

Characteristics

A child's communication is considered delayed when the child is noticeably behind his or her peers in the acquisition of speech and/or language skills. Sometimes a child will have greater receptive (understanding) than expressive (speaking) language skills, but this is not always the case.

Speech disorders refer to difficulties producing speech sounds or problems with voice quality. They might be characterized by an interruption in the flow or rhythm of speech, such as stuttering, which is called dysfluency. Speech disorders may be problems with the way sounds are formed, called articulation or phonological disorders, or they may be difficulties with the pitch, volume, or quality of the voice. There may be a combination of several problems. People with speech disorders have trouble using some speech sounds, which can also be a symptom of a delay. They may say "see" when they mean "ski" or they may have trouble using other sounds like "l" or "r." Listeners may have trouble understanding what someone with a speech disorder is trying to say. People with voice disorders may have trouble with the way their voices sound.

A language disorder is impairment in the ability to understand and/or use words in context, both verbally and nonverbally. Some characteristics of language disorders include improper use of words and their meanings, inability to express ideas, inappropriate grammatical patterns, and reduced vocabulary and inability to follow directions. One or a combination of these characteristics may occur in children who are affected by language learning disabilities or developmental language delay. Children may hear or see a word but not be able to understand its meaning. They may have trouble getting others to understand what they are trying to communicate.

Educational Implications

Because all communication disorders carry the potential to isolate individuals from their social and educational surroundings, it is essential to find appropriate timely intervention. Although many speech and language patterns can be called "baby talk" and are part of a young child's normal development, they can become problems if they are not outgrown as expected. In this way an initial delay in speech and language or an initial speech pattern can become a disorder that can cause difficulties in learning. Because of the way the brain develops, it is easier to learn language and communication skills before age 5. When children have muscular disorders, hearing problems, or developmental delays, their acquisition of speech, language, and related skills is often affected.

Speech-language pathologists assist children who have communication disorders in various ways. They provide individual therapy for the child, consult with the child's teacher about the most effective ways to facilitate the child's communication in the class setting, and work closely with the family to develop goals and techniques for effective therapy in class and at home. Technology can help children whose physical conditions make communication difficult. The use of electronic communication systems allow nonspeaking people and people with severe physical disabilities to engage in the give-and-take of shared thought.

Vocabulary and concept growth continues during the years children are in school. Reading and writing are taught and, as students get older, the understanding and use of language becomes more complex. Communication skills are at the heart of the education experience. Speech and/or language therapy may continue throughout a student's school year either in the form of direct therapy or on a consultant basis. The speech-language pathologist may assist vocational teachers and counselors in establishing communication goals related to the work experiences of students and suggest strategies that are effective for the important transition from school to employment and adult life.

Communication has many components. All serve to increase the way people learn about the world around them, utilize knowledge and skills, and interact with colleagues, family, and friends.

TRAUMATIC BRAIN INJURY

IDEA defines traumatic brain injury as . . .

> an acquired injury to the brain caused by an external physical force, resulting in total or partial functional disability or psychosocial impairment, or both, that adversely affects a child's educational performance. The term applies to open or closed head injuries resulting in impairments in one or more areas, such as cognition; language; memory; attention; reasoning; abstract thinking; judgment; problem-solving; sensory, perceptual, and motor abilities; psycho-social behavior; physical functions; information processing; and speech. The term does not apply to brain injuries that are congenital or degenerative, or to brain injuries induced by birth trauma. [34 C.F.R. §300.7(c)(12)]

A traumatic brain injury (TBI) is an injury to the brain caused by the head being hit by something or shaken violently. This injury can change how the person acts, moves, and thinks. A traumatic brain injury can also change how a student learns and acts in school. The term *TBI* is used for head injuries that can cause changes in one or more areas, such as thinking and reasoning, understanding words, remembering things, paying attention, solving problems, thinking abstractly, talking, behaving, walking and other physical activities, seeing and/or hearing, and learning. The term *TBI* is not used for a person who is born with a brain injury. It also is not used for brain injuries that happen during birth.

The definition of TBI comes from the Individuals with Disabilities Education Act (IDEA). The IDEA is the federal law that guides how schools provide special education and related services to children and youth with disabilities.

How Common Is TBI?

More than 1 million children receive brain injuries each year. More than 30,000 of these children have lifelong disabilities as a result of the brain injury.

What Are the Signs of TBI?

The signs of brain injury can be very different depending on where and how extensively the brain is injured. Children with TBI may have one or more difficulties, including:

■ Physical disabilities: Individuals with TBI may have problems speaking, seeing, hearing, and using their other senses. They may have headaches and feel tired a lot. They may also have trouble with skills such as writing or drawing. Their muscles may suddenly contract or tighten (this is called spasticity). They may also have seizures. Their balance and walking may also be affected. They may be partly or completely paralyzed on one side of the body or both sides.

■ Difficulties with thinking: Because the brain has been injured, it is common that the person's ability to use the brain changes. For example, children with TBI may have trouble with short-term memory (being able to remember something from one minute to the next, like what the teacher just said). They may also have trouble with their long-term memory (being able to remember information from a while ago, like facts learned last month). People with TBI may have trouble concentrating and only be able to focus their attention for a short time. They may think slowly. They may have trouble talking and listening to others. They may also have difficulty with reading and writing, planning, understanding the order in which events happen (sequencing), and judgment.

■ Social, behavioral, or emotional problems: These difficulties may include sudden changes in mood, anxiety, and depression. Children with TBI may have trouble relating to others. They may be restless and may laugh or cry a lot. They may not have much motivation or much control over their emotions.

A child with TBI may not have all of the preceding difficulties. Brain injuries can range from mild to severe, and so can the changes that result from the injury. This means that it's hard to predict how an individual will recover from the injury. Early and ongoing help can make a big difference in how the child recovers. This help can include physical or occupational therapy, counseling, and special education.

It's also important to know that, as the child grows and develops, parents and teachers may notice new problems. This is because, as students grow, they are expected to use their brain in new and different ways. The damage to the brain from the earlier injury can make it hard for the student to learn new skills that come with getting older. Sometimes parents and educators may not even realize that the student's difficulty comes from the earlier injury.

Educational Implications

Although TBI is very common, many medical and education professionals may not realize that some difficulties can be caused by a childhood brain injury. Often students with TBI are thought to have a learning disability, emotional disturbance, or mental retardation. As a result, they don't receive the type of educational help and support they really need.

When children with TBI return to school, their educational and emotional needs are often very different than before the injury. Their disability has happened suddenly and traumatically. They can often remember how they were before the brain injury. This can bring on many emotional and social changes. The child's family, friends, and teachers also recall what the child was like before the injury. These other people in the child's life may have trouble changing or adjusting their expectations of the child.

Therefore, it is extremely important to plan carefully for the child's return to school. Parents will want to find out ahead of time about special education services at the school. This information is usually available from the school's principal or special education teacher. The school will need to evaluate the child thoroughly. This evaluation will let the school and parents know what the student's educational needs are. The school and parents will then develop an individualized education program (IEP) that addresses those educational needs.

It's important to remember that the IEP is a flexible plan. It can be changed as the parents, the school, and the student learn more about what the student needs at school.

TIPS FOR PARENTS

- Learn about TBI. The more you know, the more you can help yourself and your child. See the list of resources and organizations at the end of this publication.
- Work with the medical team to understand your child's injury and treatment plan. Don't be shy about asking questions. Tell them what you know or think. Make suggestions.
- Keep track of your child's treatment. A three-ring binder or a box can help you store this history. As your child recovers, you may meet with many doctors, nurses, and others. Write down what they say. Put any paperwork they give you in the notebook or throw it in the box. You can't remember all this! Also, if you need to share any of this paperwork with someone else, make a copy. Don't give away your original!
- Talk to other parents whose children have TBI. There are parent groups all over the United States. Parents can share practical advice and emotional support.
- If your child was in school before the injury, plan for his or her return to school. Get in touch with the school. Ask the principal about special education services. Have the medical team share information with the school.
- When your child returns to school, ask the school to test your child as soon as possible to identify his or her special education needs. Meet with the school and help develop a plan for your child called an individualized education program (IEP).
- Keep in touch with your child's teacher. Tell the teacher about how your child is doing at home. Ask how your child is doing in school.

TIPS FOR TEACHERS

- Find out as much as you can about the child's injury and his or her present needs. Find out more about TBI. See the list of resources and organizations at the end of this publication.
- Give the student more time to finish schoolwork and tests.
- Give directions one step at a time. For tasks with many steps, it helps to give the student written directions.
- Show the student how to perform new tasks. Give examples to go with new ideas and concepts.
- Have consistent routines. This helps the student know what to expect. If the routine is going to change, let the student know ahead of time.
- Check to make sure that the student has actually learned the new skill. Give the student lots of opportunities to practice the new skill.
- Show the student how to use an assignment book and a daily schedule. This helps the student get organized.
- Realize that the student may get tired quickly. Let the student rest as needed.
- Reduce distractions.
- Keep in touch with the student's parents. Share information about how the student is doing at home and at school.
- Be flexible about expectations. Be patient. Maximize the student's chances for success.

VISUAL IMPAIRMENT

Definition

The terms *partially sighted, low vision, legally blind,* and *totally blind* are used in the educational context to describe students with visual impairments. They are defined as follows:

- *Partially sighted* indicates some type of visual problem has resulted in a need for special education.
- *Low vision* generally refers to a severe visual impairment, not necessarily limited to distance vision. Low vision applies to all individuals with sight who are unable to read the newspaper at a normal viewing distance, even with the aid of eyeglasses or contact lenses. They use a combination of vision and other senses to learn, although they may require adaptations in lighting or the size of print and, sometimes, braille.
- *Legally blind* indicates that a person has less than 20/200 vision in the better eye or a very limited field of vision (20 degrees at its widest point).

Totally blind students learn via braille or other nonvisual media. Visual impairment is the consequence of a functional loss of vision rather than the eye disorder itself. Eye disorders that can lead to visual impairments can include retinal degeneration, albinism, cataracts, and glaucoma, muscular problems that result in visual disturbances, corneal disorders, diabetic retinopathy, congenital disorders, and infection.

Incidence

The rate at which visual impairments occur in individuals under age 18 is 12.2 per 1,000. Severe visual impairments (legally or totally blind) occur at a rate of .06 per 1,000.

Characteristics

The effect of visual problems on a child's development depends on the severity, type of loss, age at which the condition appears, and overall functioning level of the child. Many children who have multiple disabilities may also have visual impairments resulting in motor, cognitive, and/or social developmental delays.

A young child with visual impairments has little reason to explore interesting objects in the environment and, thus, may miss opportunities to have experiences and to learn. This lack of exploration may continue until learning becomes motivating or until intervention begins.

Because the child cannot see parents or peers, he or she may be unable to imitate social behavior or understand nonverbal cues. Visual handicaps can create obstacles to a growing child's independence.

Educational Implications

Children with visual impairments should be assessed early to benefit from early intervention programs, when applicable. Technology in the form of computers and low-vision optical and video aids enables many partially sighted, low-vision, and blind children to participate in regular class activities. Large-print materials, books on tape, and braille books are available.

Students with visual impairments may need additional help with special equipment and modifications in the regular curriculum to emphasize listening skills, communication, orientation and mobility, vocation/career options, and daily living skills. Students with low vision or those who are legally blind may need help in using their residual vision more efficiently and in working with special aids and materials. Students who have visual impairments combined with other types of disabilities have a greater need for an interdisciplinary approach and may require greater emphasis on self-care and daily living skills.

CONCLUSION

In order to better understand transition services, it is critical to fully understand the population that will be receiving them. Because there are many factors that must be considered to ensure that each student's transition plan is practical, useful, and fulfilling, a strong working knowledge and overall sensitivity to the needs of children with exceptionalities are a basic responsibility of all special educators.

CHAPTER FOUR

TRANSITION SERVICES
IN THE IEP

OVERVIEW

Since the passage of the Education for All Handicapped Children Act (EHA), Public Law 94-142, in 1975, individualized education programs (IEP) have been a requirement of law for all children and youth with disabilities found eligible for special education. Each student's IEP must list goals and objectives for educational activities and include information about the student's assessment and educational placement, the instructional content areas to be addressed throughout the year, the time lines and persons responsible for activities corresponding to the goals and objectives, how student progress will be evaluated, and the related services that each student needs in order to benefit from his or her special education. With the newest amendments to the EHA—now entitled the Individuals with Disabilities Education Act, or IDEA (Public Law 105-17)—a new component has been added to the IEP. Beginning no later than age 16, each student now must also have included in the IEP a statement of the transition services that he or she needs in order to prepare for such postschool outcomes as employment, postsecondary education, adult services, independent living, and community participation [Individuals with Disabilities Education Act, 20 U.S.C. Chapter 33, Section 1401(a)(19)]. When appropriate, these statements must be also included in the IEPs of younger students [34 *Code of Federal Regulations* (C.F.R.) Section 300.346(b)(1)].

The new definition of "content of individualized education program" is presented in this chapter. Clearly, for students aged 16 or older and, in many cases, for students who are younger, the contents of the IEP have expanded, and this will broaden the focus of IEPs and affect how they are developed. Traditionally, the IEP has been designed for a maximum of one year, breaking annual goals into short-term objectives. With the addition of transition services, the IEP becomes longer term, with objectives spanning across several years. For the first time, planning is oriented toward life after high school, with plans including adult services agencies and community agencies, where applicable. This is an enormous step forward in the concept of preparing students educationally and will require a great deal of insight, foresight, and planning on the part of students, parents, and school and other agency professionals.

This chapter has been developed to explain transition services in the IEP. First, in order to provide a good grounding as to the meaning of these services, we will review IEPs and their purpose. The next section will discuss IEP development with respect to transition services. The last part of this chapter will examine how federal law might be translated into educational action; this includes looking closely at transition components to include in the IEP, current national trends regarding setting goals for transition, and the importance of assessment in helping each student plan for transition. After reading this chapter, you should understand the following:

OVERVIEW OF IEP DEVELOPMENT

All students in special education are expected to leave school prepared to live independently, enjoy self-determination, make choices, contribute to society, pursue meaningful careers, and enjoy integration in the economic, political, social, cultural, and educational mainstream of American society.

The IEP is the blueprint for attaining improved educational results for students with disabilities. It is used to strengthen the connection between special education programs and services and the general education curriculum. The IEP serves two major purposes:

1. It is a written plan for a student in special education: Simply stated, the IEP explains the specific educational objectives and placement for a particular student. It is a management tool for the entire assessment teaching process:
2. The IEP becomes the critical link between the student in special education and the special teaching that the student requires (Lerner, 1997).

COMPONENTS TO BE INCLUDED IN THE IEP

According to IDEA '97, the components of an IEP must include:

i) a statement of the child's present levels of educational performance, including—(I) how the child's disability affects the child's involvement and progress in the general curriculum; or (II) for preschool children, as appropriate, how the disability affects the child's participation in appropriate activities;

ii) a statement of measurable annuals goals, including *benchmarks* or short-term objectives, related to—(I) meeting the child's needs that result from the child's disability to enable the child to be involved in and progress in the general curriculum; and (II) meeting each of the child's other educational needs that result from the child's disability;

iii) a statement of the special education and related services and supplementary aids and services to be provided to the child, or on behalf of the child, and a statement of program modifications or supports for school personnel that will be provided for the child—(I) to advance appropriately toward attaining the annual goals; (II) to be involved and progress in the general curriculum in accordance with clause (i) and to participate in extracurricular and other nonacademic activities; and (III) to be educated and participate with other children with disabilities and non-disabled children in the activities described in this paragraph;

iv) an explanation of the extent, if any, to which the child will not participate with non-disabled children in the regular class and in the activities described in clause (iii);

v) a statement of any individual modifications in the administration of State or district-wide assessments of student achievement that are needed in order for the child to participate in such assessment; and (II) if the IEP Team determines that the child will not participate in a particular State or district-wide assessment of student achievement (or part of such an assessment), a statement of—(aa) why that assessment is not appropriate for the child; and (bb) how the child will be assessed;

vi) the projected date for the beginning of the services and modifications described in clause (iii), and the anticipated frequency, location, and duration of those services and modifications;

vii) beginning at age 14, and updated annually, a statement of the transition service needs of the child under the applicable components of the child's IEP that focuses on the child's courses of study (such as participation in advanced-placement courses or a vocational education program); (II) beginning at age 16 (or younger, if determined appropriate by the IEP team), a statement of needed transition services for the child, including, when appropriate, a statement of the interagency responsibilities or any needed linkages; and (III) beginning at least one year before the child reaches the age of majority under State law, a statement that the child has been informed of his or her rights under this title, if any, that will transfer to the child on reaching the age of majority under section 615(m); and

viii) a statement of—(I) how the child's progress toward the annual goals described in clause (ii) will be measured; and (II) how the child's parents will be regularly informed (by such means as periodic report cards), at least as often as parents are informed of their non-disabled children's progress, of—(aa) their child's progress toward the annual goals described in clause (ii); and (bb) the extent to which that progress is sufficient to enable the child to achieve the goals by the end of the year. [Section 614(d)(1)(A)(i) through (viii)]

INDIVIDUALIZED EDUCATION PROGRAM (IEP) REQUIREMENTS UNDER IDEA '97

The initial draft of the IEP should be developed at the eligibility meeting by the committee members, the parent(s) and, when appropriate, the student. Each student's individualized education program is a vital document, for it spells out the special education and related services that he or she will receive. A team that includes parents and school professionals and, when appropriate, the student develops the IEP. The new IDEA maintains the IEP as a document of central importance and, in the hope of improving compliance, moves all provisions related to the IEP to one place in the law—Section 614(d). (Under the prior law, IEP provisions were found in several different places.)

At the same time, several key changes have been made to what information the IEP must contain and the way in which the IEP is developed. The IEP retains many familiar components from previous legislation, such as statements regarding the student's present levels of educational performance, annual goals, special education and related services to be provided, projected dates for the beginning and end of services, and transition services for youth. However, some modifications have been made to these familiar components to place more emphasis within the law on involving students with disabilities in the general curriculum and in the general education classroom, with supplementary aids and services as appropriate.

For example, "present levels of educational performance" must now include a statement of how the child's disability affects his or her involvement and progress in the general curriculum. Similarly, the IEP must contain a statement of special education and related services, as well as the supplementary aids and services, that the child or youth needs in order to ". . . be involved and progress in the general curriculum . . . and to participate in extracurricular and other nonacademic activities; and . . . to be educated and participate with other children with disabilities and non-disabled children . . ." [Section 614(d)(1)(A)(iii)].

With these new IEP requirements, there is a clear intent to strengthen the connection between special education and the general education curriculum. As the Committee on Labor and Human Resources Report [to Accompany S. 717] states: "The new emphasis on participation in the general education curriculum . . . is intended to produce attention to the accommodations and adjustments necessary for disabled children to access the general education curriculum and the special services which may be necessary for appropriate participation in particular areas of the curriculum . . ." (p. 20).

Along the same line is the requirement that the IEP include an explanation of the extent to which the student will not be participating with children without disabilities in the general education class and in extracurricular and nonacademic activities. This explanation of the extent to which the child will be educated separately is a new component of the IEP, yet is clearly in keeping with the changes noted previously.

Other aspects of the IEP are entirely new as well. For example, each student's IEP must now include a statement of how the administration of state or district-wide assessments will be modified for the student so that he or she can participate. If the IEP team determines that the student cannot participate in such assessments, then the IEP must include a statement of (a) why the assessment is not appropriate for the child and (b) how the child will be assessed. These changes work in tandem with changes elsewhere in the IDEA requiring that students with disabilities be included in state and district-wide assessments of student achievement.

Other new IEP requirements are statements regarding (a) informing the student about the transfer of rights as he or she approaches the age of majority, (b) how parents will be regularly informed of their child's progress toward meeting the annual goals in the IEP, (c) where services will be delivered to the student, and (d) transition service needs of the student beginning at age 14.

IDEA maintains essentially the same process for developing the IEP—namely, the document is developed by a multidisciplinary team, including the parents. However, the new legislation increases the role of the general educator on the IEP team, to include, when appropriate, helping to determine positive behavioral interventions and appropriate supplementary aids and services for the student. Also added to the IEP process are "special factors" that the IEP team must consider. These factors include:

- behavior strategies and supports, if the child's behavior impedes his or her learning or that of others
- the child's language needs (as they relate to the IEP) if the child has limited English proficiency

- providing for instruction in braille and the use of braille (unless not appropriate), if a child is blind or visually impaired
- the communication needs of the child, with a list of specific factors to be considered if a child is deaf or hard of hearing
- whether the child requires assistive devices and services

The language in the new IDEA emphasizes periodic review of the IEP (at least annually, as previously required) and revision as needed. A new, separate requirement exists: Schools must report to parents on the progress of their child with disabilities at least as frequently as progress of children without disabilities is reported, which seems likely to affect the revision process for IEPs. If it becomes evident that a child is not making "expected progress toward the annual goals and in the general curriculum," the IEP team must meet and revise the IEP.

The new legislation specifically lists a variety of other circumstances under which the IEP team would also need to review and revise the IEP, including the child's anticipated needs, the results of any reevaluation conducted, or information provided by the parents.

IDEA '97 and Transition Services

The requirements for providing transition services for youth with disabilities have been modified in IDEA '97. Although the definition of transition services remains the same, two notable changes have been made to IEP requirements:

1. Beginning when a student is 14, and annually thereafter, the student's IEP must contain a statement of his or her transition service needs under the various components of that IEP that focus on the student's courses of study (e.g., vocational education or advanced placement).
2. Beginning at least one year before the student reaches the age of majority under state law, the IEP must contain a statement that the student has been informed of the rights under the law that will transfer to him or her upon reaching the age of majority.

The new law maintains 16 as the age when students' IEPs must contain statements of needed transition services. These two requirements—one for students age 14 and older and one for students age 16 and older—seem confusingly similar. However, the purpose of including certain statements for students beginning at age 14, according to the Committee on Labor and Human Resources Report [to Accompany S. 717], "is to focus attention on how the child's educational program can be planned . . . [and] the provision is designed to augment, and not replace, the separate transition services requirement, under which children with disabilities [who are 16 or older] receive transition services . . ." (p. 22).

The second mandate within IDEA that will affect IEP development of students is the law's statement of when, at the latest, the provision of transition services must begin. According to IDEA:

> The IEP for each student, beginning no later than age 16 (and at a younger age, if determined appropriate), must include a statement of the needed transition services. . . . [Section 300.346(b)(1)]

The way in which this age requirement is stated gives school districts some latitude in deciding when to begin providing transition services. At a minimum, schools must provide services to students who are age 16. As the regulations state in a note, "For all students who are 16 years or older, one of the purposes of the annual

[IEP] meeting will always be the planning of transition services, since transition services are a required component of the IEP for these students" (Section 300.344, Note 2). However, a school may provide transition services to younger students, when their needs deem it appropriate. This may be particularly important for students with severe disabilities or for those who are at risk of dropping out of school before age 16. Considering the fact that 36 percent of students with disabilities do, in fact, drop out of school (Wagner & Shaver, 1989), the need clearly exists to provide transition services to many students who have not yet turned 16 years old.

Note 3 in this section of the regulations addresses this last point directly by pointing out that Section 602(a)(2) of the Individuals with Disabilities Education Act permits transition services to students beginning at age 14 or younger, when deemed appropriate. Note 3 goes on to state:

> Although the statute does not mandate transition services for all students beginning at age 14 or younger, the provision of these services could have a significantly positive effect on the employment and independent living outcomes for many of these students in the future, especially for students who are likely to drop out before age 16.

Note 3 (in Section 300.344) goes on to quote from the Report of the House Committee on Education and Labor, which was written to accompany and explain the IDEA: Although this language leaves the final determination of when to initiate transition services for students under age 16 to the IEP process, it nonetheless makes it clear that Congress expects consideration to be given to the need for transition services for some students by age 14 or younger. The Committee encourages this approach because of their concern that age 16 may be too late for many students, particularly those at risk of dropping out of school and those with the most severe disabilities. Even for those students who will stay in school until age 18, many will need more than two years of transitional services. Students with disabilities are now dropping out of school before age 16, feeling that the education system has little to offer them. Initiating services at a younger age will be critical. [House Report 101-544, 10 (1990)]

In reference to students with severe cognitive and multiple disabilities, this House Report goes on to observe that, before these students "age out" of the public school system, "they must have time to develop the essential skills which will be critical for them throughout their lives. Transition services for this population must be considered, planned, and provided over a multi-year time period" (U.S. House of Representatives, 1990, June 18, p. 10). Thus, Congress makes its intent clear that, although providing transition services to students with disabilities under the age of 16 is not a requirement of the law, it is still highly desirable for many individuals, particularly those with severe disabilities and those at risk of dropping out of school.

INDIVIDUALS INVOLVED IN TRANSITION PLANNING

The regulations of IDEA are very clear as to which individuals should participate in determining the transition services a student needs and what these services will entail. In addition to the usual participants at an IEP meeting (e.g., the student's classroom teacher, a school representative, and the parents), the public agency is required to invite to any meeting where transition services will be discussed both "(i) the student; and (ii) a representative of any other agency that is likely to be responsible for providing or paying for transition services" [Section 300.344(c)(1)].

The Student

It is particularly important that the student be involved in the process. As mentioned earlier, the regulations specifically state that the student must be invited to attend the IEP meeting. This includes students who are younger than 16. If transition services for a younger student are discussed at a meeting where the student is not present, no decisions regarding transition services may be made without holding a subsequent IEP meeting for that purpose and inviting the student to the meeting (Section 300.344, Note 2).

Furthermore, the coordinated set of activities developed "must be based on the individual student's needs, taking into account the student's preferences and interests" [Section 300.18(b)(1)]. If the student does not attend, then the school must take "other steps to ensure that the student's preferences and interests are considered" [Section 300.344(c)(2)]. In most cases, the person most able to determine and explain the student's preferences and interests is, of course, the student.

However, perhaps the most important reason to involve the student in transition planning goes beyond what is required by law. The critical issue here is one of self-determination. "Self-determination, which includes self-actualization, assertiveness, creativity, pride, and self-advocacy, must be part of the career development process that begins in early childhood and continues throughout adult life" (Ward, 1992, p. 389). It is vital that educational systems, parents, and other service providers do everything they can to facilitate the development of each student's self-determination skills, for these are at the core of the student developing the ability to manage his or her own life. The IEP meeting is one critically important and appropriate place for the student to have an active, self-determining role. What are being discussed and planned in the IEP meeting, after all, are services that will directly affect the student's life, now and in the future.

To facilitate the student's participation in the transition process, however, many students may need to be informed about the nature of their role in the IEP meeting and afterwards—specifically, what their participation entails. Expressing personal preferences and desires and advocating for themselves, particularly in the presence of "authority figures" such as administrators, teachers, and parents, may be a new role for students, one for which they need guidance and feedback. Parents can help prepare the young person to participate in IEP meetings, talking about its purpose, describing what goes on and who typically attends, and discussing transition issues with their child before (and after) the meeting occurs. Some students may benefit from rehearsing certain aspects of the meeting (e.g., greetings, appropriate ways to express preferences or suggest alternatives). If the student requires any accommodation, such as an interpreter or an augmentative communication device, this should be arranged (by the student, parents, or teacher) in advance of the meeting, to remove any artificial obstacles to the student's participation. Ultimately, "the goal is for students to assume control (with appropriate levels of support) over their transition program and identify and manage its various components" (Ward, 1992, p. 389).

Parents must also be invited to any meeting where transition services will be discussed, and they must be informed that that is the purpose of the meeting. The school must also indicate to the parents that the student will be invited and identify any other agency that will be invited to participate [Section 300.345(b)(2)].

Participating agencies that would typically be invited to participate in discussing and determining what transition services a student should receive would be those agencies that share responsibility in some way for providing or paying for those services. Thus, the agency responsible for providing vocational rehabilitation services might be invited to send a representative. If an agency is invited to send a representative to a meeting and does not do so, the school "shall take other steps to obtain the participation of the other agency in the planning of any transition services" [Section 300.344(c)(3)].

Together, this group of people—the student, the student's teacher(s), a representative of the school, the parents, representatives from outside agencies that will be involved in planning or providing transition services, and any other invited participants—will discuss and determine what transition services the student needs.

DETERMINING WHAT TRANSITION
SERVICES ARE NEEDED

IDEA does not specifically identify how the IEP team determines what transition services a student needs, but since transition services are included as a component of the IEP, the process traditionally used to identify other needed educational or related services would apply. This process typically involves evaluation using a variety of measures, such as observations, anecdotal information, and testing (standardized and/or performance). (See Chapter 5 for a more detailed discussion of assessment issues.) Obviously, this evaluation process would focus on transition issues (employment, postsecondary education, adult services, independent living, and community participation), asking questions such as:

- What competencies and knowledge does the student need in order to move successfully into employment (postsecondary education, adult services, independent living, community participation, etc.)?
- What skills and knowledge does the student have at present in each of these areas? Is functional vocational evaluation necessary to determine the student's level of skills?
- What knowledge and skills does the student still need to acquire?

This information will be critical in determining appropriate transition services for the student and in developing the specific transition plan. In particular, the plan should address the areas in which the student most needs to increase his or her knowledge and skills in order to prepare for transition.

It must be pointed out that, although the regulations state unequivocally that "the coordinated set of activities must . . . include instruction, community experiences, and the development of employment and other adult living objectives" [Section 300.18(b)], there may be occasions when certain of these services are not provided to a student. This possibility arises from Section 300.346(b)(2), the section of the regulations defining the contents of the IEP. This section states: "If the IEP team determines that services are not needed in one or more of the areas specified in Section 300.18(b)(2)(i) through (b)(2)(iii), the IEP must include a statement to that effect and the basis upon which the determination was made" [Section 300.346(b)(2)].

Presumably, this statement is included to acknowledge that students differ from each other in terms of the nature and severity of their disability, personality, abilities, cultural values, and interests. Therefore, the type and amount of transition services needed may also differ from student to student. Just as special education and related services provided to students differ depending on student need, so, too, will transition services vary. As with other educational services provided to students with disabilities, then, transition services will be individualized to fit the person's unique needs.

Thus, an IEP team may legitimately decide that a student does not need transition services in one (or more) area(s). For example, a student might be planning on studying at a local university. To prepare for transition to this environment, he or she may need to develop objectives related to the university's application process and to investigate what accommodations the university makes available to students with disabilities and which accommodations he or she will need, if any. Some instruction may be necessary to help the student address these objectives, but community-based experiences may not be necessary. To be in compliance with the law, the IEP for this student must then state that services in community-based experiences will not be provided and give the reason(s) why the team feels that the services are not needed. However, "since it is part of the IEP, the IEP team must reconsider its determination at least annually" (Section 300.346, Note 2). Presumably, this latter requirement is intended to ensure that when new information about the student becomes available or the student's plans change, appropriate changes are made in the transition services he or she needs in order to prepare for life after high school.

Hopefully, the regulation permitting variability in the type and amount of transition services will not also permit school districts to avoid providing services that are, in fact, needed by students. Students and parents should remember that the regulations require a team approach to making decisions about which services are needed and that they are integral members of the team. In some cases, advocating for needed transition services may be an important part of obtaining the services. For disputes that cannot be settled through open discussion, compromise, or mediation, students and parents have recourse through the law's procedural safeguards (e.g., due process hearings). These safeguards are the same as those for resolving conflicts over special education and related services, for, indeed, transition services are an expansion of the IEP process and can be provided either as special education or as a related service (Section 300.18, Note).

Once the team has reached agreement on the transition areas that will be important for the student to emphasize, actually developing statements within the IEP may be different from the process used for detailing special education and related services. The most important difference is that planning for transition must look several years into the future, proactively addressing questions such as:

- How many years of public school does the student have remaining?
- Given the student's present level of performance and where he or she needs to be by the end of high school, what transition services are needed this year?
- What services are needed in each remaining year?

Especially important to the goal-setting process is the concept that skills are learned along a progressive continuum of difficulty. This means that new skills should build on the skills mastered previously and that addressing more advanced skills and knowledge can often be deferred to transition plans made in subsequent years.

A second difference is that the plan does not necessarily have to state the transition services in terms of annual goals and short-term objectives. Interestingly, the rules and regulations of the IDEA do not specifically require—nor do they specifically exclude—the use of goal and objective statements for transition services (such statements are required for other educational services). This is because "the IEP content requirements in Section 300.346(a) do not appear to be appropriate for all types of transition services" (U.S. Department of Education, 1992a, p. 44847). However, it is certainly good educational practice to plan many of the transition services using annual goal statements and short-term objectives. Such statements allow school districts, parents, and students to see clearly where they are going and to measure progress.

PROVIDING TRANSITION SERVICES

The IDEA requires that, when appropriate, the IEP of each student planning for transition should also include ". . . a statement of each public agency's and each participating agency's responsibilities or linkages, or both, before the student leaves the school setting [Section 300.346(b)(1)].

The public agency, typically the school, is primarily responsible for the provision of transition services. According to the law, the school's responsibilities in this regard—what services it will provide—must be stated clearly in the student's IEP. The responsibilities of any other participating agency (e.g., vocational rehabilitation) must also be stated in the IEP, including a statement of the agency's "commitment . . . to meet any financial responsibility it may have in the provision of transition services" (Section 300.346, Note 1). Linkages between agencies, such as cooperative agreements to provide transition services, must also be stipulated.

According to the report accompanying and explaining the IDEA, this latter requirement of the IDEA signals Congress's intention that "the preparation of students for movement from school to post-school environments not be the sole responsibility of public education. The purpose of the . . . statement pertaining to interagency linkages is to communicate shared responsibility" (U.S. House of Representatives, 1990, June 18, p. 12). This includes sharing (a) financial responsibility, in that "the local education agency should not bear the costs of transition services which according to the IEP would have been borne by another participating agency" (p. 11), and (b) personnel resources and expertise. Many of the adult agencies with which responsibility might be shared have staff with considerable expertise in transition issues—for example, rehabilitation counselors from the local rehabilitation agency. Operating within an interagency cooperative agreement, a rehabilitation counselor might become involved in helping students with disabilities plan for transition. As the report of the Committee on Education and Labor observes:

> . . . the rehabilitation counseling discipline embodies the wide range of knowledge needed for successful school to work transition, i.e., vocational implications of disability, career development, and career counseling for individuals with disabilities, job placement, and job modification. Therefore, rehabilitation counselors are professionally prepared to provide the appropriate counseling as well as to coordinate the services of the special education disciplines, adult services providers, and postsecondary education agencies to ensure effective, planned transition services for students with disabilities. (U.S. House of Representatives, 1990, June 18, pp. 7–8)

The Committee on Education and Labor states very clearly, however, that "the responsibility for developing and implementing interagency participation is an administrative-level responsibility and should not be delegated to the already heavily-burdened teacher" (U.S. House of Representatives, 1990, June 18, p. 11). Each state plan for special education sets forth policies and procedures for developing and implementing interagency agreements between the State Education Agency (SEA) and all other state and local agencies that provide or pay for services for children with disabilities (34 C.F.R. Section 300.152). Thus, developing and implementing interagency agreements is a state-level or district-level responsibility, not one that falls to the classroom teacher.

Establishing such interagency linkages can be of enormous benefit to students planning for transition. This is because, as students with disabilities leave the public school system, their entitlement to educational, vocational, and other services ends. In the place of one relatively organized service provider (the school system), there may now be a confusing array of many service providers (i.e., the local vocational rehabilitation agency, the state department of mental health, developmental disabilities councils, community services boards, the federal Social Security system, and so on). Individuals with disabilities who have left school become solely responsible for identifying where to obtain the services they need and for demonstrating their eligibility to receive the services. Therefore, for many students with disabilities, identifying relevant adult service providers, establishing eligibility to receive adult services, and having interagency responsibilities and linkages stated in the IEP, all while still in school, "will be necessary to ensure a smooth transition from school to adult life" (U.S. House of Representatives, 1990, June 18, p. 11).

WHERE TRANSITION SERVICES CAN BE PROVIDED

The IDEA does not enumerate where transition services should be provided. However, it is important to note that the definition of transition services states that the coordinated set of activities that the IEP team designs to promote the student's movement to postschool life must include:

(i) Instruction;

(ii) Community experiences;

(iii) The development of employment and other post-school adult living objectives; and

(iv) If appropriate, acquisition of daily living skills and functional vocational evaluation. [Section 300.18(b)(2)]

These requirements make it clear that transition services should be provided across a variety of locations, including within the community, as befitting the needs of the student and the particular skill or knowledge to be acquired. For example, the IEP team might determine that the student needs to learn how to operate within the community. One important facet of this general goal might involve knowing how to ride the bus. Transition services, then, might address the student's need to ride the bus by developing learning experiences within the classroom (e.g., instruction in how to identify the proper bus and pay for the ride) and then matching the classroom experience with activities within the community (e.g., actually taking the bus). More will be said later about the importance of providing students in transition with community-based experiences.

Expanding the IEP

Adding transition services to the IEP takes advantage of an already established process for deciding on and delivering educational services to students with disabilities. The IEP process under the IDEA is much the same as under the EHA, in that a multidisciplinary team—including the parents and, where appropriate, the student—meets to discuss and set appropriate goals and objectives for the student with a disability. The team also identifies the services the student needs, states how it will determine if the student has achieved the goals and objectives, and decides other important aspects of the student's special education, including the amount of time to be spent in regular education classes.

However, now that needed transition services must be stated in the IEPs of all students who are 16 years old and older (and in the IEPs of many students who are younger than 16), the basic tenets of the IEP described previously are expanded, if not in format, then in philosophy. Perhaps the largest and most significant aspect of including transition services in the IEP is the need to expand the original concept of annual goals and short-term objectives to focus on outcomes of special education and incorporate the long-range life goals of the student with disabilities. This change in philosophy does not by any means indicate that educators and agency personnel can predict or be responsible for what the rest of an individual's life will entail. It does, however, cause professionals and families to think beyond the parameters of year-long goals and school-only service systems. The subsequent challenge for IEP teams is the creation of transition goals that reflect the needs the student with disabilities will have as an adult and yet still fit within the guidelines of the IEP process.

The fact that the IDEA (P.L. 105-17) specifically defines transition services as a component within the IEP will, undoubtedly, have other ramifications for local education agencies and education professionals. For example, although many *local education agencies (LEAs)* across the country are already providing these services, they are following their own, individually styled formats for transition planning. This includes the use of a separate *individualized transition plan (ITP)* that is attached to the IEP. Since transition services are now defined as being part of the IEP, LEAs using a separate document (the ITP) may need to integrate development of this document into the IEP process.

Bringing in the World Outside of School

Another ramification of having transition services as part of the IEP is that the participants in an IEP meeting may now include individuals from outside of the school setting, such as representatives of adult service providers (i.e., vocational rehabilitation, Social Security Administration, JTPA programs, and Community Services Board). Including professionals from nonschool agencies in IEP development is important in providing transition services, because any or all of these agencies may be involved with the student during and/or after his or her public school years. Furthermore, the concept of responsibility has been expanded to include nonschool professionals. This is intended to encourage creative cooperation between the agencies to share transition responsibilities for the youth with disabilities and to forge linkages. Interagency coordination between youth and adult service providers will greatly facilitate the transition process and encourage collaborative planning and programming at the local level. Certainly, these linkages are vital to students' successful transition to the adult world.

But what happens if a participating agency, such as the vocational rehabilitation agency, fails to provide the services it has agreed to provide? The IDEA states that, in this instance:

> . . . the public agency responsible for the student's education shall, as soon as possible, initiate a meeting for the purpose of identifying alternative strategies to meet the transition objectives and, if necessary, revising the student's IEP. [Section 300.347(a)]

Thus, should an agency default on its agreed-upon obligation, the public agency—in most cases, the school—is required to reconvene the IEP team and find alternative strategies for meeting the transition objectives stated in the IEP. One potentially negative outcome of this mandate is that, when any adult service provider fails to carry out its stated obligations, the responsibility for transition services returns to the schools. This possibility is addressed in the regulations for the IDEA, which state that, even when the school reconvenes the IEP team to discuss alternative ways of meeting a student's transition objectives, the participating agency defaulting on its obligation is in no way relieved "of the responsibility to provide or pay for any transition service that the agency would otherwise provide to students with disabilities who meet the eligible criteria of that agency" [34 C.F.R. Section 300.347(b)]. How exactly the defaulting agency will be held accountable for the services it had agreed to provide is unclear, except that the policies and procedures set forth in the state plan for special education services—specifically those relating to interagency agreements (Section 300.152)—would be called into play. These policies and procedures should give the schools a mechanism for resolving disputes and for securing reimbursements from other agencies. However, because the strength of these agreements varies from location to location, some school districts may find that this particular regulation does not save them from having to assume total responsibility for paying for and providing transition services. How defaults will affect students and the services they receive also remains to be seen.

Another potentially negative outcome of this regulation governing defaults lies in the fact that the IEP team can, if necessary, revise the student's IEP. The way that the regulations state this might lead some to believe that goals and objectives stated in the IEP may be dismissed, simply because it is difficult for the school to find ways to meet them.

It is extremely important to note that revising the IEP does not mean that goals and objectives may be abandoned. The secretary of education is very clear on this point, as follows:

> When an IEP team is reconvened, an alternative strategy may be able to be identified without changing the student's IEP. In other cases, the IEP team may find it necessary to revise the IEP to include alternative ways to meet the goals that were identified. (U.S. Department of Education, 1992a, p. 44848)

Thus, it is not the goal and objective statements that may be revised; it is the ways in which the goals and objectives will be met.

Broadening Curriculum and Staff Roles

Traditionally, educators have focused on providing school-based services. Now, with transition services, schools must expand the scope of their services to include instructional and educational experiences that will occur outside of the school building and that are related to much broader outcomes: employment, independent living, functional skills, and community participation. And "as the definition of the secondary-level special education classroom expands beyond the physical structure of the school building to include the entire community, personnel capabilities must be expanded as well" (DeStefano & Wermuth, 1992, p. 543). Staff must learn new roles, new information, and new skills; they must be able to collaborate with "families, employers, community-based service providers, and other key players in the post-school environments encountered by students with disabilities" (p. 544). Clearly, these changes—expanding curriculum and expanding the competencies of staff—present schools with a significant challenge, particularly in this time of budget crunches and academically oriented educational reform.

Given all that has been said previously—the many details of federal regulations and how they govern provision of transition services—it may be useful to conclude this section by looking again at the Congressional intent behind transition services. This represents the spirit of the law and should be a guiding force in how school districts work with students with disabilities to prepare them for life after high school.

TRANSITION SERVICES AND CONGRESSIONAL INTENT

The Committee on Education and Labor issued these paragraphs as part of the report written to accompany and explain the Individuals with Disabilities Education Act:

> The Committee expects that schools, when developing a child's individualized education program each year, will (a) consider the post-school outcomes desired for that student, and (b) provide educational and related services designed to prepare the student for achieving these outcomes. This process should begin as early as possible in a child's life and must be reflected in the IEP (by no later than age 16) as a statement of the transition services to be provided.
>
> The Committee wishes to emphasize that the schools are not being asked to do what they are not intended to do. For instance, the schools are not expected to become job placement centers. However, there are many employment and employment related activities which are appropriately provided by and funded through the local education agency. In addition, the schools should facilitate linkage with other public agencies in the transition to independent living, job training preparation,

vocational rehabilitation, and post-secondary education. That is why the Committee has taken great care in its choice of the words "which promotes movement" in the definition of transition services. The Committee expects schools to familiarize themselves with the post-school opportunities and services available for students with disabilities in their communities and State, and make use of this information in the transition planning for individual students. By doing so, schools can facilitate linkage with agencies when needed by students, can ascertain requirements for access to, and participation in, the opportunities offered by these agencies, and thus can effectively communicate this information to students and their families, and identify ways in which they can prepare students with disabilities to take advantage of these opportunities. (U.S. House of Representatives, 1990, June 18, p. 12)

SUGGESTED TRANSITION COMPONENTS

Having looked at the IEP as a planning document and some ramifications of including transition services in the IEP, let us now examine more closely the specific areas or domains that are critical for IEP teams to address when planning for a student's transition to adult life. These domains are:

- employment, including supported employment
- postsecondary educational activities, including postsecondary education, vocational training, and continuing and adult education
- independent living, including exploration of residential options and daily living skills that will be needed in adult life
- eligibility for various adult services
- Community participation, including recreation and leisure activities and the development of personal and social skills

This discussion is based on the transition planning being conducted in states throughout the country and on the definition of transition services contained in the IDEA (Section 300.18). Before beginning to discuss each of these areas, however, it is important for the IEP team to realize that transition goals are not designed to predict what an individual will be doing in 20 years. Although some of the transition goals developed for a student may be related to acquiring quite specific skills (e.g., how to use a piece of equipment essential to a particular occupation), many of the goals and objectives should represent basic skills that cut across the domains listed earlier. For example, punctuality is important not only in maintaining employment, but it also has value in maintaining personal relationships, in accessing recreation and leisure activities, and in using public transportation. Similarly, the ability to use money is important in independent living environments (e.g., to buy food or pay the rent) and in recreational situations, where tickets to an event might need to be purchased. Thus, it is a good idea for a student to address transition goals that focus on developing skills that will be as relevant 20 years from now as they are at the time of IEP development.

For each student, self-determination and self-advocacy skills would certainly be relevant now and in the future. It might be suggested that four of the most fundamental skills or knowledge students can have that will serve them well in a wide variety of adult situations are the following:

- the ability to assess themselves, including their skills and abilities
- awareness of the accommodations they need because of their disability
- knowledge of their civil rights to these accommodations through legislation such as the Americans with Disabilities Act (ADA) and Section 504 of the Rehabilitation Act of 1973
- the self-advocacy skills necessary to express their needs in the workplace, in educational institutions, and in community settings

These skills will provide students with a strong base for participating in the development of IEP goals, including transition services, and for managing the many aspects of adult life that will become important after high school.

Another issue that may be important in transition planning—and one that may ultimately affect decisions made in each domain—is transportation. The IEP team may need to consider (a) the availability of public transportation in the student's community and (b) how dependent the student will be on public transportation in order to go to work or postsecondary school, travel to and from home, access adult service providers, and move about in the community. If the student can drive and expects to have access to a vehicle, then transportation may not be a critical factor in planning for the future. However, if the student will have to rely on public transportation, then this fact needs to be taken into consideration when exploring future options. Certainly, many students will want to develop the ability to use public transportation by the time they leave the school system. In some cases, decisions about what postsecondary schools to attend, where to live in the community, and so on may be driven by the availability of transportation and the student's skill in using it.

It is also important to understand that not every student with disabilities will need to receive transition services in all of the domains. The domains discussed later will need to be considered to the extent indicated by the nature and severity of a student's disability and his or her plans and desires for the future. Some students with severe disabilities will need extensive intervention to plan effectively for transition to adult life. Students with milder disabilities may require only limited services in one or two areas, with specific attention given to how their disability affects a particular aspect of transition.

IEP DEVELOPMENT AND EMPLOYMENT

Given the research presented earlier on the unemployment and underemployment of individuals with disabilities, and the fact that working has been shown to make an enormous qualitative difference in the lives of people with disabilities (Harris & Associates, 1989), all members of the IEP team must give serious consideration to planning and preparing the young person for future employment. Developing employment-related transition goals for a student will require discussion and planning of issues such as:

- In what type of work is the student interested?
- Considering the nature and severity of the student's disability and the nature of his or her job interests, is it more appropriate for the student to be involved in competitive employment or some level of supported employment?
- If the student has chosen a particular occupational field, does he or she have the skills and abilities needed to succeed in that field? What specific work skills is the student missing?
- Does the student know what employee behaviors are considered important to successful employment, and does he or she demonstrate these behaviors?
- What school activities are needed in order for the student to acquire these work-related skills and behaviors?
- What type of academic, social, and/or vocational program is needed to help the student acquire relevant work skills and behaviors before he or she exits high school? Is there such a program available within the school system or community? If not, what individuals and organizations (school, businesses, paraprofessionals, and job coaches) can collaborate to develop a personalized program to address the student's needs?
- What types of accommodations might the student need on the job? Is the student informed as to his or her rights under federal law to receive

accommodations? Does he or she have the self-advocacy skills necessary to request and obtain these accommodations?

For the IEP team to address these questions on an informed basis and develop appropriate employment goals and objectives for the student, a thorough vocational assessment of the student may be essential. *Vocational assessment*, which will be discussed in more detail later in the next chapter, can provide the IEP team with valuable information, such as what interests and aptitudes the student has, and what work skills the student has mastered and what skills need to be developed. One such model called the Life-Centered Career Education Curriculum (Kokaska & Brolin, 1985) breaks down the area of occupational skills into such goals as (a) selecting and planning occupational choices, (b) exhibiting appropriate work behaviors, and (c) seeking, securing, and maintaining employment. Within each of these general goal areas, specific corresponding objectives might include (a) identifying occupational needs, interests, and aptitudes, (b) following directions, working at a satisfactory rate, and accepting supervision, and (c) searching for a job through want ads and personal networking, applying for a job, and interviewing for a job.

Of course, these are just some of the objectives that might be developed to address general occupational goals. Each of these objectives might be broken down further or other objectives might be developed to address the specific needs of the student. When setting goals, it is important to remember that employment skills, like any skills, are learned along a progressive continuum of difficulty. For example, the suggested goal areas under "Exhibiting Appropriate Work Habits and Behaviors" range from the basic behaviors of following directions and being punctual to more advanced behaviors such as working at a satisfactory rate, working with others, and accepting supervision, and finally to a sophisticated behavior such as demonstrating occupational safety (Kokaska & Brolin, 1985).

It should also be noted that planning employment goals does not necessarily dictate specific jobs. Although it is fine to develop goals related to acquiring the skills needed to do a specific job, this should not happen to the exclusion of developing the general skills and abilities necessary for seeking, securing, and maintaining employment. An important aspect of transition planning is building skills that will generalize to adult situations and serve the student well later in life. In fact, most of the behaviors addressed in the "Work Habits" section may be practiced within the classroom setting from a very early age. This suggests that, ideally, transition planning should begin in the early elementary school years, giving students with disabilities the time and opportunity to develop a broad base of basic skills that would be transferable to the wide variety of situations they will encounter throughout their lives.

IEP DEVELOPMENT AND POSTSECONDARY EDUCATIONAL ACTIVITIES

Planning postsecondary educational activities recognizes that not all young people will seek employment immediately after they leave high school. Many students will want to pursue further education. This education may be academic in nature, such as going to a university or college, or it may be technically oriented, such as going to a trade school or vocational center to acquire the skills needed for a specific occupation (e.g., electrician, plumber, and cosmetologist).

Goals and objectives related to this option will depend on (a) whether the student is intending to pursue an academic or technically oriented education after school and (b) the nature and severity of the student's disability and how it affects pursuing postsecondary education. Some important general goals and objectives in this transition area might include:

- the learning of effective study habits
- arranging for job tryouts to allow the student to sample work in a specific area
- making arrangements for accommodations needed during college board or SAT testing (e.g., test in braille, oral presentation of questions, untimed testing, other)
- identifying postsecondary institutions that offer the sort of training or education desired
- identifying the types of accommodations and support services that the student needs because of his or her disability
- identifying postsecondary educational institutions that make available the accommodations or support services needed by the student
- applying to the schools of choice and advocating for needed accommodations

As with any transition goal setting, planning for postsecondary education should be firmly grounded in assessment. Students who wish to attend college may still consider vocational assessment as an important process in identifying postsecondary and career options (Rothenbacher & Leconte, 1990).

IEP DEVELOPMENT AND INDEPENDENT LIVING

Considering the eventual independence of an individual with disabilities is often a source of concern and excitement for both the individual and his or her family. Many issues will need to be considered under this transition domain, including (a) where the student will live (either staying in the family home or living elsewhere) and (b) the skills that are basic to taking care of oneself.

Exploring Independent Living Options

Not every student with disabilities will need to consider the question of where he or she will live after leaving high school. Some will wish to continue living in the family home. Others may be attending a postsecondary institution that provides housing for students. However, for many students, exploring the question of where to reside in the community will be an important transition issue. Options may range from independent living to group living to institutional care, and may take the following forms:

- Independent living situations do not provide the person with disabilities with supervision or support. The person is responsible for all aspects of self-care and maintenance. Renting an apartment or house alone or with a group of friends, with no more assistance than what a person without a disability might receive, would be an independent living situation.
- Foster homes are owned or rented by a family that provides some care and support to one or more nonrelated individuals with disabilities. This setting emphasizes "the individuality, diversity, and intimacy" that the family situation typically provides (Janicki, Krauss, & Seltzer, 1988, p. 6).
- Group homes have staff who provide care, supervision, and training for one or more individuals. The number of individuals may vary from group home to group home. Small group homes may have fewer than 10 people, while a large group home might serve from 21 to 40 individuals.
- Semi-independent living situations generally have separated units or apartments in one building, with staff living in a separate unit in the same building. The staff provides some care and support to the individuals with disabilities who live there, in keeping with each individual's needs.
- Board and supervision facilities have staff that provides residents with more extensive care and support than they would receive in a semi-independent living situation. For example, residents have sleeping rooms and receive meals and

supervision. However, no formal training or help with dressing, bathing, and so on is provided.

■ Personal care facilities have staff who provide residents with help in dressing, bathing, and other personal care. No formal training is provided to residents.

■ Nursing homes or institutions provide comprehensive care to individuals with disabilities, including daily nursing care. [Hill & Lakin (1986), as cited in Janicki, Krauss, & Seltzer, 1988, p. 6]

The type of living option most appropriate to an individual with disabilities will depend on his or her personal desires (e.g., whether he or she wants to live at home or outside the home, either alone or with others), the nature and severity of the disability, the amount of care, support, and supervision the person needs on a daily basis, and the amount of support available through the family and through local, state, or federal agencies (Eshilian, Haney, & Falvey, 1989, p. 120). Each student and his or her family members will need to decide which independent living option best suits the needs and preferences of the student in question. The school can provide instruction in areas that would help an individual gain independence, such as home economics, driver's education, and money management. Schools can also help the student address this postschool adult living domain by providing him or her with information about living options in the community and assessing the student's need for support. The student and his or her family can then use this information to explore options on their own. They might visit as many of the options as possible and learn the eligibility and application requirements of each. Based on the information they collect, a decision would then be made within the family about where the student will live as an adult.

Acquiring Daily Living Skills

Daily living skills are the skills involved in taking care of oneself on a daily basis. These skills are an important subcomponent of the independent living domain and include such activities as dressing, grooming, household chores, shopping, managing finances, and so on. How completely the student has mastered daily living skills may ultimately determine the type of living environment selected as most appropriate.

As with the other postschool adult living domains, a thorough assessment of student skill levels is an essential part of developing appropriate instructional activities. Parents and students can contribute a great deal of anecdotal information in this regard, as would an *ecological assessment.* Depending on what assessment reveals about a student's proficiency at daily living skills, independent living goals may accent such skills as (a) caring for personal hygiene needs, (b) managing finances, and (c) purchasing and preparing food. Each of these goals can be broken down into objectives that would range in level of difficulty. Under Kokaska and Brolin's (1985) model, for instance, the goal area of "Managing Daily Finances" includes a range of objectives that are learned in sequence, so that across one or more years a student might be required to master any or all of these skills identifying money and making change; budgeting and making wise expenditures; obtaining and using bank facilities; keeping financial records; and calculating and paying taxes.

Similarly, the general goal area of "caring for personal hygiene needs" might be broken down into objectives ranging from basic skills such as being able to dress and groom oneself appropriately to more advanced skills such as knowing how to prevent and care for illness. Stating each objective need in terms that are observable and quantifiable allows the IEP team to determine concretely if the student has mastered the skill in question.

Because acquiring daily living skills is so central to a person's ability to function independently, much care needs to be taken in how instructional activities are designed. For many students, particularly those with severe disabilities, a community-based curriculum is highly appropriate. In a community-based approach, students may initially learn and practice a skill (e.g., buying food) in the classroom but eventually practice the skill in a community or home setting. This is because many students will have difficulty transferring what they have learned in the classroom to the actual setting in which the skill is typically used (e.g., the grocery store). What happens then is that, although the student can perform the skill in class, he or she may not be able to do so in the real-world environment where the skill is actually needed. Therefore, "community environments frequented by the student and by his or her family now and in the future should be the environments used to directly teach" (Falvey, 1989b, p. 92). It is important to note that community-based instruction is most effective when only a small number of students receive instruction at a time.

For a number of logistical reasons, many school districts have been reluctant to use a community-based approach. The most typical problems include difficulty in staffing, funding, transportation, liability issues (who is responsible for injury or property damage when students are involved in community training), safety of the students, community access, and administrative, teacher, and parental support (Falvey, 1989b, pp. 94–105). Yet, there are many ways in which school districts can address and overcome these problems (see Falvey, 1989b). Now that "community experiences" are listed in IDEA's definition of transition services [Section 300.18(b)(2)(ii)], one would expect to see school districts providing some transition services through a community-based curriculum. It is certainly worthwhile for districts to develop instructional programs based in the community and for parents and student to support this type of learning experience. Such an approach to learning and teaching is often essential, if students are going to master the skills necessary to function in the community.

IEP DEVELOPMENT AND ELIGIBILITY
FOR ADULT SERVICES

For many youth, "a successful transition into the labor force is contingent on a successful transition from special education to the adult service delivery system" (DeStefano & Snauwaert, 1989, p. 37). This is because, once the young adult with disabilities exits the school system, he or she is no longer formally entitled to receive services. Rather, the youth must demonstrate his or her eligibility to receive services. Moreover, students and their families may be faced with a multitude of service options, each with its own eligibility requirements. For young people with disabilities, two of the most important service providers may be the *Social Security Administration,* which administers the *Supplemental Security Insurance (SSI)* and *Social Security Disability Insurance (SSDI)* programs (each of which can provide individuals with disabilities with cash benefits, work incentives, and Medicaid coverage), and the vocational rehabilitation system, which can provide services ranging from job training to job placement and follow-up.

Because transition planning must now involve input from community agencies that will serve the individual on exiting the school system, using IEP goals as a vehicle to investigate, identify, and satisfy these agencies' eligibility requirements will give the student a head start in accessing these service providers in the future. For example, a goal might be for the student to become familiar with at least four postsecondary service providers. Corresponding objectives and activities could then specify visiting the agencies, meeting with caseworkers, determining eligibility requirements, and completing the paperwork necessary to establish eligibility in the agencies judged to be most appropriate to the student's needs. The school system might even wish to arrange for representatives of these agencies to visit the school and meet with a group of students.

Parents and students should be aware that some adult service providers such as the Social Security Administration require several months to process applications. To avoid an unnecessary delay in receiving services on graduation, it is suggested that the student file an application six months or so before leaving school. Parents and students should also be aware that students may be placed on a waiting list to receive services from agencies such as vocational rehabilitation. Therefore, it is a good idea to explore alternatives to these traditional service providers. Often word of mouth provides the best leads to alternate service providers. The school itself or the district's special education office may be able to recommend agencies or organizations that provide services or referral within the community or county. Other organizations that parents and students might consider contacting include private nonprofit organizations within the community, local parent advocacy groups, disability advocacy groups, and the Developmental Disabilities Council. It may also be helpful to look in the Yellow Pages under "Family Services" ("Human Services" or "Social Services" in some locales) and see what service agencies are listed.

IEP DEVELOPMENT AND COMMUNITY PARTICIPATION

The IDEA specifically mentions community participation as one possible domain of transition planning. Indeed, if the end goal of transition is to live successfully in one's community (Halpern, 1985), then transition teams will need to address not just where the young adult will live in the community, and where he or she will work or go to school, but also how the individual will live. *Webster's New Collegiate Dictionary* (1980) defines *community* as "an interacting population of various kinds of individuals in a common location." Unfortunately, for many individuals with disabilities, community is merely a place of buildings and streets. There is little social interaction with other community members and little participation in community events. Through planning and preparation, however, young people with disabilities can learn to participate more fully in, as well as contribute to, the life of their community. Specific attention may need to be given to two dimensions of community participation: recreation and leisure skills, and personal and social skills.

IEP DEVELOPMENT AND RECREATION AND LEISURE

Many youth with disabilities need special assistance to learn how to use their recreation and leisure time constructively. Planning often needs to focus on developing a student's ability to identify, pursue, and participate fully in recreational and leisure activities in school and in the community. According to Falvey & Coots (1989, p. 142), positive outcomes of developing students' recreation and leisure skills are that:

- having these skills can facilitate the participation of individuals with disabilities in a variety of environments
- recreation and leisure activities are physically and emotionally beneficial to persons of all ages
- these activities provide opportunities for social interaction, communication, and the development of friendships
- constructive use of leisure time can reduce inappropriate social behavior
- these activities can be developed into vocational and career opportunities

No professional, however, should pretend to know the most enjoyable activities for a student outside of school, and most certainly the student's likes and dislikes may change with maturity. It is important that recreation and leisure activities developed to address IEP goals and objectives are ones "that are desired, preferred, and chosen by the individual" (Falvey & Coots, 1989, p. 146). Therefore, parents and professionals are cautioned against developing transition goal statements that essentially force the student to participate in a recreational activity that is not of personal interest or value. Goal statements might focus on helping the student learn to use his or her leisure time constructively and in ways that are personally enriching; the specific skills needed to participate in a chosen recreational activity (e.g., swimming, tennis, singing, bowling, card games, etc.) might also be developed. In communities that have recreational facilities and activities open to community members, goal statements might focus on developing the student's basic skills in information gathering, self-initiation, and choice making, all of which would empower the student to pursue his or her own interests. Concrete objectives, then, might include the student's learning:

- what types of assistive technology are available to facilitate his or her participation in recreational activities of interest
- what specific accommodations or adaptations can be made to help the student participate in a recreational activity
- how to find out what is happening in the community
- how to access public transportation
- how to acquire tickets to events

These objectives might be tied initially to school events, so that, depending on the interests and abilities of the student, he or she might pick a number of school events to attend (e.g., ball games, concerts, plays, dances), find out when and where the event takes place, buy a ticket, and arrange transportation to and from the event.

Extending these activities to community events would be the next logical step in the student's acquisition of the basic skills needed to participate in recreation and leisure activities. Using a community-based curriculum, as described under "Independent Living: Daily Living Skills," is highly recommended. To take advantage of events occurring in the community, it is a good idea to develop a resource bank of community organizations. (Some of these organizations may be agencies that could share responsibility for planning and implementing the transition services a student needs.) Examples of organizations in the community that may be helpful include the park and recreation department, recreation centers, YMCA and YWCA, movie theaters, bowling alleys, pools, community colleges, church groups, hobby groups or clubs, and neighborhood gyms and sports clubs (Falvey & Coots, 1989, pp. 159–160).

IEP DEVELOPMENT AND PERSONAL AND SOCIAL SKILLS

Although transition planning cannot encompass all phases of an individual's life roles, helping the student to develop good personal and social skills is likely to prove beneficial across many of the domains of adult life. For example, having good personal and social skills can help the student form and maintain friendships within the community, interact with service providers, and obtain and maintain employment. Thus, the development of personal and social skills is an appropriate transition goal for many students.

The goals and objectives developed in this area, of course, should be individualized to meet the student's particular needs. For example, if a student has difficulty in behaving in ways that are socially appropriate, objectives might include learning how to maintain eye contact; learning how to greet people; knowing the difference between strangers, acquaintances, friends, and intimates and how each should be treated; developing appropriate table manners; demonstrating the ability to take turns during conversations; and so on. If the student has difficulty with behaving in ways that are socially responsible, objectives might range from the student knowing the difference between public and private situations, to being able to recognize authority figures, to becoming aware of the laws and punishments for certain types of behavior.

Certainly, having good personal and social skills is important to functioning in the many domains of adult life. There are many resources available to assist parents and professionals in planning activities that will help the student develop these useful skills.

TYING TRANSITION GOALS AND OBJECTIVES TO SCHOOL EVENTS AND ACTIVITIES

Once transition goals and objectives have been developed for a student with disabilities, school personnel then design activities to help the student achieve each objective. With their focus on developing skills that will help the student in a variety of adult roles, some transition services may be distinct from other educational services the school system typically provides. For example, developing a student's ability to participate in community activities may be a new task for many school districts. Investigating residential options as a part of the independent living domain would be similarly new ground for many schools. It may be difficult to develop activities corresponding to some of the stated transition goals and objectives, when educational programming typically revolves around placing the student in one class for first period, another class for second period, and so on. Thinking creatively about educational programming may be necessary in order to develop a "match" between a student's transition goals and objectives and his or her class schedule (e.g., First Period—Special Education English, Second Period—Social Studies, etc.). Although not intended to imply that all transition goals can be met through programming within the school building itself—the community must clearly be the site of many transition activities—this section presents some examples of ways in which school systems can incorporate transition activities into students' educational programs, as well as take advantage of school events and activities to help students with disabilities achieve transition goals.

Many employment-related transition goals can be addressed in vocational education programs. Teachers should be alert to opportunities to place students in jobs within the school, where they can practice skills learned in vocational education class. For example, students might be required to work in the office one hour a day as a lab placement. Specific skills such as answering telephones, typing, or computer work could be practiced, and worker behaviors such as punctuality, working under supervision, and staying on task could be observed, developed, and evaluated.

Under the independent living domain, many daily living skills can be readily addressed in classes the school typically offers. For example, these "matches" could be made:

- food purchase and preparation in home economics or math class, or in the school cafeteria or store
- money management in math class
- reading survival words, using the phone book, reading the help wanted ads, movie schedule, bus schedule, and so on in English class

- personal hygiene in health or home economics class
- driving or transportation issues in driver's education class

Students could then apply the daily living skills relevant to their needs by performing "jobs" around the school. Working in the cafeteria, for example, could provide students with concrete application of food preparation skills. Selling tickets at a school event or working in the school store provides similar opportunities to apply money management skills.

Recreational and leisure skills could also be developed in a number of ways within the school. Physical education classes are a good place to learn skills that are useful to pursuing recreational activities such as swimming, baseball, or basketball. Elective courses such as music, art, dance, creative writing, or home economics offer students opportunities to develop appreciation for ways to use leisure time constructively. This can form the basis for eventual investigation of and participation in community events and clubs. After-school clubs such as astronomy, drama, band, or intramural sports offer similar opportunities for growth and involvement. Even events that require passive participation (e.g., attending school plays or sports events) can be used to develop skills and interests that will transfer to community settings.

The development of personal and social skills can be addressed through classes that allow students to interact. This would include both special education classes and mainstream classes with peers without disabilities. Places such as the school bus or the cafeteria also give students the opportunity to address goals and objectives in this area, as do after-school clubs (e.g., working on the newspaper or yearbook).

The important point here is that there are many diverse and creative ways that transition goals and objectives can be addressed, using the resources within the school and the events and activities that typically take place there. Parents and professionals can take advantage of what is naturally occurring in the school to give students the opportunity to practice and apply many of the skills important to transition. This may be essential in rural locations where the nearest town is miles away and students have limited opportunities to practice within the community those skills they are learning in school.

THE IMPORTANCE OF ASSESSMENT
IN TRANSITION PLANNING

The underlying philosophy of transition planning is the student's preparation during the school years for longer-range life roles. Planning for postschool life must be based on a thorough assessment of the individual. Assessment will reveal that person's strengths and needs, information which can then be used as the basis for making educational decisions.

Assessment should not involve the use of only one instrument or test. In order to provide a broad range of information about the student, a variety of assessment approaches and tools is necessary. For example, achievement tests used in the classroom can contribute information about the student's skills in reading, math, or other subject areas. Psychometric tests can be used to measure the attributes of the individual such as his or her interests, personality, or aptitudes. Observations of the student also contribute valuable information about the student, such as attentiveness, dexterity, attitude, and skill level at a particular task. Particularly good observational and anecdotal information about the student comes from the student's parents, because "parents and other family members are generally most familiar with the levels of skill proficiency of their sons or daughters" (Falvey & Haney, 1989, p. 18). The student, too, may also be a rich source of information about his or her skill levels, interests, and attitude.

Although achievement and psychometric testing and observations provide good information, they may not provide sufficient information for planning nonacademic goals. Vocational assessment of students with disabilities is, therefore, strongly recommended. "Vocational assessment is a systematic, ongoing process designed to help students and their parents understand the young person's vocational preferences and potential" (Rothenbacher & Leconte, 1990, p. 2). Through the assessment process, students and families have the opportunity to learn about various careers, as well as the student's personal and vocational attributes and weaknesses. Vocational assessment should contain components that gather information not available through academic testing—specifically the essential characteristics of the individual that make up his or her vocational profile. The areas to be assessed include the student's:

- occupational or vocational interests and preferences
- aptitudes in skills such as mechanical, spatial, numerical, and clerical
- worker style preferences, such as the desire to work with people or things
- learning preferences and styles, such as auditory, visual, or hands-on exposure
- worker characteristics, including student traits, values, employability skills, and other work-related behaviors
- abilities in specific technical, industrial, or other skills required in actual jobs
- functional or life skills, needed to address personal and independent living problems such as transportation, financial and housing management, and social skills (Rothenbacher & Leconte, 1990)

Most of this information can be gathered through informal means, such as inventories that measure interests, learning styles, and worker characteristics. Additional assessment methods include trying different tasks that replicate skills needed on the job, or performing actual workplace tasks during on-the-job tryouts.

A particularly useful and appropriate method of collecting information about the student in all transition domains is called ecological assessment. This method involves looking closely at the environment where an activity normally takes place and determining, through observation and through actual performance, the steps that are involved in performing the activity. For example, a teacher or paraprofessional might go to the bus stop and observe and list in detail the steps involved in waiting for and catching the bus. He or she might then actually ride a bus, to check the completeness of the list that has been developed. This list then serves as an inventory of the component skills (steps) a student needs in order to perform the activity. It is important that the inventory describe each component skill in observable terms, sequence the skills in the order needed to perform the overall activity, and include all steps required to initiate, prepare for, participate in, and terminate the activity (Black & Ford, 1989, p. 300).

After the inventory is completed, student assessment is conducted at the actual site where the activity is typically performed. It is critical that the student be somewhat familiar with the environment and activity prior to conducting the assessment; assessing the student when he or she is confronting a new situation will not give a true indication of his or her abilities (Black & Ford, 1989). Thus, continuing our example, the student would be asked to catch and ride the bus, without assistance, and an observer would use the inventory as a checklist, identifying which components of riding the bus the student can perform and which he or she cannot perform (including when he or she performs the right action but at an unacceptable rate). "In the event of an obvious error or no response, the teacher should be prepared to provide the least amount of assistance required by the student to help him or her move on to the next step" (Black & Ford, 1989, p. 298).

How the student performed the activity is then compared to the steps of the inventory and discrepancies are noted. These discrepancies form the basis for making decisions about what skills to teach the student and what to adapt. Adaptations can involve changing the sequence, developing an aid, or teaching the student to perform different but related activities (Black & Ford, 1989; Falvey, 1989a). Some students may be expected to master all of the steps in an activity; others may be expected to master some of the steps and partially participate in others.

Ecological assessment is one of the most appropriate means of determining what skills and components of skills a student needs to develop in order to address the many domains of postschool life. Its emphasis on breaking tasks down into their component steps ensures that students are, indeed, focused on learning to perform those tasks they will actually need in adult life.

Whatever the methods used in assessment, the end result should be a more thorough understanding of the student's skills in the postschool adult living objectives. This understanding should lead to more appropriate choices in setting transition goals that are sensitive to the student's interests, preferences, needs, and aptitudes.

SUGGESTIONS FOR TRANSITION PLANNING

Federal policy has encouraged the development of diverse approaches to transition planning. Accordingly, school districts involved in transition planning for students with disabilities have developed models and programs that reflect local geography and philosophy, student populations, and staff and funding resources. As a result, no nationally consistent model for IEP transition goal planning exists as of this writing.

A recent national study on transition (Repetto, White, & Snauwaert, 1990) provides insight into the transition activities within the states. The study confirmed that, from state to state, there is no consistency in transition planning documents and processes. State departments may set policy or offer guidelines concerning the age when transition planning should begin, which persons should form the transition team, and what areas need to be addressed when planning transition goals. However, the responsibility for designing the transition planning documentation and developing the actual planning process seems to rest with the local education agencies (LEAs). This means that there may be little consistency between LEAs within a state in terms of the planning age, transition team membership, and type of documentation used for planning and providing transition services. Although flexibility at the local level allows each district to provide services based on individual needs and resources into the area, this very flexibility certainly contributes to the inconsistency present nationwide.

Given that transition practices vary from state to state, and from LEA to LEA, the following general suggestions may help set the stage for positive teamwork, regardless of the transition approach taken by individual school districts.

Suggestions for Parents

Here are some ideas that may be useful to parents as their child with disabilities becomes involved in planning for transition:

■ **Become familiar with how your school or LEA approaches transition planning.** You may find it very helpful to know the specific format your school or local education agency (LEA) uses for including transition goals within the IEP. (Although formats vary among LEAs and across states, the core components of

IEPs, described earlier, appear to be present in most planning documents in some form.) You can usually get this information by contacting the director of special education in your district and asking about transition services for youth with disabilities. Be sure to ask for the name of the person in charge of developing transition services. Although there may be no one with this specific responsibility, many states and LEAs have designated contact persons. Meet with the person or persons who have responsibility for developing these services and get copies of whatever forms they use to help students plan for transition. As an informed parent, you are then able to advocate for including statements in your child's IEP regarding levels of performance, team membership, annual goals and objectives, specific services, projected dates of initiation and duration, and objective evaluation criteria. You will also be able to monitor whether these statements are adhered to in practice.

■ **Keep accurate records on your child.** Records to keep include medical episodes (including injury or serious illness), Social Security or Medicaid involvement, employment experiences, volunteer experiences, previous vocational course work, possible acquaintance networks for employment opportunities, and alternatives for family residential care. All of these records can be very useful during transition planning and after your child has left the public school system.

■ **Be aware of your rights.** You have the right to access your child's educational records, to question decisions made without your input, to demand appropriate assessment, and to advocate for positive changes in school transition curriculum.

■ **Encourage your child to express his or her views and feelings during IEP meetings.** Your child has the right to receive needed transition services and to contribute to the nature of the services he or she receives. Let your son or daughter know that his or her interests and preferences are an integral part of developing appropriate transition goals. Encourage your child to communicate those interests and preferences, and do everything you can to make sure that your child's opinions are understood and valued by other members of the transition team.

■ **Don't be reluctant to express your own views and feelings during IEP meetings.** You, as a parent, know your child better than anyone. You know his or her strengths and weaknesses, preferences and desires, and much, much more. Your observations can contribute a great deal to the planning process.

■ **Make sure you get a copy of your child's IEP stating transition and other educational goals.** Having a copy of your child's IEP will help you keep track of what needs to be accomplished in terms of your child's transition.

■ **Do what you can to reinforce your child's preparation for transition.** There are many things that you can do to help your child prepare for transition. Every day presents opportunities to reinforce your child's development of skills in self-advocacy, self-care, household management, and decision making. These skills are vital ingredients for assuming the responsibilities of adulthood.

■ **Keep in touch with other members of the transition planning team.** This helps to avoid delay or conflict in executing the objectives listed in your child's IEP or in seeking and obtaining appropriate services.

Suggestions for Professionals

Here are some ideas that professionals may find useful when developing and providing transition services:

■ **Take advantage of resources available elsewhere.** If there is no model for providing transition services available in your vicinity, or if your school system is expanding or modifying existing services, contact other professionals within and outside of your state to see what they are doing in the area of transition. Ask for copies of the specific formats they use. For example, there may be guidelines available at the state level. Other LEAs in your state may have working models for transition planning and service provision. Other states may be able to provide useful information that will help your school or LEA develop an effective process for providing transition services. Use these resources to develop a process that works for your locale.

Statewide information would be available by contacting your State Department of Special Education or other districts in your state, or, for those living on reservations, by contacting the Bureau of Indian Affairs (BIA).

- **Communicate fully with the student and his or her parents and solicit their input about transition needs and interests.** In most cases, the student can contribute vital information about his or her preferences, interests, and needs. Parents also have unique insights about their child with disabilities and can contribute information that will help the transition team develop appropriate goals and objectives for the student. Try to avoid using esoteric or jargonistic language in IEP meetings, for this can detract from the parents' or the student's perceptions of themselves as full team members.

- **Develop a curriculum or approach that allows for community-based experiences.** Many students with disabilities (particularly those with more severe disabilities) learn functional and life skills most effectively when taught in the environment where the skills are actually used. There may be many obstacles to developing and using community-based experiences for students with disabilities, but these can be overcome through planning and persistence. Students with disabilities will certainly benefit from the efforts of professionals to develop a community-based approach to teaching and learning.

- **Reminders for the IEP team.** These suggestions are actually reminders of important things to consider when the IEP team convenes to plan the transition services that a student with disabilities will need.

- **Be sure to consider student interests and aptitudes when developing a transition plan.** One of the great injustices that can occur during educational planning is charting a young adult's future needs without consulting the person who is most affected. Both parents and professionals should never be too quick to rule out a student's desires on the grounds that they are "unrealistic" or difficult to address.

- **Make sure that the IEP goals, objectives, and activities are broken down into workable segments that prepare the student for the larger postsecondary world.** Goals and objectives should be based on transition needs that have been identified for the student and should build on skills and abilities the student has already demonstrated. Goals should not be unattainable considering the school's resources. However, schools should actively seek to address goals requiring creative programming through all possible resources available to them. This includes developing shared service delivery approaches that involve adult service providers, as well as exploring resources available within the community.

- **State who will be responsible for providing each transition service.** Because transition planning involves personnel from schools and other community agencies, transition goals in the IEP should state the parties responsible for each goal, the time lines within which each goal is to be accomplished, and mutually understandable criteria for evaluation of student outcomes. Case management duties, wherein one participant serves as the overseer of the collaborative efforts of the other participants, are in most cases assumed by the school. However, all participants who sign an IEP are accountable for fulfilling their respective roles. When interagency agreements are contained within the IEP, each participant in essence agrees to work collaboratively with the others and indicates that agreement by signing the IEP.

■ **Make use of student educational placements to achieve transition goals.** It is possible to make creative use of student educational placements to achieve transition goals and objectives. For example, a transition goal might be for the student to become informed about his or her rights to reasonable accommodation under the Americans with Disabilities Act (ADA). This goal might be addressed in the student's English or social studies class through a composition or a project. The student might complete the required composition or project by focusing on what the ADA requires in terms of reasonable accommodation. This sort of project works well in integrated classrooms, giving all students the opportunity to learn about this newest civil rights legislation.

CONCLUSION

The inclusion of transition services in IEP development for youth with disabilities is a positive social and legislative move. Preparing students while they are still in school for the important roles of adulthood—employment, education, independent living, adult service providers, and community participation—is vital to reducing the disproportionately high unemployment rates and substandard wages and benefits experienced by too many individuals with disabilities.

Parents or guardians, school personnel, adult agency personnel, local education agency representatives, and, most importantly, youth with disabilities are being asked to work together in choosing goals, objectives, and activities that will best prepare youth with disabilities for future life role needs. Although there is no consensus on the "correct" format for transition goal inclusion in educational planning, the vital point is not whether the goals are in the IEP itself or in a separate ITP document. The issues of great importance are whether the goals and objectives specified for a student are in keeping with the individual and the family's real life needs, whether the goals and objectives are broken into workable segments that contribute in an organized manner to the larger picture of successful adult adjustment, and whether all resources are being utilized to achieve those goals and objectives. If these issues are addressed in a cooperative manner, based on solid assessment and rooted in solid evaluation criteria, each student and community will benefit far beyond the student's school years.

CHAPTER FIVE

VOCATIONAL ASSESSMENT

OVERVIEW

Crossing the threshold from the world of school to the world of work brings a significant change in everyone's life. School is an entitlement, meaning that it is an environment that our system of government supplies for all of our citizens. The workplace is the opposite; no one is entitled to a job.

One of the most important aspects of transition planning is the preparation of students for the world of work. Up to now, the focus has been on helping students fulfill the educational requirements for graduation from a secondary school. Now comes a very real and practical issue that can create many concerns. With the proper information and resources, this next phase of the transition process can also be very rewarding. Parents and educators must fully understand vocational options in order to help children make the best decisions for their future.

The purpose of this chapter is to give you a strong working knowledge of vocational assessments. After reading this chapter, you should understand the following:

VOCATIONAL ASSESSMENT	CONFIDENTIALITY
TRENDS IN VOCATIONAL ASSESSMENT	PROFESSIONALS TRAINED TO HELP STUDENTS WITH DISABILITIES PREPARE FOR EMPLOYMENT
THE VOCATIONAL ASSESSMENT PROCESS	
LEVELS OF VOCATIONAL ASSESSMENT	DIVISION OF REHABILITATION SERVICES (DRS)
COMPONENTS OF A VOCATIONAL ASSESSMENT	SERVICES PROVIDED BY DRS AGENCIES
OTHER ASSESSMENT OPTIONS DURING THE VOCATIONAL TRANSITION PHASE	CONFLICT RESOLUTION OPTIONS WITH A DRS AGENCY

VOCATIONAL ASSESSMENT

One of the techniques used to determine a child's interests, aptitudes, and skills is a vocational assessment. A vocational assessment has been called the critical beginning point for transition planning and services (Leconte & Neubert, 1997). Vocational assessment can be defined as a comprehensive process conducted over a period of time, usually involving a multidisciplinary team, with the purpose of identifying individual characteristics, education, training, and placement needs, which serves as a basis for planning an individual's educational program and which provides the individual with insight into vocational potential (Dowd, 1993, p. 14, cited in deFur & Patton, 1999). A vocational assessment is the responsibility of a school district's special education program. The planning of transitional services includes the development of transitional employment goals and objectives based on a child's needs, preferences, and interests. These will be identified through the child-centered vocational assessment process.

According to Hann and Levison (1998),

> Although vocational assessment and transition may be focused upon more closely in the latter school years, it is beneficial if the process can begin as soon as students enter school and ideally the process should incorporate a K–12 career development plan. This does not mean that early elementary students should be subjected to in-depth assessment batteries. It is more plausible that vocational assessment and transition in the early school years should encompass career exposure and educational activities geared to a level which is developmentally appropriate to younger students. For younger children it is important to emphasize the development of self-awareness, occupational awareness and good decision making skills. Early transition planning is also an excellent opportunity for educators and parents to introduce non-traditional employment opportunities and thereby dispel gender bias as it relates to children's understanding of traditional and non-traditional employment roles. As students approach the middle and secondary school level the need for a more formalized vocational assessment occurs. (p. 1)

A good vocational assessment should include the collection and analysis of information about a child's vocational aptitudes, skills, expressed interests, and occupational exploration history (e.g., volunteer experiences, part-time or summer employment, and club activities). The collection of this information should also take into account the child's language, culture, and family.

Through the assessment process, parents and professionals learn about the student, and the student learns about himself or herself. Students generally emerge from the vocational assessment process with increased self-awareness and a better understanding of their skills. When students are being assessed, a number of interesting changes can be observed in what they say and do. For example, students often want to discuss their vocational or career futures or specific vocational education plans; are able to say things they can do; may show excitement about the vocational activities on which they are working; may enthusiastically talk with their families and friends about what they are doing in school; may develop new, realistic career interests; may show more self-confidence and/or self-esteem; and may show more interest in school and in their academic performances.

Thus, the active participation of students in the assessment process can be an important factor in showing them how school connects to the outside world of work and in motivating them in their school work. Moreover, through the assessment process, students and families have the opportunity to gather information about various careers. Learning about various jobs, trying out work roles, exploring interests, and getting feedback on many different aspects of individual abilities and performance broaden students' knowledge base of the work world and themselves. This allows them to explore what careers might be appropriate for them and to identify those that are not.

The primary purpose of vocational assessment, then, is to gather employability-related information about an individual. This will assist and empower that individual (and his or her advocates) in making decisions regarding work and the training or services needed by the student in order to gain employment. The benefits of gathering—and using—this information are many. Among these are career awareness and exploration, improved self-awareness and motivation, the development of a vocational profile, and the identification of short- and long-term career goals that are realistic. These goals are more realistic because they are based on who the student is as an individual and what he or she is capable of doing and is interested in doing.

TRENDS IN VOCATIONAL ASSESSMENT

Vocational assessment began in industry over a century ago. As employers were trying to match people with technology in new industrially oriented occupations (moving away from an agricultural labor market), they created "trials" of actual jobs for potential employees to try, or they developed samples of work and simulated the tasks of the jobs. Similarly, the first assessment processes in rehabilitation relied heavily on work sampling and job tryouts.

This community-reality-based beginning for vocational assessment has progressed almost full circle. For several decades, assessment for training and employment centered on standardized tests (psychometrics). In an effort to make work sampling, simulated work, and job tryouts more credible, professionals began to collect "norms" in efforts to "standardize" these methods of appraisal. The increasing need to appraise the potentials and attributes of individuals with disabilities has led the field back to community-reality-based assessment. This is due, primarily, to two facts: (1) the use of most standardized instruments frequently is discriminatory to persons with different attributes; and (2) "normed" work samples and simulated work assessment tools, as they became refined, were often not representative of actual work requirements on jobs.

The emergence of community-based assessment for individuals with severe disabilities, ecological and environmental assessments, and curriculum-based vocational assessments is each indicative of the movement toward reality-based and equitable appraisals. Standardized assessments remain effective methods in vocational appraisal processes but usually are used in combination with the preceding methods.

THE VOCATIONAL ASSESSMENT PROCESS

Vocational assessment is a process that can take place at different times during the student's education and career development. It is an ongoing process that should begin during the middle of junior high school years and may continue throughout high school and, if needed, perhaps reoccur during transitional periods in adult life.

Throughout the education process, starting in kindergarten or earlier, students are involved in career awareness and vocational exploration activities. In the early years of school, children study community workers such as firefighters, police, and transportation providers. A student's performance with school work can provide sources of important information about potential careers. Extracurricular activities, such as sports, music, art, scouts, and other social organizations add to this information base and offer opportunities for the student to try out a variety of activities and roles.

These experiences can be used in informal vocational assessment, in the sense that students are developing career awareness and motivation, as well as ideas of what they like and do not like. They may also develop a fair idea of what types of jobs they would be good at and what would be difficult for them, ideas they can generally articulate, if asked.

Informal and Formal Assessment

The student may have the opportunity for informal and formal vocational assessment. Vocational assessment can be described as occurring on a continuum of appraisal procedures, which have different purposes and outcomes depending on the individual's needs and career development stage. Informal assessment is more available in schools than formal appraisal approaches.

Informal assessment differs from formal assessment in terms of the objectives, setting, personnel conducting the assessment, and the materials used in the process. Informal assessment includes the gathering of information from any number of sources other than through formal testing procedures and is conducted in classrooms or unstructured settings. Methods, such as interviewing a student or family member, making observations, conducting record reviews, and using teacher-made tests results, are examples of informal methods along the assessment continuum.

Criterion-referenced tests are another type of informal assessment. These tests measure how well a student is able to do specific tasks within a course of study. The student's performance is compared to an established level of achievement for each task or unit of the curriculum. Criterion-referenced tests are commonly used in vocational classes to determine a student's mastery of the content.

Typically, informal assessment is conducted by teachers and other professionals for the purpose of assisting a student in classroom work and for identifying possible learning difficulties. Informal assessment is an important complement to formal assessment and is essential in determining whether a referral for formal assessment is appropriate.

Formal assessment is a structured procedure conducted for a specific purpose and involves the use of norm-referenced, commercially developed, and standardized instruments. The purpose of formal assessment in vocational appraisal is to determine a student's interests, aptitudes, learning preferences, work skills, and other vocationally relevant information. Many vocational assessment instruments have been commercially developed and administered to a representative group of individuals in order to establish normative standards of performance. Normative standards allow evaluators to compare the results of one individual's performance on a test or instrument to the performances of other individuals who have taken the same test. Vocationally oriented assessment tools include interest inventories, aptitude and dexterity tests, work sample systems, and other appraisal instruments. Informal assessment information is frequently incorporated with formal assessment results in preparing comprehensive reports or vocational profiles.

Comprehensive vocational assessment or vocational evaluation is the collection of information via observations, interest inventories, aptitude tests, and so on that should occur along a continuum, with different kinds of information being collected about the student at different points in time. The use of results will vary, depending on the student's year in school. In middle, intermediate, or junior high school, for example, vocational assessment may be used to identify levels of career development and to determine career exploration and prevocational activities. During these years, vocational assessment can also help parents and teachers identify transition needs in preparing a student for high school. This type of vocational assessment is extremely helpful in guiding the student early in his or her education and should begin as early as age 12 or 13. Parents should take advantage of interdisciplinary planning sessions (i.e., IEP and three-year evaluation meetings) to learn more about the different resources available and to work with the school system to utilize all of the vocational assessment information collected on their child. This includes teacher impressions of work habits, socialization skills, and other anecdotal information about student behavior and performance. Such information can be useful during special education planning and placement decisions.

It is important to remember that when vocational assessment is begun early in a student's education, reevaluation of the student should be scheduled yearly to update recommendations. Students improve skills across time and mature in their understanding of and interaction with the world. Assessment information, when used to make decisions, should be as current as possible.

If it is available, comprehensive, formal vocational assessment should begin approximately one year prior to placement in vocational education. This is usually around the ninth or tenth grade. At this point, assessment is conducted for the specific purpose of vocational and transitional planning. In many school systems, planning for transition is being incorporated into the established IEP process as students reach about the age of 14. Because students are nearing the time when specific vocational placement choices will need to be made, the assessment process should begin to examine the match between specific aspects of occupations and the individual. Information about the student should be compiled from a variety of sources and should include all assessment information collected to date that is vocationally relevant; current teacher impressions of such areas as the student's communication skills, punctuality, ability to follow directions and to work with others, concentration, and ability to work unsupervised; medical background; survey results about interests and aptitudes; observations of the student at work or in simulated work experiences; and an analysis of strengths and needs.

Results of all assessment activities should be shared with both parents and student. The vocational profile, mentioned earlier, should be developed for the student. This profile not only details assessment results but also should include recommendations for vocational education placement, postsecondary training, or employment. A vital part of vocational and transitional planning, placement, and programming, the vocational profile also serves as a record and vehicle of communication between the student, family, school, and community personnel.

The next step in the planning process, based on the assessment results and the nature of the student's disability, is to identify the support services (e.g., transportation, assistive technology) the student will need to implement the vocational plan. An analysis of the employment or training site identified for the student should also be made. What skills are necessary for the student to perform the training or be successfully placed in the program? Does the student have these entry-level skills? This analysis will indicate any additional training the student needs before or during placement. Vocational support (supplementary) services are also mandated in the Perkins Act (P.L. 101-392).

As a teenager prepares to exit from school, parents should be aware that vocational assessment will continue to be important for a young adult's successful transition to independence in either employment or postsecondary training. In addition to identifying specific transition needs and career plans/goals, vocational assessment can assist both parents and professionals in making referrals for adult services. For many young adults with disabilities, state-sponsored vocational rehabilitation services or other community-based services may be realistic options. Vocational assessment will be necessary to determine eligibility for vocational rehabilitation and to determine appropriate vocational training programs and employment placement. The information gathered through the assessment process can help the individual with a disability, his or her family, adult service provider, and employer identify the accommodations or assistance needed for obtaining and maintaining employment.

LEVELS OF VOCATIONAL ASSESSMENT

There are three types of vocational assessments that you need to understand as special educators (Pierangelo & Crane, 1997). They are referred to as Level I, Level II, and Level III vocational assessments. A *Level I vocational assessment* is administered at the beginning of a student's transitional process and is based on the child's abilities, expressed interests, and needs. This Level I assessment may include a review of existing school information and the conduct of informal interviews. A *Level II vocational assessment* usually includes the administration of one or more formal vocational evaluations. A *Level III vocational assessment* usually involves the analysis of a child's success in a real or simulated work setting. This is usually reported by a job coach, employer, or vocational evaluator. The transitional process should not be used to limit a student's educational or career aspirations. Instead, it should allow districts to provide opportunities at an earlier age. A more detailed discussion of all three types of vocational assessments will now be addressed.

Level I Vocational Assessment

A Level I vocational assessment examines the child from a vocational perspective. A trained vocational evaluator or knowledgeable special education teacher should be designated to collect the Level I assessment data. Typically, Level I consists of a screening to determine functional skills and "where the student is" regarding vocational planning. Information is collected via such methods as interviewing, reviewing records, or interest inventories for screening. The information gathered for analysis should include existing information from:

- cumulative records
- student interviews
- parent/guardian and teacher interviews
- special education eligibility data
- a review of the child's aptitudes
- achievements
- interests
- behaviors
- occupational exploration activities

The informal student interview involved in a Level I assessment should consider the child's vocational interest, interpersonal relationship skills, and adaptive behavior.

Level II Vocational Assessment

A Level II vocational assessment is based on the analysis obtained from the Level I assessment. This may be recommended by the Committee on Special Education at any time to determine the level of a student's vocational skills, aptitudes, and interests but not before age 12. Level II occurs if the student needs more information to develop his or her vocational profile and to clarify vocational planning. Often this level is called "clinical" or "exploratory" as standardized instruments or career exploration activities may be used. Collected data should include:

- writing
- learning styles
- interest inventory
- motor (dexterity, speed, tool use, strength, coordination)
- spatial discrimination
- verbal reading
- perception (visual/auditory/tactile)
- speaking numerical (measurement, money skills)
- comprehension (task learning, problem solving)
- attention (staying on task)

Level III Vocational Assessment

A Level III vocational assessment is a comprehensive vocational evaluation that focuses on real or simulated work experiences (deFur and Patton, 1999). This assessment is the basis for vocational counseling. Level III is a more comprehensive assessment during which data are usually collected for a specified period of time. Data collection is often coordinated or conducted by a professional vocational evaluator/assessment specialist. Informal assessment (interviews, samples of classwork, situational assessments, and on-the-job tryouts) and formal assessment (work samples and standardized instruments and tests) are used in each of the three levels of service. The use of formal methods is more prevalent in Level III, which is often called a comprehensive assessment or vocational evaluation. This does not mean that only formal methods are used at this level; observations, shop or job tryouts, interviewing, and so on also play a key role in the appraisal process. Unlike the Level I and Level II assessments, a trained vocational evaluator should administer or supervise this level of assessment. Level III assessment options consist of:

- *Vocational evaluations* including aptitudes and interests that are compared to job performance to predict vocational success in specific areas. Work samples must be valid and reliable.
- *Situational vocational assessments,* which occur in real work settings. These on-the-job assessments consider what has been learned and how.
- *Work-study assessments* are progress reports from supervisors or mentors that provide information on the youth's job performance. A standard observational checklist may be utilized.

If a student plans a postsecondary educational program, he or she may benefit from two types of assessments:

- *General assessments of postsecondary education skills* are necessary to determine academic skills, critical thinking skills, requirements for reasonable accommodations, social behaviors, interpersonal skills, self-advocacy and self-determination skills, learning strategies, and time management or organizational skills. This information is usually obtained through consultation with peers or teachers, or a self-evaluation.
- *Assessments specific to field of study or setting* are necessary to assess needs, in relation to daily living skills, that may be experienced in a classroom setting or on a college campus. The identification of additional skills that a child must plan for to be an effective member of a postsecondary educational setting includes dormitory living versus commuting, lab work, and large lecture versus seminar courses.

Parents may wish to visit campuses that provide supportive services for students with disabilities. Information regarding colleges that provide these services can be obtained in local libraries, bookstores, or high school guidance offices.

Maximum benefit can be realized if an array or continuum of vocational assessment approaches and opportunities is available to students. Because the needs of individuals with disabilities are so diverse, a variety of approaches is necessary depending on the student's specific needs, age, and stage of personal and career development. It is essential that information about certain attributes of each individual be gathered. Regardless of the approach used to gather information about the youth, the following components should be included in the vocational assessment. These components represent the essential attributes of the individual that make up his or her vocational profile or identity. It is also important to remember that a student's self-concept is critical to his or her educational and vocational functioning. Vocational assessment should help clarify a student's self-concept and be included within any component of a vocational assessment.

COMPONENTS OF A VOCATIONAL ASSESSMENT

Parents and teachers involved in facilitating the student's transition should consider the developmental maturity of the student as well as the skills that the student will need to adjust to community living and employment. The skills that should be considered include daily living skills (e.g., managing money and preparing food), personal/social skills (e.g., hygiene and social skills), and occupational/vocational skills (e.g., job-seeking skills and appropriate work habits). The degree to which the student already possesses these skills and the extent to which these skills need to be developed can be determined in part by the vocational assessment.

Vocational assessment should be more formalized as the student moves through grade levels and the assessment information gathered in later years should be multilevel and include assessment at both the junior and senior high levels (Hann and Levinson, 1998).

1. Interests. What are the student's occupational or vocational preferences? Remember that these may be preferences that the student expresses, or those he or she demonstrates, or those that are identified with an interest survey or inventory. When receiving interpretations of interest inventories, make sure that the tests are truly representative of a wide range of occupations rather than being limited to one category or a few occupations. It is also important that the people who administer and interpret interest inventories represent them as occupational likes and dislikes, rather than as a measure of skills (or aptitudes) to actually do any specific occupation. Results of tests should always be verified by identifying an individual's expressed or demonstrated interests.

2. Aptitudes (abilities and capabilities). Aptitude can refer both to the ability to do and to learn certain types of skills, such as mechanical, spatial, numerical, and clerical. Many tests exist to measure a student's aptitude for performing in any one of these skill areas. Often the best measure is to have the individual try different tasks that require specific aptitudes or occupational duties.

3. Temperaments (worker style preferences). Worker style is reflected in how people behave and in the emotional responses and choices they make. Preferring to work with people, things, or data, and the ways the student organizes and makes decisions are aspects of worker style preference. Information about preferences can be gathered through observation by teachers and parents, as well as through discussion with the student or through temperament inventories.

4. Learning preferences and styles. This reflects how a person prefers to receive and process information and experiences. How does the child best retain and use input—through auditory, visual, or hands-on exposure? Does he or she have any preferences for interaction or times for learning? This type of information can be gathered through inventories of learning style, as well as through observation and discussion.

5. Developmental background (background information). This information does not represent a comprehensive case history; rather, it should include only the information that impacts on the child's performances and prognoses specifically related to vocational development. What special needs does the youth have, given his or her disability?

6. Worker characteristics. These include a student's traits, attitudes, values, employability skills, and work-related behaviors such as work habits and social skills. Positive worker characteristics are vital to successful employment and are most frequently cited as reasons for either promotions or dismissals by employers. Information about the student's statistics can be collected via inventories, observations of him or her at real or simulated work (often called situational assessments), teacher impressions, and the use of checklists that detail important worker skills (e.g., punctuality, safety awareness, etc.).

7. Vocational/occupational skills. These skills refer to specific technical, industrial, or other types of skills that are required in actual jobs. In order to know if the youth has the technical skills necessary to do a specific job, a training or job analysis must be done and compared to his or her skills. The best indicators of skills are through observations of the individual actually trying parts of the job or occupational area. For many vocational jobs, checklists of the necessary skills already exist.

8. Functional/life skills. This category refers to those skills that an individual needs in order to address personal and independent living problems that people with disabilities often encounter after leaving school. Some of these skills are use of transportation, ability to handle financial and housing management, decision making, and social skills. If the student is not at a point in the educational process at which exiting school and living and working in the community are concerns, this type of assessment may not be needed. However, for those students who are nearing this transition, functional assessment should be a part of the assessment process.

OTHER ASSESSMENT OPTIONS DURING THE VOCATIONAL TRANSITION PHASE

Functional Assessments

Functional assessment provides a comprehensive framework of factors to be considered in vocational planning and transitional preparation. A functional description of an individual with a disability includes what he or she can do, learn, and achieve, rather than simply recounting his or her academic, intellectual, or physical deficits. Functional assessment focuses on a person's skills within natural environments such as his or her home, school, and local community. The person's ability to deal with a variety of factors in each of these areas will impact on his or her overall integration in work and community living. Because of this, ecological or environmental assessment, which assists in analyzing the demands of different environments, adds an important dimension to the assessment process (Gaylord-Ross, 1986; Moon et al., 1986; Wehman, 1981).

Shifting from diagnosing "disabilities" to identifying barriers to work and community living enables professionals to plan strategies to assist individuals. For instance, an individual using a wheelchair may have no "disability" within his or her school where ramps exist, but in the office building where the student is doing an internship his or her mobility may be impeded in some way. Through functional assessment, the barrier(s) to integration in various places can be identified and adjustments can be made. Through functional assessment, a basis for defining areas needing attention and subsequent planning and problem solving can be established (Fardig, 1986; Halpern & Fuhrer, 1984).

Several professionally developed functional assessment inventories, checklists, and interview forms have been developed to evaluate areas considered to be most significant. Competencies, such as using transportation, independent living and decision-making skills, and interpersonal relationships, can be appraised through functional assessment tools (Halpern & Fuhrer, 1984).

As part of the vocational assessment process, functional assessment can serve two purposes. The information can be used to compare or verify how the student or individual functions in a work or "hands-on" training environment. Functional assessment results can also be integrated into the vocational assessment report or profile recommendations.

Functional assessment can add useful information to assist in vocational planning and decision making. The vocational implications of the individual's strengths and needs are addressed as a part of the functional assessment.

A functional assessment considers a wide variety of individual work characteristics. These include:

- ability to handle criticism
- ability to handle stress
- adaptability to change
- aggressive actions or speech

- appearance
- attention to task
- availability to work
- benefits needed
- communication
- discrimination skills
- endurance
- family support
- financial situation
- functional math
- functional reading
- independent street crossing
- independent work rate
- motivation
- physical mobility
- reinforcement needs
- social skills
- strength—lifting and carrying
- time awareness
- transportation
- travel skills
- unusual behaviors

A rehabilitation counselor, job placement specialist, or employment specialist can use information from a functional assessment to identify a job in the community with requirements that match the skills, interests, and support needs of the student.

Situational Vocational Assessment

A *situational assessment* offers a person with a severe disability the opportunity to perform job tasks in real work environments in the community. Usually, a situational assessment is conducted for a four-hour period in three different types of jobs in the community where the service provider has established a working relationship with the employer. It is important that the jobs selected are representative of the types of jobs found in the local business community (e.g., dishwasher, groundskeeper, grocery clerk).

The information obtained on the student during a situational assessment can assist in identifying the following characteristics about a potential worker:

- whether support is needed
- the type of support needed
- individual training needs and effective strategies
- the anticipated level of intervention
- the least restrictive environment
- other information needed to develop an appropriate individual written rehabilitation program

Actual performance in a job with appropriate training and support is the best predictor of an individual's performance in a supported employment situation. Observing an individual perform real work in multiple environments will provide an indication of his or her work characteristics, interests, skills, abilities, and training needs. For example:

- Does the student seem to show a preference across job types?
- Does the student work more effectively at specific times of the day?

- Does the student respond positively or negatively to factors in the environment—noise, movement, objects, people, amount of space, and so on?
- What types of prompts does the student respond to and what is the frequency?

Situational assessments can be requested from a supported employment vendor or a vocational evaluator. The purpose of such an assessment must be to determine the appropriateness of supported employment and the extent of supported employment services needed.

Finally, parents need to understand that it is important to obtain a written report from the vendor who completes the situational assessment. The report should include a description of the jobs completed, the behavioral data obtained during the assessment process, and a summary of the student's characteristics.

Curriculum-Based Vocational Assessment

An alternative vocational assessment approach, known as Curriculum-Based Vocational Assessment (CBVA), is currently gaining recognition as a useful way to gather vocationally relevant data. This emerging form of vocational assessment is similar to curriculum-based assessment, which is widely used by classroom teachers to evaluate students' mastery of concepts that are taught (Tucker, 1985). Curriculum-Based Vocational Assessment uses performance-based procedures developed and implemented by teachers from their own curriculum. It is a continuous process that teachers use to answer questions about instruction and special service needs of vocational education students (Albright & Cobb, 1988a, 1988b).

This assessment process often begins with a review of the student's records and existing assessment data. Vocationally related information is then collected by structuring the teacher's observations of the student within the classroom or vocational setting. Assessment may include how the student uses tools and how he or she works with other students in the class. This information-gathering approach enables teachers and others to observe and record behaviors in a natural setting—specifically, what a student is able to do and is interested in doing (Rothenbacher, 1989). Other appraisal techniques may be used as a part of the process, such as interest and aptitude measures.

Curriculum-Based Vocational Assessment is sometimes used to complement comprehensive vocational evaluation or it may actually supplant more formal types of appraisal services. Information from the CBVA can then be compiled with other assessment information and a vocational profile of the student can be developed more fully. This profile or report should specify classroom and vocational goals, as well as methods of instruction. It is also important to identify any needs that should be addressed.

Successful use of CBVA requires training for regular, special, and vocational educators. It also underscores the importance of school personnel working together as a team to make sure that information about the student is collected from all relevant areas. As the concept of CBVA becomes more accepted and understood, it may begin to emerge in more than the dozen or so places in which it now exists as a fully implemented system.

CONFIDENTIALITY

To bring the expertise of community-based nonschool personnel into the transitional planning process, the matter of confidentiality must be addressed. Under the Family Education Rights and Privacy Act (FERPA), also known as the Buckley Amendment (see Chapter 2), parents' rights to confidentiality must be maintained. During the transition process, families must sign releases, giving written consent, in order to benefit from available community resources. This does not commit a parent or the child to a specific service if at a later date it is not wanted or needed. Parents must ask their district about the rules of confidentiality regarding the release of information, the use of information by community agencies, and the storage of information once it is released by the district.

PROFESSIONALS TRAINED TO HELP STUDENTS WITH DISABILITIES PREPARE FOR EMPLOYMENT

There is a variety of people who are specifically trained to support students in planning and preparing for employment or other postsecondary school options. These people may include vocational counselors, special and regular educators, counselors from the Department of Rehabilitation Services (DRS), and county case managers.

Prevocational Skills

If families have been properly advised through earlier stages of the transition process, their children should have learned job-related skills and behaviors, or prevocational skills, that can be fostered to help each child be successful in future employment. Examples of these skills include physical stamina, promptness, problem solving, hygiene, ability to follow directions, independence in completing assigned tasks, and ability to establish social relationships with coworkers.

Upon graduation from high school or the end of secondary school eligibility, the student will be faced with several options, depending on the nature and severity of his or her disability. Many individuals with disabilities choose to pursue continued employment training in a postsecondary institution whereas others choose to begin working right away. This direction usually follows along with the student's vocational education plan, sometimes referred to as the transitional individual educational plan that was developed while he or she was still in high school. This comprehensive plan should have assisted the student in developing the skills needed to find and keep a job after graduation. Schools may offer a vocational work experience with a job coach. In some schools, a student may have been assigned to a vocationally licensed teacher who operated as the work experience coordinator within the job site. If a school does not have such an individual, then a special education teacher would be responsible for developing the student's vocational goals.

While the student is still in school, the vocational counselor or individual assigned to develop a vocational plan begins to observe and develop a general transition checklist of possible vocational skills. These general observations may change from year to year as the student matures, or they may remain the same because of the nature of the disability. Whatever the case, these observations are the beginning of what will be defined as vocational skills and needs. A sample checklist follows. This is not intended to be comprehensive but merely a beginning tool in assessing the student's needs and skills.

Skills Checklist

DOMESTIC SKILLS
The student can:
_____ prepare a breakfast
_____ prepare a lunch
_____ prepare a supper
_____ prepare a snack
_____ pack own lunch

_____ clean own room
_____ clean own apartment
_____ do own laundry
_____ use a washer or dryer
_____ make own meal plans
_____ budget own time

VOCATIONAL SKILLS
The student can:
_____ get to/from work on time
_____ punch/sign in appropriately
_____ perform work satisfactorily
_____ work cooperatively with coworkers
_____ take break/lunch appropriately
_____ wear suitable clothing
_____ use appropriate safety measures
_____ follow directions
_____ accept supervision

RECREATION/LEISURE SKILLS
The student can:
_____ use free time for pleasure
_____ choose reasonable activities
_____ pick a hobby
_____ perform required activities
_____ use community resources

COMMUNITY SKILLS
The student can:
_____ use public transportation
_____ shop for groceries
_____ shop for clothing
_____ make necessary appointments
_____ use the phone
_____ use bank accounts
_____ be safe in traffic
_____ respond appropriately to strangers
_____ know how to seek help
_____ handle money

SOCIAL/PERSONAL SKILLS
The student can:
_____ supply appropriate personal identification, if necessary
_____ greet people appropriately
_____ wear contemporary style of dress, hair style, makeup
_____ use good grooming/hygiene
_____ "communicate" with friends/coworkers
_____ be courteous and friendly

DIVISION OF REHABILITATION SERVICES (DRS)

Many students with disabilities will seek out a counselor from the Division of Rehabilitation Services (DRS) located within their state. These services are usually well known to school counselors, who should have a brochure that is put out by this agency.

A counselor from DRS will work with the school, parents, and the student to help plan for employment needs. DRS primarily serves adults or individuals who have graduated or aged out from secondary education. However, it is important to involve the counselor during the transition process, so that when the student graduates and enters the workforce, appropriate supports are in place that will allow him or her to be successfully employed.

To receive services from DRS, a student must meet two requirements:

- The student must have a documented physical or mental disability that presents difficulties or barriers to employment.
- There must be a good chance that DRS services will help him or her get and keep a job.

If a student is still being provided public school assistance, then the school will usually make an appointment for DRS involvement somewhere in the transitional process. If the student has more severe limitations, a DRS counselor can become involved during the very early stages of the planning. Also, keep in mind that DRS services are time limited. For example, the agency will provide job-placement services, ensure that the student with disabilities is satisfactorily employed, and provide follow-up services for at least 60 days and up to 18 months after the initial job placement.

Files can be reopened if the student needs assistance to retain his or her current employment, find a new job, or reestablish a vocational program. When a DRS agency is contacted, a VR (vocational rehabilitation) counselor will be assigned to work closely with the student and the family. The VR counselor will ask for background information that will help him or her work with the student. Questions usually focus on the following: goals interests, educational history, work history, financial situation, and physical and emotional health.

With parental permission, the counselor may want to collect information from the student's doctor, hospital, or school or to ask for evaluations at the expense of the DRS agency. The purpose of this information-gathering process is to give the counselor knowledge about how the student's disability affects the ability to work and to help the counselor decide whether the student is eligible for services.

SERVICES PROVIDED BY DRS AGENCIES

Based on all available information, the DRS counselor will plan a program along with the family. Depending on what the student needs to meet the vocational goal, the student may receive one or more of the following services that the agency buys and/or provides (Pierangelo & Crane, 1997):

1. a vocational assessment to help identify, skills, abilities, and interests; possible job goals; and services necessary to get a job and live as independently as possible
2. a physical and/or psychological examination to help understand how the student's disability affects his or her ability to work
3. guidance, counseling, and referral to help the student with problems he or she may have
4. vocational counseling and career planning
5. short-term medical intervention to improve the student's ability to work (if not covered by family insurance)
6. training to learn the skills the student will need for the job he or she wants to enter, which may include on-the-job training, job coach services, college and university programs, trade and business school programs, personal adjustment programs, and work adjustment programs

7. transition services
8. driver evaluation and training
9. homemaker evaluation and training
10. services that may assist the student during assessment or training, including special transportation; some maintenance expenses; attendants, note takers, and interpreters; and reader's aid for matriculated students
11. supported employment (more on this later in the chapter)
12. books, tools, and equipment that may be needed for training or employment
13. telecommunications aids and adaptive devices that may be needed for employment
14. assistance with some costs of modifications needed for employment: work site modifications, van or other vehicle modifications, and home modifications
15. training in job-seeking skills to learn how to fill out a job application or develop a résumé, handle job interviews successfully, and develop other job-related skills
16. occupational licenses, tools, initial stock, and supplies for a small business
17. job placement services to help the student find suitable work
18. follow-up services to make sure of job satisfaction and deal with any problems relating to work
19. referral to independent living services for peer counseling, advice on other benefits, housing assistance, and training in independent living skills
20. assistance in working with agencies such as the Social Security Administration, Department of Social Services, Office of Mental Health, and Veterans Administration

Keep in mind that there is no guarantee that all agencies will pay for or provide all of these services. Parents need to investigate the agency in their particular community. Although there is usually no cost for such services, sponsorship for some services may be based on the individual's income and/or family resources.

Following are the rights individuals have when involved with DRS services:

- to have the student's eligibility for VR services determined in a timely way regardless of age, color, religion, creed, disability, marital status, national origin, sexual orientation, or gender
- if eligible, to take part in planning vocational goals and the services needed to reach these goals
- if eligible, to receive services to reach the student's vocational goal
- to have goals tailored to the student's personal needs
- to receive an individual written rehabilitation program (IWRP)
- to have all information kept confidential
- to be informed of all decisions and actions of the DRS related to the case
- to be informed of rights as a consumer of DRS services
- to request and receive a timely review if there is any dissatisfaction with any actions or decisions by the DRS staff

Along with the student, families will have their own responsibilities if they get involved in DRS services. Families play an important role in working toward a successful outcome with the student. Both have the responsibility to:

- Work closely with the DRS counselor to provide all information needed to plan a program.
- Ask questions if they don't understand any aspect of the program.
- Keep in touch with the counselor by letter or telephone. If the family moves, let the counselor know the new address and telephone number.
- Participate fully in developing an individual written rehabilitation program.

- Make every effort to identify and apply for sources of funding that will help pay for the vocational rehabilitation program.
- Help the child maintain satisfactory performance and regular attendance, whether in a training program or in a job.
- Let the counselor know, on a regular basis, how well the child is doing or what problems there are with the program.
- Work with the counselor to look for job openings and go on interviews when the student is ready for work.
- Let the counselor know if the student becomes employed. For at least two months after the student is employed, maintain contact with the counselor to let him or her know how things are working out and whether assistance of any kind is needed.

CONFLICT RESOLUTION OPTIONS WITH A DRS AGENCY

Applying for DRS services is not a guarantee of eligibility. Many factors are considered, and each case is very different. If there is a rejection for services or a need to resolve disagreements or concerns the family has about DRS services, parents should ask for a review of the case. There is a variety of ways in which disagreements or concerns can be resolved as quickly as possible. Any individual—a lawyer or a relative—may represent the student and parents at this meeting. The options include:

- **Informal meeting.** Parents meet with the child's counselor, his or her supervisor, and a representative, and try to quickly resolve problems.
- **Administrative review.** Parents can ask for a review by a district office manager. They must ask for this review, in writing, within 90 days of the decision or action, unless they have a good reason for waiting longer than 90 days.
- **Impartial hearing.** Parents can ask for a formal hearing before an impartial hearing officer who does not work for DRS. They must ask for a hearing, in writing, within 90 days of the decision or action, unless they have a good reason for waiting longer than 90 days.

CONCLUSION

Vocational assessments can be the most important part of a student's educational career. They have been shown to be an effective intervention for improving the vocational and career outcomes of students with disabilities (Thomas, Hiltenbrand, & Tibbs, 1997). Vocational assessment can help parents, professionals, and the young person with a disability to think strategically about the young person's vocational future—both training and employment—and to make decisions that are based on the student's interests, abilities, and potential. As vocational assessment becomes more a part of transition planning for youth with disabilities, students, parents, and professionals can look forward to having the information necessary to ensure that students select postsecondary options and employment appropriate for them—who they are as individuals and what they are capable of and interested in becoming. By determining where the student's strengths and needs may lie in the area of vocational abilities, you can help the student on a path to career success.

CHAPTER SIX

EMPLOYMENT PLANNING

OVERVIEW

The purpose of this chapter is to provide an overview of employment options and procedures necessary for the preparation of a student with disabilities to adult life. After reading this chapter, you should understand the following:

INTERNSHIPS AND APPRENTICESHIPS	OTHER AVENUES TO EMPLOYMENT
ADULT EDUCATION	JOB SEARCH METHODS
TRADE AND TECHNICAL SCHOOLS	APPLYING AND INTERVIEWING FOR JOBS
COMPETITIVE EMPLOYMENT	
SUPPORTED EMPLOYMENT	APPLICANTS OR EMPLOYEES WITH DISABILITIES IN STATE OR LOCAL
SHELTERED WORKSHOPS	GOVERNMENT AGENCIES

Once the vocational assessment process is complete (see Chapter 5), the student will be presented with a variety of training and work options, depending on the results of the evaluation. Many options and directions are available.

INTERNSHIPS AND APPRENTICESHIPS

Internships are similar to on-the-job training. They are time limited, paid or unpaid jobs that permit the intern to sample the type of work available in a general field. Many high school and community transition programs offer individuals the opportunity to participate in an internship prior to competitive employment. By participating in an internship, individuals can learn more about the job and have the opportunity to familiarize themselves with the work environment.

Apprenticeship programs have been a historical means of preparing competent and skilled workers. Apprenticeships offer individuals the opportunity to learn the skills necessary for an occupation by working under the supervision of experienced workers. These programs generally take from three to four years to complete, but participants are paid for their labor. In the beginning, wages may not be more than minimum wage, but by the end of the program, wages are usually nearly those earned by an experienced worker. Generally, the sponsor of the apprenticeship is a company or a group of companies, a public agency, or a union. Over 700 organizations are currently involved in apprenticeship programs.

Local unions, vocational education programs in the community, the state office of vocational rehabilitation, and the state employment office are all sources of more information about apprenticeship opportunities. Each state also has a state occupational informational coordinating committee (overseen at the federal level by the National Occupational Informational Coordinating Committee). These committees, to differing degrees in each state, provide systems for individuals to obtain information about apprenticeships. The Bureau of Apprenticeship and Training also has regional offices throughout the United States.

Training Offered by Disability-Specific Organizations

Organizations such as ARC (formerly the Association for Retarded Citizens), the United Cerebral Palsy Foundation (UCPF), and others serving people with a specific disability may provide vocational assessment and training. The types of training provided vary, but the goals of the training are that individuals with disabilities will obtain employment and become as independent as possible. As an example, many regional offices of ARC provide training in computer skills and other office skills to persons with mental retardation who have been referred to the ARC program. This training often leads to competitive employment for these individuals.

ADULT EDUCATION

Adult education programs are designed to provide instruction below the college level to any person age 16 or older who is no longer being served by the public education system. There are many different programs available, and you can find them in a variety of settings. One setting of importance to youth seeking vocational training is an area vocational center. In many states, area vocational centers operate as part of the public school system. Secondary school students may receive vocational instruction in the area vocational center during the day, whereas instruction for adults in the community would generally be available there at night. Vocational courses may include training in such areas as health care, business education, home economics, industrial arts, marketing, or trades such as carpentry or automotive mechanics. The course of study might involve students in apprenticeships (discussed previously), which can lead to certification in a trade or recognized occupation. Adult education programs may also be available to prepare individuals for GED (general equivalency diploma) tests or to teach English as a second language (ESL). Continuing education programs may also be offered under the auspices of adult education; however, continuing education is generally meant to provide personal enrichment rather than vocational training. For example, continuing education classes may be offered in areas such as cooking, gardening, or sewing.

Information about adult education programs—whether they are intended as vocational training or personal enrichment—can usually be obtained by contacting the local education agency.

TRADE AND TECHNICAL SCHOOLS

Trade and technical schools are designed to prepare students for gainful employment in recognized occupations. Examples include occupations such as air-conditioning technician, bank teller, cosmetologist, dental assistant, data processor, electrician, medical secretary, surveyor, and welder. Vocational training is provided so that an individual can obtain skills in a specific area of interest or increase the level of skills he or she has already achieved. A course of study may take anywhere from two weeks to two years to complete, with the general entrance requirement of a GED or high school diploma. These schools typically place great importance on job placement for their graduates. If students are working with a high school counselor or a vocational counselor at the VR office in or near their community, one of these schools may be recommended to them as a way of getting the training they need.

COMPETITIVE EMPLOYMENT

Competitive employment can be defined as full-time or part-time jobs in the open labor market with competitive wages and responsibilities. Competitive employment is employment that the individual maintains with no more outside support than a coworker without a disability would receive. The key word here is *maintains*. Although a student may make use of transition services available in the community in order to prepare for and find competitive employment, these services are temporary. Once the individual has the job, support from outside agencies is terminated, and the individual maintains, or does, the job on his or her own.

The types of jobs that are normally considered competitive employment are as vast in number as they are varied. Waitresses, service station attendants, clerks, secretaries, mechanics, professional drivers, factory workers, computer programmers and managers, teacher's aides, teachers, health care workers, lawyers, scientists, and engineers are just some examples of people who are competitively employed. As can be seen by these examples, the amount of training an individual needs varies considerably from job to job. Some jobs are entry level and require little or no specific training. Other jobs require vocational preparation and training, whereas still others require extensive academic schooling.

Recently, a training model known as *transitional employment* has been useful in helping many young people prepare for competitive employment. Transitional employment is aimed at those individuals who cannot enter into competitive work on their own. With training and support, however, they may be able to handle a full wage job. Among those who have benefited from transitional employment are individuals who are mentally disabled, learning disabled, or developmentally disabled, and persons with hearing and vision impairments.

The important thing to remember about competitive employment, however, is that the assistance and supports offered by a human services agency are time limited in nature and end once the student has secured employment.

SUPPORTED EMPLOYMENT

Two aspects must be considered when confronted with vocational decisions—finding a job and keeping a job. The student may require little or no help with one or both aspects, or he or she may require a great deal of help. As we have seen, help with finding a job comes from the school system, in partnership with the vocational rehabilitation agency.

Supported employment (SE) enables people with disabilities who have not been successfully employed to work and contribute to society. SE focuses on a person's abilities and provides the supports the individual needs to be successful on a long-term basis. It allows people experiencing disabilities, their families, businesses, and their communities to experience the successes of people with disabilities. The partnership that SE has established between individuals experiencing disabilities and their communities is having a lasting impact on the way the public perceives people with disabilities. SE affords the public the opportunity to see people for who they are rather than seeing the disability (Association for Persons in Supported Employment, 2003).

Supported employment is a job with pay at a business in the community. Supported employment is for adults who traditionally have not been considered part of the workforce; need long-term support to be employed; have one or more disabilities, such as mental retardation, autism, mental illness, traumatic brain injury, physical disabilities, severe learning disabilities, or severe behavioral challenges; and require intensive, repetitive, or adaptive assistance to learn new tasks.

How Do Parents Know If Their Children Need Supported Employment?

If a student is already involved in a work situation or has been involved in the past, parents should be aware of several signals that may indicate the need for supported employment services. These include but are not limited to:

- repeated failures to maintain employment without support
- failure or inability to generalize skills from preemployment training programs
- problems acquiring skills
- significant communication problems where job-site advocacy would help social integration with coworkers and supervisors
- the need for extended training and support to develop production rates

Help for the student is provided by the same companies that specialize in finding employment for adults with disabilities. They can provide a job coach to give help directly to the student with disabilities. Optimally, the job coach will train the student's coworkers and supervisors to provide the supports that are needed to maintain the student's effectiveness on the job. Other services that are provided by job coaches include:

- travel training
- task analysis
- hands-on instruction
- developing job-modification accommodations
- developing visual or other tools to improve productivity
- training in appropriate job behaviors
- developing natural supports and social skills
- employee liaison problem solving
- parent liaison
- advocate for employee with disability

The amount and kind of help that is provided to find and keep a job should be based on the needs and abilities of the student with disabilities. When a parent is involved with an agency that will provide employment services for the student, the parent will need to learn as much as possible about the agency in order to assess its ability to meet the student's vocational needs and goals. Therefore, parents should ask the following questions:

1. What types of jobs are available?
2. How does the agency select a job for an individual with disabilities?
3. Where are the actual job locations?
4. Does the agency provide individual or group placements?
5. How does the agency promote integration?
6. What are the average wages of employees?
7. What is the average number of hours worked per week?
8. What type of support does the agency provide?
9. Is transportation provided? What type, and by whom?

10. What are the average benefit packages available to employees?
11. What provisions does the agency have for employee and parent or family input?

Supported employment is a major avenue to inclusion of persons with disabilities in their communities. As a service, it also reflects the growing conviction by persons with disabilities and their families that they have the right to be involved in decisions affecting the quality of their lives.

Although the transition from high school to adult life is a complex time for all students, it can be especially challenging for young people with disabilities. The goal of parents and professionals is to help the student make this transition to the world of work as easily as possible. Being informed and educated as to options, rights, and resources can only enhance the student's transition into the vocational phase of his or her life.

SHELTERED WORKSHOPS

In *sheltered employment options (sheltered workshops)* individuals with disabilities work in a self-contained unit; they are not integrated with workers who do not have disabilities. Sheltered employment options typically range along a continuum from adult day programs to work activity centers to sheltered workshops. In adult day programs, individuals generally receive training in daily living skills, social skills, recreational skills, and prevocational skills. Work activity centers offer individuals similar training but may also include training in vocational skills. In sheltered workshops, individuals perform subcontracted tasks such as sewing, packaging, collating, or machine assembly and are usually paid on a piece-rate basis. Typically, people do not advance to the workshop until they have demonstrated certain mastery levels. Sheltered employment options are generally supported by federal and/or state funds and are operated by private, nonprofit corporations governed by a volunteer board of directors (Pierangelo & Crane, 1997).

Traditionally, sheltered employment options were thought to be the only options available for individuals with severe disabilities. There is now evidence from supported employment models that individuals with severe disabilities can work in community settings if provided with adequate support. With the emergence of supported employment, many facilities began to modify their sheltered employment programs to provide workers with integrated options. Advocates of this trend away from sheltered employment point to the advantages of supported employment, which include higher wages, more meaningful work, and integration with workers who do not have disabilities.

OTHER AVENUES TO EMPLOYMENT

There are many avenues that lead to stable, satisfying employment. This section addresses other avenues a young person with a disability can take to employment—learning and growing along the way. For young people with disabilities, early job experiences are vital learning situations wherein they gain good work habits such as punctuality, responsibility, insight into appropriate behaviors, and standards of personal grooming. As such, initial jobs need not always place the individual on a career ladder. Sometimes it is useful to take jobs as stepping-stones in one's training, rather than as the final step in employment. Temporary work can be one such stepping-stone. Employers often have trouble finding a person to take a job that will last only several weeks or months. For a young person with a disability, a temporary job may offer the opportunity to get valuable work experience, earn wages, and develop a work history. Part-time work is a similar stepping-stone in many ways. Part-time employment offers many advantages for persons who need to attend school part of the day or who may be uncertain as to their work stamina or tolerance. Job-sharing is another stepping-stone, where two workers share the responsibilities of one full-time job. All of these examples can offer individuals meaningful employment that suits their schedule or their mental or physical abilities. These are also excellent ways by which to enter an organization, establish a reputation as a worker, and possibly move into a full-time job when one becomes available or is desired.

Programs also exist that are designed to provide experience outside of a traditional classroom, for example, volunteering and international exchange programs. Both types of programs offer personal enrichment to young adults and enhance their independence, self-advocacy skills, and their ability to make informed choices about further education and careers.

Volunteering

Volunteering enables a student or adult with a disability to develop a work history and can lead to paid employment. Some transition programs provide opportunities for young adults with disabilities to have volunteer experiences in several career areas as part of career exploration and selection. A volunteer organization in your community, county, or state may also be able to provide you with information about volunteer opportunities. At the national level, VOLUNTEER: The National Center for Citizen Involvement has been developing projects on the use of volunteers who have disabilities; this organization may be able to provide information specific to your locality. Contact VOLUNTEER at P.O. Box 1807, Boulder, CO 80306. Also at the national level is AmeriCorps, a federal agency that runs the VISTA program (Volunteers in Service to America). VISTA can be contacted, toll free, at (800) 424-8867 for information and recruitment and current projects, as well as information about state and regional offices. The number for AmeriCorps is (800) 94-ACORPS.

International Exchange Programs

International exchange programs can also serve as stepping stones for young people with disabilities. Although the programs cannot be considered employment, they nevertheless are personally enriching and, for a young person with a disability, lead to increased independence. There are two general types of international exchange programs: educational exchanges and international work camps. *Educational exchange programs* enable young adults to live, study, or volunteer in another country while living with a host family or with other participants in a dormitory. *International work camps* bring persons with disabilities and persons without disabilities together to work on community projects in host countries. Individuals with disabilities have participated successfully in both kinds of international programs. For more information about exchange programs, contact Mobility International USA, P.O. Box 10767, Eugene, OR 97440, (503) 343-1284 (Voice/TDD) or the U.S. Committee of the International Christian Youth Exchange (ICYE), 134 West 26th Street, New York, NY 10001, (212) 206-7307.

The Military

The military may also offer viable postsecondary options for many young adults with disabilities. Some individuals with learning disabilities, for example, "can benefit from the highly structured, repetitive, and physically active regime of military life" (Scheiber & Talpers, 1987, p. 64). However, in order to pursue a career in the military, individuals must meet the qualifications of the specific branch of interest (e.g., the Navy). A student and/or parent should talk to a recruiter in the particular branch of interest prior to graduation in order to find out about requirements. It is also important to know that Section 504 of the Rehabilitation Act does not cover uniformed personnel branches of the military; therefore, no particular accommodations are made regarding a person's disability unless that person is a civilian employee.

There are also opportunities for civilian service employees in military installations. The majority of these positions is in an administrative or support staff capacity. These provide opportunities for persons skilled in the areas of accounting, computer technology, contracting, and clerical duties. The best avenue for a person with a disability to take in order to obtain employment as a civilian is to be certified by the vocational rehabilitation system for Schedule A employment. The person may then apply directly to the federal government agency in which he or she is interested, including military installations around the nation and the world. Each installation in the military has to adhere to equal opportunity standards for employees in civilian positions.

Entrepreneurship

Entrepreneurship is a nontraditional avenue many individuals with disabilities have taken to employment. Rather than work for someone else, they decided to start a business of their own. For some persons, the focus of the business grew out of a hobby or a personal interest. An example of this is Don Krebs, who became a quadriplegic as a result of a waterskiing accident. After his recovery, Don searched for adaptive equipment to allow him to return to waterskiing, a sport he loved, and in the process recognized the great need for adaptive recreation equipment. Using money from SSDI and his Plan for Achieving Self Support (PASS), Don started Access to Recreation, a mail-order company specializing in adaptive recreation equipment (Marks & Lewis, 1983).

Business Opportunities

Some individuals with disabilities who have successfully created their own business began with the desire to work out of their homes. Betty, for instance, is mobility impaired and uses a wheelchair. She operates a mail-order business from her home and sells eyeglass frames wholesale to optometrists and opticians.

Other people with disabilities have become involved in businesses their parents have created. Laura and Charles, for example, have a son who is severely mentally retarded. Concerned about Harold's employment prospects, Laura and Charles joined forces several years ago with two other families whose children are mentally retarded. Together, the parents purchased 10 vending machines that they then situated in strategic locations. The young adults, who now range in age from 18 to 25, are responsible for tending to the machines—restocking them with sodas, retrieving the coins and rolling them up for deposit in the bank, and reporting any machine malfunctions to their parents. Although it took the families several months to identify the most lucrative spots to place the vending machines, the amount of income generated by this small business has surprised them all.

Starting and Maintaining a Business

Starting and maintaining a business is a serious enterprise. The ingenuity, determination, and stamina of participants are important factors in producing success or failure. Operating a small business can offer many advantages to individuals with disabilities, however, such as minimizing transportation concerns, setting one's own work hours, and having the freedom to modify the job in whatever way is necessary to get the job done most efficiently, given the personality and disability of the individual. Persons interested in starting a business can contact the Small Business Administration (SBA) for assistance and advice. SBA can also help you secure a loan through a bank or other commercial lender. SBA operates more than 100 local offices across the country. To find out if an office exists in your vicinity, consult your telephone directory or contact the SBA central office at 409 3rd Street, S.W., Information Center, Room 100, Washington, D.C. 20416, (202) 606-4000 (in the D.C. area) or (800) 827-5722.

JOB SEARCH METHODS

The remaining sections of this chapter are addressed to the young person who will be engaged in the job search—with assistance as needed from parents and professionals.

People look for jobs for many different reasons: They are laid off, they want to reenter the workforce, they want or need to relocate, they dislike their present job, they want to get a better job, or they are entering the labor force for the first time. This section provides guidelines that will help the special educator assist the student with disabilities in preparing for and conducting a job search. Steps discussed include:

- developing a résumé
- locating prospective employers
- applying for the job
- interviewing
- following through

These are only guidelines; you will find additional detailed information at your public library or at high school or college career centers.

Developing a Résumé

The two main types of résumés are chronological and functional. A *chronological résumé* is used when an individual has had a fairly direct path of development from one position to another in the same field. A *functional résumé* emphasizes the student's skills and is used by people who change jobs or careers frequently. A good résumé will be one page long and will capture the individual's career goals, education, and work history. For some positions, the student may have to include a sample of his or her writing.

A résumé should include the following information: name; address; telephone number; job objective or career goal; educational history (degrees, certificates, courses, accomplishments); work history, including military service (skills, experience); and memberships related to job objective. Depending on the position for which the student is applying, it might also include work-related honors or achievements, knowledge of foreign languages, ability to travel or relocate, and security clearance information.

Job Application Forms

Some jobs do not require a formal résumé but may call for a written application. Most application forms require such basic information as name, address and telephone number, Social Security number, dates of previous jobs, names and addresses of former employers, and dates of schooling or training.

Before you have the student begin to fill out the application, have him or her read it through to be sure that all required information is available. It is very important that the student print the information neatly and legibly. He or she may need your assistance with this part of the application depending on the disability. If the application makes a poor impression, the student is unlikely to go further with that employer.

Although not every job calls for letters of reference, you may want to help the student ask people whom they know if they would be willing to write one for the student. Make sure the student does not list someone as a reference unless the student has his or her permission to do so. Candidates for references include former employers, teachers, volunteer supervisors, and other people who can assess the student's character.

Locating Employers

When the student has determined the kind of job he or she wants, the student must locate potential employers. Among the most frequently used methods of finding them are making *cold calls;* getting information from friends, relatives, or colleagues; reading want ads; and using employment agencies. Usually, more than one source will be used and there are advantages and disadvantages to all methods.

Cold Calls.   This technique involves visiting employers to see if there are openings. A person using this method of finding a job needs high motivation and good interpersonal skills. Sometimes talking directly to the person who makes the hiring decision rather than the personnel office produces better results. Before calling on small companies, it is a good idea to call or write ahead of time; they may not appreciate interruptions. Letters, followed by phone calls, can be effective for small and medium-sized businesses. Advantages of cold calls are that some jobs are not listed anywhere, the opening may be new, and you may be in the right place at the right time. Disadvantages include the time involved and the high rejection rate.

Networking.   *Networking* is an approach to getting employment by discussing your situation, wants, and needs with people whom you know who could help you enter a particular field or get a specific job. Learning about an opening through friends, relatives, or coworkers is the most successful way to get a job; most employers do not like to hire strangers. They know that people who are referred to a company tend to be more stable and, therefore, will stay longer in the job. Advantages of networking are that referrals often guarantee an interview, jobs offered often are better with higher pay, and it is easier to develop a relationship with the potential employer when referred by a colleague.

Newspaper Ads.   Many people start their job search with want ads. This is unfortunate because it is frequently a last resort for employers. Advantages of classified ads are that they list specific openings and have frequent new listings. Disadvantages are that the jobs are often undesirable or hard to fill, or have a high turnover rate; positions are often at the high and low ends of the skill/experience spectrum—few in the middle; there is little information about the job or employer; competition is intense; and ads list a small proportion of available jobs.

Employment Agencies.   Public employment services are funded by the federal government and administered by states. They are widely viewed as ineffective, primarily offering low-paying, low-status jobs. Their main advantage is that there is no cost to the client or employer. Disadvantages are that they are usually looking for unskilled or casual labor, there are fewer occupations offered than are listed in want ads, and they offer limited opportunities.

Employment agencies will, for a fee, try to match employers and employees. Depending on the agency and the position offered, the fee may be paid entirely by the employer or by the employee, or they may split it. Some agencies specialize in a particular field such as clerical work or sales. Private agencies tend to be more successful with experienced people who have sharply defined skills, good work histories, and employment in a single field. Advantages are that they offer a chance for employer and prospective employee to explore the possibility of a permanent relationship, and they may list positions not offered elsewhere. The main disadvantage is the fee.

APPLYING AND INTERVIEWING FOR JOBS

Once the student has found a job that sounds good, he or she must apply for it. This involves writing to the company offering the job and including a résumé or job application. In either case, a cover letter is very important; it is the first thing that the prospective employer will see. The letter should be personalized and contain information such as where the student heard about the job, an indication of his or her interests, why the student is suited for the position, and his or her interest in interviewing. It should include the student's name, address, and phone number.

The next step in the job search is the job interview, which involves an exchange between people trying to find out whether they can work together to mutual benefit. Before you have the student go to the interview, help him or her learn as much as possible about a prospective employer by reading brochures, talking to present employees, calling the chamber of commerce, or visiting the public library. Some interviewing dos and don'ts: do be honest; be prompt (better 10 minutes early than 1 minute late); use a firm handshake; dress appropriately; make eye contact; address interviewer by name—pronounced correctly; use good grammar; know something about the company; prepare to ask intelligent and thoughtful questions; don't sound arrogant; don't be too personal; don't smoke or chew gum; don't make excuses; and don't bring up salary at the first interview.

After the interview, it is important to maintain contact with the prospective employer. Have the student write a thank-you letter, indicating that he or she will call at a specific time to find out his or her status regarding the position. Have the student call as indicated. If the student is not hired, have the student ask why. Knowing why he or she did not get a job may help him or her get the next one.

APPLICANTS OR EMPLOYEES WITH DISABILITIES IN STATE OR LOCAL GOVERNMENT AGENCIES

If a state or local government employer employs 15 or more people, an individual with a disability is covered by Title I of the ADA, enforced by the EEOC. A state or local government agency that employs 15 or more employees is also covered by Title II of the ADA, which is enforced by the U.S. Department of Justice. To file a complaint, contact the nearest EEOC office or call (800) 669-4000 (voice) or (800) 800-3302 (TTY/TDD).

If a state or local government employer employs fewer than 15 employees, an individual with a disability is covered by Title II of the ADA, enforced by the U.S. Department of Justice. To file a complaint, send it to the U.S. Department of Justice, Civil Rights Division, Coordination and Review Section, P.O. Box 66118, Washington, D.C., 20035-6118.

If a state or local employer receives federal financial assistance, an individual with a disability is also covered by Section 504 of the Rehabilitation Act of 1973, as amended, enforced by the federal agency that provided the federal financial assistance. The enforcement of Section 504 is coordinated by the U.S. Department of Justice. To file a complaint, send it to the agency that provided the funds or to the U.S. Department of Justice, Civil Rights Division, Coordination and Review Section, P.O. Box 66118, Washington, D.C., 20035-6118.

Individuals do not have to exhaust administrative procedures under Section 504 of the Rehabilitation Act. They may file suit against a public entity in federal district court without filing a complaint with an administrative agency.

CONCLUSION

Transition from the secondary school system to the world of adult life and adult responsibilities is a complex time for all young people. Young adults with disabilities and their families often find this time particularly challenging. To achieve the end goal of transition—which, according to Halpern (1985) is to live successfully in one's community—requires much planning, consideration, exploration, and self-determination. Young people with disabilities must make decisions and take action regarding three critical areas in their lives that are likely to undergo a transition as they become adults. These areas are their residence, or where they will live in the community; their personal life, which involves self-esteem, maturity, family, friends, and intimate relationships; and employment, which requires appropriate training and education, job search skills, and knowledge of important employee behaviors (Halpern, 1985). Successfully addressing these three issues is what will lead young people—those with disabilities and those without—to a successful life as an adult in the community.

CHAPTER SEVEN

SOCIAL AND SEXUAL ISSUES

OVERVIEW

Today, because of the work of advocates and people with disabilities over the past 50 years, American society is acknowledging that those with disabilities have the same rights as other citizens to contribute to and benefit from our society. This includes the right to education, employment, self-determination, and independence. We are also coming to recognize, albeit more slowly, that persons with disabilities have the right to experience and fulfill an important aspect of their individuality, namely, their social life and sexuality. As with all rights, this right brings with it responsibilities, not only for the person with disabilities but also for that individual's parents and caregivers. Adequately preparing an individual for the transition to adulthood, with its many choices and responsibilities, is certainly one of the greatest challenges that parents and others face.

The focus of this chapter will be to address various concerns related to individuals with disabilities and their social and sexual issues. After reading this chapter, you should understand the following:

THE IMPORTANCE OF DEVELOPING SOCIAL SKILLS

ACQUIRING SOCIAL SKILLS

HOW PARENTS AND PROFESSIONALS CAN HELP WIDEN SOCIAL EXPERIENCES

AVOIDING SOCIAL MISTAKES

MISCONCEPTIONS ABOUT SEXUALITY AND DISABILITY

DEFINING SEXUALITY

HOW SEXUALITY DEVELOPS

SEXUALITY EDUCATION

SUGGESTIONS FOR TEACHING CHILDREN AND YOUTH ABOUT SEXUALITY

EARLY SIGNS OF PUBERTY

ISSUES TO ADDRESS WITH THE ADOLESCENT

HOW PARTICULAR DISABILITIES AFFECT SEXUALITY AND SEXUALITY EDUCATION

THE IMPORTANCE OF DEVELOPING SOCIAL SKILLS

In the course of human development, there is probably no greater need than to attach, connect, or build gratifying human relationships. This human need is felt by all, whether one has a disability or not. It is vital that all children be given the opportunities to learn and practice the social skills considered appropriate by society. All children must learn how to conduct themselves in ways that allow them to develop relationships with other people. Parents must keep in mind that social skills pervade an individual's entire life, at home, in school, in the community, and at the workplace. An example of the significance of a deficit in social skills appears to be that a large percentage (nearly 90 percent) of employees lost their jobs because of poor attitude and inappropriate behavior rather than the lack of job skills.

Children with disabilities may find developing these skills more difficult than their peers without disabilities. As a result of a variety of learning or other cognitive disabilities, visual or hearing impairments, or a physical disability that limits their chances to socialize, children with disabilities may lack the exposure and experiences required to develop appropriate social skills. Most, however, are capable of learning these important "rules" (Duncan & Canty-Lemke, 1986) and should be given opportunities to learn and practice them by teachers, parents, and professionals.

ACQUIRING SOCIAL SKILLS

The development of social skills is a process that begins very early. We usually learn these skills from modeling significant individuals in our lives. The road to social skill development is filled with successes and mistakes. When the mistakes occur, parents usually provide us with a clear frame of reference so that we learn from our mistakes. The change in our behavior to more appropriate responses usually results from reward or punishment, both tending to shape our behavior. Rewards tell us what to do and punishments should tell us what not to do.

A very important source of social skill modeling comes from friends. A child who is able to maintain a social awareness of other people's reactions will modify his or her behavior in accordance with the positive or negative responses from others. In the case of individuals with disabilities, however, this important feedback on performance may be denied (Duncan & Canty-Lemke, 1986); some cannot learn the basics of social behavior. For others, social isolation plays a key role; how can a person get feedback on his or her social skills when little socializing takes place?

Socialization takes time. We are always fine-tuning socialization skills throughout our lives, as we are exposed to many new social situations at different developmental periods. The development of social skills relies on the ability of children and adults to observe the behavior of others as well as their own, discuss possible behavioral options, practice different skills in a variety of situations to see which ones result in positive feedback, and listen to constructive feedback from individuals whom they trust and respect.

Individuals with disabilities may have difficulty with many of the skills mentioned previously, and as a result they may:

- find it hard to take turns during conversations
- not be able to maintain eye contact
- experience difficulty being polite
- have problems maintaining attention
- not know how to repair misunderstandings
- not be able to find topics that are of mutual interest
- have problems distinguishing social cues (both verbal and nonverbal), for example, facial expressions or tone of voice
- find it hard to express what they mean if language problems exist
- have difficulty judging how close to stand to another person

To compound the problem, many individuals with disabilities are completely oblivious to their social clumsiness and do not understand why their social lives are not fulfilling.

Clearly, appropriate behaviors can be taught to those with disabilities. Teaching can begin at home, with the parent playing a vital role in helping a child to socialize. Children should be included in family social activities where they have a part to play in the gatherings. They might greet people at the door, take their coats, show them where the chairs are, and offer them food. Remember, these early interactions lay the foundation for interactions in the future, many of which will take place outside the home, and in many cases, skills will have to be practiced one at a time.

To a certain degree, children may be protected and rescued from uncomfortable social situations by their parents and teachers throughout their years in school. As most children grow older, however, they interact more and more with people in situations in which direct supervision by concerned adults is not possible. Children can learn how to incorporate the early teachings so that they can make friends within their peer groups, learn more about socializing, and refine their social skills as they grow and mature. Friendships are important for all children to develop because contact, understanding, and sharing with others are basic human needs. As children develop, the natural movement is away from parents and more toward a peer group attachment. Friends "serve central functions for children that parents do not, and they play a crucial role in shaping children's social skills and their sense of identity" (Rubin, 1980, p. 12).

Unfortunately, many children with disabilities are socially isolated as a result of several factors:

- The presence of a disability may make peers shy away.
- Transportation to and from social events may be difficult.
- Special health care may be required, for example, a respirator.
- The individual with the disability may be reluctant to venture out socially.

Because a lack of appropriate social skills may contribute to a person's social isolation, the child is caught in a vicious cycle. The current educational trend toward inclusion is an attempt to remedy this social isolation and provide all students with positive social role models.

HOW PARENTS AND PROFESSIONALS CAN HELP WIDEN SOCIAL EXPERIENCES

Teaching social skills is one of the most difficult and frustrating experiences confronted by parents and professionals, particularly when the disability is characterized by concrete thinking. What makes it so difficult is that our social behavior varies in different contexts, and children with disabilities may not be able to adjust as quickly as the situation requires.

Parents and professionals can provide a variety of experiences that widen their social circle in a number of ways. These include (Pierangelo & Crane, 1997):

- Emphasize good grooming and personal hygiene, and teach children the basics of self-care.
- Discuss and explore the characteristics of good friendships: what makes for good friendships, how friendships are formed and maintained, and some reasons why friendships may end.
- Model important social behaviors and then have the individual role-play any number of typical friendly interactions. Such interactions might include phone conversations, how to ask about another person's interests or describe

one's own interests, how to invite a friend to the house, or how to suggest or share an activity with a friend.
- Help the child develop hobbies or pursue special interests.
- Encourage the child to pursue recreational and leisure activities in the community.
- Encourage the child to participate in extracurricular activities at school.
- Help the teenager find employment or volunteer positions in the community.
- Try not to overprotect. Although it is natural to want to shield a child from the possibility of failure, hurt feelings, and others' rejection, parents, particularly, must allow their children the opportunity to grow and stretch socially.

AVOIDING SOCIAL MISTAKES

Many individuals with disabilities need special help to avoid two types of social mistakes. The first includes those that occur when the person with a disability treats an acquaintance or a total stranger as if he or she were a dear and trusted friend. Individuals with mental retardation are particularly vulnerable to making these kinds of mistakes (e.g., hugging or kissing a stranger who comes to the family home).

The second error generally involves doing or saying something in public that society considers unacceptable in that context, such as touching one's genitals or undressing in plain view of others. Committing either type of error can put the person with a disability into a vulnerable position in terms of breaking the law or opening the door to sexual exploitation. As a special educator, you can help parents understand these situations and how to handle them. Present parents with the following information concerning how to handle their child when they exhibit socially inappropriate behaviors:

- Teach the distinction between public and private through modeling, explanation, and persistence.
- When a child commits public–private errors, such as touching his or her genitals, immediately and calmly say, "No, that's private. We don't touch ourselves in public." Then, if possible, allow the child to go to a private place.
- Provide a place of privacy for the child to go to. Not only does this allow the child to understand the difference between public and private but it also acknowledges his or her right as an individual to have and enjoy time alone.

MISCONCEPTIONS ABOUT SEXUALITY AND DISABILITY

The natural course of human development means that, at some point in time, children will assume responsibility for their own lives, including their bodies. A parent faces this inescapable fact with powerful and often conflicting emotions: pride, alarm, nostalgia, disquiet, outright trepidation, and the bittersweet realization that the child soon will not be a child any longer. The role that parents and professionals play in a child's social-sexual development is a unique and crucial one. Through daily words and actions and through what they do not say or do, parents and caregivers teach children the fundamentals of life: the meaning of love, human contact and interaction, friendship, fear, anger, laughter, kindness, self-assertiveness, and so on.

Although a parent is expected to be a child's primary educator of values, morals, and sexuality, this may often not be the case. For many reasons, some personal and some societal, parents often find sexuality a difficult subject to approach. Discussing *sexuality* with one's child may make a parent uncomfortable, regardless of whether the child has a disability, and regardless of culture or educational background, religious affiliation, beliefs, or life experiences. For many people, the word *sexuality* conjures up many images, both good (joy, family, warmth, pleasure, love) and fearful (sexually transmitted diseases, exploitation, unwanted pregnancies). Anxieties and misgivings are often heightened for parents of children with disabilities.

A physically disabled individual engaging in sexual activity has been an image not entertained much by mainstream society. However, if an individual is born with or acquires a physical disability during his or her life span, the issue of sexuality becomes one of the most important factors of existence (Mona, 2003). Unfortunately, there are many misconceptions about the sexuality of children with disabilities. The most common myth is that children and youth with disabilities are asexual and, consequently, do not need education about their sexuality. The truth is that all children are social and sexual beings from the day they are born (Sugar, 1990). They grow and become adolescents with physically maturing bodies and a host of emerging social and sexual feelings and needs; this is true for the vast majority of young people, including those with disabilities. Many people also think that individuals with disabilities will not marry or have children, so they have no need to learn about sexuality. This is not true either. With increased realization of their rights, and more independence and self-sufficiency, people with disabilities are choosing to marry or to become sexually involved. As a consequence of increased choice and wider opportunity, children and youth with disabilities do have a genuine need to learn about sexuality, including what sexuality is, its meaning in adolescent and adult life, and the responsibilities that go along with exploring and experiencing one's own sexuality. They need information about values, morals, and the subtleties of friendship, dating, love, and intimacy. They also need to know how to protect themselves against unwanted pregnancies, sexually transmitted diseases, and sexual exploitation.

DEFINING SEXUALITY

According to the Sex Information and Education Council of the United States (SIECUS), *human sexuality* encompasses the sexual knowledge, beliefs, attitudes, values, and behaviors of individuals. It deals with the anatomy, physiology, and biochemistry of the sexual response system; with roles, identity, and personality; with individual thoughts, feelings, behaviors, and relationships. It addresses ethical, spiritual, and moral concerns, and group and cultural variations (Haffner, 1990, p. 28).

How Sexuality Develops

An understanding of sexuality begins with looking at how the social and sexual self develops. These two facets of the total self must be examined in conjunction with one another, for sexuality is not something that develops in isolation from other aspects of identity (Edwards & Elkins, 1988). Indeed, much of what is appropriate sexual behavior is appropriate social behavior and involves learning to behave in socially acceptable ways.

From the time we are born, we are sexual beings, deriving enormous satisfaction from our own bodies and from our interactions with others, particularly the warm embraces of our mothers and fathers. Most infants delight in being stroked, rocked, held, and touched. Research shows that the amount of intimate and loving care we receive as infants "is essential to the development of healthy human sexuality" (Gardner, 1986, p. 45). The tenderness and love babies receive during this period contribute to their ability to trust and to eventually receive and display tenderness and affection.

We form many of our ideas about life, affection, and relationships from our early observations. These ideas may last a lifetime, influencing how we view ourselves and interact with others. Because children are great imitators of the behaviors they observe, the environment of the home forms the foundation for their reactions and expectations in social situations. Some homes are warm, and affection is freely expressed through hugs and kisses. In other homes, people are more formal, and family members may seldom touch. The amount of humor, conversation, and interaction between various family members also differs from home to home. Some families share their deep feelings, whereas others do not. Children observe and absorb these early lessons about human interaction, and much of their later behaviors and expectations may reflect what they have seen those closest to them say or do.

In the preschool and early school years, children continue to be curious about their bodies and the bodies of the opposite sex. They make many explorations, using all their senses. Friendships, playmates, games, and activities are important during this period to the continuing development of the sense of self within a social sphere.

With puberty, which normally starts between the ages of 9 and 13, children begin to undergo great physical change brought about by changes in hormonal balance (Dacey, 1986). Physical changes are usually accompanied by a heightened sexual drive and some emotional upheaval due to self-consciousness and uncertainty as to what all the changes mean. Before the changes actually begin, it is important that parents talk calmly with their children about what lies ahead. This is a most important time for youth; many are filled with extreme sensitivity, self-consciousness, and feelings of inadequacy regarding their physical and social selves. Their bodies are changing, sometimes daily, displaying concrete evidence of their femaleness or maleness.

During *puberty* (the onset of sexual maturation), all children need help in maintaining a good self-image. Adolescence follows puberty and often brings with it conflicts between children and parents or caregivers. As humans advance into adolescence, physical changes are often matched by new cognitive abilities and a desire to achieve greater independence from the family unit and others in authority. The desire for independence generally manifests itself in a number of ways. One is that adolescents may want to dress according to their own tastes, sporting unconventional clothes and hairstyles that may annoy or alarm their parents. Another is that adolescents often begin to place great importance on having their own friends and ideas, sometimes purposefully different from what parents desire. The influence of peers in particular seems to threaten parental influence.

Both parents and adolescents may experience the strain of this period in physical and emotional development. A parent, on the one hand, may feel an intense need to protect the adolescent from engaging in behavior for which he or she is not cognitively or emotionally ready (Tharinger, 1987). A parent may fear that the child will be hurt or that deeply held cultural or religious values will be sacrificed. On the other side of the equation, young people may be primarily concerned with developing an identity separate from their parents and with experiencing their rapidly developing physical, emotional, and cognitive selves (Dacey, 1986). All children follow this developmental pattern, whether they have a disability or not, some at a slower and perhaps less intense rate, but they all eventually grow up.

SEXUALITY EDUCATION

What does it mean to provide sexuality education to children and youth? What type of information is provided and why? What goals do parents, caregivers, and professionals have when they teach children and youth about human sexuality? Sexuality education should encompass many things. It should not just mean providing information about the basic facts of life, reproduction, and sexual intercourse. "Comprehensive *sexuality education* addresses the biological, sociocultural, psychological, and spiritual dimensions of sexuality" (Haffner, 1990, p. 28). According to the Sex Information and Education Council of the United States, comprehensive sexuality education should address (1) facts, data, and information, (2) feelings, values, and attitudes, and (3) the skills to communicate effectively and to make responsible decisions (Haffner 1990, p. 28).

This approach to providing sexuality education clearly addresses the many facets of human sexuality. Stated in broader terms, the goals of comprehensive sexuality education are as follows:

■ **Provide information.** All people have the right to accurate information about human growth and development, human reproduction, anatomy, physiology, masturbation, family life, pregnancy, childbirth, parenthood, sexual response, sexual orientation, contraception, abortion, sexual abuse, HIV/AIDS, and other sexually transmitted diseases.

■ **Develop values.** Sexuality education gives young people the opportunity to question, explore, and assess attitudes, values, and insights about human sexuality. The goals of this exploration are to help young people understand family, religious, and cultural values, develop their own values, increase their self-esteem, develop insights about relationships with members of both genders, and understand their responsibilities to others.

■ **Develop interpersonal skills.** Sexuality education can help young people develop skills in communication, decision making, assertiveness, peer refusal skills, and the ability to create satisfying relationships.

■ **Develop responsibility.** Providing sexuality education helps young people to develop their concept of responsibility and to exercise that responsibility in sexual relationships. This is achieved by providing information about and helping young people to consider abstinence, resist pressure to become prematurely involved in sexual relationships, properly use contraception and take other health measures to prevent sexually related medical problems (such as teenage pregnancy and sexually transmitted diseases), and to resist sexual exploitation or abuse (Haffner, 1990, p. 4).

Considering this list, it becomes clear that a great deal of information about sexuality, relationships, and the self must be communicated to children and youth. In addition to providing this information, parents and professionals must allow children and youth opportunities for discussion and observation, as well as to practice important skills such as decision making, assertiveness, and socializing. Sexuality education is not achieved in a series of lectures that takes place when children are approaching or experiencing puberty; sexuality education is a lifelong process and should begin as early in a child's life as possible.

Providing comprehensive sexuality education to children and youth with disabilities is particularly important and challenging because of their unique needs. These individuals often have fewer opportunities to acquire information from their peers, have fewer chances to observe, develop, and practice appropriate social and sexual behavior, may have a reading level that limits their access to information, may require special materials that explain sexuality in ways they can understand, and may need more time and repetition in order to understand the concepts presented to them.

With opportunities to learn about and discuss the many dimensions of human sexuality, young people with disabilities can gain an understanding of the role that sexuality plays in all our lives, the social aspects to human sexuality, and values and attitudes about sexuality and social and sexual behavior. They also can learn valuable interpersonal skills and develop an awareness of their own responsibility for their bodies and their actions. Ultimately, all that they learn prepares them to assume the responsibilities of adulthood, living, working, and socializing in personally meaningful ways within the community.

SUGGESTIONS FOR TEACHING CHILDREN AND YOUTH ABOUT SEXUALITY

This section offers some practical suggestions to teach parents on how to take an active role in teaching their children with disabilities about sexuality. The discussion is organized by age groupings and the specific types of sexuality training that can be provided to individuals as they grow and mature. Although physical development is not much delayed for most individuals with disabilities, a child may not show certain behaviors or growth at the times indicated later. Depending on the nature of the disability, emotional maturity may not develop in some adolescents at the same rate as physical maturity. This does not mean that physical development won't occur. It will. Parents can help children to cope with physical and emotional development by anticipating it and talking openly about sexuality and the values and choices surrounding sexual expression. This will help prepare children and youth with disabilities to deal with their feelings in a healthy and responsible manner. It's important to realize that discussing sexuality will not create sexual feelings in young people. Those feelings are already there, because sexuality is a part of each human being throughout the entire life cycle.

Basic sexual education occurs over a long period of time, from infancy through age 11. During this period some of the topics that have to be addressed include:

- the correct names for the body parts and their functions
- the similarities and differences between girls and boys
- the fundamentals of reproduction and pregnancy
- the qualities of good relationships (friendship, love, communication, respect)
- decision-making skills, and the fact that all decisions have consequences
- the beginnings of social responsibility, values, and morals
- the acknowledgment that masturbation can be pleasurable but should be done in private
- avoiding and reporting sexual exploitation

Also during the later part of this developmental age range, preteens are usually busy with social development. They are becoming more preoccupied with what their peers think of them and, for many, body image may become an issue. If we think of the emphasis placed on physical beauty within our society—"perfect bodies," exercise, sports, makeup—it is not difficult to imagine why many preteens with disabilities (and certainly teenagers) have trouble feeling good about their bodies. Those with disabilities affecting the body may be particularly vulnerable to low self-esteem.

There are a number of things parents and professionals can do to help children and youth with disabilities improve self-esteem with regard to body image.

The first action parents and professionals can take is to listen to the child and to allow the freedom and space for feelings of sensitivity, inadequacy, or unhappiness to be expressed. Be careful not to wave aside a child's concerns, particularly as they relate to his or her disability. If the disability is one that can cause a child to have legitimate difficulties with body image, then parents and professionals need to acknowledge that fact calmly and tactfully. The disability is there; others know it and the child knows it. Pretending otherwise will not help a child develop a balanced and realistic sense of self.

Encourage children with disabilities to focus on and develop their strengths, not what they perceive as bad points about their physical appearance; this is called *refocusing* (Pope, McHale, & Craighead 1988). Many people have also helped a child with a disability improve negative body image by encouraging improvements that can be made through good grooming, diet, and exercise. Although it's important not to teach conformity for its own sake, fashionable clothes can often help any child feel more confident about body image.

One of the most important things that parents can do during their children's prepubescent years is to prepare them for the changes that their bodies will soon undergo. No female should have to experience her first menses (*menarche*, the onset of menstruation) without knowing what is going on in her body; similarly, boys should be told that nocturnal emissions (or "wet dreams," as they are sometimes called) are a normal part of their physical development. To have these experiences without any prior knowledge of them can be very upsetting to a young person, a trauma that can easily be avoided by timely discussions between parent and child. Professionals need to explain to parents so that they teach their children (with or without disabilities) that these experiences are a natural part of growing up. Above all, parents must do so before these experiences occur.

EARLY SIGNS OF PUBERTY

Early signs of puberty include a rapid growth spurt, developing breast buds in girls, and sometimes an increase in "acting out" and other emotional behaviors. Additional topics of importance to address with children approaching puberty are

- sexuality as part of the total self
- more information on reproduction and pregnancy
- the importance of values in decision making
- communication within the family unit about sexuality
- masturbation (see discussion later)
- abstinence from sexual intercourse
- avoiding and reporting sexual abuse
- sexually transmitted diseases, including HIV/AIDS

During this period of adolescence, it is important for parents to let their child assume greater responsibility in terms of decision making. It is also important that adolescents have privacy and, as they demonstrate trustworthiness, increasingly greater degrees of independence. For many teenagers, this is an active social time, with many school functions and outings with friends. Many teenagers are dating; statistics show that many become sexually involved. According to Morris (2000), over 70 percent of all boys and 60 percent of all girls have had sexual intercourse by age 17. For youth with disabilities, there may be some restrictions in opportunities for socializing and in their degree of independence. For some, it may be necessary to continue to teach distinctions between public and private. Appropriate sexuality means taking responsibility and knowing that sexual matters have their time and place.

ISSUES TO ADDRESS WITH THE ADOLESCENT

Puberty and adolescence are usually marked by feelings of extreme sensitivity about the body. An adolescent's concerns over body image may become more extreme during this time. Teach parents to let the adolescent voice these concerns, while they reinforce ideas they've hopefully introduced about refocusing, good grooming, diet, and exercise. Without dismissing the feelings as a "phase you are going through," they need to try to help their adolescent understand that some of the feelings are a part of growing up. Parents may arrange for the youth to talk with the family doctor without the parent being present. If necessary, parents can also talk to the doctor in advance to be sure he or she will be clear about the adolescent's concerns. If, however, an individual remains deeply troubled or angry about body image after supportive discussion within the family unit, it may be helpful to engage the services of a professional counselor. Counseling can be a good outlet for intense feelings, and often counselors can make recommendations that are useful to young people in their journey toward adulthood.

One topic that many parents find embarrassing to talk about with their children is masturbation. They will probably notice an increase in self-pleasuring behavior at this point in their child's development (and often before) and may feel in conflict about what to do because of personal beliefs. Beliefs about the acceptability of this behavior are changing, however; the medical community as well as many religious groups now recognize masturbation as normal and harmless.

Masturbation "can be a way of becoming more comfortable with and enjoying one's sexuality by getting to know and like one's body" (Sex Information and Education Council of the United States, 1991, p. 3). Masturbation only becomes a problem when it is practiced in an inappropriate place or is accompanied by strong feelings of guilt or fear (Edwards & Elkins 1988). How can parents avoid teaching their children guilt over normal behavior, especially if they themselves are not convinced? First, they may wish to talk to a family doctor, school nurse, or clergy and may be surprised to find that what they were taught as children is no longer being approached in the same way. In dealing with children, parents must recognize that they communicate a great deal through their actions and reactions; they have the power to teach children guilt and fear, and that there are appropriate and inappropriate places for this behavior.

The adolescent with a disability must be taught that touching one's genitals in public is socially inappropriate and that such behavior is acceptable only when one is alone and in a private place. Starting from very early in the child's life, when a parent first notices such behavior, it is important to accept the behavior calmly. When young children touch themselves in public, it is usually possible to distract them. During adolescence (and sometimes before), masturbation generally becomes more than an infrequent behavior of childhood and distracting the youth's attention will not work. Furthermore, it denies the real needs of the person, instead of helping him or her to meet those needs in acceptable ways (Edwards & Elkins 1988).

Among the many other topics that an adolescent will need to know about are

- health care, including health-promoting behaviors such as regular checkups and breast and testicular self-exam
- sexuality as part of the total self
- communication, dating, love, and intimacy
- the importance of values in guiding one's behavior
- how alcohol and drug use influence decision making
- sexual intercourse and other ways to express sexuality

- birth control and the responsibilities of childbearing
- reproduction and pregnancy (more detailed information than has previously been presented)
- condoms and disease prevention

Depending on the nature of an individual's disability, parents may have to present information in very simple, concrete ways or discuss the topics in conjunction with other issues. Remember, young people are receiving information from other sources as well; it may be essential to include the entire family in the resolve to be frank and forthright, for a lot of information comes from siblings. Children may feel more comfortable asking their brothers and sisters questions than directly asking parents.

Parents and professionals must encourage a child to be involved in activities with others that provide social outlets, such as going to the community recreation center on weekends, going to sports events or a movie, joining a club or group at school or in the community, or having a friend over after school. These interactions help build social skills, develop a social network for a child, and provide him or her with opportunities to channel sexual energies in healthy, socially acceptable directions (Murphy & Corte, 1986).

HOW PARTICULAR DISABILITIES AFFECT SEXUALITY AND SEXUALITY EDUCATION

Tailoring the pace and presentation of information to the needs of each young person with disabilities is very important. Parents and professionals must take into consideration how the child's particular disability may affect his or her social-sexual development, how the disability affects the child's ability to learn information about sexual issues, and what extra information may have to be provided to address a child's special needs.

Fostering Social and Sexual Relationships: Suggestions for Young Adults

Some very common questions asked by students with disabilities pertaining to social relationships are:

- Will I ever have an adult relationship (e.g., a boyfriend or girlfriend, a lover, a spouse)?
- How will I meet this person?
- What will I talk about?
- What will I say about my disability?
- Will my disability distract the other person from seeing me for the whole and unique person I am?
- What can I do to foster a relationship and help it grow into something strong and meaningful for me?

Here are some ideas about relationships, selfhood, disability, love, sexuality, friendship, patience, hope, and fulfillment that you, as a special educator, can tell an individual with a disability about the realities of adult relationships:

- Don't ever believe that no one will love you because you have a disability. People with disabilities can both love and be loved. Relationships are based on friendship, trust, laughter, and respect—all of which combine to spark and maintain the love you find in a relationship.

■ Involve yourself in a variety of such activities as work, community projects, and recreation. These activities will give you the opportunity to meet people. They will also help you grow as a person and avoid boredom and loneliness.

■ A relationship is fostered through being a good listener and companion, a person who genuinely cares about others. Build trust and respect between you and the other person. Share activities and ideas. Romance can grow out of such solid ground.

■ Keep up on current events. Being able to discuss a variety of topics can help conversations flow.

■ Be patient in your search for connection with others. Relationships take time to develop. They cannot be forced. Don't settle for the first person who expresses an interest in you as a woman or a man, unless you are also interested in that person!

■ Be open about your disability. Communicate how your disability will affect, and might interfere with, specific aspects of everyday life. Bring it up yourself, as the other person is often uncomfortable with introducing the topic. The burden of a disability requires that you make other people comfortable with it. How you talk about your disability with openness and humor will set the tone for the relationship.

■ Open and frank discussion between you and your partner is the key to solving whatever unique considerations your disability presents. Between loving and trusting partners, however, mutual pleasure and fulfillment are possible.

CONCLUSION

Although the issue of sexuality is often difficult for parents and professionals to discuss with children and youth, it is also one that is highly important to address in an open, frank, and matter-of-fact manner. Yet, sexuality education is not something that is accomplished in a limited number of lessons parents deliver; it is a lifelong process of learning about ourselves and growing as social and sexual beings. Because children and youth with disabilities will mature and one day be adults functioning within the community, they have a right to be fully and accurately informed about what sexuality means, what responsibilities it involves, and what unique pleasures, joys, and pain this aspect to identity can bring. The special needs of individuals with disabilities must be taken into consideration when parents and professionals present information on attitudes, values, behaviors, and facts about social skills and sexuality.

CHAPTER EIGHT

TRANSPORTATION EDUCATION

OVERVIEW

Transportation provides us all with access to the wider opportunities of society—employment, postsecondary education, job training programs, and recreation. Traveling by car, by cab, or by public transportation systems such as bus and subway enables us to go to work and come home, go to school or other training programs, visit friends, take care of daily needs such as grocery shopping, and enjoy recreational activities.

Yet, many individuals with disabilities have traditionally been isolated from these societal opportunities because they lacked a means of transportation. For many, driving a car was not possible due to a visual, physical, or cognitive disability. Public transportation systems were often inaccessible due to structural barriers. Still other individuals were unable to use the transportation systems that were available because they lacked the training, or "know-how," to use these systems safely.

Today, the lack of access to transportation that many individuals with disabilities have experienced is changing. Recently enacted federal legislation clearly intends to ensure that people with disabilities have an equal opportunity to participate independently and successfully in society. The Americans with Disabilities Act (ADA) recognizes the critical role that public transportation plays in the lives of many people and mandates that public transportation systems become accessible to people with disabilities. It also mandates that paratransit services are available and accessible to individuals who are unable to use public transportation.

Unfortunately, availability of transportation is not the only impediment to independent travel for people with disabilities. They must also know *what* systems of transport are available, how to access these, how to plan their travel, and how to execute their travel plans safely. For many individuals, learning how to travel on public transportation requires systematic training. Travel training, then, is often a crucial element in empowering people with disabilities to use the newly accessible transportation systems in our country.

To this end, the Individuals with Disabilities Education Act (IDEA) can be of particular importance. The IDEA requires public schools to provide transition services to youth with disabilities to prepare them for the transition from school to adult life. Although accessible transportation and transportation training are not specifically mentioned within IDEA, clearly the ability to use available transportation systems may be critical to a student's transition into the adult world. Thus, both the ADA and the IDEA provide individuals with disabilities, their families, school systems, service providers, community agencies, and transit systems with compelling incentives to work together to ensure that individuals with disabilities learn how to use accessible transportation.

The focus of this chapter will be to discuss transportation concerns of students and adults with disabilities. After reading this chapter, you should understand the following:

TRAVEL TRAINING

SKILLS REQUIRED FOR TRAVELING INDEPENDENTLY

BEGINNING TRAVEL TRAINING

THE PROCESS OF TRAVEL TRAINING

THE NECESSITY OF TRAVEL TRAINING PROGRAMS

WHO BENEFITS FROM TRAVEL TRAINING PROGRAMS?

THE IMPORTANCE OF EQUAL ACCESS TO TRANSPORTATION

WHERE TO LOOK FOR TRAVEL TRAINING PROGRAMS

TRAVEL TRAINING GUIDELINES FOR PEOPLE WITH A COGNITIVE DISABILITY

TRAVEL TRAINING GUIDELINES FOR PEOPLE WITH A PHYSICAL DISABILITY

WHAT TO LOOK FOR IN A TRAVEL TRAINING PROGRAM

TEACHING TRAVEL SKILLS TO PERSONS WHO ARE BLIND OR VISUALLY IMPAIRED

EVALUATING THE QUALITY OF PROGRAMS THAT TEACH TRAVEL SKILLS

PUBLIC TRANSPORTATION AND THE ADA

TRAVEL TRAINING

Travel training is short-term, comprehensive, intensive instruction designed to teach students with disabilities how to travel safely and independently on public transportation. The goal of travel training is to train students to travel independently to a regularly visited destination and back. Specially trained personnel provide the travel training on a one-to-one basis. Students learn travel skills while following a particular route, generally to school or a work site, and are taught the safest, most direct route. The travel trainer is responsible for making sure the student experiences and understands the realities of public transportation and learns the skills required for safe and independent travel using a program that provides instruction in travel skills to individuals with any disability except visual impairment. Individuals who have a visual impairment receive travel training from orientation and mobility specialists. Travel trainers have the task of understanding how different disabilities affect a person's ability to travel independently and devising customized strategies to teach travel skills that address the specific needs of people with those disabilities.

Individuals who need assistance to learn the public transportation system can receive one or both of the following types of travel training (GATRA, 2003):

- **Destination travel training.** This type of training teaches the individual to go to and from a specific destination, usually on a daily basis.
- **General travel training.** This type of training provides the individual with more complex instructions. The individual is taught to use the bus and other public transportation for general travel, selecting destinations of his or her choice. Included in this training is learning to read the bus and other public transportation schedules.

Interest in travel training increased in the 1990s. Recently enacted federal legislation clearly intends to ensure that people with disabilities have an equal opportunity to participate independently and successfully in society. Of significance are the 1990 passage of the Americans with Disabilities Act (ADA) and the 1990 passage of the Individuals with Disabilities Education Act (IDEA), which reauthorized and amended Public Law 94-142.

The ADA recognizes the critical role that public transportation plays in the lives of many people and mandates that public transit systems become accessible to people who have disabilities and that paratransit services are available and accessible to individuals who are unable to use public transportation. In recognition of the ADA, architectural barriers are being removed, new transit vehicles are being purchased, equipment is being modified, paratransit certification and eligibility practices are being established, and transit personnel are being trained to provide service to people who have disabilities. Nationwide, the transit industry is expecting to serve increasing numbers of individuals who have disabilities.

Together, the ADA and the IDEA provide individuals with disabilities, their families, school systems, service providers, community agencies, and transit systems with compelling incentives to work together to ensure that students learn how to use accessible transportation.

Providing students with travel training can reduce expenses for school districts, local governments, transit providers, agencies, or organizations that provide transportation. The cost of using public transportation is significantly less than the cost of using a contracted private car or private bus service. Although the cost of training a student can be substantial, in the long run that cost is a worthwhile investment because the student will gain independence and henceforth will assume responsibility for the cost of using public transportation.

SKILLS REQUIRED FOR TRAVELING INDEPENDENTLY

Experienced travel trainers agree that simply teaching students to follow a route is not enough to ensure safe travel. A quality travel training program will require students to demonstrate certain skills before travel training in real-life situations begins and will require students to practice certain skills with 100 percent consistency before they can be recommended for independent travel. For instance, Pierce Transit's Training Program (2003) consists of four components:

1. **General instruction.** Basic orientation to the mechanics of the bus system, fare structure, reading a schedule, calling a customer service representative for a trip plan, and one-on-one training for specific trips.
2. **Group orientation.** Basic orientation to the mechanics of the bus system, fare structure, reading a schedule, calling a customer service representative for a trip plan in a group setting.
3. **Mobility training.** Teaches participants to utilize the fixed route system with a mobility device.
4. **Destination training.** Trains participants to travel to specific destinations gaining the knowledge to use the fixed route system for some or all of their needs.

Before being allowed to enter travel training, students should possess three general skills: (1) an awareness of personal space, meaning a clear idea of where their personal space ends and that of others begins, (2) an awareness of their environment, and (3) the ability to recognize and respond to danger. Before being allowed to travel independently, students should demonstrate a number of other skills. Specifically, they should be able to:

- cross streets safely, with and without traffic signals
- board the correct bus or subway
- recognize and disembark at the correct destination
- make decisions
- initiate actions
- recognize the need for assistance and request help from an appropriate source
- follow directions

- recognize and avoid dangerous situations and obstacles
- maintain appropriate behavior
- handle unexpected situations, such as rerouted buses or subways, or getting lost
- deal appropriately with strangers

Before graduating from a travel training program, students must demonstrate mastery of these skills and employ them with 100 percent consistency. Although students find it useful to be able to read, tell time, and calculate simple math, these skills are not mandatory for independent travel or for travel training, and no individual should be denied training if she or he lacks these skills. A good travel training program accounts for a student's disabilities while making full use of a student's abilities.

BEGINNING TRAVEL TRAINING

Most people enter travel training between the ages of 15 and 21. However, it may be appropriate for some children to be introduced to travel training at an earlier age. This specialized instruction may occur as part of a student's educational program (as defined in the individualized education program), as part of the services of a Competitive Supported Employment provider (usually through coaching), or by an Orientation and Mobility instructor through education or through public or private vocational rehabilitation services (Parent Education Network, 2003).

A student can request training for himself or herself or be referred to travel training by his or her family or by school personnel or anyone closely involved in the daily life of the student. It is important to note that travel training may need to be included as a crucial component of a student's individualized education plan (IEP).

The candidate for travel training then goes through an assessment process. A travel training professional gathers information about the student's functioning and behavior by observing and conducting personal interviews with the student. By assessing the student's performance of various tasks, the travel trainer develops a profile of the student's functional abilities, needs, experiences, and motivation. The travel trainer fully explains the process and desired outcomes of travel training to the student and his or her family, who must give consent before travel training can begin. Everyone involved in travel training must agree that the student will be allowed to travel independently if she or he successfully completes travel training.

Initially, many students express anxiety about traveling alone. A student's anxiety may be a reflection of his or her family's anxiety about the prospect of the student traveling independently or simply a genuine insecurity on the part of the student, who is entering the complex world of public transportation at a disadvantage.

The assessment process often indicates that students, especially those with moderate to severe developmental disabilities, have little or no concept of the meaning of being "alone" and may have difficulty understanding the concept of independent travel. Beginning with the assessment process, travel training should gradually but fully introduce students to independent travel, taking care to slowly reduce their anxiety and that of their families.

THE PROCESS OF TRAVEL TRAINING

A travel trainer usually begins training a student at the student's residence, which allows the trainer to observe the student in a familiar environment, reassure the family through daily contact, assess the student's home environment at regular travel times for potential problems, and remind the student's family of the independent aspect of independent travel; that is, the student will be acting independently in the everyday world outside the family's care.

The training is sometimes broken down into four separate techniques (Westchester County Department of Community Mental Health Travel Training Program, 2003):

1. **Modeling.** Trainee is accompanied to ensure familiarity with the route and process.
2. **Prompting.** Trainer uses verbal cues to ensure success.
3. **Fading.** Trainee rides independently while the trainer observes to guarantee success and determine if further training is warranted.
4. **Shadowing.** Trainer follows trainee by car to ensure safety and proficiency. There are also follow-ups done on an as-needed basis to determine if further training is required.

Travel training should occur at the time of day when a student will later be traveling independently, so that a trainer can assess the effectiveness with which the student handles the noise, varying light, crowds, fatigue, busy intersections, and empty streets associated with a particular route, and adjust travel training accordingly. Travel training should continue through inclement weather, so students can get used to using an umbrella, traveling through snow and ice, and dressing appropriately for the weather. Regardless of the nature of their disability, most students need to learn the various skills required for traveling in all kinds of conditions. In a quality travel training program, a travel trainer works with one student at a time. The trainer follows the travel route with the student and instructs the student in dealing with problems such as getting lost or taking a detour around a construction site. The trainer should teach the student to make decisions, deal with the consequences of decisions, and maintain appropriate safety and behavior standards.

When a student successfully performs all the skills necessary for safe travel along a chosen route in the company of a trainer, most travel training programs send the student on a "solo" trip, during which the student travels alone on a bus or train, and the trainer follows behind in a car or in an adjacent train car. During this initial solo trip, the student is aware that she or he is being followed by the trainer.

Although the "solo" trip is an appropriate means of determining a student's travel skills, the "solo" trip does not give the trainer information on how the student manages while traveling alone and independently. Different travel training programs will obtain this information using different methods. For example, a student in the New York City Board of Education Travel Training Program is followed again after successfully completing a "solo" trip, this time by a travel trainer unknown to the student. This new travel trainer assesses the student's performance when the student believes he or she is truly traveling alone and independently or an "observation solo" trip. The trainer, remaining unknown, observes the manner in which the student handles the responsibilities of traveling alone but stays close enough to ensure the student's safety if intervention is required. Whether or not a travel training curriculum includes an "observation solo" trip at the end of a travel training program, a travel trainer should give the student, the student's family, and whoever initially referred the student for travel training a recommendation or written report regarding the student's ability to travel safely and independently.

THE NECESSITY OF TRAVEL TRAINING PROGRAMS

Being able to get around on one's own is an important component of independence; this is as true for people with disabilities as it is for those without disabilities.

Nearly all people who have disabilities can (with training and the use of accessible vehicles) board, travel on, and exit a public transportation vehicle. However, a certified travel training program is often needed to teach people who have a disability to do so safely and independently. Programs that maintain high-quality procedures for travel training are crucial in helping people who have a disability to develop autonomy and practice their right to move freely through a community.

A logical place to implement travel training programs is within the public school system. As the primary providers of education for students with a disability, local school districts have a full range of resources available to develop quality travel training programs. Because students are part of a school system for many consecutive years, educators can plan and deliver a full program of travel instruction. When a student enters the school system, this instruction can begin with activities that develop a student's sense of purposeful movement. *Purposeful movement* is the cognitive and physical ability to move safely and independently through the complex environments of school, home, and neighborhood and includes such movements as negotiating stairs, using a telephone, boarding a bus, or crossing a street.

As students progress through the school years, the various travel skills can be introduced and practiced routinely. Then, as students become young adults and are close to exiting the school system, explicit travel training can become part of their education and can form the basis of the transition from school transportation to public transportation.

Most students who successfully complete a comprehensive travel training program along one route require little additional training to learn other routes and reach other destinations. Learning purposeful movement skills early in school, then entering a travel training program in high school, reduces the time and expense required for additional travel training and helps individuals with disabilities acquire the transportation skills they will need once they leave secondary school.

Although the public school system is the optimal environment in which to begin travel training, individuals with disabilities can also get travel training from independent living centers or similar agencies. More information about local travel training programs may be obtained from state offices that deal with developmental disabilities or by contacting some of the organizations listed in the "Resources" section of this book.

WHO BENEFITS FROM TRAVEL TRAINING PROGRAMS?

The individual with a disability, the family, the school system, and society have much to gain from standardized, quality travel training programs. Individuals with a disability gain self-esteem by traveling independently, and many students remark on how much it means to them to be "treated just like anybody else" and to be able to say "I can do it myself." Learning the skills they need also increases their access to the wider opportunities of society, including employment, postsecondary education, job training programs, and recreation. The ability to travel independently and at will provides people who have disabilities with a vital key to achieving as much participation in society as they desire.

Society, too, benefits when people with disabilities participate actively in everyday life. Travel training programs can enable students with disabilities to become adults who can travel to and from their jobs without support, who are involved citizens of their communities, and who have the opportunity to live independently.

THE IMPORTANCE OF EQUAL ACCESS TO TRANSPORTATION

Access to transportation is the key to independence, productivity, and inclusion in educational or vocational training. When individuals are ready to enter the workforce, most discover that their choices of employment are limited by the availability of accessible transportation. Their opportunities to participate in and enjoy other activities—going to the mall, the coffeehouse, the movies, the public swimming pool, or other recreational places—may be similarly limited. If people with disabilities don't have access to public transportation or don't know how to use it safely, their lives can become isolated.

It's important that people with disabilities receive training on how to use existing transportation services safely, including public transportation. Some individuals live in communities where there are no public transportation services and must rely solely on the goodwill of others for transportation to work, school, medical services, or anywhere else they need or wish to go. It is very beneficial for everyone to learn about the transportation services that are offered in their communities by private organizations and federal, state, and local governments. All people with disabilities should be aware of their right to equal access to transportation under the Americans with Disabilities Act (ADA).

WHERE TO LOOK FOR TRAVEL TRAINING PROGRAMS

Various service providers and community projects offer travel training programs to their service populations. As is the case with most disability-related programs, each training program has its own eligibility criteria and guidelines for program participation. Many programs concentrate on specific types of disability, which makes it easier for staff members to become experts on training techniques and possible accommodations for the specific needs of their students. Whereas some programs offer their services solely on an individual basis or in small groups, others offer a combination of services that can provide the necessary flexibility for many individuals with various disabilities.

Public and private schools, Centers for Independent Living, Vocational Rehabilitation Services, MR/DD Programs, and the Lighthouses for the Blind Program either directly offer travel training programs or can make referrals to community providers of travel training. High schools may offer travel training courses or may make arrangements with a community travel training program to offer travel training to students with disabilities. Often organizations that train seeing, hearing, and companion dogs will train individuals who apply for their services on how to use public transportation safely with the assistance of their service animal.

Many training projects are funded through government grants and are offered at no cost to the individual. Training curricula vary from project to project, according to the varieties of transportation services available in the community and the project's targeted student population. The curricula of a travel training program should be flexible enough to accommodate individual learning styles, various types and levels of disabilities, and the goals and needs of the individual selecting a travel training program. It is important to select a program that has worked with people who have a particular disability. It is critically important that the trainers have enough flexibility to modify the training program to accommodate students' learning style and needs. Ask about the qualifications of the trainers, about safety policies, and for references from people with similar disabilities.

Although it may be useful for the program to include classroom instruction, the greater part of a training program should emphasize hands-on travel training. The trainer should be available if necessary to assist an individual in learning routes of travel, such as from home to work, work to the movies, school to home, or home to the grocery store. The training program and its staff should be sensitive to the various desires and lifestyles of the individuals who are participating in their program. Some training programs, notably Centers for Independent Living, employ individuals with disabilities as their trainers.

For some individuals with disabilities, the Americans with Disabilities Act has opened up new doors to their community and has enabled them to access transportation services for the first time. However, the majority of individuals with disabilities still remain unaware of their rights under the ADA and lack information and training on how to use public transportation systems. Community services organizations, educational and vocational programs, and transportation providers can work together to reach people with disabilities and to develop creative projects and solutions to meet their transportation needs. With access to dependable transportation, the goals of independence, productivity, and inclusion for many people with disabilities will be greatly enhanced.

TRAVEL TRAINING GUIDELINES FOR PEOPLE WITH A COGNITIVE DISABILITY

Traveling independently on public transportation is one occasion when a person with a cognitive impairment must perform with absolutely no assistance. Training a person with a cognitive impairment to use public transportation requires a comprehensive and individualized instructional program. Before a person with a cognitive disability can safely use public transportation, she or he must demonstrate 100 percent consistency in many functional skill areas, beyond simply learning the travel route to and from a destination.

Before travel training begins, a travel trainer determines a student's strengths and weaknesses, assesses how much support the student can expect from her or his parents or guardians, and reviews the travel route to determine the feasibility of traveling to a specific destination. Travel training begins only when the student is ready to learn the travel route and has support from parents or guardians. It's notable that a student with a cognitive disability does not necessarily have to know how to read a clock, make change, or understand survival signs to succeed in a travel training program, though these skills certainly are assets.

A comprehensive travel training program for people with a cognitive disability should consist of the following:

Phase 1. Detailed instruction in specific travel routes, fare costs, boarding and deboarding sites, and the demonstration of pedestrian skills necessary for this travel route, as well as constant practice in life skills such as appropriate interaction with community workers and with strangers, use of a public telephone, and appropriate behavior in public places.

Phase 2. Direct observation of the student by the travel trainer to verify that the student has learned all necessary travel skills taught in Phase 1.

Phase 3. Instruction in emergency procedures. Emergencies can include boarding the wrong transit vehicle, missing a stop, or losing one's fare or transfer pass.

Phase 4. Assessment of the student's interactive skills with strangers. Travel training programs may use plainclothes police officers or travel trainers (whom the student has not met) to approach the traveling student and try to extract personal information from him or her. Students pass this assessment procedure if they do not impart personal information to or leave with a stranger.

Phase 5. Indirect observation of the student. As the student walks to and from the transit stop and rides the transit vehicle independently, her or his performance is assessed at a distance by a travel trainer, who follows in a car. The student is aware that she or he is being observed.

Phase 6. Covert observation and assessment. The student is not aware that she or he is being observed.

Phase 7. Follow-up observations. Periodically, a student who successfully completes a travel training program should be covertly observed to verify that she or he is still practicing safe travel skills.

Although different travel training programs may vary the order in which they teach travel skills, the teaching methods of travel training programs should be the same. The average length of a quality travel training program is 15 sessions, though training time will vary according to the complexity of the travel route and the nature of the student's disability.

Once a person with a cognitive impairment begins to travel independently along one travel route, typically she or he learns other travel routes with relative ease. Sometimes the individual will generalize to a new route the training she or he received for the initial route. Other students may simply need "routing," a brief review of a new travel route. Still others may need the same intense instruction to travel to a new destination, especially if reaching the new destination requires new or more advanced pedestrian skills or different modes of transportation.

TRAVEL TRAINING GUIDELINES FOR PEOPLE WITH A PHYSICAL DISABILITY

Persons who have physical impairments may not require the intensive travel training that persons with a cognitive impairment require. Instead, travel training for people with a physical disability often focuses on developing life skills and self-assertiveness. For example, a person in a wheelchair may learn how to use a wheelchair lift, or a person with cerebral palsy may learn how to safely use an escalator or how to enter and leave a crowded subway. Individuals with physical disabilities may also learn how to appropriately ask for assistance or how to assert their rights in traveling and other social situations. Above all, a program should first and always consider the personal safety of the student.

Practical travel training should also teach students to investigate a destination to make certain, for example, that curb cuts exist on both sides of a street or that a restaurant has accessible restrooms. Students with a physical impairment need to learn problem-solving techniques to cope with unexpected emergencies, such as missing the last train home or negotiating a large mud puddle after a rainstorm. Students may also find it valuable to develop a community with persons who have similar impairments, because sharing experiences and advice within a community can be reassuring and informative and can reinforce productive behaviors.

Learning how to contact their local transit authority to obtain information on accessible transportation in their area is also a necessary skill for individuals with a physical disability. This includes finding out about regularly scheduled, fixed route services, such as buses and trains, and paratransit and special travel services. Many persons who have a physical impairment never contact these providers but typically allow a family member or a friend to make contacts and procure information. A comprehensive travel training program should teach students to get this information for themselves. Students who learn to make contacts, procure information, and arrange for travel services will gain independence and confidence.

WHAT TO LOOK FOR IN A TRAVEL TRAINING PROGRAM

When investigating travel training programs, one should thoroughly review the training procedures each program offers. Although a national movement to establish travel training standards is underway, no standards presently exist.

Some travel training programs encourage individuals with a disability, as they travel, to seek assistance from "natural helpers," that is, other passengers who frequently ride the same transit vehicle. However, professional travel trainers would not advocate this practice as safe or realistic. Establishing reliance on natural helpers may cause problems for the trainee, because a natural helper is likely to occasionally absent himself or herself from the transit vehicle, leaving the trainee on his or her own. It is never wise to "link" a person with a cognitive impairment to a stranger; in fact, a responsible travel training program will advocate wariness toward strangers.

Another travel training technique that some programs advocate is the use of peer trainers. One should be leery of using a developmentally disabled peer to teach travel training because training in pedestrian skills and emergency procedures can be a complex task for instruction. These and other safety issues can arise with this practice. When teaching travel training, safety should be the foremost concern of any quality program.

Many travel trainees must "unlearn" certain travel behaviors that they were encouraged in the past. Trainees must learn to avoid being too friendly to strangers, to solve unexpected problems, to make decisions, and to make judgments independently of others (such as not running across a street when the light is red to try and "beat" an oncoming car). The family and educators of a person with a cognitive impairment should consider whether they unconsciously encourage unsafe travel practices in the student.

Students and adults with disabilities who are found eligible for services available through job coaching providers may receive travel training as a part of their job placement supports. Coaches work one-to-one to provide needed instruction and supports for the individual with a disability to develop independent and safe travel skills. For persons investigating coaching services as a possible avenue for travel training, ask for information regarding this service. Individuals with disabilities or parents may wish to ask some of the following questions (Parent Education Network, 2003):

1. How do you assess my child's current skill levels in travel?
2. What are some examples of specialized instructional methods and accommodations you offer for someone with my child's disability?
3. How long does the coach accompany me or my child during the travel training?
4. How do you determine when it is appropriate to fade coaching services from the travel training?
5. How do you handle the fading process in order to assure me or my child's safety?
6. What follow-up services are available to assure continued safety?
7. What training has the coach received in travel training and safety?
8. What are some examples of personal safety skills that are taught as a part of the travel training?
9. Is interaction with strangers any part of the instructional program related to safety (if appropriate to individual needs)?

Travel Training for Persons with Physical Disabilities

A journey by public transit begins the moment a person decides to travel by public transit from one place to another. When they travel, people with disabilities have to consider and plan every minute detail of their journey. They have to choose a destination and a route of travel, decide how much money to bring for fares, and select appropriate clothing. After making these decisions, they must then physically execute certain actions: exiting the home, getting to the transit stop, and boarding the transit vehicle. Independent travel requires a coordination of planning and action that many of us perform every day and take for granted but that people with disabilities must consider with care.

Laying the Foundations for Traveling When Children Are Young

With many children, travel training begins at a very early age, when parents begin to teach the child to watch the changing of the traffic light and teach them to associate its colors (red, yellow, green) with the actions of stopping or going. This instruction continues with teaching the child to look both ways before crossing a street, asking for input on locating bus stops, depositing transit fare, and asking for transfers or where to stand on a subway platform or whom to go to should they get lost. Eventually, the young child is equipped with the safety information, travel knowledge, and physical skills necessary to travel independently.

However, children with physical disabilities, unlike their peers without disabilities, often do not have a chance to develop the cognitive and physical skills that they need for traveling independently on public transportation. Because they have a physical disability, they often rely on other people to transport them from place to place, and so they never learn the essential skills for traveling safely. Children with physical disabilities may find their range of movement restricted if, for example, they are not taught to safely get across a street to a bus stop, or if they do not learn to use subway tokens or bus transfer passes. Without such instruction, these children cannot be expected to safely and independently use public transportation.

Experience helps children develop travel skills, and all children should be allowed to have travel experience beginning with basic personal mobility. Even children who have severe physical disabilities, such as a child who uses a wheelchair but requires someone to push the chair, should be allowed to gain the experience needed to develop travel skills. Using this case as an example, the child in the wheelchair should be instructed in basic travel skills, such as obeying traffic signals, and then should be allowed to demonstrate these skills by telling the person pushing the wheelchair when to cross the street. As a child verbally directs travel, she or he is gaining the knowledge and skills necessary to eventually travel independently.

Beyond the Basics: The Role of Travel Training Programs

Travel training programs offer travel training beyond the basic training that parents or guardians give to growing children with physical disabilities. These programs are customized to fit the needs of each student's unique abilities and disabilities. When a professional travel training instructor designs a travel training program for a young student, she or he will assess the physical and cognitive abilities and disabilities of the student.

The Travel Skills That Students Must Learn. Students will need to move through indoor and outdoor environments. Skills such as opening doors and negotiating hills, ramps, curbs, curb cuts, and steps are important, and a student's capacity to accomplish these tasks should be assessed at the start of the training program. Endurance is also very important to a child's ability to travel independently. Is the student physically able to leave her or his home, travel to a transportation stop, wait for a bus or subway, board, and then reach and disembark at the final destination? Another important consideration is the student's standing and ambulatory balance. Will wind, rain, snow, ice, or crowds cause the student to fall easily? Can the student maneuver in tight spaces, as during rush hours when subway platforms and cars are packed? A student who has poor balance or poor endurance can still be expected to travel independently, but modifications should be made to the training program to accommodate his or her needs. The student might be instructed to use a less crowded route or to travel only during nonrush hours. Bus stops near places to sit down might be suggested if the student cannot stand for long periods. If a bus stop is at the top of a hill and the student cannot climb the hill, then another route should be planned. A student who cannot use the steps to enter the bus will need to be taught how to use a bus lift. Students who are ambulatory will need to practice walking forward, backward, and sideways, going up and down steps (including curbs, ramps, and curb cuts), and opening doors, sitting down and getting up, and operating a traffic signal.

Using a Wheelchair.   Many of the students who enter travel training programs use wheelchairs for mobility. Students who use wheelchairs will need to acquire the skills described above and must be able to propel the wheelchair forward and backward and make turns in tight spaces. A student who uses a manual wheelchair should be taught (if possible) how to do a wheelie to jump small ledges. Students using motorized wheelchairs, however, cannot do wheelies, because a motorized chair is too heavy. Because of this, their wheelchairs might not be able to go over the difference in height between a train and the platform level. In these cases—and in the case of students who cannot propel a manual wheelchair but who do not have a motorized wheelchair—it is necessary to teach students how to verbally direct someone to assist them. When a student can verbally direct a helper, then independent travel is an attainable goal.

Often people with physical disabilities travel by private car or van, an ambulate service, or an accessible school bus. When riding a bus, students who use a wheelchair are instructed to enter the bus lift backward, engage their brakes, and tell the bus operator when they are ready. Having boarded the bus, the student is instructed to use the tie down and the seat belt and to lock the wheelchair brakes. The student must then inform the bus operator of his or her stop in advance and also signal for the stop. The student is taught to exit the bus by entering the lift facing forward or out of the bus and locking the brakes.

The present tie-down system for wheelchairs on most buses cannot accommodate most motorized wheelchairs. Students in a motorized wheelchair should be instructed to position the wheelchair so that the front casters are facing the inside wall of the bus and to ensure that the motor is turned off and that the brakes are engaged. Students using manual wheelchairs should also be instructed to turn their front casters to face the side of the bus and to engage the brakes, as the tie downs sometimes will pop open.

TEACHING TRAVEL SKILLS TO PERSONS WHO ARE BLIND OR VISUALLY IMPAIRED

What Are Some Key Travel Issues That People with a Visual Impairment Face?

Gathering information, whether from physical surroundings, posted signs, or other passengers, is an important concern for travelers who are blind or visually impaired.

When traveling by bus, rail, or paratransit vehicle, individuals with a visual impairment require information to plan their travel; to establish and maintain orientation or sense of direction, to find their way when traveling to or within transit facilities and vehicles, and to protect themselves from potential hazards in their environment. When they use mass transit, travelers who are blind or visually impaired must consider their entire journey—from their point of origin to their final destination—when gathering information for travel.

Print signs and other displayed information in mass transit environments are usually inaccessible to persons with visual impairments, thus limiting the information that is readily available for effective and efficient travel. Travelers with visual impairments are specifically concerned about access to the following features of mass transit facilities:

- route, timetable, and fare information
- print or graphic messages on displayed signs, monitors, and maps
- information about the layout of transit stations, bus stops and depots, and transit vehicles
- information about the location of fare gates, token booths, vending machines, information kiosks, stairs, elevators, escalators, and boarding platforms

Once travelers with visual impairments have boarded a transit vehicle, it's very important for them to know each stop the vehicle arrives at, and to have access to information displayed on monitors, signs, and system maps within the vehicle itself.

Safety during travel in transit environments, as in all environments, is another serious concern for persons who are blind or visually impaired. Common hazards that people with visual impairments encounter in transit environments include parcels left haphazardly on narrow rail boarding platforms, crowds that jostle and push, and unprotected platform edges that precipitate into an open track bed—which travelers with visual impairments often refer to as "the pit." Effective use of specialized travel techniques, known as orientation and mobility (O&M) techniques, and certain environmental design features required by the Americans with Disabilities Act, such as tactile warning strips installed along the edges of train platforms and information in braille, enable travelers to secure the information and protection they need for safe and effective travel.

How Can Children and Youth with Visual Impairments Enter a Travel Training Program?

Children and youth who have a visual impairment are eligible to receive travel training as part of their special education program. These services can be provided starting in early intervention programs for infants and toddlers and should be written into a student's individual family service plan. School-aged students need to have these services specifically included in their individualized education program (IEP) or individualized transition program.

O&M instruction is provided by licensed or certified teachers of the visually impaired who have received specialized training in orientation and mobility. O&M instruction provided through a school program is individualized to address a student's needs during the school years and focuses on teaching the skills required for daily travel. Instruction often takes place in both school and community settings and is provided on a one-to-one basis, with the student's family and entire educational team assuming integral roles in the O&M program.

Young adults who have completed their public or private school education and who have entered the vocational rehabilitation system may require O&M services to successfully complete the transition to an adult lifestyle. These services can be provided directly by O&M instructors on the staff of a state vocational rehabilitation agency, by private rehabilitation agencies for the blind working under contract with a state agency, or by private instructors retained on a fee basis by either a state agency or a private rehabilitation service provider. These services may be delivered using a center-based program model, a field-based program model, or a combination of the two. For example, a young adult learning to travel from home to a job site may receive O&M instruction at a rehabilitation center to develop specific travel skills and then receive field-based O&M services to learn the travel route from home to work.

Who Are the Service Providers That Teach Travel Skills to Persons with Visual Impairments?

O&M services in schools and rehabilitation settings are provided by O&M instructors, who are also known as O&M therapists, O&M specialists, or peripatologists. O&M instructors in schools are teachers of the visually impaired who have certification in O&M from the Association for the Education and Rehabilitation of the Blind or Visually Impaired (AER). They can be assisted by O&M Assistants (OMAs), who are paraprofessional instructors trained, by O&M specialists to perform certain teaching and monitoring tasks. There are 17 university teacher training programs in the United States at which O&M specialists can receive training at the undergraduate and graduate levels. Some of these universities offer certificate programs that allow individuals with bachelor's or master's degrees to complete a concentration in O&M course work without completing the requirements for a master's degree.

When Is the Best Time for Children and Youth with a Visual Impairment to Learn Travel Skills?

Children and youth should begin learning travel skills as soon as possible—that is, as soon as a child's visual impairment is identified by the family physician or immediately after a vision loss occurs later in childhood. Early instruction in moving safely and purposefully through the daily living environment will enhance a student's capacity for effective independent travel. Early intervention programs for infants and toddlers who have a visual impairment include instruction in basic indoor and outdoor O&M skills and techniques, while focusing on the child's development of conceptual, social, and environmental awareness as well as the sensorimotor skills related to travel. O&M instruction for toddlers may also include an introduction to the use of mobility tools such as small travel canes or modified cane devices, depending on the individual needs of the student.

What Are Some Methods of Teaching Orientation and Mobility?

It is important that students with visual impairments learn travel skills in their natural daily travel environments, preferably in the actual settings where they will use their mobility skills. For example, when students learn to use their arms and hands to trail along a wall or similar surface or learn to use a cane to follow along a grass line, this instruction should take place at home and at school to facilitate daily living activities, such as traveling from the classroom to the cafeteria or leaving the school building to go to the playground. Similarly, students need to learn to cross streets by developing auditory, motor control, judgment, and cane skills at intersections in their home and school communities or at locations that are characteristic of intersections found in the communities where they will be traveling.

Instruction in the use of mass transit—trains and buses—should also be community based. Often a transit system will make a bus or a train available to O&M instructors to use for initial lessons in familiarizing students with the layout of the vehicle and for introducing methods of boarding, paying a fare, locating a seat, maintaining orientation en route, and disembarking at the desired destination.

Students who have other impairments besides their visual impairment can and do learn to travel safely and efficiently. O&M and communication techniques and instructional approaches are modified to accommodate these students' unique learning needs. O&M instructors collaborate with occupational and physical therapists to teach students with sensorimotor or orthopedic impairments to use mobility devices and adapted techniques, to install electronic probes or curb feelers on wheelchairs and walkers, to coordinate the use of a support cane with the use of a mobility cane, and to develop exercises to facilitate maximum motor use for travel.

O&M instructors work with communication specialists to teach students with cognitive, speech, or hearing impairments to develop effective communication skills for use when traveling. Instructors also work with students' families and educational teams to assure repetitive and consistent opportunities for students to use mobility skills throughout the day. When teaching travel skills to students with multiple impairments, it is crucial to adopt a team approach in which the responsibility for the student's education is shared among team members.

What Can Children and Youth with a Visual Impairment and Their Families Expect from O&M Services?

O&M services will teach purposeful, graceful, safe, and effective travel skills that will allow children and youth to carry out their daily living needs and keep pace with the increasingly complex environments they will encounter as they mature. Families and students can expect to be involved in all aspects of assessment, goal setting, planning, and implementation of O&M instruction.

EVALUATING THE QUALITY OF PROGRAMS THAT TEACH TRAVEL SKILLS

Three important elements should be considered when reviewing the quality of an orientation and mobility (O&M) program provided by an educational system: the program's structure, the instructional process, and outcomes of instruction. With respect to each element, the following needs to be considered:

> **Program structure.** How extensive is the instructor's caseload, and how often is service provided? Service that is provided sporadically is likely to be of little impact. Is an OMA available to assist the O&M instructor and to practice selected travel skills with the student? Does the O&M instructor receive adequate supervision and support from the school or agency at which he or she is employed? Does the instructor have access to professional journals, in-service training, and professional mentoring? Have the O&M instructors graduated from a recognized university personnel preparation program in orientation and mobility? Are instructors in rehabilitation programs and teachers in educational settings certified by AER in orientation and mobility?

> **Instructional process.** Are the student and family involved in all critical aspects of assessment, goal setting, program planning, and implementation? Does the O&M instructor provide adequate in-service education and support to the educational team, including the student's family? Are student records maintained in a professional and confidential manner, and in conformity with IEP requirements? Are families satisfied with the frequency and quality of the communication between the O&M instructor and home? Are services provided in environments in which the student will need to travel and in accordance with the family's preferences and values?

Instructional outcomes. Do the student and family believe that the student is working toward realistic goals—that is, goals that are neither too ambitious nor too modest? Is the student acquiring travel skills during the school years to carry out age-appropriate school and daily living activities? Are the student and family comfortable with the student's knowledge of travel and safety skills and the student's level of independence? After the student completes the program, is he or she able to comfortably and safely carry out travel for personal, social, and vocational activities?

Visual impairment, including blindness, brings with it a host of special needs and concerns when an individual with such a disability travels. Gathering information from and about one's environment is a certain challenge to the traveler who is visually impaired, and safety is always a concern. Yet, with the help of a properly trained and certified orientation and mobility instructor and with training that begins early in the individual's life and continues to evolve in terms of skill development, individuals who have visual impairments can learn the skills they need to travel safely on public transportation.

PUBLIC TRANSPORTATION AND THE ADA

An Introduction to the ADA

The Americans with Disabilities Act (the ADA) of 1990 is a comprehensive civil rights law that sets forth provisions for full societal access for individuals with disabilities. As a result of this legislation, people with disabilities have gained sweeping protection against discrimination in public and private establishments and when using public services such as public transportation. The next section of this chapter provides an overview of the ADA's requirements for accessible transportation, the varieties of accessible transportation that are utilized in this country, and the steps that still need to be taken to bring about full accessibility and compliance with the ADA.

The effect of the ADA is to make unlawful any discrimination against people who have disabilities. The purpose of the ADA is: (1) to provide a clear and comprehensive national mandate for the elimination of discrimination against individuals with disabilities; (2) to provide clear, strong, consistent, enforceable standards addressing discrimination against individuals with disabilities; (3) to ensure that the Federal Government plays a central role in enforcing the standards established in this Act on behalf of individuals with disabilities; and (4) to invoke the sweep of Congressional authority, in order to address the major areas of discrimination faced day-to-day by people with disabilities.

People with disabilities, according to the ADA, include individuals who have physical or mental impairments that substantially limit one or more major life functions, such as seeing, hearing, speaking, walking, breathing, learning, and performing manual tasks. This definition applies to about 49 million Americans—a conservative estimate, given the increasing numbers of elderly people and other people with conditions that are covered by the ADA.

The ADA mandates full accessibility to transportation services and basically changes the manner in which public and private transportation is provided in the United States. The ADA has far-reaching implications for the transportation industry. Its requirements for accessibility affect all modes of transportation except air travel, which is regulated by the Air Carriers Access Act of 1986 and related U.S. Department of Transportation (U.S. DOT) regulations. The ADA also affects federal highways, transit systems, private transportation systems, airports, and water transportation systems. What follows is a summary description of the ADA requirements for providers of public fixed route transportation; local and state governments; federal highways; paratransit services; transportation stations, stops, and facilities; making communication services available; private providers of transportation; and providers of water transportation.

Requirements for Providers of Public Fixed Route Transportation

The ADA requires providers of public, fixed route transportation services (public transportation that follows an established route, such as a bus or subway system) to phase in accessibility as new public transportation vehicles are purchased or leased and as public transportation facilities are constructed or refurbished. Providers must furnish paratransit services to persons with disabilities who cannot use fixed route transportation services.

The ADA does not require providers to replace nonaccessible vehicles with new, accessible vehicles or to retrofit nonaccessible vehicles to make them accessible. However, since August 26, 1990, the ADA requires public transportation providers, when they acquire new vehicles, to purchase or lease *only* accessible vehicles.

New or leased rail and commuter trains must have at least one car per train that is accessible, as of August 26, 1995. Providers of rail and commuter train transportation must make "good faith" efforts to locate accessible train cars before purchasing or leasing inaccessible used ones. Train cars that are remanufactured to extend their use by five years or more must also be made accessible.

Requirements for State and Local Governments

State and local governments that are responsible for maintaining public streets, roads, and walkways must provide curb ramps at existing pedestrian crosswalks. As accommodations are installed in existing walkways to comply with the ADA, governments must give priority to walkways that service government offices, transportation depots, public places such as parks and theaters, and places of employment. Curb ramps must be provided at any intersection that has curbs or other barriers. New construction must be designed to accommodate people with disabilities.

Requirements for Federal Highways

The Federal Highway Act of 1973, the Rehabilitation Act of 1973, and the Surface Transportation Act of 1978 mandate accessibility to walkways, roads, highways, overpasses, underpasses, rest areas, and emergency roadside communication systems constructed with federal funds. Although some existing facilities are exempt from this mandate, all plans for new construction must comply. Facilities must be accessible to persons with either physical or sensory disabilities.

Paratransit Requirements

This is one of the more sweeping changes that the ADA requires—fixed route public transportation operators must provide paratransit services (transportation services that do not follow a fixed route) to people with disabilities who cannot use fixed route transportation. The service area, days and hours of service, fares, response time, and passenger capacity of paratransit services must be comparable to those of fixed route public transportation services. The U.S. DOT has established three categories of riders who are eligible to use paratransit services:

1. Riders who cannot independently ride, board, or disembark from a fixed route vehicle
2. Riders who can independently use the fixed route service but for whom a fixed route vehicle is not available at the rider's time or place of travel

3. Riders who, due to the combination of a disability-related condition and environmental barriers, cannot reach the bus or rail stop

All fixed route public transportation providers operated by municipal, state, and federal governments must submit to the Federal Transit Authority (FTA) an initial ADA Paratransit Plan, along with annual updates describing progress toward compliance. Full compliance with all service criteria was required by January 26, 1997. Only those providers who showed that compliance would cause an undue financial burden were granted a time extension from compliance.

Requirements for Transportation Stations, Stops, and Facilities

After January 26, 1992, any facility that is constructed or modified to provide fixed route or paratransit public transportation must be accessible to people with disabilities, including those who use wheelchairs. Intercity train and commuter rail stations must be accessible, unless the FTA grants a time extension to the provider. Time extensions for intercity rail systems can extend to 30 years, provided that two-thirds of the provider's key stations are accessible within 20 years; the FTA may give key commuter rail stations extensions of up to 20 years. New commuter and Amtrak rail systems must be constructed so that they are accessible, unless a waiver is granted. Existing Amtrak stations must be made fully accessible by July 26, 2010.

Requirements for Making Communication Services Accessible

The ADA requires public transportation providers to afford persons with disabilities, including persons with sensory or cognitive impairments, an effective means of communicating with transportation system personnel, while these travelers are within or utilizing transportation facilities. This regulation applies to a public facility's vehicle operation, print materials, and public address system. For example, information about transportation services must be available in accessible formats such as braille, large print, or audiotapes. Teletypewriters (TTYs), interpreters, or qualified readers must be available to supplement public telephones. To facilitate onboard announcements and other communication, public address systems are required in new buses longer than 22 feet. Vehicle operators are required to announce major stops, intersections, and transfer points. At vehicle transfer points, operators are required to assist persons with a visual impairment in identifying specific buses or trains. Public address systems within transportation facilities must have a means of conveying the same or equivalent information to people with hearing loss.

Requirements for Private Providers of Transportation

The ADA prohibits discrimination against persons with disabilities who use privately operated transportation services. The law, however, distinguishes private providers of transportation into primary and secondary providers. Primary private providers are those whose main business is providing transportation to a specific clientele or to the public. An example of a primary private provider is an airport shuttle. Secondary private providers are those who provide transportation to a specific clientele or to the public but whose vehicles are used for other purposes as well. An example of a secondary private provider is a hotel service. As in the domain of public transportation, discrimination by primary and secondary private providers on the basis of disability is illegal under the ADA. Discriminatory practices include maintaining inaccessible facilities, refusing to provide auxiliary aids and services, and refusing to remove barriers.

Although taxi companies are subject to the ADA requirements for private providers, they do not have to purchase accessible automobiles. Taxi companies that choose to purchase accessible vehicles must ensure that the vehicles are truly accessible. Taxi companies may not refuse assistance to persons with disabilities in stowing wheelchairs or mobility aids during a ride or charge such people higher fares.

The Debate over Accessible Transportation

The ADA resolves a long-standing debate over accessible transportation services between the disability community, which has argued that people with disabilities have a basic right to accessible fixed route transportation, and the transportation industry, which has argued that the cost of making transit systems fully accessible was excessive. For more than two decades, federal policy vacillated between these opposing views, creating confusion among state and local governments, transit systems, and the disability community. But in passing the ADA, the federal government issued a clear mandate that supports full accessibility, standardizes accessible transportation services, and establishes requirements for both public and private operators of transportation services.

Some of the Complications Associated with Implementing the ADA

A law as fundamental and sweeping as the ADA is inevitably accompanied by complications. There are valid and serious problems associated with fully complying with the ADA, which are discussed next.

Senior Displacement.   The ADA may well be the only civil rights legislation that may cause a loss of services to certain consumers. According to a recent study completed by the American Association of Retired Persons (AARP), many paratransit users who are senior citizens may be displaced by people with disabilities. According to the AARP study, one in five paratransit systems have indicated that, given their limited financial resources, they may have to deny service to senior customers who, because they have no disability, are not eligible for ADA protection, so that the transportation provider can transport customers who fall within ADA eligibility standards.

Operating Costs of Paratransit Transportation Systems.   State and municipal governments have expressed grave concerns about the costs of operating or hiring the paratransit systems that are required under the ADA. The uncertainty of obtaining funds, coupled with increasing demand for services, has made it difficult for many paratransit systems to meet ADA requirements. Some paratransit systems have requested waivers to delay compliance. These requests have been refused so far, but as the compliance deadline draws near, waiver requests are likely to be submitted and accepted more frequently. One way to lessen the number of people who use paratransit services is to train people with disabilities to use fixed route public transportation.

Detectable Warnings.   The U.S. DOT regulations requiring detectable warnings along rail platform edges sparked controversy in the disability community and the transit industry. These detectable warnings are placed to warn people who have visual impairments of the proximity of the rail tracks. Although transit systems did not argue directly against the need for detectable warnings, they have raised concerns about the maintenance requirements and safety of detectable warnings. Transit systems voiced concerns about the large monetary investment that installing detectable warnings would require and noted that detectable warnings have had limited testing in actual use. At the center of this issue are the safety of passengers with a visual impairment and the high cost of installing detectable warnings. Despite these concerns, U.S. DOT and the U.S. Access Board ruled in favor of detectable warning strips. Installation along key station platform edges was required by July 26, 1994.

CONCLUSION

Although many transportation options for individuals with disabilities exist in certain areas, there is still work to be done in making all public transportation accessible. The availability of these options must be coordinated with the skills required to use such services. These skills begin early in life and must be reinforced continuously if one is to move toward a world of independence.

CHAPTER NINE

RECREATIONAL AND LEISURE OPTIONS

OVERVIEW

Studies indicate that between 12 and 20 percent of the American population—perhaps 40 million people—have some type of disability. That's a huge segment of U.S. society that historically has been denied access to outdoor recreation by facilities built with only able-bodied people in mind, by a lack of special equipment, and by a lack of special consideration.

In recent years, however, two things have helped open the outdoors to people with disabilities: First, across the nation there are several nonprofit groups with the mission of improving the quality of life for people with disabilities by providing opportunities for outdoor recreation, often using specially adapted equipment.

Another door to the outside opened in 1990, when Congress passed the landmark Americans with Disabilities Act. It ensures basic civil rights for people with disabilities and requires that, on any facility built for public use, reasonable efforts be made to provide access to people with a lack of mobility.

Since then, hundreds of outdoor recreational facilities built with government funds have been designed to make access easier for the wheelchair-bound and people using walkers, canes, or crutches.

Armed with the law, activists for disabled access began lobbying state and local agencies for other opportunities. Access for people with disabilities in the outdoors has multiplied exponentially over the past 10 years with the construction of state and federal projects. In this chapter you will learn about:

IMPORTANCE OF LEISURE ACTIVITIES	**ADVANTAGES OF SPECIAL LEISURE PROGRAMS**
WHICH ACTIVITIES TO EXPLORE	
ISSUES FOR SPECIAL EDUCATORS	**INDIVIDUAL CONCERNS ABOUT LEISURE ACTIVITIES**
PLANNING FOR SUCCESS	**MASTERING LEISURE ACTIVITY SKILLS**

Recreation and leisure form a vital part of our lives. We all need to enjoy ourselves and have fun. Sadly, many adults with disabilities have unnecessarily limited lives often because the people involved with them do not know where to turn for support. Recreation and leisure activities are a critical dimension of the quality of life for all people, including those with developmental disabilities. These activities are a vehicle through which people have fun, meet new friends, and develop skills and competencies. Yet, traditionally, recreation and leisure activities are given low priority as an area in which support and assistance are provided. Many people are still limited to segregated recreation and leisure choices. When other opportunities are offered, they often involve taking groupings of people with disabilities to large public settings (e.g., malls, theaters, restaurants), while very little support is offered for individualized participation in community settings that offer greater opportunities for social connections and relationships. Although not all people with disabilities need support to participate in recreation and leisure activities, others, particularly those with more severe disabilities, may not have any access to integrated recreation and leisure unless supports are available (Walker, 1999).

IMPORTANCE OF LEISURE ACTIVITIES

Successful participation in leisure activities can raise the self-esteem of students who may have had few successes. It can help people take pride in their achievements when the rest of their lives may be dull and unrewarding. Leisure is also an ideal way of developing warm and positive relationships with other people and extending networks of friends and acquaintances. When people enjoy themselves together in a relaxed environment, friendships can flourish.

Many people with disabilities receive little encouragement to feel good about themselves. They may have been taught by "sighted" methods, so they found it hard to learn. They may wrongly believe that this "failure" is their fault and have feelings of worthlessness. They may be aware that other people have very low expectations of them. People with disabilities may then be reluctant to try anything new—so they may have sound reasons for "opting out" or for avoiding an activity. Alternatively, parents may have been overly concerned about making their child's world safer, so that as adults they may have missed out on activities they might have enjoyed.

It is vital, therefore, that special educators consider carefully how to involve their students so that the pleasure and potential benefits of leisure activities are not missed. It is often the environment, inadequate help, and the negative attitudes of others that limit the participation of people with disabilities in leisure activities. This means the setting, the individual issues, and the support available (if any is necessary) all have to be considered.

WHICH ACTIVITIES TO EXPLORE

By adopting an "anything is possible" approach to leisure for your students, individuals with disabilities can enjoy almost any leisure pursuit, provided that:

- You know the individual and know how he or she might express pleasure, fear, and so on.
- It is not too complicated or vastly beyond a person's ability.
- You think through the activity carefully.
- Appropriate individual support is available.

Unfortunately, most people are unaware of the range of possible leisure activities that individuals with disabilities might and do enjoy. Often teachers and parents decide how individuals with disabilities should spend their time.

Many people have never been told that they do not have to participate in every activity organized within a day center, club, or household. Alternatively, they may lack communication skills to explain that they would rather do something else. Sometimes people's wishes are simply overlooked or ignored—not always accidentally!

If people have spent all their leisure time in groups, they may not know how many things become possible if they have one-to-one help. Others know exactly what they would like to do, perhaps opting to do something that has offered friends or family status or has allowed them to join in with their peers.

Choosing leisure activities with and for people who may have had limited opportunity in life can feel like an overwhelming task—particularly if they have no obvious means of communication. But nearly everyone can show their pleasure or displeasure and, thus, provide teachers with many pointers as to what they might like to do. You might consider what someone likes doing and how it can be built on.

When people have had little success in life, it may be appropriate for them to take part in an activity in which no one wins or loses or in which a person has such a warm relationship with his or her caregiver that failure does not matter.

Other people need to be allowed to fail in order, perhaps, to learn that they cannot be good at everything, or that there are other people who are better at this activity, or even simply to help them make other choices. It is also worth considering age appropriateness. Young adults may not want to be stigmatized by taking part in childish activities. Older people with learning difficulties may find energetic activities too tiring. Some activities (such as joining a country dance group or a local computer club) may provide opportunities to develop new relationships. Other activities are more solitary, such as doing jigsaw puzzles alone, and do not help people make friends.

Recreation and leisure activities should begin with the individual. Explore over several meetings the needs, interests, skills, fears, and limitations of the individual. Keep in mind that leisure and recreation activities should be enjoyable, not frustrating and overwhelming. Questions that should be considered include (Lieberman, 1998):

- What types of recreation has he or she participated in previously?
- What are this person's favorite activities?
- With whom does he or she prefer to spend leisure time?
- At what time of day is recreation most enjoyable for this person?

People with disabilities are as diverse in their interests as everyone else. Check the following list for some ideas. Remember, this list is only a start.

FITNESS ACTIVITIES
aerobics
running
swimming
cross-country skiing
walking
weight lifting
track and field
gymnastics
wrestling
bicycling (stationary/tandem)

OUTDOOR ACTIVITIES
fishing
camping
hiking
canoeing
kayaking
horseback riding
sledding
rowing

HOME ACTIVITIES
cooking
gardening
needlepoint
knitting
arts and crafts
listening to music
table games
card games
bingo
dominoes
board games (chess, checkers, etc.)

COMMUNITY ACTIVITIES
bowling
ice skating
roller skating
dancing (folk/social)
martial arts
diving

SPORTS ACTIVITIES AND ORGANIZATIONS
Special Olympics
community leagues
goal ball (persons with hearing)
American Athletic Association for the Deaf
school sports
U.S. Association for Blind Athletes

ISSUES FOR SPECIAL EDUCATORS

It is important that special educators realize that some people can be very anxious about new activities. They may worry about looking stupid or be embarrassed at how slowly they may learn. They may have no idea that sighted people might find the activity just as difficult! People who have taken part in an activity before may feel much more confident than those without previous experience.

Individuals with disabilities need clear instructions that make sense to them. Staff members need to give precise advice that is relevant to the specific disability. For instance, individuals with visual impairments will need different explanations depending on their level of vision, for example, a totally blind person might need more detailed information than a person with some useful vision. It is important that explanations and instructions are given in a way that people can both hear and understand. In some situations, verbal explanations will not be enough. People will need staff to consider providing information in other ways, perhaps through other senses, usually touch or smell.

Depending on the activity being considered, it could be very important that staff know the individual well. Knowledge of that person's level of understanding and the implications of his or her disability will assist staff in deciding what sort of help that person may need initially. Staff or volunteer helpers often need to consider what information and skills a participant should have before the activity is introduced. Some, for example, may need to learn reaching and grasping skills before being able to catch or throw a ball. Others may need to learn how to find their way around first, perhaps to the changing rooms or toilet.

It is important that people have some method of expressing choice or refusing to take part. They may need to learn the sign for an activity, such as for swimming. If they do not speak or use sign, alternative methods of communication need to be employed so their wishes can be taken into account. People might understand that a riding hat will be handed to them to feel before they are lifted on to a horse.

PLANNING FOR SUCCESS

Thinking through an activity from start to finish and paying attention to detail may prevent problems that could easily have been identified in advance. Organizing sufficient friendly help for individuals takes time. Individuals may need several "taster sessions" to discover if they like doing new things, and it is important to consider who might accompany them. The fact that an escort might love or loathe an activity might affect another person's enjoyment.

This is a brief list of important things to consider before embarking on new leisure pursuits:

- Who has chosen the activity? Why?
- How, where, and by whom is the activity to be introduced?
- What assistance does the person require?
- Can the individual choose his or her escort or helper?

- Is it age appropriate?
- What is the age of staff member or helper?
- Would the activity be more successful with a male or female helper or some-one from a particular ethnic group?
- What is the escort's role?
- Is the escort really helping or taking over?
- How much should the escort or helper actually do?
- Is the escort helping more than one person?
- Does the person need to have or learn any particular skills before the activity is attempted?
- What do staff need to know?
- Are there personal safety or individual eye safety issues?
- Is the activity taking place when it suits the individual? Have the individual's preferences and comfort been considered?
- Has the person a sign for the activity or an object reference to help him or her understand what is going to happen next? Can he or she make choices?
- Do staff or helpers know where to get appropriate advice?

When the student is involved in the transition from school to adult life, a healthy part of this journey should include leisure activities. You can discover a child's leisure interests by having him or her sample a variety of activities. Parents of very young children in today's society normally expose them to a wide variety of experiences such as dance classes, Little League, music lessons, scouting, sports activities, cultural experiences, travel, and, art lessons.

As the student without disabilities grows older, this process of sampling leisure interests depends less on the parents and more on the peer group. For young people with disabilities, however, parents and other family members may continue to guide or structure leisure experiences. This extended period of parental guidance and involvement should be considered a realistic part of the transitional process to adulthood for a student with disabilities. Learning specific leisure skills can be an important component for successful integration into community recreation programs. Research has shown that leisure skill training contributes to a sense of competence, social interaction, and appropriate behavior.

ADVANTAGES OF SPECIAL LEISURE PROGRAMS

One of the issues that parents and professionals have to address is whether a child should participate in activities designed specifically for people with disabilities or enter activities geared for a more mainstreamed population. The advantages of a special program designed for children with disabilities are that it may be the only opportunity for some children with severe disabilities to participate, for example, *Special Olympics;* allows for a sense of group identity; provides a setting for social interaction; and creates a more level playing field so that the individual's abilities become the focus rather than the disability.

On the other hand, concentrating on "disabled only" activities may unnecessarily exclude individuals from many leisure opportunities and prevent interaction with the community of people without disabilities.

INDIVIDUAL CONCERNS ABOUT LEISURE ACTIVITIES

One of the greatest concerns of individuals with disabilities is the problems they may face assimilating into the social world. Many students receive special services while in school that expose them to other children with disabilities. This social interaction and connection provides a foundation for improving social skills. Once school experience ends and the child is confronted with the mainstream world, however, many of these social opportunities are not available and social isolation is often the result. Social isolation is probably the most painful aspect that individuals with disabilities face when they enter adulthood. Therefore, parents, particularly, play a crucial role in assisting the child by providing the exposure to leisure and recreational activities. Parents may often find themselves the only agent for this particular aspect of life—especially once the child leaves the school setting.

MASTERING LEISURE ACTIVITY SKILLS

In order to best assist people to participate in integrated settings, it may be necessary to provide some supports or accommodations. Supports must be both individualized and flexible (Schleien, Ray, & Green, 1997; Taylor, Knoll, & Biklen, 1987; Walker & Edinger, 1988; Walker, Edinger, Willis, & Kenney, 1988); both the types and levels of support should be based on the needs and desires of the particular person. These supports should fit into the rhythms and routines of the setting or activity. There are many different types of possible supports and accommodations; many of these will benefit all participants, not just those with disabilities (Komissar, Hart, Friedlander, Tufts, & Paiewonsky, 1997).

Support can involve such things as physically assisting the person to be part of the activity and/or assisting him or her to be a part of social interactions. It can involve helping the person acquire particular skills and competencies, adaptation of part or all of an activity, and/or use of adaptive devices and equipment (Walker, 1999).

Mastering a leisure activity skill provides many advantages for individuals with disabilities. This process will increase the individual's interest level, increase self-esteem and confidence through the mastery of skills, provide the individual with communication topics for social interaction, and broaden the individual's knowledge base.

As opportunities for recreation and leisure are investigated by both the parents and the child, several considerations may arise:

1. What is the experiential and sensitivity level of the people running the program in an integrated activity?
2. How much will the activity or program cost?
3. How will the individual get to the activity?
4. Is the activity integrated?
5. Does the individual need or want to have someone supervise or accompany him or her while participating in the activity?
6. Will the activity occur regularly? An optimal leisure plan would include a balance of ongoing and one-time-only activities.

CONCLUSION

Once the leisure activities available within a community have been examined, options must be weighed and selected to ensure continuous and growing experiences. The value that individuals with disabilities attach to each of the preceding questions will depend on their interests, residential situation, and accessibility.

A wide variety of leisure activities is available; these activities may be either integrated or specifically geared to those with disabilities. Although integrated or mainstreamed activities abound, special programs may be harder to find.

CHAPTER TEN

ASSISTIVE TECHNOLOGY

OVERVIEW

Raising a child with a disability presents families and professionals with many challenges. Today, one of the major challenges facing people who care for and about children and youth with disabilities is technology—what to get, where to get it, how to use it, how to pay for it, how to evaluate its effectiveness, and where to put it.

Technology is receiving the attention of families, advocates, legislators, and professionals due to its potential for enhancing the lives of individuals with disabilities. From computers to communication devices to environmental controls, the world of technology offers many children and adolescents with disabilities the tools necessary to be more successful in school, at work, and at achieving independence in daily living. Indeed, opportunities not thought of years ago are now becoming available to some children with disabilities with the assistance of new technology, and rumors of emerging technology are raising new hopes.

Yet, the diversity of available technology, its ever changing nature, the lack of general sophistication regarding it, and the decisions to be made prior to purchase, prompt many and continuous questions. Presently, much information does exist on all issues related to the choice and purchase of any piece of technology; much of the information is, however, of varying degrees of readability, in many and disparate places, and often requires the skills of a super sleuth to uncover or decode.

Technology is bursting into the classroom at all levels, as a tool for teachers to develop, monitor, and provide instructions, and for students to access and engage in learning. P.L. 100-407, Technology-Related Assistance for Individuals with Disabilities Act of 1988 (Tech Act), was designed to enhance the availability and quality of assistive technology (AT) devices and services to all individuals and their families throughout the United States.

Computer and other technologies have expanded and enriched lives and given many children with disabilities options not imagined 20 years ago. Just as there is a wide array of assistive technology, so too are there many decisions, choices, and options for families and professionals. Making informed decisions about technology is a challenge that many consumers will encounter in coming years. Resources are available to assist consumers, such as current periodicals; disability, parent, and professional organizations; national technology centers; and private companies. Walking the assistive technology maze can be made less complex and confusing by understanding the implications of technology in the lives of children and youth with disabilities and by knowing where to go for help.

This chapter will present an overview of assistive technology devices available to individuals with disabilities. After reading this chapter, you should understand the following:

ASSISTIVE TECHNOLOGY DEFINED

ASSISTIVE TECHNOLOGY DEVICES

ASSISTIVE TECHNOLOGY DEVICES: A HISTORICAL OVERVIEW

ASSISTIVE TECHNOLOGY DEFINED

Assistive technologies are the tools and strategies that act to liberate the use of technology for all students as well as to provide new ways to "assist" interactions and learning. They act to "augment abilities and bypass or compensate for a disability" (Lewis, 1993, cited in AT Basics, 2003).

Over the past 10 years, the percentage of students with disabilities served in schools and classes with their peers without disabilities has gradually increased and continues to grow. In fact, approximately 95.9 percent of students with disabilities, ages 6 to 11, receive their education in regular education classrooms/resource rooms (OSEP, 2002). The 1997 reauthorization of the Individuals with Disabilities Education Act (IDEA) calls for providing access to the general education curriculum in order to improve outcomes for all students.

As we enter the twenty-first century, we find that recent legislation and technology innovations are changing the ways teachers teach and children learn. Since 1990, the Individuals with Disabilities Education Act (IDEA) has mandated that "to the maximum extent appropriate, children with disabilities . . . are educated with children who are not disabled." Broadly defined, assistive technology includes any device or piece of equipment that increases the independence of a person with disabilities. Assistive technology for those with disabilities, of course, is not new. For instance, the wheelchair has long been an indispensable assistive device for those with impaired mobility.

The distinction between adaptive technologies employed by individuals without disabilities and assistive technologies for individuals with disabilities blurs at times. Some of the assistive technologies designed for individuals with disabilities have proven so ergonomically sound that they have been incorporated as standard features. One such example is the placement of the keyboard on/off switch, which was designed so that people with motor impairments would not have to reach to the back of the machine to turn the power on and off.

Assistive technology has increased enormously the ability of those with disabilities to lead independent lives. Computer-based environmental control units allow users to turn on lights and appliances and open doors from a wheelchair. Augmentative communication devices enable those who cannot speak to voice thoughts and needs using touch- or light-activated keyboards coupled to synthetic speech systems. Screen reading programs for the blind, screen magnification systems for those with low vision, and special ability switches that permit the mobility impaired to use a computer are only a few examples of the technology by which individuals gain access to the computer screen and keyboard.

ASSISTIVE TECHNOLOGY DEVICES

Assistive technology devices can be anything from a simple tool with no moving parts (e.g., a toothbrush with a built-up handle) to a sophisticated mechanical/electronic system (e.g., a robotic arm). Simple mechanical devices are often referred to as *low-tech devices* whereas computer-driven or complex assistive technology may be called *high tech*. However, many people in the assistive technology field have argued that this complexity-based classification is not a useful one as there is no clear division between "simple" or low-tech and "complex" or high-tech devices. Many low-tech devices can be purchased at a hardware store, selected from a catalog, or fabricated using tools and materials found in home workshops (Franklin, 1991). Examples might be note-taking cassette recorders, pencil grips, NCR paper/copy machine, simple switches, head pointers, picture boards, taped instructions, or workbooks. High-tech devices frequently incorporate some type of computer chip, such as a handheld calculator or a "talking clock." Examples might be optical character recognition (OCR) calculators, word processors with spelling and grammar checking, word prediction, voice recognition, speech synthesizers, augmentative communication devices, alternative keyboards, or instructional software.

ASSISTIVE TECHNOLOGY DEVICES: A HISTORICAL OVERVIEW

In the late 1800s, the population of the United States was growing rapidly. Census information, gathered by hand, resulted in long delays and inaccuracy in the information reported about the nation's population. In fact, the 1880 census took eight years to count. Estimates at that time indicated that if the census process continued in the same manner, the 1890 census would take 12 years to complete and the 1930 census would be available in 1985.

Help arrived in the form of the 1890 Census Machine developed by John Shaw Billings and Herman Hollerith. The 1890 census took three years to complete and computerization was underway. Hollerith turned to big business to market the invention, now called the Tabulating Machine. He joined a company that eventually called itself International Business Machines (IBM). IBM joined with Harvard in 1938 to create the first electronic computer, the Mark I. The Mark I required 46,000 vacuum tubes to perform its operations.

The ENIAC computer, completed in 1947, weighed 30 tons, stood 9 feet tall, and took up 1,500 square feet. In 1951 the UNIVAC computer was completed. Weighing in at a mere 3 tons and occupying only 575 square feet, UNIVAC was the first computer to handle numbers and words. Commercially produced computers continued to evolve, with more power packed into less space at a lower price.

In 1973, the first computer chip, the 8080, was manufactured by Intel. Less than a square inch in area and thin as cardboard, this chip could perform a million calculations per second (like the ENIAC) but only cost about $4 to purchase. These chips were inexpensive because their main ingredient was silicon, which is more common than sand, and they were produced in enormous quantities (Budoff, Thormann, & Gras, 1985).

The interest in using computer technology with people with disabilities began in October 1981 with the Johns Hopkins First National Search for Applications of Personal Computing to Aid the Handicapped. In November 1980, the Applied Physics Laboratory at Johns Hopkins University began a national search for applications of personal computing to aid people with disabilities. Enthusiastic responses from professionals, amateurs, and students resulted in introductory workshops and regional fairs and culminated in an exhibit of the top national entries at the National Academy of Sciences, an awards ceremony in Washington, D.C., and a two-day workshop on computing for people with disabilities at Johns Hopkins in October 1981.

In March 1983, the Council for Exceptional Children held its First National Conference on the Use of Microcomputers in Education. This conference reflected the need for basic workshops on microcomputer use and for information on practical applications of computers in special education. In 1983 CEC/ERIC published *Microcomputers in Special Education* by Florence M. Tabor; *The Exceptional Parent* magazine published its first annual technology issue; and the IEEE held its first Computer Society Workshop on Computers in the Education and Employment of the Handicapped.

The year 1984 saw the first U.S. Office of Special Education Programs (OSEP) document published by COSMOS Corporation: *Microcomputer Implementation in Schools,* by Robert K. Yin and J. Lunne White. The document described and analyzed the use of microcomputers in the schools and district offices of 12 school districts. In September 1984, *Closing the Gap* held its first conference on Computer Technology for the Handicapped. A 1985 OSEP publication, *Robotics, Artificial Intelligence, and Computer Simulation: Future Applications in Special Education,* by Gwendolyn B. Moore, Robert K. Yin, and Elizabeth A. Lahm, identified ways in which technologies might be used to help special education students in the future.

The vehicle for introducing technological devices for educational use was put into place in 1975 with the passage of the Education of the Handicapped Act (EHA), P.L. 94-142. Increased federal interest was demonstrated with the passage of the Amendments to the Education of the Handicapped Act of 1986, P.L. 99-457. These amendments created a new Part G designed to promote the use of new technology, media, and materials in the education of students with disabilities. Discretionary grants under this new authority were targeted to assess usage and promote effectiveness; design and adapt new technology, media, and materials; assist public and private sectors in development and marketing; and disseminate information.

Following P.L. 99-457, the Technology-Related Assistance for Individuals with Disabilities Act of 1988, P.L. 100-407, was signed into law. The primary purpose of the act is to assist states in developing and implementing statewide programs of technology-related assistance for meeting the needs of individuals with disabilities. The program enabled individuals with disabilities to acquire assistive technology devices and services.

IDEA 1997 AND ASSISTIVE TECHNOLOGY

The 1997 reauthorization of the Individuals with Disabilities Education Act (IDEA) emphasizes the importance of technology and the need to share cutting-edge information about advances in the field. The law requires that assistive technology devices and services be considered for all children identified as having an exceptional education need. These amendments mark a significant shift in how educators view assistive technology, which previously had been viewed almost exclusively within a rehabilitative or remediative context. Now, within the context of planning individualized education plans (IEP), technology is being considered as a viable tool for expanding access to the general education curriculum. However, there is still much work to be done to ensure that IEP teams consider the maximum benefits of technology use.

Assistive devices are not a new area of interest created by the new law. As shown previously, interest in the new higher technologies began shortly after the silicon chip invention. Prior to that, low-technology assistive devices were being developed and used for centuries. Consequently, definitions of what an assistive device is are numerous and are often based on the perspective of a specific agency or disability group.

The wide variety of assistive devices and their applications to children and youth with disabilities are currently receiving a great deal of attention from many disability-related fields. This flurry of activity stems from the potential that new and emerging technologies hold for individuals with disabilities to lead full and independent lives.

According to AT Basics (2003, p. 1), "School districts are required under law to provide appropriate AT to students with disabilities when it supports their acquisition of a free and appropriate public education (FAPE)." In order to support the inclusion and participation of students with disabilities in regular education classrooms, all IEPs developed for children identified as needing special education services must indicate that AT has been considered to "to provide meaningful access to the general curriculum" (IDEA, 1997). More specifically, IDEA indicates that AT devices and services must be made available to a child with a disability if required as a part of the child's special education, related services, or supplementary aids and services.

There have been several clarifications from the Office of Special Education and Rehabilitative Services (OSERS) on the use of AT by students with disabilities. These include:

- AT must be provided by the school district at no cost to the family.
- AT must be determined on a case-by-case basis; it is required if needed to ensure access to free and appropriate public education (FAPE).
- If the IEP team determines that AT is needed for home use to ensure FAPE, it must be provided.
- The student's IEP must reflect the nature of the AT and amount of supportive AT services required.
- A parent is accorded an extensive set of procedural safeguards, including the provision of AT to the child.

Keep in mind that AT is any item that is used to increase, maintain, or improve functional capabilities of a child with a disability. For some students with disabilities, AT may be the *only way* that access to the general curriculum can be ensured!

APPLYING ASSISTIVE TECHNOLOGY IN INSTRUCTION

Lahm and Morrissette (1994) outlined seven areas of instruction in which AT could assist students with mild disabilities. These areas include organization, note taking, writing assistance, productivity, access to reference materials, cognitive assistance, and materials modification. A number of approaches are available to assist students with mild disabilities in these areas of instruction:

1. Organization. Low-tech solutions include teaching students to organize their thoughts or work using flow charting, task analysis, webbing or networking ideas, and outlining. These strategies can be accomplished using graphic organizers to visually assist students in developing and structuring ideas. A high-tech solution might be the outline function of word-processing software, which lets students set out major ideas or topics and then add subcategories of information.

2. Note taking. A simple approach is for the teacher to provide copies of structured outlines for students to use in filling in information. A high-tech approach might include optical character recognition, which is software that can transform typewritten material into computer-readable text using a scanner.

A teacher's typewritten notes can be duplicated using either NCR paper (carbonless copies) or a copy machine. A slightly more high-tech method is to use microcassette recorders. Or notes can be read by a voice synthesizer, allowing students with reading difficulty to review the notes much the same as reviewing a tape recording. Recorders are beneficial for students with auditory receptive strength, but they may be less useful for those needing visual input. Videotaping class sessions may be helpful for visual learners who pick up on images or body language or for students who are unable to attend class for extended periods of time. Laptop or notebook computers can provide high-tech note taking for many students with disabilities. An inexpensive alternative to a full-function portable computer is the portable keyboard. The limitations of these keyboards are in formatting information and a screen display limited to four lines of text.

3. Writing assistance. Word processing may be the most important application of assistive technology for students with mild disabilities. Many of these students have been identified as needing assistance in the language arts, specifically in writing. Computers and word processing software enable students to put ideas on paper without the barriers imposed by paper and pencil. Writing barriers for students with mild disabilities include mechanics, such as spelling, grammar and punctuation errors, process, generating ideas, organizing and drafting, editing and revising, motivation, clarity and neatness of final copy, reading ability, and interest in writing.

Grammar/spellcheckers, dictionaries, and thesaurus programs assist in the mechanics of writing. Macros, a feature that allows keystrokes to be recorded in a file that can be used over and over, also assist in mechanics. Macros can be used for spelling difficult text, for repetitive strings of words, or for formatting paragraphs and pages. Macros also save time for students who have difficulty with either the cognitive or motor (keyboarding) requirements of writing. Word prediction is assistive software that functions similarly to macros. If a student has difficulty with word recall or spelling and cannot easily use the dictionary or thesaurus feature, then word prediction software offers several choices of words that can be selected.

Teachers can use the editing capabilities of the word processor during the writing process, making electronic suggestions on the student's disk. If the computer is on a network, students can read each other's work and make comments for revision. Painter (1994) indicated that peer feedback was an effective way to assist students in generating and revising text. Computer editing also reduces or eliminates problems such as multiple erasures, torn papers, poor handwriting, and the need to constantly rewrite text that needs only minor modifications. The final copy is neat and legible.

Motivation is often increased through the desktop-publishing and multimedia capabilities of newer computers. A variety of fonts and styles is available, allowing students to customize their writing and highlight important features. Graphic images, drawings, and even video and audio can be added to the project to provide interest or highlight ideas. Multimedia often gives the student the means and the motivation to generate new and more complex ideas.

4. Productivity. Assistive productivity tools can be hardware based, software based, or both. Calculators, for example, can be the credit card type or software based, which can be popped up and used during word processing. Spreadsheets, databases, and graphics software also offer productivity tools, enabling students to work on math or other subjects that may require calculating, categorizing, grouping, and predicting events. Productivity tools also can be found in small, portable devices called personal digital assistants (PDAs). Newer PDAs can be used as note-taking devices via a small keyboard or graphics-based pen input. Some PDAs can translate words printed with the pen input device to computer-readable text, which can then be edited with the word processor and transmitted to a full-function computer.

5. Access to reference materials. Many students with mild disabilities have difficulty gathering and synthesizing information for their academic work. In this arena, telecommunications and multimedia are providing new learning tools for the students.

A computer and a modem can transport students beyond their physical environment to access electronic information. This is particularly appropriate for individuals who are easily distracted when going to new and busy environments such as the library. Telecommunications networks offer access to the information superhighway. Students can establish "CompuPals" with other student, which often motivates them to generate more text, and, thus gain more experience in writing. Students can also access electronic encyclopedias, library references, and online publications. However, these experiences should be structured, because the information highway is complex and it is easy to get distracted or lost as opportunities are explored. Multimedia-based tools are another way in which information can be made accessible to students. Multimedia's use of text, speech, graphics, pictures, audio, and video in reference-based software is especially effective in meeting the heterogeneous learning needs of students with mild disabilities.

6. Cognitive assistance. A vast array of application program software is available for instructing students through tutorials, drill and practice, problem solving, and simulations. Many of the assistive technologies described previously can be combined with instructional programs to develop and improve cognitive and problem-solving skills. Multimedia CD-ROM–based application programs offer another tool for assisted reading. Similar to talking word processors, CD-based books include high-interest stories that use the power of multimedia to motivate students to read. These books read each page of the story, highlighting the words as they are read. Additional clicks of the mouse result in pronunciation of syllables and a definition of the word. When the student clicks on a picture, a label appears. A verbal pronunciation of the label is offered when the student clicks the mouse again. These books are available in both English and Spanish, so students can read in their native language while being exposed to a second language.

7. Materials modification. Special educators are familiar with the need to create instructional materials or customize materials to meet the varied needs of students with disabilities. Today there are powerful multimedia authoring and presentation tools that educators can use to develop and modify computer-based instructional materials for students with mild disabilities, providing a learning tool that these students can access and use to balance their weak areas of learning with their strong areas.

Authoring software allows teachers and students to develop instructional software that can incorporate video, pictures, animation, and text into hypermedia-based instruction. Multimedia authoring software is very easy to learn and use. In fact, authoring software packages are even available for young children. For example, if the objective is to teach map reading, an image of a local map can be scanned in and specific locations can be made into buttons that the students can click on, causing a short video clip playing of the familiar location. A set of questions might be asked using both text and synthesized speech to have students give directions on how to get to the location shown on the video. Students could then write directions (or draw their own map). Digitized pictures of landmarks could also be incorporated into the directions. These directions, along with the images, could then be printed for use in completing the assignment. Without the ability to author and incorporate multimedia easily into instructional software, such computer-based training would be impossible because of the need to incorporate the shared learning concepts inherent in local environments into the assisted learning process.

Such instruction can make learning more efficient and certainly more real for students for whom abstract learning and generalization may be difficult.

COMPUTER TECHNOLOGY

Another major classroom change is the use of computer technology. Computers have become an essential literacy tool in our society, their use crucial for future success in the workplace. Over 76 percent of American students use a computer at school; 83 percent use one at home for school assignments and word processing (NCES, 2001). Internet access in public schools has increased to 78 percent, with 27 percent of classrooms having Internet access (NCES, 2001). However, to best take advantage of the potential of technology, teachers and students must have adequate and equitable access; schools must build the capacity to use technology, develop a technology plan, and offer adequate training and technical support, and teachers and students must use technology in effective ways (Jerald, 1998).

With increased access to education technology, it can be used to create more accessible curricular materials in fast and easy ways for students with disabilities (Research Connections, 1999). As classrooms materials are created in digital format, they can then be accessed and manipulated in a variety of ways to be heard, seen, and manipulated. For example, students can change how they interact with digitized materials by:

- enlarging the size of the text
- changing the color or font of the text
- having the text read aloud
- hearing labels read of pictures and simulations
- speaking into a computer microphone to write
- using alternate input options: trackballs, larger keyboards, touch screens, and so on.

Software companies are designing programs that meet a wider range of needs. CD textbooks and e-Books are just two examples. Universal Access features are embedded in programs that present content in alternate ways, with multiple options for student control (e.g., text-to-speech, enlarged fonts and tool bars with large, well-labeled buttons) (CAST, 1998). Other characteristics promote student engagement, interest, and motivation. These "built-in" options make learning more relevant.

COMPUTER TECHNOLOGY AND
EDUCATIONAL SOFTWARE

Many of the computers purchased each year are bought for use in the home. Well over 50 percent of home computer owners report that the major reason for buying a computer is for educational applications. Exactly how computers are used depends on the software selected. Depending on the design and content, software can present new skills or concepts, reinforce previously learned skills, or require the learner to apply skills to a task or problem. Educational software generally falls into four categories: drill and practice, tutorial, simulations, and games. Tool software such as word processing is another option. Each type of software can be used for instruction at home.

Drill and practice. These programs provide opportunities for the child to practice previously learned skills. The content of the drill and practice program is usually structured, focusing on a specific sequence or kind of skill building. For many students with disabilities, drill and practice activities are very important for mastering skills, and using this kind of software at home can reinforce learning that takes place at school.

Tutorials. These programs introduce new skills or concepts. It is assumed that the learner has not been introduced to the material presented in the software. The child may have learned related skills, but the content of the software is essentially new. Because the content is new, the learner will need guidance and supervision to aid understanding and teach correct use from the beginning.

Simulations. Simulations are a type of problem-solving software. The learner applies skills and information that he or she has mastered. Simulations place the learner in real-life situations. The learner applies rules, uses facts, and draws conclusions to solve a problem. In addition to academic skills, simulations require good coordination and keyboarding ability. The necessary academic and physical skills should be assessed when considering this type of program for a child with a disability.

Games. Computer-based games can be either drill and practice or problem-solving activities. Arcade-style games are usually drill and practice programs. The learner practices skills by competing with the program in which facts or problems are presented. The learner is timed and gets points for giving the correct answer within the time limit.

Tool software. This software helps the user find, organize, and reorganize information. Word processing programs, database management systems, and music or graphics editors are all examples of tool software. No content is specified with tool software. Instead, the program provides a framework for writing, creating files, or drawing. To use a word processing program or a spreadsheet, the learner must become familiar with its features. Tool programs are more versatile for home use than drill and practice or tutorial programs, and family members can use them for different purposes.

Many possibilities exist for computer learning at home. Yet, because of differences in age, skills, and interests, few products will appeal to all members of the family. Knowing how a child learns and thinks about his or her strengths or weaknesses is important for it can affect learning.

TECHNOLOGY APPLICATIONS: CASE STUDIES

Following are three case studies of how AT is used every day by individuals with disabilities.

Case 1. A high school student with a visual impairment in a current events class has an assignment to follow a recent major event, present available facts about it, write a report, and complete a presentation about the event to his classmates. A major source of information for his sighted classmates is the newspaper, but unless someone reads it to him, he cannot use that source. The radio is an available option, but typically radio news coverage contains too little detail. With the available computer technologies, though, he can receive the newspaper on a computer disk and, using his personal computer equipped with synthesized speech, he can auditorily scan the newspaper, find relevant articles, and have the computer read them to him. Using the same computer, he can begin to write his paper, print it out in braille so he can check it and change it if necessary, and then print it in standard text to hand into his teacher.

Case 2. An adolescent with quadraparalysis shows all the signs of becoming a teenager. She wants control of her own life: to decide which radio station to listen to, to decide when to turn the reading light off at night, to call her friends and have a private conversation, and to stay home alone when her parents go out. Without assistive devices she would be unable to be an independent teenager, but with a single switch connected to an environmental control unit and placed on her head, she can control her personal radio, turn the lights on and off, access the telephone for calling friends, and call for emergency help when her parents are out.

Case 3. A toddler with severe disabilities attends a special education preschool program. The teachers are unable to determine the child's cognitive abilities because the child has no verbal skills and very few motor skills. In the past, teachers had few ideas for appropriate educational programs for this type of child. As a result of available technologies, the child's educational program includes motor training and language and communication training, and teachers can more easily see the child's potential and can build on it. Now the teachers are working on training him to use a consistent motor response using switches and battery-operated toys. The child is learning to reach and touch a switch that turns on a battery-operated teddy bear. At other times the child has two or three switches to choose from and must decide which toy is preferable. The language therapist is using the same switches to teach the child to make consistent "yes" and "no" responses for communication.

SELECTING ASSISTIVE TECHNOLOGY EQUIPMENT: BECOMING INFORMED

Technology is an investment. Therefore, consumers should become more informed and critical of the limitations of technology. Consumers should also be aware of alternate possibilities for achieving a specific goal.

In addition to standard considerations such as cost, available software, expandability, ease of use, and available peripherals, it is also important to consider the adaptability of the hardware. For students with special needs, adaptability in most types of materials is necessary. For example, students with physical disabilities might need to use switches that are operated by a head movement, a head wand, a foot switch, an eye blink, or a sip and puff method. Students with a visual impairment may need a speech synthesizer. For students with a moderate disability, a combination of speech synthesis and alternative inputs may be necessary. For students with behavioral or attention disabilities, timing is important. In addition, a special feature that is essential to these students is just how fast the computer can load programs from the disk.

Fortunately, there is a wealth of information that parents and professionals can access, thus allowing them to make informed choices about the products they purchase and the services they select.

1. **Where to begin.** If professionals or parents are interested in using computers or assistive technology with a student but do not know where to being, start by reading general information on the subject. There are books available as well as publications, some of which are specific to special needs.

2. **School and community services.** Print information alone may not be enough to help with technology decisions. You may need to contact agencies and organizations that provide special services. To do this, first become aware of re-

sources that exist in the community. Local resources can supply personalized assistance to fit technology to children.

Perhaps the most important community resource is the school. Professionals can often help parents assess the potential of using technology at home given their child's needs. Professionals may also be able to guide parents in selecting appropriate software for their child. Some districts allow parents to borrow computer equipment for home use.

Another local resource is a computer users' group. User groups can provide valuable information about the use of software and hardware. Technical questions can be answered by members who are experienced with both. Check with a local computer dealer or telephone directory to find a user group in your area. Computer manufacturers may also know of a local user group.

3. Specific information. For information about using technology with a student with a specific disability, try contacting the local chapter of the disability organization serving that population. For example, if the child has a learning disability, contact the local Learning Disabilities Association of America (LDAA). Other organizations such as the Easter Seal Society and the United Cerebral Palsy Association often provide direct services to families and to local schools in the use of technology.

Given the number and different types of computers that are available today, it is almost impossible to do a comparison. Generally, though, one or two factors tend to influence the decision to purchase particular equipment. These factors might include specific software compatibility, cost, or compatibility with other computers in the school.

Some questions to ask when considering a computer system are:

- Do the software programs you plan to use run on this computer?
- Is the amount of computer memory sufficient to operate the software you plan to use?
- Can the memory be expanded?
- Is a color monitor necessary?
- Does the software you plan to use work with the printer?
- Can the printer print graphics?
- How much will the total computer system cost (including monitor, printer, disk drives)?

Although parents may not be able to afford all the options they want initially, get them to think of the future. They will want a computer that can be useful in a number of situations and that can be adapted to suit different needs.

4. Hardware. Hardware information may be harder to find locally. Computer dealers that sell computer systems can usually be found in most cities. Companies that sell assistive or adaptive equipment may need to be contacted directly.

5. Software. The local public library can be a gold mine for information on computer software. Some libraries set up mini computer labs for public use.

6. Assistive technology. If you don't know what assistive equipment is needed, local hospitals and community rehabilitation or vocational centers may be active in designing and fitting assistive devices to complement a child's capabilities. Some states have established centers to provide information about particular devices.

7. Funding. Finding funding for technology devices requires an individualized approach. To begin your search, check out resources that are available locally, such as the Lions or Kiwanis Clubs and religious organizations.

Nationally, the Easter Seal Society in connection with IBM has an assistance project that allows eligible persons with disabilities to purchase discounted computer systems. Additional funding sources may soon emerge with new federal legislation and more national interest in technology by insurance companies.

To really make technology work for parents and their children, it is important to become an informed consumer. Inform them to use the abundant resources available; read about technology, talk to others who use it, and try out various technology options before purchasing anything.

INTEGRATING TECHNOLOGY INTO THE STUDENT'S IEP

The new requirements in IDEA '97 to consider assistive technology devices and services for all students with disabilities create a massive task for school districts. Special educators across the country have begun reporting an increased number of referrals for children with mild disabilities in which the issue is access to the curriculum and productivity once in the curriculum. School-based professionals are finding that the "fix-it" approach taken with traditional assistive technology applications is not appropriate for these new types of technology referrals. More often than not, instructional issues are at the heart of these referrals—they require educators to start with the curriculum and then ask how tools might assist students in achieving the outcomes.

The student assessment/evaluation process, as outlined in the Individuals with Disabilities Education Act (IDEA), specifically states that a student's need for assistive technology devices and services is to be considered and addressed when his or her individualized education program is planned. These devices and services can be provided by the school as either a part of special education or as related services.

This next section will examine various types of technology that may be integrated into a student's IEP.

Sensory Enhancers

Sensory enhancers are adaptive/assistive devices and/or software to allow a sensory-deficient student access to the environment through the use of technology. Individuals in the following categories can be served: hard of hearing, deaf, speech impaired, visually impaired, seriously emotionally disturbed, orthopedically impaired, other health impaired, deaf-blind, multiple disabilities, and specific learning disabilities. Following are examples of types of sensory enhancers:

- audio output devices
- braille writers (input/output)
- character magnification devices
- digitizers
- electronic scanners (with speech synthesizers)
- eye movement detectors/eye sensor devices
- voice analyzers and recognizers

Keyboard Adaptation and Emulators

Keyboard adaptations are alternatives to using the standard keyboard to input data. Keyboard emulators are peripheral products that make the computer "think" that its own keyboard is being used. Examples of keyboard adaptions/emulators are alternative key pads (sketch pad, graphic pad), bar code scanners, fist/foot keyboard, firmward card, joystick, key guard, light pen, membrane keyboard, mouse, and touch screen.

Environmental Controls and Manipulators

Environmental controls and manipulators modify the operation of a device to compensate for environmental restrictions due to a student's handicap. Some examples of environmental controls and manipulators are adaptations of timers, light switches, telephone/radio amplifiers, headphones, buzzers (environmental control systems); control mechanisms with sonar sensing devices; pressure plates; robotics; additional external switches and sensors (eyebrow switch, breath switch, pressure switch); and telecommunication devices for the deaf (TDDs).

Instructional Uses of Technology

Instructional uses of technology are those that utilize software and/or related applications of technology that allow the student full educational opportunity. Examples of the instructional uses of technology are computer-assisted instruction (software for drill and practice, simulations, tutorials, demonstrations, problem solving), computer-managed instruction (tracking and placement, grading display and analysis, scheduling, and various information management tasks), computer-supported activities (word processing, databases, spreadsheets, utilities), video disks, telecommunications, and alternative languages (LOGO).

Motivational Devices

Motivational devices encourage the student to interact with his or her environment through exploration, manipulation, and play. Two motivational devices are battery-operated devices and modifications of toys and games.

Traditional and Technological Considerations in the IEP

The following questions identify content of traditional assessment/evaluation reporting and suggest the addition of questions that would support technological considerations in the IEP.

Health

TRADITIONAL

Does the student have any acute, subacute, or chronic health problems?

Does the student have a progressive and/or degenerative condition?

TECHNOLOGICAL

Given the student's attendance record, could the use of technology allow the student more continuous access to school and the curricula?

How can technology be used to compensate for the effects of a degenerative condition?

Visual

TRADITIONAL

What is the student's visual acuity?

What is the student's tracking ability?

TECHNOLOGICAL

What kinds of physical adaptions need to be made to allow the student to access technology?

How will technology allow the student to utilize compensatory senses (e.g., could a student use a magnified screen or does he or she need large print on the screen)?

Is the student able to discriminate presented visual stimuli? Would speech-produced input facilitate learning?

Hearing

TRADITIONAL

Is there a decibel loss?

How will the decibel loss affect the student's ability to learn?

TECHNOLOGICAL

What adaptions will allow the student access to the instructional program; for example, how can technology (microcomputer, software, and a voice entry system) help to produce vocalization training?

Would speech output facilitate learning? Is the student able to discriminate presented auditory stimuli?

Social and Emotional Status

TRADITIONAL

How does the student respond to differing social situations?

What are the student's basic character traits?

TECHNOLOGICAL

What is the positive and negative psychological impact of the use of a computer with certain students? For example, how will the student who has normal intelligence but no means of expressive communication deal with the use of a computer to provide his or her voice?

What is the impact of the use of technology on the environment, peers, and the class?

General Intelligence

TRADITIONAL

How does the student perform on a standard IQ test?

What is the student's potential for learning?

TECHNOLOGICAL

Does the student have the ability or will the student develop the ability for higher cognitive functions that will allow for conceptualization, symbolization, generalization and abstraction? For example, will the student be able to understand cause-and-effect relationships when making a selection on the computer, causing it to output information?

Does the student have the notion of causality and the desire to bring about an effect?

Does the student have the cognitive ability to learn and remember the use and operation of given devices?

Does the student have symbolic functioning, for example, the ability to associate a symbol or set of symbols with units of experience?

Academic Performance

TRADITIONAL

How does the student perform on a wide range of screening measures that reflect achievement?

TECHNOLOGICAL

How can the current level of achievement be affected by the use of technology? That is, how will the use of drill and practice, educational games, simulation, demonstrations, tutorials, problem solving, word processing, information search and retrieval, graphics, and/or spreadsheets affect academic performance?

Will the use of technology affect the speed of learning?

Will the probability of the learner achieving his or her goals and objectives set forth in the curriculum be increased?

Communication Status

TRADITIONAL

What is the student's receptive and expressive language ability?

Does the student have any problems with voice, articulation, and fluency that affect the production of spoken language?

TECHNOLOGICAL

What is the relationship between the student's level of expressive and receptive language? That is, how will the use of technology affect the student's ability to communicate?

What skills are present (spoken, incomprehensible but consistent, written, speed of communication with and without device)?

What is the present language structure (nonvocal from birth, nonvocal from injury)?

Does the student understand the intent to communicate?

What is the symbolic level of functioning?
How will speech output affect the student?

STATE LEVEL SUPPORT FOR ASSISTIVE TECHNOLOGY

States can support local education agencies in meeting these new requirements to consider assistive technology in each child's IEP. To ensure that technology benefits children with disabilities, states need to implement policies and practices that support its effective use. Louis Danielson, director of the Division of Research to Practice at OSEP, suggests that state directors of special education put into place a clear policy on assistive technology that includes:

- a statement of desired AT outcomes
- policies for delivering AT services
- staff development and technical assistance policies
- verification that the technology plan includes research-based practices
- mechanisms for interdisciplinary involvement
- policies for purchasing, using, and managing equipment
- strategies for obtaining adequate funding
- strategies for communicating these policies

Promoting Access to the Curriculum: Promising Practices

As a result of the new law, technology is increasingly being recommended to help students with cognitive disabilities achieve in a challenging curriculum. Technology that supports students in accessing the curriculum does not need to be expensive or complicated to make a difference in learning. Both low-tech and high-tech applications have been used successfully to ensure students' success in the general education curriculum. What do we know about the positive benefits of using technology in academic subject areas to help children with disabilities achieve to high standards? The following research-based applications have been selected to show how technology is being integrated into curricula and instruction to support a wide range of student abilities.

ELEMENTS TO CONSIDER IN IMPLEMENTING TECHNOLOGY

- Locate equipment where instruction and learning are taking place. Technology needs to be in the classroom and accessible to the child.
- Select low-tech applications whenever possible.
- Integrate the use of technology into lessons in a purposeful and meaningful way.
- Have the same equipment used in the classroom available in the child's home to promote continuity of learning, if possible.
- Offer training and technical support to classroom teachers initially. When the technology is available in the home, provide training to family members.
- View the initial fiscal and human resources as an investment that the child will continue to benefit from in subsequent years.
- Don't reinvent the wheel each year—when possible use the technology that is already in place.

FACTORS FOR SUCCESS

Ongoing research identifies key factors in the successful use of AT in educational settings (Todis, 1997, cited in AT Basics, p. 3):

- Student and family goals and values form the basis of the student's educational programs.
- The acquisition and use of AT are tied directly to student academic and personal goals.
- Students, family, and educators (including teachers, therapists, and instructional assistants) work as a team to select, obtain, implement, and monitor AT.
- Communication about all aspects of the student's school program is frequent and honest.
- Devices and equipment that are worn or outgrown are replaced. Those that are not meeting student needs are modified, replaced, or abandoned, either temporarily or permanently.
- Both major and minor glitches are regarded as inevitable but solvable problems are dealt with quickly and systematically by the team.

FUNDING FOR ASSISTIVE TECHNOLOGY DEVICES AND SERVICES

Despite what they are now or have been called in the past, there has never been any justification for schools to refuse to consider, provide, or pay for assistive technology devices or services. The key to access has always been how the device or service in question is to be used: the purposes it will serve, not its label. Before the term *assistive technology* became part of policy discussions, schools were required to provide computers and other adaptive equipment, augmentative communication devices, typewriters, tape recorders, word processors, braille printed materials, auditory trainers, wheelchairs, and other types of devices and services to students who needed them. In addition, other decisions and policy letters established some core principles related to assistive technology device funding.

The best-known policy letter concerning school provision of assistive technology devices and services is the so-called "Goodman Letter" (OSEP, Aug. 10, 1999). In this letter, the Department of Education made it clear that schools are prohibited from refusing to consider assistive technology devices and services as part of the IEP writing process. However, this was based on the law before there was any mention of assistive technology devices and services—it was issued before the 1990 IDEA amendments.

Thus, in 1990, the IDEA merely clarified existing law, rather than adding a new benefit when it added the definitions of assistive technology devices and services to the statute. In 1992, the Department of Education clarified the existing definitions of "special education," "related services," and "supplemental aids and services" when it promulgated the IDEA regulations. These regulations made an express connection between assistive technology devices and services and these three components of a FAPE, special education, related services, and supplementary aids and services.

In the years since the 1990 IDEA amendments, there have been additional policy letters and decisions related to use of assistive technology devices and services. Overall, there has been an ongoing expansion of use of assistive technology in the public schools. However, the pace of this growth has been slow and many students with severe disabilities still do not have access to appropriate technology because of various unlawful restrictions placed on their use by the school district.

School district or statewide policies regarding assistive technology access are rare. Policies regarding functional goals or outcomes related to technology use are all but nonexistent, and school districts continue to excuse their nonuse of technology on cost grounds. Clearly, there is still a long way to go regarding schools' provision of assistive technology to students with disabilities.

CONCLUSION

The potential of assistive technology to improve and enhance the lives of individuals with disabilities is virtually unlimited. Now, with the help of current federal laws, assistive technology will provide more children with the opportunity to maximize their learning in a challenging curriculum. The benefits of technology are as extensive as the abilities and goals of the students using them. However, professionals and parents should exercise certain cautions. Technology must not been seen as a panacea; it alone will not "fix" a disability or guarantee a successful inclusion program.

CHAPTER ELEVEN

RESIDENTIAL OPPORTUNITIES AND RESPITE CARE

OVERVIEW

There may be times after a student with disabilities leaves secondary education when parents will have to explore housing alternatives other than the family home. A variety of motivations for this decision may include the following:

- The physical, medical, economic, and psychological resources of some families to care for the needs of a family member with disabilities may diminish over time.
- The need to foster independence and autonomy may dictate the desirability of separate housing.

Parents who are confronted with the need for residential options may face a confusing and sometimes overwhelming fund of information. A large part of this confusion is attributable to the variety of terms used to describe these available programs, for example, group homes or community residences.

Three major factors will influence the types of service available to persons with disabilities.

First, some residential services are available only to those who are eligible for medical assistance and county mental retardation services. Second, service options are based on the level of care needed. The family subsidy program aids families in keeping children with disabilities at home rather than placing them in a residential facility. For those who need some supervision and training to live independently but do not need care 24 hours a day, *semi-independent living services (SILS)* may be an option. *Community-based waivered services* or placement in an *intermediate care facility (group home)* are options for persons who need 24-hour supervision.

The third factor influencing the type of residential services available is the funding level for the programs. Unfortunately, the need for *residential facilities* far outweighs the availability of these resources. Some of this is due to a lack of funding, but there has also been tremendous resistance on the part of local communities to have such residences in their midst ("not in my backyard"). Historically, costly and lengthy legal fights have addressed this issue.

Therefore, those working with the student with disabilities must begin addressing these issues years before this need arises. Some parents report waiting five to six or more years for a space to open up at a facility. One of the pathways, in addition to putting their names on a list, is to get parents and their children involved in the activities of a local service provider. This will enable the family to develop an ongoing relationship with that service provider, which will be helpful when space in a facility becomes available. When parents begin their search for residential options, their goal should be to identify as many as possible. Knowing where to look will enable them to find contacts who can answer their questions.

In this chapter we will try to reduce the confusion caused by the different labels. In trying to unravel the many options, it is important to be as open as possible, as two group homes may be vastly different because they serve people with different levels of disability.

Raising a child with a disability or chronic illness poses other challenges. As families meet these challenges, time off can become a necessity for the caretakers. In recent years, the growth of *respite care services*—short-term specialized child care—has begun to provide families with some temporary relief.

The birth of a child with a disability or chronic illness or the discovery that a child has a disability has profound effects on a family. When parents learn that their child has a disability or special health care need, they begin a process of continuous, lifelong adjustment. Adjustment is characterized by periods of stress and, during this time, family members' individual feelings of loss can be overwhelming, shutting out almost all other feelings. Coping with uncertainty about the child's development may interfere with the parents' ability to provide support to each other and to other family members. Even when the diagnosis is clear, there are still many uncertainties—health, programmatic, and financial.

Social and community support can reduce the stress experienced by families. The support of relatives, friends, service providers, and the community can help families ease the adjustment period.

After reading this chapter, you should understand the following:

RESOURCES TO CONSIDER	**HOUSING SUBSIDIES**
CENTERS FOR INDEPENDENT LIVING (CILs)	**OVERVIEW OF RESPITE CARE**
	BENEFITS OF RESPITE CARE
RESIDENTIAL SERVICES	**RESPITE CARE SUGGESTIONS FOR PARENTS**
GROUP HOMES	
INTERMEDIATE CARE FACILITY (ICF/MR)	**HOW TO TELL IF A FAMILY COULD BENEFIT FROM RESPITE CARE**
EVALUATING RESIDENTIAL PROGRAMS	**WHAT PARENTS NEED TO KNOW WHEN SEEKING RESPITE CARE SERVICES**
MAKING A RESIDENCE ACCESSIBLE	

RESOURCES TO CONSIDER

Every state has numerous public agencies that are responsible for meeting the various needs of people with disabilities and their families. The names of these agencies will vary from state to state, and those involved may have to investigate or cross-reference using available agencies that assist with residential resources. Parents should start their search with the following sources of information:

- local school district's director of special education services
- Internet
- public and university libraries
- special education departments at universities
- other families or individuals who may have similar experiences
- child advocacy services

CENTERS FOR INDEPENDENT LIVING (CILs)

Centers for Independent Living (CILs) are nonresidential places of action and coalition, where persons with disabilities learn empowerment and develop the skills necessary to make lifestyle choices. Centers provide services and advocacy to promote the leadership, independence, and productivity of people with disabilities.

Centers work with both individuals as well as with local communities to remove barriers to independence and ensure equality of persons with disabilities (Department of Rehabilitative Services, 2003).

According to the Department of Rehabilitative Services (2003), CILs are nonprofit organizations that are funded by state, federal, local, and private dollars. Part C of Title VII of the Federal Rehabilitation Act provides general operations money for CILs in Virginia in an amount over $1.3 million. Additional funds under Title VII, Part B of the act are granted to centers under the State Plan for Independent Living. The plan, which is jointly developed and signed by the Statewide Independent Living Council, the Department of Rehabilitative Services, and Department of the Blind and Vision Impaired, provides Part B funds to centers for systems change activities in an amount over $450,000. General fund dollars for center operations and Youth Transition Services currently exceed $4.5 million. A portion of the State General Fund dollars was used to expand Centers for Independent Living during the last five years. Six new consumer-based centers were established during this time period. Centers also solicit local and private funding to meet service needs that have been identified at the local level. The centers are run by people with disabilities who themselves have been successful in establishing independent lives. These people have both the training and personal experience to know exactly what is needed to live independently, and they have a deep commitment to assisting other people with disabilities in becoming more independent.

These centers are community, consumer controlled, noninstitutional organizations. They generally offer services free of charge. There are approximately 250 CILs nationally, with at least one located in every state.

Funded by the Rehabilitation Services Administration (RSA), CILs offer a varied combination of independent living services such as:

- referral services
- independent living skills training
- peer counseling
- individual advocacy
- counseling services
- services related to securing housing or shelter
- rehabilitation technology
- mobility training
- life skills training
- interpreter and reader services
- personnel assistance services
- consumer information programs
- transportation assistance
- physical rehabilitation
- therapeutic treatment
- prostheses
- individual and group recreational services
- self-employment skills
- advocacy skills
- career options
- services to children
- preventive services
- community awareness programs

RESIDENTIAL SERVICES

A *residential program* offers housing other than the individual's natural home, and it is usually designed for persons with similar needs in terms of age, independence, or abilities. A residential program usually provides a homelike environment with supervision and guidance as needed, living experiences appropriate to the functioning level and learning needs of the individual, a location within the mainstream of community life, and access to necessary supportive, habilitative programs.

The goal of residential programs is to provide access to the highest possible quality of services that a person with certain disabilities needs, while at the same time permitting and encouraging the person to be as independent as possible.

Adult Foster Care

Adult foster care homes are provided by families that for altruistic, religious, or monetary reasons provide a home care environment for the adult with disabilities. In this residential option, the foster care family receives government reimbursement for this service. Although this living arrangement is meant to be a permanent situation, no guarantees exist.

According to Adult Foster Care Services (2003), Adult Foster Care is a licensed family setting for adults who are unable to live alone due to physical, emotional, or developmental impairments. These homes often provide 24-hour care for a small number of impaired residents. Residents receive meals, support, supervision, and some assistance with personal care and living skills, as needed.

There is a minimum room and board payment made to providers per month, which is set by the state. Adult Foster Care is not a therapeutic residential facility where a resident receives awake night or nursing care assistance.

Boarding Homes

A *boarding home* is a residential facility that provides minimal structure and training for the adult with disabilities. These homes may provide sleeping and meal arrangements and deal with clientele with a variety of disabilities.

Family Subsidy Program

This program provides financial assistance to families to enable them to care for their children with disabilities up to age 22 at home. The Department of Human Services pays eligible families a monthly allowance for certain home care costs, such as medical equipment, respite care, transportation, and special diets. Eligibility for the program is based on the needs of the family and its ability to provide the necessary level of care in the home. The program is not based on financial need.

Freestanding Weekend Respite

This is a community-based program for families in need of respite on a planned or emergency basis. The overall objective is to afford families a reprieve from the day-to-day caregiving responsibilities. Respite provides room and board, 24-hour supervision, and appropriate recreational activities to individuals with developmental disabilities.

GROUP HOMES

Ensuring nondiscrimination in housing means ensuring an essential element of independence and integration into the community for disabled individuals. The right to vote, to work, and to travel freely are all important aspects of an individual's life, but none is more elementary than having the freedom to choose where and how one lives. Housing is shelter, but it is much more. It's the opportunity to be part of a community. It's a chance to enjoy the social and recreational aspects of being a neighbor. It can be the independence to flourish in a lifestyle of one's own choosing. In short, housing is a basic right that we cannot allow to be denied on the basis of disability (Cranston 1990).

Until the 1950s and 1960s, our society relied on large institutions such as state hospitals, training centers, nursing homes, and detention facilities to house and care for people with disabilities and addiction disorders, at-risk and delinquent children, and adults who had been found not guilty by reason of insanity. Over the last several decades, however, many of these large institutions have been closed, and state agencies have come to see group homes and other congregate living arrangements as one of the ways to provide a transition back into the community for these individuals. The passage of the Fair Housing Amendments Act of 1988 accelerated this trend for people with disabilities and children (Whitman & Parnas, 1999).

The general characteristics of group homes include a home with fewer than 16 people with a family-like structure, that is similar to surrounding homes in the community. Tasks are performed by the residents of the home to the extent of their abilities, for example, cooking, mowing the lawn, doing laundry, and so on. The expectation is that the individual with disabilities will graduate to a more independent situation that will meet his or her needs and preferences.

The term *group home* has taken on many meanings. The concept has certain general characteristics, but these may vary from facility to facility. Specifically, group homes are divided into two arrangements: semi-independent living arrangements and supervised living arrangements. These options differ in staffing arrangements, level of disability, and the need for supervision.

Some people with disabilities, however, live in group homes either because they require a high level of support or because there is a lack of resources, such as funding for individual rental assistance or for personal care attendants, that would allow them to live independently. Group homes allow people with disabilities to be reintegrated into single- and multifamily residential neighborhoods where their needs can be met and where they can fit naturally into the community. Well-run homes provide access to a safe, healthy living environment and the same quality of housing and community opportunities available to other families in the neighborhood (Whitman & Parnas, 1999).

Semi-Independent Living Arrangements (SILs)

These services provide intensive support and training to persons with disabilities 18 years of age and over to enable them to learn to live independently in the community or to maintain semi-independence. Persons eligible for SILs do not require daily support services but are unable to live independently without some training or occasional support. SIL recipients live in their own homes or apartments, in rooming houses, or in foster homes. They often share living arrangements with other persons who have disabilities. The key characteristic is that the staff does not live in the facility. In some cases, they may be on call in cases of emergency.

Home Care Attendants or Personal Assistant Services

These auxiliary services are available to assist consumers in housekeeping and personal care needs; they enable the consumer to live more independently. They may be paid for by the individual or by public funds through Medicaid.

Supervised Living Arrangements

These services provide intensive support and training for persons with severe disabilities. Unlike semi-independent living arrangements, these facilities have full-time residential staff. This type of arrangement is usually provided for individuals who are not able to care for themselves and need full-time supervision.

INTERMEDIATE CARE FACILITY (ICF/MR)

ICF/MR facilities are specially licensed residential settings for persons who require 24-hour care and supervision and are supported by Medicaid funds. An ICF/MR is a nursing home, recognized under the Medicaid program, which provides health-related care and services to individuals who do not require acute or skilled nursing care but who, because of their mental or physical condition, require care and services above the level of room and board available only through facility placement (*Insurance Glossary,* 2003).

Specific requirements for ICFs vary by state. Institutions for care of the mentally retarded or people with related conditions (ICF/MR) are also included. The distinction between "health-related care and services" and "room and board" is important because ICFs are subject to different regulations and coverage requirements than institutions that do not provide health-related care and services. Group homes may range in size from small six-person homes to larger institutions. Most of them are small residences, serving under 16 people. The ICF provides a full array of direct-care and clinical services within the program model. Clinical services include psychology, social work, speech therapy, nursing, nutrition, pharmacology, and medical services. ICF admission requires that participants be Medicaid eligible, have an IQ below 59, and manifest deficits in basic skills such as grooming and hygiene.

Supportive Living Units (SLUs)

SLUs are state-funded, small residential sites, typically housing one to three high-functioning individuals. These individuals may or may not be Medicaid eligible, are typically competitively employed, and require 21 hours or less per week individual protection and oversight by a direct-care person.

Waivered Services

The term *waivered services* applies to persons with mental retardation who are currently in ICF/MRs or who are at risk of being placed in ICF/MRs unless the waivered services can be provided to them in a home or community setting. The possible living arrangements are intended to be much less restrictive and isolated from the mainstream world than the traditional ICF/MR settings. The home or community-based residence could include a person's own parental home, a foster home, an apartment, or a small group home. These services are available to individuals who would otherwise qualify for Medicaid only if they were in an out-of-home setting.

EVALUATING RESIDENTIAL PROGRAMS

There is no substitute for firsthand observation. When the professional and the parents have organized a list of potential residential programs, the parents (and the professional if possible) should make appointments to visit each one. Do not hesitate to ask the following questions:

- What are the entry requirements?
- How many people live at the particular residence?
- Is there a waiting list?
- How long is the waiting list?
- What is the staffing pattern?
- What other services are provided at this residence?
- What are the expectations for activities outside the residence?
- Can the resident go to a day program?
- Can the resident have a part-time or weekend job?
- What will the costs be for the specific services provided by this residence?
- How is the personal money of the resident monitored?
- Are family visits encouraged?
- What kinds of household chores will the resident be responsible for?
- Are leisure activities part of the resident's program?

MAKING A RESIDENCE ACCESSIBLE

Whether one is building an accessible home or modifying an existing residence, the cost can be prohibitive. A home equity or other bank loan may be one financing alternative. Depending on one's circumstances and the nature of the disability, assistance may also be obtained through medical insurance, medical and social services, income support, or vocational services from any of a number of different resources. Consumer-oriented disability organizations and rehabilitation facilities may also provide information resources on funding assistance available in the local community.

HOUSING SUBSIDIES

Section 8 Housing

Section 8 refers to rent subsidy payments by the government to allow an individual to secure decent, safe, and sanitary housing in private accommodations. The income limitations for eligibility are determined by information from the local housing authorities. This program comes under the U.S. Department of Housing and Urban Development (HUD). The specific steps required in applying for rental assistance are:

1. An application must be completed and filed with the local housing authority.
2. Eligibility is then determined, based on the intended type of occupancy (elderly or disabled) and income.
3. It is up to the parent or the young person to find suitable housing on the open market.
4. This housing must be inspected by the local housing authority and meet demanding quality standards.
5. Once the housing has passed inspection, it must be determined if the landlord is interested in participating in Section 8 housing.
6. If it is determined that rent and utilities do not exceed the fair market rent, and the landlord is in agreement, the housing may be leased.

Section 202 Housing

Section 202 refers to a program that provides direct loans for the construction of housing for three specific populations: individuals with developmental disabilities, those with chronic mental illness, and those with physical disabilities.

These funds are intended for the construction of group facilities for those with disabilities. Parents can get further information on this subsidy from their local housing authority.

OVERVIEW OF RESPITE CARE

Over the years, there has been a growing awareness that adjustment to the special needs of a child influences all family members. This awareness has generated interest and has led to the development of support services for families to assist them throughout the lifelong adjustment process. Within the diversity of family support services, respite care consistently has been identified by families as a priority need (Cohen & Warren, 1985).

All parents need a break now and then, to have time for themselves away from the responsibilities of caring for their children. This is true for families of children with disabilities or chronic health care needs, too; only for these families it may be more difficult to arrange.

Although *respite* may be a new word for some people, it is not a new phenomenon; it emerged in the late 1960s with the *deinstitutionalization movement*. One of the most important principles of this movement was the belief that the best place to care for a child with special needs is in the child's home and community. Families with a child who has a disability or chronic illness know the commitment and intensity of care necessary for their children. The level of dedication and care becomes part of daily life, part of the family routine, but this same commitment can make stress routine, too. Parents can become accustomed to having no time for themselves. According to Salisbury and Intagliata (1986), "The need of families for support in general and for respite care in particular has emerged as one of the most important issues to be addressed in the 1980s by policymakers, service providers, and researchers in the field of developmental disabilities" (p. xiii).

Respite care is an essential part of the overall support that families may need to keep their child with a disability or chronic illness at home. United Cerebral Palsy Associations, Inc. (UCPA) defines respite care as "a system of temporary supports for families of developmentally disabled individuals which provides the family with relief." "Temporary" may mean anything from an hour to three months. It may also mean "periodically or on a regular basis." It can be provided in the client's home or in a variety of out-of-home settings," (Warren & Dickman, 1981, p. 3). Respite services are intended to provide assistance to the family and to prevent "burnout" and family disintegration. Because not all families have the same needs, respite care should always be geared to individual family needs by identifying the type of respite needed and matching the need to the services currently available or using this information to develop services where none exist. Once identified, it is also important for families to have ready access to that type of respite in an affordable form.

Regardless of the type of respite program utilized, the emphasis should be on orienting services toward the entire family. The birth of a child with a disability or the discovery that a child has a disability or chronic illness is obviously a difficult time for the entire family, including siblings, grandparents, and other relatives. Families need to adjust to major changes in their daily lifestyles and in their dreams. Extended family and friends will also need to adjust to these changes. These changes will take planning and time. We are accustomed to typical family life; a child with a significant disability or chronic illness is not typical. Therefore, plans for an untypical lifestyle call for creativity and flexibility. It is also important to bear in mind that the child will change as he or she grows and develops into an individual with his or her own personality and ideas.

Many families will find these changes difficult to handle. Many communities may be limited in their resources or in their interest in meeting the special needs such families present. These combined factors can leave the immediate family with the full-time care of their child and can lead to feelings of isolation from other family members, friends, and community activities and religious and social functions. Even performing the basic necessities of daily life, such as grocery shopping or carpooling, can become difficult to impossible.

It is obvious to anyone who has lived this life that respite care becomes a vital service—a necessity, not a luxury. Parents, of course, are clearly the experts about the need and importance of respite care. Just as families differ, so will the necessity for respite care. Basically, however, all families require some relaxation, diversion, and the security of knowing that their children are safe and happy. The most difficult problem for the family with a child who has a disability is finding the quality of care and expertise the child needs.

As one parent put it,

> Families need an uncomplicated, easily accessible means of arranging respite care to suit their wants and needs. When a potential pleasure becomes more trouble than it's worth, then I give it up. I always measure the event against the complications involved in making it happen. Time off is no relaxation if I spend the entire time worrying if the kids are OK. I can't enjoy myself if I think they are unhappy, and certainly I can't relax if I'm not confident about the reliability of the person watching my children. I think many professionals are under the misconception that time away from the cares of rearing a child with a disability is what I need to maintain my sanity. I need much more than time—I need the security that comes from knowing that the person I've left my son with is as capable as I am of providing for his needs. You simply can't relax and enjoy yourself and worry at the same time. It's peace of mind I need—not just time.

BENEFITS OF RESPITE CARE

In addition to providing direct relief, respite has added benefits for families, including:

Relaxation. Respite gives families peace of mind, helps them relax, and renews their humor and their energy.

Enjoyment. Respite allows families to enjoy favorite pastimes and pursue new activities.

Stability. Respite improves the family's ability to cope with daily responsibilities and maintain stability during crisis.

Preservation. Respite helps preserve the family unit and lessens the pressures that might lead to institutionalization, divorce, neglect, and child abuse.

Involvement. Respite allows families to become involved in community activities and to feel less isolated.

Time off. Respite allows families to take that needed vacation and spend time together and time alone.

Enrichment. Respite makes it possible for family members to establish individual identities and enrich their own growth and development.

Often we hear the question, "Who takes care of the caretakers?" Caretakers can include not only parents but also brothers and sisters, grandparents, and extended family and friends. Respite gives caretakers the opportunity to have a rest, to take care of personal matters, to enjoy some leisure time, and occasionally to be relieved of the constant need to care for a child with a disability or chronic illness.

The child or youth with disabilities also benefits from respite care, gaining the opportunity to build new relationships and to move toward independence. In many families, it is common for children to attend day care or after-school care, interact with peers and adults outside the family, and stay with a child care provider while their parents enjoy an evening out. Respite provides these same opportunities for children with special needs.

For older individuals with a disability, respite can assist in building skills needed for independent living. Because the most appropriate living situation for many adults with a disability is in a group home or other supported environment, out-of-home respite care can enable families to test this option, explore community resources, and prepare themselves and their family member with a disability for this change.

States and communities are recognizing that respite care also benefits them. On average, the costs for respite services are 65 to 70 percent less than the costs of maintaining people in institutions (Salisbury & Intagliata, 1986). The cost-effectiveness of respite services allows scarce tax dollars to be used for additional community-based services. During the previous decade, over 30 states passed legislation for in-home family support services, including respite care, using either direct services or voucher systems (Agosta & Bradley, 1985).

With the 1986 passage of the Children's Justice Act (Public Law 99-401) and its amendment, the Children with Disabilities Temporary Care Reauthorization Act (P.L. 101-127), respite care has gained support at the federal level. This legislation authorized funding to states to develop and implement affordable respite care programs and crisis nurseries. Unfortunately, although this federal funding provides relief for some families, access and affordability continue to be issues for many families in need. As Brill (1994) observes: "Families soon discovered that the law fell short of providing national guidelines for respite care. Every state dispensed different versions of the services, and individual agencies devised their own criteria for length of time and funding allotments" (p. 49).

Thus, in spite of the availability of government funding in some areas, many respite care programs must charge for their services. This practice reduces expenses for providers and makes it possible to serve more families. However, charging for respite services can limit their availability to those families who can afford the fees (Cohen & Warren, 1985).

For children and youth with disabilities, their families and communities, and federal, state, and local governments, the benefits of respite care are enormous. However, the need for maintaining and expanding the levels of available respite services is tremendous.

RESPITE CARE SUGGESTIONS FOR PARENTS

Parents deciding to leave their child who has special needs in the care of someone else, either in or outside their home, may experience a variety of hesitations. They can have feelings of guilt, anxiety, or even a sense of loss of control.

Jeanne Borfitz-Mescon (1988) suggests that a number of fears and concerns are common to parents in this situation: that the child may not get as much attention or that the care may not be as good, that something may be missed, that the caretaker or staff may not be able to comfort their child, and that he or she might be left crying. The anxiety resulting from these very normal and real concerns or fears can in fact cause parents to believe that respite is just not worth it.

It is important that a parent becomes comfortable with his or her decision and develop the trust critical to maintaining the peace of mind necessary for relaxation and enjoyment. One way to accomplish this goal is to help parents begin to think about respite care and whether their family and their child with special needs would benefit from it. The following suggestions may help.

HOW TO TELL IF A FAMILY COULD BENEFIT FROM RESPITE CARE

If parents are considering respite care, they need to ask themselves the following questions:

1. Is finding temporary care for the child a problem?
2. Is it important that the parents enjoy an evening alone together, or with friends, without the children?
3. If parents had appropriate care for their child with special needs, would they use the time for a special activity with their other children?
4. Do they think that they would be a better parent if they had a break now and then?
5. Are they concerned that in the event of a family emergency there is no one with whom they would feel secure about leaving their child?
6. Would they feel comfortable going to a trained and reputable respite provider to arrange for care for their child?

If parents answered "yes" to several of these questions, they and their family could benefit from respite care and should investigate the resources in their community.

Many agencies and organizations have information on respite care services. (For a referral, contact the National Respite Locator Service, operated by the ARC National Resource Center: 1-800-773-5433). In general, assist parents in seeking out groups or professionals who work with children their child's age. For example, if their child is in preschool, have them contact the school and discuss the need for respite care with the staff. If there is a parent group associated with their school, or if there is a local parent group concerned with children who have needs similar to their child's, the parent should ask them. If the child is an adolescent, the parents should talk to the staff at their child's school or identify parent groups in the area with needs similar to theirs.

The following list presents some of the types of groups parents may want to contact in seeking services. Many will be listed in the telephone book. If parents experience difficulty locating the organization in their community, often a state contact can be made. Examples include:

- state and local government agencies
- State Department of Mental Retardation
- State Developmental Disabilities Council
- State Program for Children with Special Health Care Needs (formerly Crippled Children's Services)
- Departments of Health and Human Services, or Social Services
- Department of Mental Health
- state and local departments of education
- State Protection and Advocacy Agency

Also, state and local disability support groups and agencies may be helpful in assisting parents with respite care. Examples of these include:

- the Arc
- United Cerebral Palsy Associations, Inc.
- Autism Society of America
- Brain Injury Association
- Mental Health Association and CASSP
- Spina Bifida Association
- National Easter Seal Society
- Parent Training and Information Center
- Parent-to-Parent
- University Affiliated Program(s)
- Community Services Board
- YMCA/YWCA
- churches

WHAT PARENTS NEED TO KNOW WHEN SEEKING RESPITE CARE SERVICES

Parents seeking respite care services in their community should ask themselves the following questions. The information will be helpful when contacting agencies in their local community about respite care (Bradley, 1988).

1. What kind of services do they need? (Long term, short term, or both? Why?)
2. Do they prefer services in their home, a cooperative, or in an outside setting? (This will depend on the type of service they need.)
3. Can they donate time to a cooperative, or is it better for them to obtain help from a respite agency?
4. Does this agency provide the types of service they need?
5. Is there a cost for the service?
6. Are the parents able to afford this service?
7. If they can't afford the service, are there funds available to assist them?
8. Who is responsible for the direct payment to the provider?
9. How are respite providers selected?
10. Are the providers trained?
11. How many hours of training have they had?
12. Do these providers have training in first aid and CPR?
13. What other areas are covered in their training?
14. For out-of-home care, does anyone monitor the facility for safety and health measures?
15. Will they be able to have a prior meeting with the care provider?
16. Will they have an opportunity to provide written care instructions to the provider?
17. Will they have an opportunity to assist in training the provider with reference to their son or daughter's needs?
18. What is the policy that covers emergency situations?
19. Will they have to carry additional insurance to cover the provider while he or she is in the home?
20. Is there a policy that deals with mismatches between providers and the family?
21. Can they request a specific care provider and have the same person with the child each time?
22. Will the respite care provider care for the other children, too?

CONCLUSION

Just as in the school setting, where the policy fosters the least restrictive educational environment, it follows that the same philosophy should be encouraged in seeking out adult living arrangements. This least restrictive independent arrangement may require utilization of many agencies, support personnel, family, and so on. Everything should be done to attain an individual's personal least restrictive living arrangement.

Furthermore, individuals with disabilities should be aware that funding may be available to assist in making residences adaptive to personal needs—ramps and modifications in doorways or bathrooms. As a special educator, you must teach parents to explore this option with their local center for independent living.

Caring for a child with disabilities or severe health problems can be a full-time job. It is easy for parents to become overwhelmed with the care needs of a child with a disability or chronic illness. Often families who would not hesitate to call for relief from the constant care of their typical children hesitate to call for relief from the care of their child with a disability or special health care need. That is why respite, as the word implies, is truly an interval of rest. Respite can be a parent's answer to renewed energies and a new perspective. If respite care is not available in the parents' community, help them make it happen. The best advocate for the family and the child is the parent. However, as a special educator you can also play a role in facilitating such services by having an active knowledge of what is available. One of the most important goals to strive for is family unity and well-being. It is important to remember that a parent, too, needs the gift of time that respite care represents.

CHAPTER TWELVE

POSTSECONDARY EDUCATIONAL OPTIONS

OVERVIEW

A number of years ago, students with disabilities had limited choices when it came to choosing a college or university that could provide accommodations. With the advent of the Americans with Disabilities Act and the disabilities rights movement, accommodations for students with disabilities became commonplace. Now students with disabilities are able to apply to several different types of postsecondary educational institutions. After reading this chapter, you should understand the following:

COLLEGES AND CAREER
EDUCATION OPPORTUNITIES

THE LAW AND
ITS IMPACT

DISABILITY-RELATED
SUPPORT SERVICES

FINANCIAL AID

ISSUES TO CONSIDER WHEN LOOKING
INTO POSTSECONDARY EDUCATION

CHECKLIST FOR ASSESSING COLLEGES
FOR ACCESSIBILITY

ACCOMMODATIONS
FOR SPECIFIC DISABILITIES

DISTANCE LEARNING

COLLEGES AND CAREER EDUCATION OPPORTUNITIES

Colleges offer an opportunity for individuals with disabilities to continue their education and earn tangible evidence of education such as a certificate or degree. Junior and community colleges offer a variety of courses that, upon successful completion of the prescribed courses, may lead to a certificate or associate's degree. Community colleges are publicly funded, have either no or low-cost tuition, and offer a wide range of programs, including vocational and occupational courses. They exist in or near many communities; generally the only admissions requirement is a high school diploma or its equivalent. Junior colleges are usually privately supported, and the majority provides programs in the liberal arts field. Four-year colleges and universities offer programs of study that lead to a bachelor's degree after successful completion of four years of prescribed course work.

THE LAW AND ITS IMPACT

In high school, the school district was responsible for providing any or all support services necessary for an individual with disabilities to participate in the educational process. The college or university does not have the same legal obligation. It is required by law to provide any reasonable accommodation that may be necessary for those with disabilities to have equal access to educational opportunities and services available to peers without disabilities, if requested.

175

Title II of the ADA covers state-funded schools such as universities, community colleges, and vocational schools. Title III covers private colleges and vocational schools. If a school receives federal dollars, regardless of whether it is private or public, it is also covered by the regulation of Section 504 of the Rehabilitation Act, requiring schools to make their programs accessible to qualified students with disabilities.

Under the provisions of Section 504, universities and colleges may not:

- limit the number of students with disabilities
- make preadmission inquiries as to whether an applicant has disabilities
- exclude a qualified student with a disability from a course of study
- discriminate in administering scholarships, fellowships, and so on, on the basis of a disability
- establish rules or policies that may adversely affect students with disabilities

For college students with disabilities, academic adjustments may include adaptations in the way specific courses are conducted, the use of auxiliary equipment, and support staff and modifications in academic requirements. These modifications may include:

- removing architectural barriers
- providing services such as readers, qualified interpreters, or note takers for deaf or hard-of-hearing students
- providing modifications, substitutions, or waivers of courses, major fields of study, or degree requirements on a case-by-case basis
- allowing extra time to complete exams
- using alternative forms for students to demonstrate course mastery
- permitting the use of computer software programs or other assistive technological devices to facilitate test taking and study skills

DISABILITY-RELATED SUPPORT SERVICES

One of the most important things to consider is to have the student become familiar with the colleges or institution's disability-related support services. Every college will have someone or several individuals whose responsibility is to oversee the needs and accommodations for these students. Making contact is crucial because this type of support will facilitate any problems or concerns in transitioning to college. The need for this contact is also very important in light of the many difficulties faced by some college students with disabilities.

The Northern New York Post Secondary Transition Team (1998) lists several common difficulties faced by some college students with disabilities.

READING
1. Reading too slowly or too fast
2. Difficulty understanding what was read
3. Difficulty remembering what was read
4. Difficulty identifying important information
5. Trouble sounding out new words
6. Difficulty turning pages
7. Difficulty with print size and/or format

WRITTEN LANGUAGE
1. Difficulty using proper sentence structure
2. Misspelling words

3. Difficulty copying correctly from a book or blackboard
4. Writing too slowly or too fast
5. Poor penmanship
6. Able to express ideas verbally better than in writing

ORAL LANGUAGE
1. Difficulties concentrating on conversations
2. Difficulty in expressing ideas
3. Writing better than speaking
4. Difficulty speaking in a grammatically correct manner
5. Difficulty telling a story in proper sequence

MATHEMATICS
1. Difficulty remembering basic facts
2. Reversing numbers
3. Confusing operational symbols
4. Copying problems incorrectly from one line to another
5. Difficulty following the sequence of operational processes
6. Difficulty understanding and retaining abstract concepts
7. Difficulty comprehending word problems
8. Reasoning deficits

ORGANIZATION AND STUDY SKILLS
1. Time management difficulties
2. Slow starting and completing tasks
3. Difficulty remembering information
4. Difficulty following oral and/or written directions
5. Difficulty with organization
6. Short attention span
7. Difficulty focusing
8. Inefficiently using reference materials

Small (1996) indicates that there are many colleges and universities in the United States that have good track records when it comes to accommodating learning disabilities. The quality of any given college's response is subject to the vagaries of funding, administrative fiat, and the current image an institution is trying to promote. What was once an effective, coordinated support program one year may turn into a vague assortment of academic support services the next. The commercially available guidebooks to colleges and universities for students with learning disabilities do a fine job capturing most of the institutions and what they offer the students.

Small (1996) addresses the services/accommodations that may be available to students with disabilities at selected colleges and universities:

- Preferential or early registration
- Counsel on which courses to take given an instructor's style and sensitivity to learning disabilities
- Reduced or redistributed course load (e.g., not taking a number of heavy reading courses simultaneously)
- Skills development and remediation (reading, spelling, writing, math)
- Modified exam arrangements (oral, untimed, extended time, scribe, use of word processor for essays)
- Assistance with note taking (note taking buddy, taping lectures)
- Course waivers and substitutions (foreign language, sometimes in math)
- Assistance with proofreading
- Use of calculators, spelling aces, lap computers in classes

- Taped textbooks, readers, electronic text readers (text recognition synthesized speech machines)
- Assistance with developing oral expression
- Speech and language specialists
- Assistance with personal organization
- Assistance with time management
- Writing, reading, math, study skills centers (be careful, some have personnel who know little about the needs of students with learning disabilities)
- Support for students on medication (e.g., students with ADHD)
- Social skills training
- Training and support in developing and maintaining motivation and attention

Social Skills

Some students may have problems with social skills due to their inconsistent perceptual abilities. They may be unable to detect the difference between a joking wink and a disgusted glance or notice the difference between sincere and sarcastic comments or other subtle changes in tone of voice. These difficulties in interpreting nonverbal messages may result in lower self-esteem for some and may cause them to have trouble meeting people, working with others, and making friends.

Many college campuses have an Office for Disabled Student Services or Office of Special Services. Others have designated the dean of students or some other administrator to provide this information and to coordinate necessary services and accommodations. At vocational schools or other training programs, the person responsible for disability services can usually provide this information.

There are also many publications that can tell more about the policies and programs that individual colleges and universities have established to address the needs of students with disabilities.

FINANCIAL AID

Another major question regarding postsecondary education or training opportunities is the availability of financial aid to help pay for tuition and living expenses. Obtaining financial aid can be a complex process because laws are amended and eligibility requirements, policies, and disbursement of government funds change each year. Most money called "financial aid" is available to those studying only above the high school level (thus, financial aid is usually not available for adult education). The student must usually demonstrate the ability to benefit from the education or training in order to receive traditional financial aid.

The financial aid system is based on a partnership among the student, parents, postsecondary educational institutions, state and federal government, and available private resources. For the student with a disability, the partnership may be extended to include a vocational rehabilitation agency and the Social Security Administration. Such a partnership requires the cooperation of all and an understanding by each of their responsibilities within the financial aid process.

Heath (2001) created the following precollege checklist for students with disabilities.

Pre-College Financial Aid Checklist

DURING THE JUNIOR YEAR OF HIGH SCHOOL:

_____ Explore college profiles and programs. If possible, visit the colleges that most interest you.

_____ Investigate financial aid opportunities with your high school counselor.

_____ Write to the college(s) of your choice for applications and financial aid information.

_____ Begin the application process with Vocational Rehabilitation and/or Social Security.

_____ If you are involved in Special Education services at your high school, be sure that your Individual Transition Plan (ITP) includes your academic and vocational goals.

_____ Collect information and document expenses for completing the financial aid forms.

BY THE SENIOR YEAR OF HIGH SCHOOL:

_____ Obtain the FAFSA from your high school counselor. Using the most accurate income tax information possible, complete the form.

_____ Mail the financial aid form as soon as possible after January 1, since forms postmarked before then do not count. (Be sure to check the application deadline for each college to which you plan to apply.)

_____ Complete and return to the college(s) all application materials and any financial aid documents requested by the college by the date indicated by the institution (usually February/March).

_____ Keep track of the date on which you sent in each form. You should receive a Student Aid Report (SAR) within four weeks. If you have not received any response within four weeks, call the student aid center at the number listed on the FAFSA.

_____ When the SAR arrives, contact the financial aid offices of the college(s) on your list to see if they need a copy of it.

_____ Keep in touch with the college financial aid offices during the course of the application process to verify that they have received your application data and that they are processing your aid package.

_____ If you are a VR client, be sure that your counselor is in touch with the financial aid offices at the colleges(s) on your list. Be on time and accurate in filling out the application forms. If possible, have a third party read them and check for accuracy. Keep at least one photocopy of each completed form for your own record in case problems arise.

What Is Financial Aid?

Financial aid is a system of financial assistance to help individuals meet their educational expenses when their own resources are not sufficient. Four types of aid are available:

1. Grants—Aid that generally does not have to be repaid.
2. Loans—Money borrowed to cover school costs, which must be repaid (usually with interest) over a specified period of time (usually after the student has left school or graduated).
3. Work-study—Employment that enables a student to earn money toward a portion of school costs during or between periods of enrollment.
4. Scholarships—Gifts and awards based on a student's academic achievement, background, or other criteria.

The federal government contributes to all three types of student financial aid. These programs are explained in a booklet called _The Student Guide: Financial Aid from the U.S. Department of Education_. The programs described in the booklet are:

■ Federal Pell Grants
■ Federal Supplemental Educational Opportunity Grants (SEOG)

- Federal Work-Study (FW-S)
- Federal Perkins Loans
- Federal Family Education Loans (FFEL)
    - Federal Stafford Loans (subsidized and unsubsidized)
    - Federal PLUS Loans

All of these programs are based on financial need of the student and his or her family, except the unsubsidized Stafford and PLUS programs.

What Expenses Are Considered Disability Related?

In addition to the financial aid that students may receive for tuition, room, and board, there may be times when additional expenses requiring further financial assistance are incurred. These may include:

- special equipment related to the disability and its maintenance
- expenses of services for personal use or study such as readers, interpreters, note takers, or personal care attendants
- transportation necessary to pursue an academic program, if regular transportation is not accessible
- medical expenses relating directly to the individual's disability that are not covered by insurance

Students should be sure to inform the aid administrator of disability-related expenses that may previously have been covered by the family budget. These may include food and veterinary bills for dog guides, batteries for hearing aids and a telecommunication device for the deaf (TDD) (now called a Typed Text QTT) or the cost of recruiting and training readers or personal care attendants. Leaving home often necessitates the purchase of new or additional equipment that will allow the student to be independent at school. Students with disabilities should seek assistance from the Office of Disability Support Services and/or Financial Aid Office to determine disability-related expenses.

Regardless of whether the student is able to obtain any special equipment or services through the institution or elsewhere, it is still important to let the financial aid administrator know of any anticipated expenses. Such information is considered in the determination of the student's financial need, on which all aid decisions are based.

Vocational Rehabilitation and Financial Aid

The local vocational rehabilitation agency has VR counselors who can help a person with a disability determine eligibility for assistance. The VR program is an eligibility program rather than an entitlement program. To be eligible for services, an individual must have a disability that is a substantial handicap to employment and must have potential for employment as a result of rehabilitation services. The primary goal of a VR counselor is to make the client employable; therefore, the counselor will look closely at a student's educational plans in terms of job potential. Although initial counseling and evaluation are open to all, the counselor may determine that a client is not eligible for other services based on state agency policies governing economic need, order of selection, and other policies of the agency.

Among the services that may be provided by VR agencies to a student who is a client are:

- tuition expenses
- reader services for persons who are blind or learning disabled
- interpreter services for people who are hearing impaired; individually prescribed aids and devices, which are authorized in advance in an individual-

ized written rehabilitation program (I WRP) developed jointly by the client and the counselor

- telecommunications, sensory, and other technological aids and devices
- other goods and services, which help render an individual who is handicapped employable

The preceding items may differ from state to state or be subject to a test of a client's ability to pay or the use of available resources from another social service agency before a commitment of VR funds is made. To understand why there are differences among and between states' VR programs, students and parents need to know that although the U.S. Department of Education, Rehabilitation Services Administration (RSA) administers the Rehabilitation Act, each participating state administers its own program through the provisions of a state plan that has been developed under the guidelines of the act and that has been approved by RSA.

ISSUES TO CONSIDER WHEN LOOKING INTO POSTSECONDARY EDUCATION

1. What are admission requirements?
2. What is the grade point average? ACT? SAT?
3. Are there special accommodations for individuals with disabilities to take entrance exams?
4. Are there special incentive programs?
5. Is there a disabled student service office on campus? How does one contact the office? Does it have a full-time or part-time person there?
6. What kind of documentation is required to verify disabilities?
7. Is there a disabled student organization on campus? How does one contact this organization?.
8. How are the faculty informed of the necessary accommodations, if needed?
9. Is tutoring available? Is it individualized or group? Is there a cost involved?
10. Are note takers and readers available? Is there a cost involved? How are they trained?
11. Is it possible to arrange for tape recorder classes, computers, untimed testing, and test readers?
12. Is it possible to relocate classes to more accessible sites?
13. What is the college's policy regarding course substitutes or waiver of curriculum requirements?
14. Are there developmental courses available? In what areas?

CHECKLIST FOR ASSESSING COLLEGES FOR ACCESSIBILITY

When looking for the right college, make sure to find what services are available through the Office of Services for Students with Disabilities on each campus. The office may be located in the Office of Student Affairs, or it may be listed independently. It is essential to obtain as much information as possible about services for students with disabilities and services that pertain to particular disabilities before beginning classes.

Following are samples of questions for parents and students to consider when speaking to a college representative:

1. What services are offered (e.g., readers, note takers, bus service)? Are there fees?
2. What are the names of the director and staff people connected to these services? Is there a document that describes the various services?

3. Can you introduce me to a student with my disability (or another disability) so I can learn from that person's experience? What arrangements do other students make in the same situation as mine?

4. Who is available to assist in finding services on and off campus (e.g., accessible apartments, restaurants, other)?

5. Is there an office for the local vocational rehabilitation agency on campus? If not, where is it?

6. What are the local organizations for individuals with disabilities such as mine? What services can I get through them (e.g., Center for Independent Living and Personal Care Association)?

7. How many students with disabilities attend this college until graduation? What history is there of my major department making accommodations?

8. If accommodations are ever denied, what is the procedure to follow to contest the decision?

9. How early does a qualified student have to start to make arrangements for putting textbooks on audiotape?

ACCOMMODATIONS FOR SPECIFIC DISABILITIES

The student should be sufficiently knowledgeable about his or her disability to address every concern, or potential concern, with those who will be offering services.

VISUAL IMPAIRMENT

- Does the college offer training in finding one's way around campus? If not, how do I get the training? Do you have a list of qualified instructors?

- Are readers paid or volunteer? Who pays? (Whether using a volunteer or paid reader, assess whether your needs are being provided for, and find a gracious but clear way to communicate to them if they are not. Ask the office: "Do you help locate readers? Do you have any suggestions for finding them?")

- Are large-print computer programs available to me? What other assistive technology is available? Where is the equipment located? Is there training to help me use the computers and accompanying software?

- What accommodations are there for taking exams? How and where are they usually taken? What responsibility do I have in the whole process? Can I work out my own arrangements if I so choose? Can I get the exams in an alternative medium, like large print, or braille, or recorded?

- Is campus transportation accessible for me? Is there campus or city public transportation and is it accessible to me?

HEARING IMPAIRMENT

- Will the Office of Services for Students with Disabilities arrange for interpreters? If so, how do I set that up with my class schedule? If not, will they provide assistance in locating them? Who pays?

- Are oral and sign language interpreters available?

- Are note takers available to record lectures for me, or do I have to find my own? Are they paid, and who pays? What is the procedure for payment?

- Does the campus have TDDs (Telecommunication Devices for the Deaf, sometimes called Text Telephones)?

- What are the provisions for safety in the dormitory in case of fire or other emergency? Do dormitory telephones have the capacity to have the volume turned up?

- Is captioning of speakers while they are speaking available?

- What amplification equipment is available? Can I borrow any of it for my own use?

MOBILITY IMPAIRMENT

- Is there accessibility to buildings, classrooms, laboratories, and dormitories? How wide are the residence hall doorways and what is the accessibility of the bathrooms?
- Will there be any special problems or assistance with class registration?
- Will anyone assist me in arranging my schedule to include the required classes and still have enough time to go from one classroom in one building to another classroom in another building?
- Will I be able to reach and use all the equipment in the laboratory? If not, what arrangements must I make?
- If I need special adaptations to access computers, who will provide them?
- If I need adaptations to access the library catalog system, who will arrange for them?
- If the college has a large campus, is there accessible transportation, such as a lift-equipped van, to get from one area to another? Are there curb cuts and smooth sidewalks that I can manage with a wheelchair?
- Is driver evaluation and training available?
- If my wheelchair needs repair, can I get it done locally?
- Is there a dormitory or other residence that can assist people who require help with daily activities such as eating or dressing?

Learning Disability

Remember that academic accommodations are based on the documented type of learning disability and its severity. Diagnostic papers must be written by a licensed medical or psychological examiner. Subtest standard scores must be listed as legal evidence of severity. School skills levels will not be sufficient, nor will an old individualized education plan (IEP) contract.

There is a high probability that whatever the accommodations recommended by the examiner, they will not exactly meet your needs in college. In some classes you will need no accommodations but in others you may face demands on your learning disability that no one thought of. For these reasons, it is imperative you understand your learning disability thoroughly enough to explain how it works to a person unfamiliar with learning disabilities.

Although the laws allow accommodations for diagnosed disabilities, the law does not entitle anyone to misrepresent his or her needs for the purpose of gaining advantage over people without disabilities. The law probably will not protect past accommodations in a different academic circumstance unless the need can be documented. If the student finds himself or herself in a resistant environment within a college or university after he or she begins attending, the student will need to have available his or her diagnostic papers and the current request for accommodations in order to be successful in advocating for his or her needs. Other things to consider include:

- Are academic accommodations uniform for everyone, or are they individualized according to the diagnostic papers (e.g., note takers, extended test time)?
- Are the students with more severe learning disabilities expected to manage their own lives (e.g., getting homework in on time, money management, school schedules)? Who is available to help when help is needed?
- How early does a qualified student have to start making arrangements for special exam conditions with the professor?
- If the learning disability causes more trouble than anticipated, can the course load be reworked?
- Are there counseling services available in case a student gets overwhelmed?

- May a student have additional time for tests? Who arranges for the extra time—the student, the professor, the Office of Services for Students with Disabilities, or the dean?
- May the student tape class lectures?

Heiser (2000) indicates that the following questions should be considered in order to find the "best match" for the student, the postsecondary institution, and the learning disability (LD) support services.

1. Does the student qualify for a learning support service college program?
2. Have his or her high school courses prepared the student to successfully compete in college?
3. Are there special admission procedures?
4. Are there additional fees for the LD support services program?
5. What kind of college (small or large) and location (urban or rural) would provide the best opportunity for academic success?
6. Is the learning support services program "specifically" directed toward the LD student? Are there services available to students with disabilities and the general student body?
7. How many students are enrolled in the program and what is the proportion of LD students to the general student population?
8. When was the program started?
9. How long have the personnel been in the program?
10. Does the program have faculty and administrative support?
11. Who does the academic advising for the LD student?
12. Are the academic advisors (those persons who help the student select courses) familiar with the goals and procedures of the learning support services program and the general characteristics and needs of the LD student in particular?
13. Does the institution have course waivers (e.g., foreign language requirements)?
14. Are special courses required of LD students? Do they carry college credits? Can these credits be used toward graduation?
15. Are there remedial or developmental courses available?
16. Are students in this program required to remain in the program throughout college?
17. Is counseling available and what kind (e.g., personal, academic and career, group or individual), and is it required or optional?
18. Is there assistance available for improving social/interpersonal skills?
19. Are there support groups available for the LD student?
20. What kind of tutoring is available to the student?
21. Are all textbooks available on tape?
22. What kind of additional resources are available (e.g., word processors, tape recorders, etc.)?
23. Are students permitted to tape lectures?
24. Is there a summer "precollege" session available for entering freshmen?
25. Should the student visit more than one college before making a decision?

CHRONIC HEALTH CONDITION

- What medical services are available locally? Are there rehabilitation units in local hospitals?
- How can the student arrange his or her schedule to accommodate fatigue?
- Can arrangements be made for a personal care attendant if the student needs one?

The answers to these questions will give the student an idea of how easy or difficult college is going to be in terms of accommodations. The student may need to change some strategies, and may need to push for support in areas where the services do not appear to meet his or her needs. The more the student knows in advance, the more effective the student will be in beginning this process.

DISTANCE LEARNING

Off-campus education, or *distance learning,* is becoming increasingly popular in the adult or higher education community. To reach the growing number of nontraditional students (those who are other than 18 to 23 years old, embarking on postsecondary education directly from high school), some postsecondary institutions have become decentralized with campuses in several locations. A result of decentralization is that education can be available to those unable to attend classes during the day or on a specific campus due to work, family, or other commitments.

Distance learning includes courses offered by educational institutions, businesses, or other entities away from the regular campus site through computer conferencing, cable TV, telephone conference calls, videocassettes, correspondence courses, or any combination of these. Some courses may be accessed by the student at home. Others may be offered at a public library, business headquarters, factory meeting room, or other community site. Such nontraditional settings, or "schools without walls," can provide nontraditional students with the flexibility they need in order to earn college degrees or obtain training for new careers. One result of the diverse demographic patterns emerging in the late 1990s is that a growing number of adults with disabilities are seeking educational and career opportunities.

Distance learning is an option for adults with disabilities who are unable to participate in regular campus classes. Distance learning programs constitute a part of the system of lifelong learning, which has been steadily expanding for many years. Change itself has become the rule, not the exception. Educational services are moving from the classroom at formal institutions of higher education to sites in businesses and community agencies, as well as being totally off site, using electronic technology.

Students with disabilities may participate in distance learning opportunities for various reasons. Some students may be unable to leave home or the hospital. Others may participate in such programs to increase flexibility regarding scheduling and to increase control over the environment in which they perform their academic work. Because institutions offer different types of distance learning programs, students are advised to investigate the options.

Enrolling in a Distance Learning Program

Distance learners are strongly advised to be sure the school is accredited. An accredited institution has earned recognition from an appropriate accrediting commission or association that determined the institution has met acceptable levels of educational quality. Students must check with the institution concerning its accreditation before they enroll in any program. In addition, all states have an agency overseeing higher education that can be consulted about accreditation.

When choosing a particular postsecondary institution, students should be aware of the importance of academic advising and ask whether it will be offered through computer, telephone, or in person. Academic advisors for distance learners are usually available to discuss degree plans, course selection, prerequisite courses, course content, preparation of portfolios, graduate school, study skills, and other areas of concern. Students and advisors should be able to develop a degree program plan that outlines how the student will complete all or part of the remaining academic requirements. Most advisors realize that adults have numerous responsibilities, and they are usually ready to accommodate varied schedules and widely differing needs.

Access to the Student Services at the College

Many individuals with disabilities who access distance learning programs do not realize that they can use and benefit from the institution's student services, through the Dean of Students, Office of Special Services, or Office of Disability Support Services. To obtain such accommodations as print materials in alternate formats, extended time for completing the work, or use of an interpreter or note taker, students with disabilities must disclose and document their disability to the Disability Support Services Office. Students who are not able to visit the office are encouraged to fax or mail a letter of application, résumé, or other documentation to the office, so a career counselor can provide feedback. Students with disabilities have been able to perform practice interviews over the telephone with a career counselor. Students may also communicate with the campus financial aid office.

Students in distance learning programs should be able to access most of the programs in student services at community colleges and universities. Some distance learning programs operate from very small offices and are themselves not able to offer extensive student services but will try to accommodate by referring the student to the services offered to on-campus students. To increase the success of students enrolled in distance learning programs, faculty and administrators are encouraged to be creative when seeking to provide academic and student services to students with disabilities.

As demand for education by persons with disabilities continues to grow, distance learning will be an important factor in facilitating access. Many adults with disabilities who have already successfully completed a traditional program can also participate in distance learning programs as a means of continuing lifelong learning.

CONCLUSION

One of the major goals of the transition process is to facilitate an individual's arrival at his or her maximum potential. Within the last 10 years, the opportunities for an individual with disabilities to achieve higher education have expanded greatly. Every year, more and more colleges and universities develop the necessary programs that allow these individuals to participate in this educational environment.

CHAPTER THIRTEEN

FINANCIAL AND HEALTH INSURANCE ISSUES

OVERVIEW

To properly plan for the financial future of a student with disabilities, students and parents must be aware of the options and incentives that are available during the transition process. A very important part of this process is helping children with disabilities manage to the best of their ability their finances or other affairs. The purpose of this chapter is to give you, the special educator, a strong working knowledge of the financial considerations that all children with disabilities must face in their transition to adult life.

This chapter will also focus on health insurance issues facing parents and individuals with disabilities. Chronic illness, disability, or severe injury creates great stress for family and friends. The adjustment for a family with a child who has a severe or complex health issue can be very intense and taxing; the special needs of this child require a focus on many issues. Concerns surrounding the child's well-being, health, daily life, and constantly changing future expectations are magnified. As the health field changes and technology and terminology expand, parents must learn new skills and acquire a wide range of knowledge to ensure that a child's ongoing health needs are properly addressed.

With the expansion of technology and improved medical care also comes the burden of growing medical costs. As a result, parents of children with chronic disabilities have the added anxiety of finding the resources necessary for medical attention and recommended equipment.

The purpose of this chapter is to give you a strong working knowledge of health insurance issues for individuals with disabilities. After reading this chapter, you should understand the following:

SOCIAL SECURITY ADMINISTRATION	**FOOD STAMPS**
SUPPLEMENTAL SECURITY INCOME (SSI)	**HEALTH INSURANCE ISSUES**
CRITERIA FOR DETERMINING SSI BENEFITS	**EXPLORING INSURANCE OPTIONS**
	KINDS OF INSURANCE POLICIES
HOW TO SIGN UP FOR SSI BENEFITS	**MEDICARE**
WORK INCENTIVES	**MEDICAID**
SOCIAL SECURITY DISABILITY INSURANCE (SSDI)	**MEDICAID WAIVERS**

Many people with disabilities are eligible for benefits under one or more of several government programs. These programs are designed to protect the person with a disability by making sure that the person's financial resources are sufficient to provide the basic necessities of life—food, clothing, and health care.

To plan for the future of a child with disabilities, individuals must be aware of and use the many programs sponsored by the federal government and operated through a federal state partnership. These are called *entitlement programs*. Some of them are provided for large portions of the population in general—not just for persons with disabilities; other programs are specifically for people with disabilities. With a well-planned combination of services and, when possible, by supplementing these services with private assets, a parent can establish a relatively secure financial future for a son or daughter.

Benefits include more than money. The individual may also be eligible for valuable services such as health care, vocational rehabilitation, supported employment, subsidized housing, and personal attendant care. Assets acquired through inheritance may affect eligibility for those benefits. Therefore, in order to protect the individual's eligibility for government benefits at some point in the future and to provide for his or her long-term needs, the parent may want to consider establishing an individual estate plan.

The need for a clear-cut, long-range plan is needed in cases in which a daughter or son has cognitive or mental disabilities. Mental illness and cognitive disabilities often impair a person's ability to manage his or her own finances. Parents will, therefore, have to provide for the present as well as the future of their daughter or son.

Planning will entail taking inventory of a family's financial assets. Most families are surprised to learn that they do have a variety of resources within their reach. Some of them may include standard government benefits, savings, family assistance, parents' estate, inheritances, property, investments, military benefits, insurance, house or home, and, resources from other family members and friends.

Although a family's financial situation is confidential, when it comes to parents' financing their children's future there are several paths to explore depending on the nature and severity of the child's disability and the personal assets of the family.

The professional's role in this area is not to be a financial advisor but to inform and assist students and their parents in fully understanding their options and rights. The following options should be explored and either one or a combination may be sufficient for a particular situation: using the family's own financial assets or government assistance through a variety of programs.

Because support from a parent's personal assets is self-explanatory, we will focus on the government programs that can provide financial support for individuals with disabilities.

SOCIAL SECURITY ADMINISTRATION

The Social Security Administration (SSA) directs two programs that can be of financial benefit to eligible individuals with disabilities throughout the transition process. These programs are the Supplemental Security Income (SSI) program and the Social Security Disability Insurance (SSDI) program.

Because the Social Security Administration considers many variables before determining if a person is eligible for SSI or SSDI benefits, the discussion here is intended only as an overview to the benefits of these programs. Ultimately, an individual's eligibility can be determined only by contacting the Social Security Administration and filing an application. Your awareness of these entitlement programs will assist parents in this very crucial aspect of the transition process.

SUPPLEMENTAL SECURITY INCOME (SSI)

The SSI program is targeted for individuals who are both (a) in financial need and (b) blind or disabled. People who get SSI usually receive food stamps and Medicaid, too. The evaluation process to determine eligibility varies, depending on whether the applicant is under age 18 or over. Recently, there have been many significant changes in how the SSA determines the SSI eligibility of individuals under age 18. These changes are expected to make it easier for children and youth with disabilities to qualify for SSI benefits. More information about these changes and the specific evaluation process the SSA now uses for individuals under age 18 is available by contacting the Social Security Administration directly. When a child reaches age 18, the Social Security Administration no longer considers the income and resources of parents in determining if the youth is eligible for benefits.

Under the SSI program, individuals over age 18 are eligible to receive monthly payments if they have little or no income or resources such as savings accounts, are considered medically disabled or blind, and do not work or earn less than a certain amount, defined by the Social Security Administration as substantial gainful activity (SGA).

CRITERIA FOR DETERMINING SSI BENEFITS

To determine a person's financial need, the Social Security Administration considers the following:

- **The person's place of residence.** SSI payments may be reduced by different percentages, depending on the individual's residence. People who live in city or county rest homes, halfway houses, or other public institutions usually cannot get SSI checks, but there are some exceptions. A person living in a publicly operated community residence that serves no more than 16 people may get SSI. Anyone living in a public institution mainly to attend approved educational or job training that will help him or her get a job may get SSI. Those living in a public emergency shelter for the homeless may be able to get SSI checks. If an individual lives in a public or private institution and Medicaid is paying more than half the cost of the care, he or she may get a small SSI check.
- **The parent's employment status.** An individual's SSI payments may be determined by parental income and employment status. This issue should be explored fully so that an individual with a disability can receive the proper assistance.
- **Income and things owned by an individual with a disability.** Whether an individual can get SSI also depends on what he or she owns and how much income is coming in, such as wages, Social Security checks, and pensions. Income also includes such noncash items received as food, clothing, or shelter. If a person is married, the SSA will also look at the income of the spouse and the things the spouse owns. For someone under age 18, SSA may look at the income of the parents and the things they own. For a sponsored alien, they may also look at the income of the sponsor and what he or she owns.

For specific information and criteria for any of the foregoing factors have the parents contact their local Social Security Administration office.

Before an individual with a disability can get SSI, he or she must also meet other rules. These rules are that one must live in the United States or Northern Mariana Islands and one must be a U.S. citizen or be in the United States legally.

If an individual is eligible for Social Security or other benefits, then he or she must apply for them. (Eligible persons can get both SSI and Social Security checks if eligible for both.) If disabled, one must accept vocational rehabilitation services if they're offered.

HOW TO SIGN UP FOR SSI BENEFITS

It's easy. Just have the student and his or her parents visit the local Social Security office or call (800) 772-1213 for an appointment with a Social Security representative who will help them sign up. SSI should be applied for right away; this benefit cannot start before the day one applies. Parents or guardians can apply for children under age 18 who are blind or disabled.

What to Bring When Signing Up for SSI Benefits

Help your students and their parents understand that the following things are required before applying for SSI benefits. Even if applicants don't have all of the things listed, however, suggest they sign up anyway. The people in the Social Security office are there to help applicants get whatever is needed.

- Social Security card or a record of Social Security number
- Birth certificate or other proof of age
- Information about residence, for example, a home with a mortgage or a lease and landlord's name
- Payroll slips, bank books, insurance policies, car registration, burial fund records, and other information about income and the things that are owned
- Medical information supporting the disability. When signing up for disability, the names, addresses, and telephone numbers of doctors, hospitals, and clinics are required. SSI checks can go directly into an individual's bank account, so have the family bring a checkbook or any other papers that show names and account numbers. Many people choose to have their checks sent to the bank because they find it safer and easier than getting their checks by mail.

WORK INCENTIVES

The Social Security Administration offers two programs that can be of benefit to individuals with disabilities. The SSI and SSDI programs offer financial and medical benefits to eligible persons with disabilities. In addition, both programs have work incentives that make it possible for individuals with disabilities to work without an immediate loss of benefits.

SSI Program Work Incentives

SSI work incentives are exactly that—additional incentives that allow students with disabilities to increase their income while maintaining needed SSI cash assistance benefits. SSI work incentives allow students to participate in paid work situations and maintain their SSI benefits while they are in school. As a planning tool, work incentives provide students, parents, school personnel, and other IEP/transition team members with potential resources for additional postsecondary training and other forms of support when a student exits school. SSI program work incentives protect SSI benefits for students while they participate in paid employment.

Accessing SSI work incentives during the transition process expands current and future opportunities for many students with disabilities. Students with disabilities can:

- engage in paid employment
- increase their income without decreasing their SSI benefits or eligibility for other benefits such as Medicaid (*in most states*)

- offset expenses incurred as a result of their work
- save for further postsecondary education and training or to start their own business

According to the the National Transition Network (1998), the transition planning process must include establishing the student's eligibility for SSI benefits and providing the student with real work experience during the transition period—age 14 (or younger, if appropriate) to age 21. For a student with a disability to benefit from SSI work incentives, the student must be (1) receiving or eligible for SSI cash assistance benefits and (2) engaged in work experiences as part of the transition program.

SSI work incentives available to transition-age students include Earned Income Exclusion, Student Earned Income Exclusion (SEIE), Impairment-Related Work expenses (IRWE), Plan for Achieving Self-Support (PASS), Blind Work Expense (BWE), and Property Essential to Self-Support (PESS). Each of the SSI work incentives is an income or resource exclusion that combines to assist individuals with disabilities in maintaining necessary SSI benefits until they are self-sufficient. These incentives can be particularly helpful in designing community-based, paid employment transition programs for students without decreasing the cash assistance benefits provided by the SSI program.

There are a number of work incentives under the SSI program. These include:

Section 1619a. Provisions under Section 1619a of the Employment Opportunities for Disabled Americans Act allow people to continue to receive special SSI monthly cash payments after their earned income is at the amount designated as the Substantial Gainful Activity (SGA) level (currently $500 a month). The Social Security Administration uses a formula to determine the amount of SSI benefits an individual with a disability will continue to receive. In most cases, people remain eligible for Medicaid and state-funded attendant care benefits (U.S. Department of Health and Human Services, 1990, October).

Section 1619b. Provisions under Section 1619b of the Employment Opportunities for Disabled Americans Act allow most individuals to keep Medicaid benefits after they stop receiving monthly SSI checks. The law requires that a person's medical condition be reviewed within 12 months of entering the 1619b status to ensure the person still has a disability. A person must apply for these benefits before his or her regular SSI benefits actually stop.

Impairment-related work expenses (IRWE). IRWEs are the costs for services or materials a person needs to be able to work. Social Security deducts these costs from an individual's SGA when calculating how much money that person should receive in his or her monthly check. Services and materials can be deducted as IRWEs only if the person pays for the costs himself or herself and receives no reimbursement for them. The services or materials must be necessary because of a person's disability. They cannot be costs that a person without a disability would have if she or he were to hold the same type of job. According to the U.S. Department of Health and Human Services (1990, August), examples of IRWEs are the cost of wheelchairs, pacemakers, respirators, braces, and artificial limbs. Work-related equipment such as one-handed typewriters, electronic visual aids, and braille devices may also be deductible. Other costs such as attendant care needed to prepare for and go to or from work are often deductible as well. The cost of a job coach has just recently been allowed as an IRWE.

Plan for Achieving Self-Support (PASS). PASS is a work incentive program that enables a person with a disability to receive earned and unearned income and to set some or all of these funds aside for up to 48 months. The purpose of the program is to help individuals accumulate resources in order to pursue a specific work goal, such as "education, vocational training, or starting a business, or purchase of work-related equipment" (U.S. Department of Health and Human Services, 1990, October, p. 3). Thus, the PASS program is a means of encouraging and empowering individuals to become financially self-supporting.

A PASS program must be in writing and must include a realistic work goal, a date for achieving the goal, a clear savings/spending plan, and a method for keeping track of the funds that are set aside. Social Security must approve an individual's PASS program. It is helpful to initiate a PASS prior to receiving transitional and/or supported employment services, but a PASS program can also be established after a person goes to work. The income and resources set aside under a plan are excluded from the SSI income and resource tests. SSI payments themselves cannot be set aside in a PASS, and individuals must have some type of resources or income other than the SSI check to establish a PASS.

SSDI Program Work Incentives

The SSDI program also has work incentives. As with SSI work incentives, impairment-related work expenses can be deducted from the earnings on which Substantial Gainful Activity (SGA) is calculated. Other work incentives include a trial work period, extended period of eligibility, and extended Medicare coverage.

The trial work period allows individuals with disabilities to test their ability to work without fear of losing SSDI benefits. The trial period is for nine months of work, which need not be consecutive. During or after this time, if an individual demonstrates the ability to earn above the SGA limit of $500 a month, despite his or her disability, he or she may no longer be considered disabled by the Social Security Administration. Benefits would be discontinued three months later (considered a grace period).

The extended period of eligibility is an additional work incentive tied to the nine-month trial period. This incentive exists to ensure that the individual with a disability has sufficient time to develop the financial and occupational stability necessary in order to maintain independence. Basically, individuals can be reinstated to SSDI benefits if their earnings fall below the SGA level at any time during the extended period (36 months). Furthermore, individuals do not need to file a new application or have a new disability determination. Benefits are reinstated without a waiting period.

Most people with disabilities would rather work than try to live on disability benefits. There are a number of special rules for providing cash benefits and Medicare while they attempt to work. These rules are called work incentives. Be familiar with these disability work incentives so they can be used to the individual's advantage.

If an individual is receiving Social Security disability benefits, the following work incentives apply:

Trial work period. For nine months (not necessarily consecutive), people may earn as much as they can without affecting their benefits. (The nine months of work must fall within a five-year period before the trial work period can end.) A trial work month is any month in which an individual earns more than $200. After the trial work period ends, the work is evaluated to see if it is "substantial." If earnings do not average more than $500 a month, benefits will generally continue. If earnings do average more than $500 a month, benefits will continue for a three-month grace period before they stop.

Extended period of eligibility. For 36 months after a successful trial work period, an individual who is still disabled will be eligible to receive a monthly benefit without a new application for any month earnings drop below $500.

Deductions for impairment-related expenses. Work expenses related to the disability will be discounted in figuring whether earnings constitute substantial work.

Medicare continuation. Medicare coverage will continue for 39 months beyond the trial work period. If Medicare coverage stops because of work, monthly premiums may be purchased.

Different rules apply to SSI recipients who work. For more information about Social Security and SSI work incentives, you may want to ask for a copy of the booklet Working While Disabled—How Social Security Can Help (Publication No. 05-10095).

SOCIAL SECURITY DISABILITY INSURANCE (SSDI)

The SSDI program is a bit different because it considers the employment status of the applicant's parents. "SSDI benefits are paid to persons who become disabled before the age of 22 if at least one of their parents had worked a certain amount of time under Social Security but is now disabled, retired, and/or deceased" (National Association of State Directors of Special Education, 1990, p. 9). As with SSI, eligibility for SSDI generally makes an individual eligible for food stamps and Medicaid benefits as well.

Be aware that changes in legislation might result in a reduction of benefits. Recent legislation, however, has made major changes in both the SSI and SSDI programs to encourage people receiving these benefits to try to work and become independent. These changes are called work incentives because they make it possible for individuals with disabilities to work without an immediate loss of benefits.

Whatever financial status a family has at the time a child turns 18, assist your students and their families by providing a thorough knowledge of the student's financial entitlements.

Plan for Achieving Self-Support (PASS)

The Plan for Achieving Self-Support (PASS) is a work incentive that allows an individual to set aside income and/or resources for a specified period of time to achieve a work goal. For example, an individual may set aside money for postsecondary education, the purchase of job-coaching support, personal transportation, job-related equipment, or to start a business. The income and/or resources set aside in a PASS do not count in determining SSI benefits. Nor may SSI cash benefits be used to support a PASS. When appropriate, a PASS may be used in conjunction with other SSI work incentives. If a student under age 18 cannot satisfy the SSI income eligibility requirement *only* because his or her parents' income is too high, the student may apply for a PASS incentive through which his or her parents can set aside enough income to make the student eligible for SSI benefits.

The PASS is similar to the IEP/transition plan: It establishes job-related goals and objectives. Because of these similarities, it is possible to incorporate a PASS into the IEP/transition plan. A transition student may benefit from a PASS while in school or upon exiting. The basic requirements for a PASS include a feasible and reasonable occupational goal; a defined timetable; the need for income or resources, other than SSI benefits, to be set aside; and an explanation of expenditures to be covered by the set-aside funds.

A student wishing to incorporate a PASS into his or her transition program should:

- Request assistance if needed from teachers, counselors, or other IEP/transition team members.

- Obtain the eight-page PASS application (see Appendix E), instruction sheet, and SSA publication *Red Book On Work Incentives* from the school counseling office, special education office, or from the local SSA office.
- Gather all income and resource information that will be required.
- Identify the job goal and steps for achieving it (which may be incorporated into the IEP/transition plan).
- Work with his or her vocational rehabilitation counselor to develop the plan.
- Make and keep an appointment with the local SSA office.
- Complete the PASS application and submit it to local SSA office.
- Answer questions from the SSI-PASS Cadre about the application.

The PASS should be considered during the IEP/transition development process even if it is not to be used while the individual is still a student. A PASS may be used by any individual participating in SSI at any age. Some students can benefit from a PASS while they are in school and also after they leave school to further their vocational goal by purchasing additional training or transportation, for example. As part of the transition planning process, the planning team may incorporate the future use of a PASS into the student's IEP/transition plan.

The most likely candidates for a PASS incentive are students who currently are receiving SSI benefits, want to work and have work goals in their IEP, are in school or a training program or plan to complete postsecondary training, or plan to start their own business.

A PASS incentive can be used to support a number of expenses related to employment goals, including tuition, fees, books, and supplies for school or training programs; supported employment services, including a job coach; attendant care; equipment and tools needed to work; and transportation.

A PASS incentive must:

- be specifically designed for the individual with a disability
- be in writing
- have a specific career goal that the individual is capable of achieving
- have a specific time frame for reaching the goal
- show what money or other resources the individual will use to reach the goal
- show how the money and resources will be used.
- show how the money set aside in the PASS will be kept separate from other funds (e.g., a separate bank account)
- be approved by the SSA
- be reviewed periodically to assure compliance

Income and resources that are set aside in a PASS are excluded under the SSI income and resources tests. Any transition student who receives SSI benefits or could qualify for them can have a PASS. A student, for example, whose income exceeds SSI requirements, may develop a PASS to maintain his or her SSI eligibility while pursuing work goals.

To receive a PASS an individual must complete a PASS application and submit it to the SSA office. Each PASS is reviewed for approval by the local PASS cadre. This process can take up to three months to complete. Anyone may help a student develop a PASS, including special education teachers and other school personnel, vocational counselors, social workers, employers, and private PASS vendors. A distinct advantage of a PASS is that it allows the student to be proactive in securing necessary training, support, or services to enhance employment opportunities.

Blind Work Expenses (BWE)

SSA has special rules for people who are blind, including allowing them to earn a higher income (Substantial Gainful Activity [SGA]) and maintain SSI eligibility.

Blindness is defined as central visual acuity of 20/200 or less in the better eye with best correction that has lasted or is expected to last a year or longer. Blind Work Expenses (BWE) is a work incentive that allows a blind person to deduct certain expenses needed to earn an income from their earned income when determining SSI eligibility and payment amount. For individuals who are blind, the BWE work incentive is more advantageous than the IRWE. Examples of BWE include guide dog expenses; transportation; federal, state, and local income taxes; Social Security taxes; attendant care services; visual and sensory aids; translation of materials into braille; professional association fees; and union dues. When developing transition plans for students who are blind, school personnel and parents should contact their regional SSA office to get more specific information on SSA programs and benefits available.

Property Essential to Self-Support (PESS)

PESS allows a person to exclude certain resources that are essential to employment for self-support. For example, property that is used in a trade or business or is required by a person as an employee is totally excluded when determining resources for SSI eligibility or payment determination. Although the PESS may have little application for secondary transition students, it may have utility for some students when they enter the workforce. A student, for example, who is trained in carpentry may be required to supply his or her own tools as terms of employment. Under a PESS, the value of these tools would not be counted as a resource.

The Role of School Personnel in Accessing
SSI Work Incentives

School personnel responsible for the successful transition of students from school to work and independent living can perform several functions to support the use of SSI work incentives as a viable part of transition planning. Specifically school personnel can:

- Identify students who are currently receiving SSI benefits and students who may be or will eligible.
- Incorporate SSI work incentives into the IEP/transition planning process and community-based employment.
- Inform students and parents about SSI program benefits and eligibility and work incentives when transition planning begins (age 14, or younger, if appropriate).
- Assist students and parents in collecting appropriate documentation on student's disability, limitations, performance, and behaviors that will assist SSA in determination or redetermination of eligibility.
- Establish a close relationship with local SSA staff to facilitate communication among students, parents, school personnel, and SSA staff.
- Collaborate with and engage other professionals (e.g., vocational rehabilitation, SSA, and human services) who share a common interest in students' secondary and postsecondary success.

Identify Potentially Eligible Students

Students eligible to receive SSI benefits can be identified through medical and psychological data alone. Some disabilities (e.g., blindness, hearing impairments, significant speech impairments, mental retardation, and autism as measured by an IQ under 60, and cerebral palsy with severe motor involvement) can be assumed to meet SSA's medically based criteria. Students who exhibit cognitive and emotional problems that will interfere with their ability to work may also be eligible. Students who are not receiving SSI benefits who may be, or will become, eligible at age 18 should be identified during the initial transition planning process. School personnel can also identify students who are receiving or will be eligible to receive SSDI benefits.

Incorporate SSI Work Incentives into the IEP/Transition Planning Process

Incorporating SSI work incentives into a student's IEP/transition plan can provide excellent opportunities for students, parents, and other IEP/transition team members to explore employment opportunities while the student is still in school. These incentives can also benefit students after they are out of school. To be eligible for SSI work incentives, a student must first be receiving SSI benefits and be engaged in paid work experiences (CBVE) as part of their transition plan. Therefore, it is important to explore and include work incentives in a student's transition plan in the very early stages of the process. This will assist students, parents, and other IEP/transition plan members in identifying specific steps that will be required to allow students to establish postschool goals and objectives and participate in school-sponsored employment opportunities. SSI work incentives can also help students plan for and save money toward a future career goal. Participating in SSI work incentives will, in most cases, allow students to increase their monthly income while still retaining their SSI benefits, including Medicaid.

Inform Students and Parents of SSI Program Benefits

School personnel can introduce and explain SSI work incentives to students and parents during the early stages of transition planning. Successful transition planning requires that school personnel, parents, students, and adult service providers work together to design a sequence of activities that will lead toward community participation and employment when a student exits school. Typically, community-based vocational education will be a focus of the initial transition discussions. Introducing work incentives early in the transition process establishes paid employment as a viable transition goal and allows students, parents, and other IEP/transition team members to broaden their collective thinking regarding available resources and the potential benefits of SSI work incentives. Just as school personnel inform parents and students about vocational rehabilitation and other adult services, so should they inform parents and help them gain knowledge about the SSI program eligibility requirements, benefits, and work incentives. As part of the transition planning process, school personnel routinely collect information on students and their families to assist in the design of plans that meet the goals and circumstances of the students and their family. Information regarding SSI eligibility or potential eligibility should be included in this information.

Applying and Reapplying for SSI Benefits

Many students and parents are unfamiliar with the SSI program and its application. School personnel can assist students and parents in the SSI application process by helping them complete the application form and referring them to the appropriate local SSA representatives. Once the student is determined eligible for benefits, the greater the opportunities for incorporating work incentives into the transition plan. It takes an average of three months to complete the application process; thus, it is crucial to begin the process during the early stages of the student's transition planning.

It is very important that all relevant documents—including medical history, school history, and functional limitations associated with any transition program work experiences—are gathered and organized for submission to the local SSA office. School staff can help gather appropriate school, social, and medical records, both past and present; make a list of all persons SSA may need to contact; and prepare school-based reports on the functional limitations of the student observed in school and in community-based settings. These reports may be excerpted from current assessment reports and/or IEPs/transition plans.

Short written reports with formal records that include specific examples of the student's functional limitations are extremely important. Information from clergy, relatives, family, and friends also can be useful when they describe specific examples of the student's functional limitations (Bazelton Center for Mental Health Law, 1997).

School personnel can also help parents develop their own anecdotal information on their son's or daughter's performance at home. Staff can assist students and parents in obtaining short, written reports from other people who have close contact or work with the student. These may include employers, job-site supervisors, or coworkers of students in community work settings. It's helpful when school staff and parents keep a diary of activities and functional limitations of students they observe over time.

Students and parents should ask all doctors who have seen the student for hospital, medical, and prescription records including reasons for medications. Hospital records should include dates, names of hospitals and attending doctors, and reasons for hospitalization. Sources for such documentation include doctors, psychologists, nurses, clinics, and hospitals; developmental centers, day care and preschool, school counselors and teachers; therapists; mental health counselors; and social workers and welfare agencies.

One of the most significant roles school personnel can play is providing SSA with information that documents observed student limitations in a variety of settings including school and community training and employment sites. Special education teachers, related service personnel, job coaches, and other school staff are in an excellent position to provide this information because they work with the student on a regular basis. Documented observations of the student's functional limitations by school personnel that impact or will impact on work performance will assist SSA examiners in the determination process.

School personnel can also assist students and parents with the redetermination process of SSI eligibility, which is required once the student reaches age 18. School personnel can help students and parents understand the differences in eligibility criteria for adults (18 and over) and children (under 18 years of age), and should be prepared to address questions regarding potential benefit loss, including Medicaid, if appropriate.Knowing and understanding the eligibility criteria allows school personnel and students and parents to develop appropriate documentation and records for the redetermination process. Often school assessment reports and IEPs/transition plans contain pertinent information regarding the student's functional limitations across environments; this is a critical component for initial determination and redetermination of eligibility.

Cooperative Working Relationships

It has been pointed out in this handbook that SSA staff have in-depth knowledge and experience in assisting youth with disabilities and parents in applying for SSI benefits and work incentives. Many local SSA offices have specific staff (e.g., work incentives liaisons and PASS specialists) assigned to work with transitioning youth and the SSI program. It is important for school personnel and other IEP/transition team members to establish a rapport with these individuals. This rapport will assist school personnel, the student and his or her parents, and other IEP/transition team members in facilitating the application process.

Regional PASS cadres have been established and operate throughout the country to specifically assist school personnel and the IEP/transition team in writing, reviewing, and evaluating PASSes. These cadres can be very helpful in developing a successful PASS application.

Applying for SSI Benefits and Work Incentives

Just as all members of the IEP team and others involved in the transition of youth with disabilities must support the goals and objectives of the student's IEP/transition plan, so is it important that they be familiar with and support the SSI application and work incentives processes for the student, especially when it is a component of the student's plan. Both application processes require submitting detailed documentation about the student to the SSA office. Various members of the student's IEP/transition team may have different knowledge about the student. For example, a student's family and friends will interact with the student in different environments than school personnel and will be familiar with different aspects of the student's behavior (e.g., basic skills levels and how the student functions in interpersonal relationships). Vocational rehabilitation and medical personnel are very likely to have critical information regarding the student's functional limitations. Engaging all of these individuals at some point in these SSI application processes will provide the SSA office with a complete and detailed picture of the student. All this information will assist state Disability Determination Services and SSA staff in determining the student's eligibility for SSI benefits and work incentives. IEP/transition team members and other professionals can also offer their previous knowledge of how to access SSI benefits and work incentives in an efficient manner.

FOOD STAMPS

The Food Stamp Program provides financial assistance by enabling recipients to exchange the stamps for food. It is a major supplement for income if an individual with a disability meets the income requirements. This program is federally funded through the Department of Agriculture's Food and Nutrition Service (FNS). It is administered by state and local social service agencies. In most cases, if an individual is eligible for SSI, food stamps will also be available. For more information, contact your local department of social services.

According to Schirm and Castner (2000), the Food Stamp Program is a central component of American policy to alleviate hunger and poverty. The program's main purpose is "to permit low income households to obtain a more nutritious diet . . . by increasing their purchasing power" (Food Stamp Act of 1977, as amended). The Food Stamp Program is the largest of the domestic food and nutrition assistance programs administered by the U.S. Department of Agriculture's Food and Nutrition Service. During fiscal year 2002, the program served over 19 million people in an average month at a total annual cost of over $18 billion in benefits. The average monthly food stamp benefit was about $185 per household.

Although the costs of the Food Stamp Program and other assistance programs are scrutinized during federal budget debates, the Government Performance and Results Act calls for policymakers to pay close attention to the effects of programs, not just total dollars spent. One important measure of a program's performance is its ability to reach its target population. The national food stamp participation rate—the percentage of eligible people in the United States who actually participate in the program—has been a standard for assessing performance for over 15 years. Recent studies have also examined participation rates for socioeconomic and demographic subgroups of the national population (Cunnyngham, cited in Schirm and Castner, 2002) and rates for states (Schirm and Castner, 2002b).

The U.S. Department of Agriculture (USDA) prohibits discrimination in all its programs and activities on the basis of race, color, national origin, sex, religion, age, disability, political beliefs, sexual orientation, or marital or family status. (Not all pro-hibited bases apply to all programs.) Persons with disabilities who require alternative means for communication of program information (braille, large print, audiotape, etc.) should contact USDA's TARGET Center at (202) 720-2600 (voice and TDD).

To file a complaint of discrimination, write USDA, Director, Office of Civil Rights, Room 326-W, Whitten Building, 1400 Independence Avenue, S.W., Washington, D.C. 20250-9410 or call (202) 720-5964 (voice and TDD). USDA is an equal opportunity provider and employer.

HEALTH INSURANCE ISSUES

A great deal of financial, social, and medical support is available within the community, state, or country, but it is up to the parent to wade through the vast amount of terminology, forms, agencies, issues, and so on to find the best direction for a particular child. As a special educator involved in the transition process, it is crucial for you to be knowledgeable about all the areas of health insurance that exist so that you can assist the parents in this very important area. The path to the correct resources will differ from family to family as a result of the family's personal financial situation, the type of available health insurance, the child's specific medical needs, the state in which the family resides, and the family's understanding of its rights and responsibilities.

EXPLORING INSURANCE OPTIONS

The importance of exploring all the available options and avenues of assistance cannot be stressed enough; being proactive in this area is essential. The first thing parents need to know is how to locate general sources of medical, financial, and insurance assistance. Through these sources parents will find the best-quality health care at the least risk. Following this process can help the family discover several options that may reduce their costs.

Medical care and insurance have gone through major changes in the last five years with the advent of *health maintenance organizations (HMOs)*. These organizations assist insurance companies by evaluating and authorizing appropriate medical care. The best available medical insurance policy for a child with disabilities may already have been determined by the parents' company's insurance carrier. If the parents do not currently have a policy or are considering changing their current policy, they will be confronted with many different options. Several individuals and agencies can be contacted for assistance in making this decision. They include:

- the office of social services in the medical facility where the child is treated or cared for
- the primary care physician
- the agent or claims representative in the company with which the parent may have health insurance
- the billing department for a specific physician or medical facility
- the state department of health

When contacting these individuals or agencies, have the parent develop a script beforehand and keep a piece of paper or notebook handy to take notes on each conversation. They will also have to keep track of the offices to which they are referred, insurance policy details, and state support systems.

There are people who can help parents identify resources in their own community and in their state, as well as help them learn the questions to ask. These people are the parents and care providers who have been there. They can empathize with the complexity of the details—phone calls, correspondence, medical forms, financial forms, and lingering questions. It may be helpful to contact parent groups and disability organizations near the school or community to ask for help in research. Associations concerned with specific disabilities can provide helpful information. Even if there is not an association for the child's specific needs, another group whose members also have complex medical needs will have information on financing these needs.

When parents contact these individuals or agencies, they will need to offer the following information so that they may be given the best options for their situation: the health care needs of the child, the family medical insurance situation, outstanding expenses, and what the family needs.

KINDS OF INSURANCE POLICIES

Before choosing an insurance policy, contact your personnel department, insurance broker, or state department of insurance. You may want to consider one of the following three kinds of policies: a health maintenance organization (HMO), an indemnity plan, or a preferred provider organization (PPO).

Health maintenance organizations (HMOs) represent prepaid or "capitated" insurance plans in which individuals or their employers pay a fixed monthly fee for services instead of a separate charge for each visit or service. The monthly fees remain the same, regardless of the types or levels of services provided. There is usually a small copayment required for approved doctor's visits. Services are provided by physicians employed by, or under contract with, the HMO. HMOs vary in design. Depending on the type of HMO, services may be provided in a central facility or in a physician's own office.

A health maintenance organization (HMO) is a type of managed health care system. HMOs and their close cousins, preferred provider organizations (PPOs), share the goal of reducing health care costs by focusing on preventative care and implementing utilization management controls.

Unlike many traditional insurers, HMOs do not merely provide financing for medical care. The HMO actually delivers the treatment as well. Doctors, hospitals, and insurers all participate in the business arrangement known as an HMO.

HMOs provide medical treatment on a prepaid basis, which means that HMO members pay a fixed monthly fee, regardless of how much medical care is needed in a given month. In return for this fee, most HMOs provide a wide variety of medical services, from office visits to hospitalization and surgery. With a few exceptions, HMO members must receive their medical treatment from physicians and facilities within the HMO network. The size of this network varies depending on the individual HMO (Fidelity Investments, 2002). When you join an HMO, you choose a primary care physician (PCP) who is your first contact for all medical care needs. The primary care physician provides your general medical care and must be consulted before you can see a specialist. Because of this control system, HMO costs tend to increase less rapidly than other insurance plans.

Indemnity health insurance plans are also called fee-for-service plans. These plans existed before the rise of HMOs. With indemnity plans, the individual pays a predetermined percentage of the cost of health care services, and the insurance company (or self-insured employer) pays the other percentage. For example, an individual might pay 20 percent for services and the insurance company pays 80 percent. The fees for services are defined by the providers and vary from physician to physician. Indemnity health plans offer individuals the freedom to choose their health care professionals (*Insurance Glossary,* 2003).

Preferred provider organizations (PPOs) offer discounted rates if the patient uses doctors from a preselected group. If an individual uses a physician outside the PPO plan, the individual must pay more for the medical care.

Calculated Decisions

Deciding between an HMO, PPO, or indemnity plan is usually based on personal preferences with respect to freedom of choice and one's ability to pay for that freedom. There are medical factors, however, that may influence an individual's informed decision. Parents may also want to consider the following by estimating the expected, predictable health care needs of each family member over the next year:

- How many visits to the doctor are expected for such preventive services as childhood immunizations, mammograms, Pap tests, or sigmoidoscopies?
- Is the individual planning to start a family? Will a child be born in the current year or next?
- Is the condition chronic, such as diabetes that requires ongoing medication?
- What is the individual's philosophy about medical services and health care professionals? Does the individual tend to go to the doctor for minor problems that in most cases would clear up on their own? Does the individual practice medical self-care in attempts to avoid going to the physician?
- What was the average cost for health care services for the family over the past two years?

Have parents try to estimate the likelihood of unpredictable health care needs of each family member over the next year. Have parents ask the following questions:

- How healthy have family members been in the past?
- Does a member of the family have a chronic condition that requires sporadic visits to a health care professional?
- Does anyone in the family smoke?
- Does anyone consume more than a reasonable amount of alcohol, that is, according to state standards?
- Is the individual sedentary or does he or she exercise regularly?

Although answers to the preceding questions will not tell you which plan is best for the individual and his or her family, they can help estimate health care costs over the next year. Then the family can compare the estimated costs of the various plans to see which plan is likely to be the best.

MEDICARE

Born out of the 1960s, *Medicare* was a response to growing concerns about the high cost of medical care for older Americans. Since that time, however, the program has expanded to include not only older Americans but also millions of adults with disabilities. Unlike Medicaid (discussed later), which is based solely on financial need, the right to Medicare benefits is established primarily by payroll tax contributions. Medicare is a federal health care insurance program that provides some medical coverage to people over 65 and also to individuals with disabilities for a limited period of time. Medicare will help meet some bills for long-term care but will not fund unlimited long-term care. To meet uncovered costs, you may need supplemental or *medigap* insurance policies. Medigap insurance is offered by private insurance companies, not the government. It is not the same as Medicare or Medicaid. These policies are designed to pay for some of the costs that Medicare does not cover.

Medicare is a federal program that provides health insurance to retired individuals, regardless of their medical condition. Following are some basic facts about Medicare you should know (Fidelity Investments, 2002):

Medicare coverage consists of two parts—Medicare Part A (hospital insurance) and Medicare Part B (medical insurance). A third part, Medicare Part C (Medicare + Choice) is a program that allows you to choose from several types of health care plans.

> **Medicare Part A (hospital insurance).** Generally known as hospital insurance, Part A covers services associated with inpatient hospital care (e.g., the costs associated with an overnight stay in a hospital, skilled nursing facility, or psychiatric hospital, such as charges for the hospital room, meals, and nursing services). Part A also covers hospice care and home health care.
>
> **Medicare Part B (medical insurance).** Generally known as medical insurance, Part B covers other medical care. Physician care—whether it was received while you were an inpatient at a hospital, at a doctor's office, or as an outpatient at a hospital or other health care facility—is covered under Part B. Also covered are laboratory tests, physical therapy or rehabilitation services, and ambulance service.
>
> **Medicare Part C (Medicare + Choice).** The 1997 Balanced Budget Act expanded the kinds of private health care plans that may offer Medicare benefits to include managed care plans, medical savings accounts, and private fee-for-service plans. The new Medicare Part C programs are in addition to the fee-for-service options available under Medicare Parts A and B.

MEDICAID

Medicaid is a federal-state program that helps pay for health care for nonelderly people who are financially needy or who have a disability. Individual states determine who is eligible for Medicaid and which health services will be covered. Most people do not qualify for Medicaid until the majority of their money has been spent. It is important to realize, however, that some individuals whose incomes are not in the lowest category but who have substantial medical expenses do qualify for Medicaid. These individuals—who either have incomes higher than the AFDC (Aid for Families with Dependent Children) cutoff or have very high medical bills that drop their incomes below the level established for "categorically needy"—are considered "medically needy." Once an individual is covered by Medicaid, he or she is entitled to receive the following minimal services:

- physician services
- laboratory and X-ray services
- outpatient hospital services
- skilled nursing facilities (SNF) for persons over 21
- family planning services
- medical diagnosis and treatment for persons under 21
- home health services for individuals
- inpatient hospital service

In many states, Medicaid will also pay for some or all of the following:

- dental care
- medically necessary drugs

- eyeglasses
- prosthetic devices
- physical, speech, and occupational therapy
- private-duty nursing
- alternative medical care, for example, chiropractors, acupuncturists
- diagnostic, preventive, screening, and rehabilitative services
- inpatient psychiatric care

Federal law dictates that states may not reduce other welfare benefits people receive when they become eligible for Medicaid. Also, states may not impose citizenship or residency requirements other than requiring that an applicant be a resident of the state. Neither the age of the applicant nor the fact that he or she works restrict eligibility to receive Medicaid.

Since its inception, the program has been plagued by fraud from both health care providers and patients. To curb this fraud, Congress passed a law in 1996 making persons criminally liable for committing fraud in order to become eligible for medical assistance (Legal Information Institute, 2003).

MEDICAID WAIVERS

Waivers are intended to provide the flexibility needed to enable states to try new or different approaches to the efficient and cost-effective delivery of health care services or to adapt their programs to the special needs of particular areas or groups of recipients.

A waiver under Section 1915(c) of the Social Security Act allows a state to include as "medical assistance" under its Medicaid plan home- and community-based services furnished to recipients who would otherwise need inpatient care that is furnished in a hospital, skilled nursing facility, intermediate-care facility, or intermediate-care facility for individuals with mental retardation (ICF/MR), and is reimbursable under the state plan (Assistive Technology Partners, 2003). Each state determines which services will be reimbursed by Medicaid. If you have any questions, contact your local social services agency.

Beginning in 1981, states have been able to obtain formal permission from the federal Medicaid agency (HCFA—Health Care Financing Administration) to set aside typical Medicaid restrictions. This permission allows for services to be provided in the home or community to certain individuals who would otherwise have to be institutionalized in order to be eligible for Medicaid.

Now in states with Medicaid waivers, children can stay at home when medically possible and, under certain conditions, not have their parents' income deemed (counted as belonging) to them. Also, under some waivers, some nonmedical services, such as *respite care* (discussed in Chapter 11), may now be covered by Medicaid.

The types of Medicaid waivers include the following:

Model Medicaid waiver. Under this provision, states apply to the federal government for waivers before they can cover services traditionally covered by the Medicaid program in that state for persons who would have to be institutionalized. The requirement to consider income is waived to allow medically eligible persons to qualify for this program. Each state defines requirements for eligibility.

Home- and community-based medical waiver. Under this provision, states that apply to the federal government for waivers can cover services typically financed under Medicaid (as the model Medicaid waiver does) and go beyond to cover additional services in the community. These additional services are identified as "waivered services" in the community. Home- and community-based waivers are available for certain categories of individuals who otherwise would be institutionalized and who meet qualifications specified by the state for this waiver.

State Medicaid Plan Option. Another strategy states can use to help families become eligible for Medicaid is to amend the state plan. With this approach, states can provide, without obtaining special permission from the federal government, medical services to certain designated categories of children who would otherwise be institutionalized or hospitalized. Instead, a state plan, approved by the federal government, certifies categories of children who meet these qualifications.

CONCLUSION

Dealing with the issue of entitlements is often frustrating, but it's important to persevere. For specific information about the benefits provided through SSDI and SSI, contact your local Social Security Office (listed in the telephone directory under "Social Security Administration") and request a copy of the publications addressing SSI and SSDI. Single copies are free. You can also contact the SSA through its toll-free number: (800) 234-5772 (voice) or (800)325-0778 (TDD); it is available 24 hours a day. Because of the volume of inquiries that SSA receives, it is best to call early in the morning or late in the afternoon. SSA also recommends calling later in the week.

Remember, not every service is available and not every person can be helped 100 percent. Keep in mind that every year new programs begin and some old ones end, particularly at the state and local levels. Have your students and their parents keep in touch with their contacts and stay as aware as they can, through reading and talking to knowledgeable people about what is happening in the area of services for individuals with disabilities. There are many excellent voluntary organizations as well as state, local, and federal offices that can help you. Numerous newsletters are produced by groups of and for individuals with disabilities. Using the Internet can connect people to much information and innumerable resources.

One of the major aspects of coping with a disability is educating oneself about both the disabling condition and what is available to enhance one's quality of life. Initially, the task of acquiring information falls to the families and the professionals they encounter. This information, however, must be passed on to the young person so that, as much as possible, he or she can achieve a satisfying independent life.

As of the spring of 1996, vast changes have been made in the Welfare Reform Act. Consequently, each state is in the process of revising its legislation in accordance with the new federal guidelines. The ultimate effect will not be known for some time. It is clear, however, that in many cases, benefits will be diminished. Each individual situation should be explored with the local Department of Social Service and Social Security Administration.

Because of these changes, this may be a time to help the student and his or her family become proactive or to renew their commitment to advocate for the needs of their family and community.

CHAPTER FOURTEEN

ESTATE PLANNING

OVERVIEW

This chapter will focus on one very important and often complicated issue that parents confront when they have a son or daughter with any type of disability—how to plan their estate to best provide for the child's future security. Parents often may ask themselves:

- What will our son or daughter do when we are no longer here to provide help when it's needed?
- Where and how will our child live?
- Will he or she have enough income to sustain a decent quality of life?

Other questions parents may ask themselves focus on the estate planning process itself:

- How do I know that my estate plan is going to work?
- Do I have enough money to hire a lawyer and write a will?
- Do I even have anything to leave my children?

These are very difficult questions for parents to consider and difficult ones to answer. When a child has a disability—whether it is mild, moderate, or severe—parents have concerns about that child's future. The information provided in this chapter is relevant both to a family whose child is already independent or is expected to be so and to one whose child will need moderate or extensive support or supervision throughout life.

Parents may have a tentative plan in the back of their minds that one day, in the near or distant future, they will write a will that leaves their son or daughter with a disability sufficient resources to make his or her life secure. Many of them may have already written such a will; yet there are many things to know and consider when planning an estate.

For example, bequeathing a person with a disability any assets worth more than $2,000 may cause the person to become ineligible for government benefits such as SSI and Medicaid. For many individuals with disabilities, the loss of these benefits would be a devastating blow. In addition to the cash benefits and medical coverage that would be lost, the person would also lose any number of other government benefits that may be available to eligible persons with disabilities, such as supported employment and vocational rehabilitation services, group housing, job coaches, personal attendant care, and transportation assistance. Therefore, it is our hope that you, as a special educator, will read and thoroughly consider the information presented in this chapter. The future security of many parents' sons or daughters with a disability may well depend on the actions you take to help them establish an estate plan appropriate to their child's needs. After reading this chapter, you should understand the following:

HOW THE TYPE OF DISABILITY AFFECTS ESTATE PLANNING

Disabilities, of course, can take many forms and have varying degrees of severity. The nature and severity of a child's disability will affect the nature of the estate plan that parents develop. According to Hill, Glowacki, Jaeger, and Hughes, LLP (2001), an individual with disabilities often can't manage assets and income without assistance. In some cases, the individual requires the protection of guardianship. Individuals with a disability or diminished capacity sometimes qualify for and receive government benefits, such as SSI, SSDI, Medicare, Medicaid (MA, also known as Medical Assistance or Title 19), COP, CIP, and/or other similar benefits. Some but not all of these benefits programs are unavailable to individuals with assets over $2,000 plus certain exempt assets. There also are income limitations for the benefits programs with asset limitations.

If an individual receiving SSI and MA receives income or a gift or inheritance, he or she may lose those government benefits. With proper planning, there are legal ways to avoid this problem. Thus, parents, grandparents, siblings, and other relatives or friends desiring to provide for their family member or friend with disabilities should see an attorney experienced in estate planning for persons with disabilities who stays current with the constantly changing federal and state laws, regulations, and policies concerning qualification for these benefits programs. Even if an individual with disabilities does not receive SSI or MA, acquiring income, a gift, or an inheritance may create problems due to the recipient's inability to manage the increased financial resources. Appropriate estate planning can avoid these potential problems, too.

Physical Disabilities or Health Impairments

Many individuals have *physical disabilities* or *health impairments* that do not affect their ability to manage financial or other affairs. If a student with a disability has such a condition, how to leave an estate depends on a number of factors. The primary factor will be whether he or she receives (or may one day need to depend on) government benefits such as Supplemental Security Insurance (SSI), subsidized housing, personal attendant care, or Medicaid. If a child does receive (or may one day need to depend on) government benefits, then it is most important for parents to create a special estate plan that does not negate his or her eligibility for those benefits. How to do this is discussed in some detail in this chapter.

If a child with a physical disability or health impairment is not eligible for or is not receiving government benefits, parents may be able to dispense with elaborate planning devices and merely leave their child money outright, as they would to any other individual. If they believe that the disability may reduce their son's or daughter's financial earning capability, they may want to take special care to leave a greater portion of their estate to this child. There are some exceptions to this simplified approach; for example, if parents are concerned that a son or daughter with a disability may not responsibly handle an inheritance, then they can utilize a trust, just as they would for any other heir.

Another exception is if a child's disability or health impairment involves the possibility of deteriorating health and more involved health care needs in the future. Although the child may be capable of earning money and managing an inheritance at present or in the immediate future, in 20 or 30 years' time, deteriorating health may make it difficult for him or her to maintain employment or pay for health care. Government benefits might then become critical to the child's security. Remember, benefits include much more than money; the child may also be eligible for valuable services such as health care, vocational rehabilitation, supported employment, subsidized housing, and personal attendant care. If, however, a child acquires too many assets through inheriting all or part of an estate, he or she may be ineligible for these benefits. Therefore, in order to protect a child's eligibility for government benefits at some point in the future and to provide for his or her long-range needs, you should inform parents that they may have to consider establishing a special estate plan.

Cognitive Disabilities or Mental Illness

If a child's disability affects his or her mental capability, the need to create a special estate plan is clearer. Mental illness and *cognitive disabilities* often impair a person's ability to manage his or her own financial affairs while simultaneously increasing financial need. As a result, parents must take care to ensure that there are assets available after their death to help their son or daughter, while also providing that the assets are protected from his or her inability to manage them. More information will be given later in this chapter.

HOW TO START PLANNING AN ESTATE

Parents who have a son or daughter with a disability should give careful consideration to developing an estate plan that provides for that person's future best interests. Here are some suggestions that you, as a special educator, can give parents to help them approach planning their estate:

1. Realistically assess your son's or daughter's disability and the prognosis for future development. If necessary, obtain a professional evaluation of your child's prospects and capability to earn a living and to manage financial assets. If your son or daughter is already an adult, you should have a fairly clear understanding of his or her capabilities, but if your child is younger, it may be more difficult to predict the future. In such cases, you should take a conservative view. It is better to anticipate all possibilities, good and bad, in such a way that you do not limit your loved one's potential or set him or her up for unrealistic expectations. Remember, too, that you can change your estate plan as more information about your child becomes available.

2. Carefully inventory your financial affairs. Estimate the size of your estate (what you own) if you should die within the next year or the next 10 years. Keep in mind that the will you write governs your affairs at the time of your death, and so it must be flexible enough to meet a variety of situations. Of course, you can always write a new will, but you may never actually write it because of a hectic schedule, procrastination, or oversight.

3. Consider the living arrangements of your son or daughter with a disability. Your child's living arrangements after your death are of paramount importance. Every parent of an individual with a disability should give thought to the questions, "If (my spouse and) I should die tomorrow, where would our child live? What are the possibilities available to him or her?" The prospective living arrangements of your son or daughter will have a tremendous impact on how your estate should be distributed. Involved in answering the question of living arrangements is whether or not your child will need a guardian or conservator to make decisions for him or her after your death. If you conclude that a guardian or conservator is necessary, you should be prepared to recommend a potential guardian or conservator in your will.

4. Analyze the earning potential of your son or daughter; it is important to determine how much your child can be expected to earn as a result of employment. If he or she is currently employed, does this employment meet all of his or her living expenses, or only some? If your child is currently too young to be employed, you will have to project into the future. In many cases, even if your son or daughter is employed or expected to be employed at some point in the future, he or she will require additional financial assistance.

5. Consider which *government benefits* your son or daughter needs and is eligible to receive. Support for a person with a disability will usually come from state and federal benefits. These might be actual case grants, such as Social Security or Supplemental Security Income, or they might be in-kind support programs, such as subsidized housing or sheltered workshop employment.

Financial concerns and government benefits can be divided into the following three categories.

1. Those categories that are unaffected by the financial resources of the beneficiary. For example, Social Security Disability Insurance (SSDI) beneficiaries receive their benefits without regard to financial need. Regardless of what a parent leaves to a son or daughter with a disability, the Social Security payments will still be forthcoming once the person has qualified for them.

2. Some government benefits, such as supplemental security income (SSI) and Medicaid, have financial eligibility requirements. If a person with a disability has too many assets or too much income, he or she is not eligible to receive some or all of these benefits. Someone who is eligible due to a lack of financial resources can become ineligible on inheriting money, property, or other assets, leading to a reduction or termination of the SSI benefits for that person. Therefore, if your son or daughter is receiving government benefits that have financial eligibility requirements, it is important to arrange your estate in a manner that will minimize his or her loss of benefits, especially SSI or Medicaid.

3. Government programs are available to individuals with disabilities where payment for services is determined according to the person's ability to pay. Many states will charge the individual with a disability for programmatic benefits if he or she has sufficient assets or income. The most striking is the charge that can be levied against residents of state mental institutions. For example, if a resident of a state hospital inherits a substantial sum of money, the state will begin charging the resident for the cost of residency in the state hospital and will continue to charge until all the money is exhausted, yet the services provided will be no different from the ones that he or she was previously receiving.

GUARDIANSHIP

Parents are the natural guardians of their children until age 18, when the power to make decisions on their behalf ends. A court must authorize any future guardianship powers once a person legally becomes an adult. In the past, most individuals with disabilities had public guardians or conservators. Although the commissioner of human services was the technical guardian, the acting guardian or conservator was usually a staff member from the county social service department. In recent years, an effort has been made to recruit family members and other concerned individuals to assume the role of guardian or conservator.

Guardianship is the result of a court hearing that establishes the need to appoint an individual (guardian) to assume substitute decision-making powers for another person (ward) who is not capable of exercising his or her rights due to incapacity or incompetence. The standard for determining incapacity generally requires that a person is functionally unable to care for self or property and cannot communicate decisions regarding care for self or property. This incapacity must be the result of a disorder or disability.

Guardianship is the most restrictive limitation on personal decision-making authority that a court can impose on a person. The ward automatically loses the right to vote, the right to choose where to live, the right to approve medical procedures, the right to enter contracts, and other essential decisions. The role of the guardian is to act in the best interests of the ward in making decisions regarding financial matters or personal needs that have been authorized by the court. The duties of a guardian are defined by law. Only a court can establish guardianship.

CONSERVATORSHIP (LIMITED GUARDIANSHIP)

Conservatorship is a less restrictive form of substitute decision making by a person (*conservator*) for another person (*conservatee*) that may include some, but not all, of the duties of guardianship. The conservatee does not automatically lose the right to vote because he or she is not considered incapacitated in all areas. Conservatorships can be tailored to include assistance with certain activities only. If the conservatee is capable of making some essential decisions, conservatorship is preferable to guardianship. A conservator's duties are established by the court based on law, and a formal hearing similar to a guardianship proceeding is required.

TYPES OF GUARDIANSHIP AND CONSERVATORSHIP

An individual can be appointed a guardian or conservator of the person, the estate, or both:

> **Guardian of the person and estate.** Has the full scope of powers and duties concerning every major aspect of the ward's life.
>
> **Conservator of the person and estate.** Has only some of the powers of the guardian.

Guardian of the person. Makes decisions concerning the ward's place of living, care, comfort, maintenance, employment, training, personal effects, medical procedures, entering into contracts, and social/recreational needs.

Conservator of the person. Has some of the powers of the guardian depending on the person's needs.

Guardian of the estate. Assumes responsibilities for taking control of the ward's property, preparing a written inventory, keeping adequate records, determining and collecting all income, paying debts from the ward's assets, paying taxes, and filing an annual written report to the court about the assets, receipts, and disbursements of the estate.

Conservator of the estate. Assists the conservatee with those specific financial matters that the court has authorized.

Unless the person has substantial assets, it may not be necessary to seek guardianship or conservatorship of the estate since there are detailed accounting procedures required. If your family member does not have significant assets, consult the clerk of your local county probate court to see if the court will allow you to avoid seeking guardianship or conservatorship of the estate.

Choosing a Guardian or Conservator

A close relative or friend over age 18 is usually the best choice to be a guardian or conservator, as long as that person is willing and able to meet all the responsibilities. If a close relative or friend is not available, a concerned professional or representative from an organization offering guardianship or conservatorship services may be appropriate.

It is important to note that although parents may state in their will that they want a particular individual to serve as guardian or conservator after their death, this is not legally binding. That individual must still go to court and go through the same proceedings that the original guardian or conservator went through to obtain guardianship or conservatorship. Therefore, it is advisable to consider adding another family member or friend in the original petition to the court.

ALTERNATIVES TO GUARDIANSHIP AND CONSERVATORSHIP

Based on an assessment of the functional and decisional skill level of a family member, parents may decide that one of the several alternatives to guardianship or conservatorship may be more appropriate. The alternatives that follow are considered "less restrictive" because they do not restrict an individual's rights as severely as guardianship or conservatorship.

Appointment of a Representative Payee

Individuals receiving Supplemental Security Income (SSI) or Social Security Disability Income (SSDI) may receive the benefit checks directly, or the checks can be sent to a representative payee who will assist the beneficiary with financial management and payment of obligations. A representative payee is appointed by the Social Security Administration and is typically a parent or social worker. Court action is not needed to establish a representative payee, but regular reports must be submitted to the Social Security Administration detailing how the money was spent. A separate bank account must also be maintained for the beneficiary's money.

Contact the Social Security Administration for further information on the appointment of a representative payee.

Power of Attorney

If the person is a competent adult, he or she may authorize, in a private written agreement, another individual to assume power of attorney. A *power-of-attorney* agreement authorizes a person to enter into legal agreements and manage financial affairs in the name of another person. The person given power of attorney does not have to be a lawyer; any competent person can play this role. A power-of-attorney agreement terminates on the death of the principal or if the principal is determined to be incompetent. Parents should consult with a lawyer before setting up a power-of-attorney agreement.

Special Needs Trust

The only reliable method of making sure that the inheritance actually reaches a person with a disability when he or she needs it is through the legal device known as a *special needs trust (SNT)*. The SNT is developed to manage resources while maintaining the individual's eligibility for public assistance benefits.

This trust agreement for the benefit of a person with a disability allows for a fund to be created that will pay for items and services not covered by Medicaid and other governmental benefits. The trust should be set up by an attorney, and parents may want to consult a financial planner for additional assistance. A trustee will be authorized to spend money on behalf of the individual with disabilities for supplemental purposes such as recreational opportunities, vacations, personal items, Christmas and birthday gifts, and so forth. It is essential that parents consult with an attorney so that all of the implications of any changes in the interpretation of the law are clearly understood and communicated to you. The Social Security Administration has publications, entitled *Understanding SSI,* that discuss special needs trusts and should be carefully reviewed by parents.

Joint Bank Account

An account set up by a bank allowing joint access to the account may allow parents to supervise or assist their family member with finances. This type of informal assistance may be sufficient to monitor finances when minimal supervision is required.

Informal Advocacy

For families who choose not to go the route of guardianship, the other alternative is to seek out an informal advocate who will carry out the conditions as stated in a letter of intent. Be aware that parents can appoint more than one advocate—each responsible for a different area of concern (e.g., financial or legal needs)—or a public agency to oversee their child's well-being. Relatives usually make the best advocates because of their special knowledge of the needs of the family member. A friend or professional may be able to assist on an occasional basis. You can inform parents not to overlook the assistance that can be provided by natural support systems such as other family members, church communities, neighbors, social clubs, and so on. This informal advocate can assist their family member in meetings with case managers, social service providers, and individuals in the community, as well as in financial, social, employment, residence, or recreational issues that may be faced by their child.

CONSEQUENCES OF NOT FILING FOR GUARDIANSHIP OR CONSERVATORSHIP

Because the natural guardianship powers of parents ends when a son or daughter turns 18, parents may lose the right to access records and to make decisions unless authorization is obtained from the court. If guardianship or conservatorship is appropriate for an individual with a disability, failure to seek these powers may result in a loss of power to consent to ordinary or necessary medical care, loss of access to medical records, loss of authority to challenge school or residential facility programs, and other rights previously held. He or she may also have trouble having an individual service plan (ISP) developed. For an exact explanation of rights under this section, you should tell parents to contact a lawyer who specializes in the rights of those with disabilities.

LETTER OF INTENT

A *letter of intent* is a document written by the parents or guardians or other family members that describe their son's or daughter's history, his or her current status, and what they hope for their child in the future. Parents would be wise to write this letter today and add to it as the years go by, updating it when information about their son or daughter changes. To the maximum extent possible, it is also a good idea to involve their child in the writing of this letter, so that the letter truly represents him or her. The letter is then ready at any moment to be used by all the individuals who will be involved in caring for their son or daughter should the parents become ill or disabled themselves or when the parents die. Even though the letter of intent is not a legal document, the courts and others can rely on the letter for guidance in understanding their son or daughter and following their wishes. In this way, parents can continue to "speak out" on behalf of their son or daughter, providing insight and knowledge about his or her own best possible care.

What Happens Once the Letter of Intent Is Written?

Once parents have written the letter of intent about their son or daughter, the first, most important thing to do is to let people know that there is a letter of intent available to be consulted. This might mean telling their other children (or relatives, neighbors, friends, workshop director, pastor, or case manager) why they have written the letter, what type of information it contains, and where the letter can be found. Tell parents to put the letter in an easily accessible place and make it clearly identifiable. Many parents also make copies of the letter and give it to their other children (or other concerned individuals).

Second, parents should update the letter on a regular basis. They should select one day out of each year (such as the last day of school or perhaps your son's or daughter's birthday) where they will review what they have written and add any new information of importance. They should talk with their child each time and incorporate his or her ideas. After each addition, sign and date the letter. Should something change in their child's life, such as his or her caseworker or the medication he or she is taking, update the letter immediately. In conclusion, will the letter of intent overcome all of the obstacles to their son's or daughter's transition into someone else's care? No, of course not. The letter is of immediate usefulness, however, in coping with their son's or daughter's changed situation and, in the long term, will certainly help care providers understand and care for their child.

How to Involve an Individual with a Disability in Writing the Letter of Intent

How much a parent involves their son or daughter in writing the letter of intent will depend in large part on his or her age and the nature and severity of the disability. It is only fitting that young adults and adult children be involved in planning their own lives to the maximum extent possible. Many individuals have disabilities that do not prevent their full or partial participation in the letter-writing process.

Before involving a child, however, parents might want to talk first between themselves about the content of the letter and their ideas regarding their child's future. When they've agreed on the basic information they feel should go in the letter, they should discuss each area with their son or daughter. Ask for their child's input about his or her favorite things to do, what type of education has been enjoyable and what might be pursued in the future, and what type of employment he or she enjoys or envisions. Equally crucial to discuss are their child's future living arrangements: How does their child feel about the options they are considering listing in the letter of intent?

It's important for a child to realize that the letter is not a binding, legal document; it is written to give guidance, not edicts, to all those involved in caregiving in the future. If you or the parents fear that the child will be upset by talking about a future that does not involve parents, then you may wish to make the discussion simply about the future—what will happen when the child leaves high school or a postsecondary training program, what the child wants to be or do in the next 10 years, and where he or she wants to live. You, and especially parents, may be surprised to find that discussing the future actually relieves a child. He or she may very well be worrying about what will happen when his or her parents are no longer there to provide whatever assistance is needed.

Involving a child in discussing and making decisions about the future may be more difficult if the individual has a disability that severely limits his or her ability to communicate or to judge among a variety of options. You, as a special educator, and the parents are probably the best judges of how much—and how—you can involve a child with a severe cognitive disability. For these children, the letter is especially critical; it will serve to communicate the vital information about themselves that they cannot.

What to Include in the Letter of Intent

Although a letter of intent is not a legal document, it gives the future caregiver a very thorough specific description of the child, his or her need, and the parents' wishes on their child's care in case they are no longer able. Keep in mind that the letters may vary in their content and scope; however, there are several general areas that should be addressed. These include:

- **Behavior management.** What consistent approach has worked best in the parents' absence?
- **Daily living skills.** Average daily schedule, activities.
- **Day program or work.** Present, past, and future.
- **Education.** The parents have a lifelong perspective of their son's or daughter's educational history and goals.
- **Employment.** What has the child enjoyed? Consider his or her goals, aspirations, and limitations.
- **Financial issues.** Benefits, services, financial holdings, assets.

- **General information on the parents.** Vital statistics on the parents, that is, names, addresses, phone, Social Security numbers, blood type.
- **Leisure and recreation.** Structured and unstructured activities, vacations, fitness programs.
- **Marital status of the individual with disabilities.** If the student with disabilities is married, wife's or husband's name, address, phone.
- **Number of dependents.** List the names and birthdates of dependent children.
- **Medical care.** What has and has not worked with the child?
- **Medical history and care.** Diagnosis, function, facilities, blood type, insurance, doctors' and dentists' names and addresses, mental status, other therapies, allergies, diseases, procedures, operations.
- **Other relationships.** Friends and relatives with whom the individual has close relationships.
- **Religion.** Is there a special church, synagogue, or person your son or daughter relates to in the religious community? Faith, name of clergy, and participation.
- **Residence.** If something should happen to the parents tomorrow, where will their son or daughter live? What would be the best living arrangement? Does their child need adaptive devices?
- **Siblings information.** Names, phone numbers, addresses, nature of relationship.
- **Social.** What activities make life meaningful for the child?

Additional Considerations for the Letter of Intent

Advocate/Guardian.   Who will look after, fight for, and be a friend to the child? (Parents should list three to four people.)

Trustee(s).   Whom do the parents trust to manage their son's or daughter's supplementary funds? (List three or four people.)

For each applicable area mentioned in the letter of intent, consider the child's future. Parents should list three or four options to guide future caregivers in decision making and interaction with their child. They should draw on what they know about their son or daughter, through observation and through discussion with their child, and share what they've learned.

WRITING A WILL

All parents, and particularly parents of individuals with disabilities, should have a will. The object of the will is to ensure that all of the assets of the deceased parent are distributed according to his or her wishes. If at death parents have no will, their property will be dispersed according to the law of the state in which they live at the time of their death. This law is called the *state's law of intestacy.* Although laws of intestacy vary from state to state, in general they provide that some percentage of assets of the decedent passes to the surviving spouse and the rest is distributed to the children in equal shares. Writing a will is highly recommended, since the laws of intestacy are rarely the most desirable way to pass property to one's heirs.

Although it is theoretically possible for any individual to write a will on his or her own, it is unwise to do so. Because of the technical nature of wills, it is highly advisable to have a lawyer prepare one. Parents of individuals with disabilities particularly need legal advice because they often have special planning concerns. If parents do not have a lawyer, they can call the local bar association, which will provide them with the name of an attorney in their vicinity, but it is preferable to contact a local disabilities group, which may be able to put you in contact with an attorney familiar with estate planning for parents of persons with disabilities. Not all lawyers are familiar with the special needs associated with caring and providing for individuals with disabilities, and it is best to find one who has prepared estates for other parents who have sons or daughters with disabilities.

The cost of an attorney varies according to the attorney's standard fee and the complexities of the estate. The attorney can quote the parents a fee based on an estimation of the work. If the fee quoted is beyond their immediate means, it may be possible to negotiate a lower fee or devise a payment plan with the attorney. Remember, a will goes into effect only on the death of the person who created it. Until death, the creator of the will can freely revoke, alter, or replace it.

ESTABLISHING A WILL: FOUR POSSIBLE APPROACHES

The following is a very brief summary of four options in establishing a will. A more thorough explanation of these options should be discussed with a lawyer who specializes in disability law. Having decided what the parents' son or daughter needs and what they own, the parents can now consider how best to assist him or her. There are four possible ways to do so:

First, parents can *disinherit* their son or daughter with the disability. No state requires parents to leave money to their children, with or without a disability. If the parents' assets are relatively modest and their son's or daughter's needs relatively great, the best advice may be to disinherit their child by name and have him or her rely on federal and state supports after their death. This may be the most prudent decision, particularly if they wish to help their other children.

Second, parents can leave their son or daughter with a disability an *outright gift*. If their child with a disability is not receiving (and is not expected in the future to need) government benefits, this may prove to be a desirable course of action. Their son or daughter, if mentally competent, can hire whatever assistance he or she needs to help with managing the gift. If their child has a mental illness or cognitive disability, an outright gift is rarely a good idea, because he or she may not be able to handle the financial responsibilities.

Third, parents can leave a *morally obligated gift* to another of their children. Morally obligated gifts are not a complete solution, because they may not be legally protected. They can be useful, however, for parents who have a modest amount of money and do not expect a lifetime of care for a son or daughter with a disability. If they merely want their other sons or daughters to use some of the inherited money to assist their sibling with special needs, this may be the best approach for them.

Fourth, parents can establish a *trust* for their son or daughter with a disability. The point of a trust is to keep assets in a form that will be available to their son or daughter but that will not disqualify him or her for government benefits, if he or she might otherwise be eligible for them.

WORKSHEET FOR COSTING OUT EXPENSES OF THE PERSON WITH A DISABILITY

Before contacting a lawyer, parents should do some preliminary estimates on the expenses and monetary needs that their child may require. As a special educator, you can discuss these estimates with the parents and then have them consult with an attorney or financial planner to establish what needs to be done.

INCOME

Government Benefits   _____

Employment   _____

Other   _____

Total Monthly Income   _____

EXPENSES

Housing:

Rental   _____

Utilities   _____

Maintenance   _____

Cleaning items   _____

Laundry costs   _____

Other   _____

Care Assistance:

Live-in   _____

Respite   _____

Custodial   _____

Other   _____

Personal Needs:

Haircuts, beauty shop   _____

Telephone (basic, TT)   _____

Books, magazines, etc.   _____

Allowance   _____

Clothing   _____

Other   _____

Employment:

Transportation   _____

Workshop fees   _____

Attendant   _____

Training   _____

Other   _____

Education:

Transportation   _____

Fees   _____

Books, materials   _____

Other   _____

Special Equipment:

Environment control   _____

Elevator   _____

Repair of equipment   _____

Computer   _____

Audio books   _____

Ramp   _____

Guide dog   _____

Technical instruction   _____

Hearing aids/batteries   _____

Wheelchair   _____

Other   _____

Medical/Dental Care:

Medical/dental visits   _____

Therapy   _____

Nursing services   _____
Meals of attendants   _____
Drugs, medicine, etc.   _____
Transportation   _____
Other   _____

Food:
Meals, snacks—home   _____
Outside of home   _____
Special foods   _____
Other   _____

Social/Recreational:
Sports   _____
Special Olympics   _____
Spectator sports   _____
Vacation   _____
TV/VCR or rental   _____
Camps   _____
Transportation   _____
Other   _____

Automobile/Van:
Payments   _____
Gas/oil/maintenance   _____
Other   _____

Insurance:
Medical/dental   _____
Burial   _____
Automobile/van   _____
Housing/rental   _____
Other   _____

Miscellaneous:
Total Expenses   _____
(Subtract)
Monthly Income
+ Government Benefits   _____
(Equals)
Supplementary Needs   _____

CONCLUSION

This chapter was intended to provide updated and accurate information. It is not intended, however, to render any legal, tax, accounting, or other professional advice or services. Use this chapter as a general guide only. This book contains information that was available only up to the time of printing, and laws do change with some frequency. As a special educator, you should *never* give legal advice. Rather, you should inform parents to discuss their estate planning with a qualified attorney; don't rely solely on the information that you find here or in any other book.

TRANSITION PLANNING TIME LINE

The following is a series of events that needs to be considered during a child's transition process. All items will not be applicable to all students or to all state regulations. The list is provided to serve as an optional planning tool.

AGE RANGE	ACTION
12–15	____ Initial vocational assessment.
	____ Develop and implement strategies to increase responsibilities and independence at home.
	____ Discuss the following curriculum areas at CSE meetings: Academic Social Language/communication Occupational Self-help skills Self-advocacy skills
14–16	____ Introduce and discuss transition services.
	____ Notify parents that transition services will be incorporated into the IEP beginning at age 15.
	____ Assure that copies of work-related documents are available: Social Security card Birth certificate Obtain working papers (if appropriate)
	____ Obtain parental consent so that the appropriate adult agency representative can be involved.
	____ Develop transition component of IEP and annually thereafter.
	____ Complete periodic vocational evaluations.
15–21	____ Discuss adult transition with CSE.
	____ Consider summer employment/volunteer experience.
	____ Explore community leisure activities.
	____ Consider the need for residential opportunities, including completing applications, as appropriate.
	____ Complete periodic vocational evaluations.

AGE RANGE	ACTION
16–21	____ Obtain personal ID card.
	____ Obtain driver's training and license.

	____ Develop transportation/mobility strategies such as:
	    Independent travel skills training
	    Public or paratransit transportation
	    Needs for travel attendant

	____ Investigate SSDI/SSI/Medicaid programs.
	____ Consider guardianship or emancipation.
	____ Develop and update employment plans.
	____ Involve state vocational rehabilitation agencies, as appropriate within two years of school exit.
	____ Research possible adult living situations.
	____ Investigate postschool opportunities (further educational vocational training, college, military, etc.).
18–21	____ Complete periodic vocational evaluations.
	____ Seek legal guardianship.
	____ Apply for postschool, college, and other training programs.
	____ Male students register for the draft (no exceptions).
	____ Register to vote.
	____ Review health insurance coverage: inform insurance company of child's disability and investigate rider of continued eligibility.

	____ Complete transition to employment, further education or training, and community living, affirming arrangements are in place for the following:
	  1. Postsecondary/continuing education
	  2. Employment
	  3. Legal/advocacy
	  4. Personal independence/residential
	  5. Recreation/leisure
	  6. Medical/health
	  7. Counseling
	  8. Financial/income
	  9. Transportation/independent travel skills
	 10. Other

TRANSITION CHECKLIST

The following is a checklist of transition activities that families may wish to consider when preparing transition plans with the IEP team. The student's skills and interests will determine which items on the checklist are relevant and whether or not these transition issues should be addressed at IEP transition meetings. The checklist can also help identify who should be part of the IEP transition team. Responsibility for carrying out the specific transition activities should be determined at the IEP transition meetings.

FOUR TO FIVE YEARS BEFORE LEAVING THE SCHOOL DISTRICT

- Identify personal learning styles and the necessary accommodations to be a successful learner and worker.
- Identify career interests and skills, complete interest and career inventories, and identify additional education or training requirements.
- Explore options for postsecondary education and admission criteria.
- Identify interests and options for future living arrangements, including supports.
- Learn to help the child communicate effectively his or her interests, preferences, and needs.
- The student should be able to explain his or her disability and the necessary accommodations.
- Learn and practice informed decision-making skills.
- Investigate assistive technology tools that can increase community involvement and employment opportunities.
- Broaden the child's experiences with community activities and help him or her form friendships.
- Pursue and use transportation options.
- Investigate money management and identify necessary skills.
- Acquire identification card and the ability to communicate personal information.
- Identify and begin learning skills necessary for independent living.
- Learn and practice personal health care.

TWO TO THREE YEARS BEFORE LEAVING THE SCHOOL DISTRICT

- Identify community support services and programs (vocational rehabilitation, county services, Centers for Independent Living, etc.).
- Invite adult service providers, peers, and others to the IEP transition meeting.
- Match career interests and skills with vocational course work and community work experiences.
- Gather more information on postsecondary programs and the support services offered, and make arrangements for accommodations to take college entrance exams.
- Identify health care providers and become informed about sexuality and family planning issues.

- Determine the need for financial support (Supplemental Security Income, state financial supplemental programs, Medicare).
- Learn and practice appropriate interpersonal, communication, and social skills for different settings (employment, school, recreation, with peers, etc.).
- Explore legal status with regard to decision making prior to age of majority (e.g., wills, guardianship, special needs trust).
- Begin a résumé and update it as needed.
- Practice independent living skills (e.g., budgeting, shopping, cooking, and housekeeping).
- Identify needed personal assistant services and, if appropriate, learn to direct and manage these services.

ONE YEAR BEFORE LEAVING THE SCHOOL DISTRICT
- Apply for financial support programs (Supplemental Security Income, vocational rehabilitation, and personal assistant services).
- Identify the postsecondary school plan and arrange for accommodations.
- Practice effective communication by developing interview skills, asking for help, and identifying necessary accommodations at postsecondary and work environments.
- Specify desired job and obtain paid employment with supports as needed.
- Take responsibility for arriving on time to work, appointments, and social activities.
- Assume responsibility for health care needs (making appointments, filling and taking prescriptions, etc.).
- Register to vote and, if a male, for selective service.

SAMPLE TRANSITIONAL IEP

DESCRIPTIVE INFORMATION

Date Plan Initiated: _____   Student Name: _____

Age: _____   DOB: _____   Case Coordinator: _____

Social Security #: _____   Disability: _____   Phone: _____

Parent/Guardian name: _____   Father's home phone: _____

Home address: _____   Father's work phone: _____

Grade: _____   Teacher: _____   County of residence: _____

Class location: _____   School phone: _____   Social worker: _____

Vocational education placement: _____   Home school district: _____

Contact person (name and phone):
Contact person (CSE): _____

Additional vocational/technical placements/program: _____
_____
_____

PARTICIPANTS IN TRANSITION PLANNING

Name: _____   Role/agency name: _____

Role/agency: _____

Additional services needed: _____

EMPLOYMENT	**DATE**	**ACTIVITIES ACCOMPLISHED**
Responsibilies		
_____ Competitive employment (no need for services)		
_____ Competitive employment (time-limited support)		
_____ Supported employment (infrequent support)		
_____ Supportive employment (daily support)		
_____ Sheltered workshop		
_____ Day treatment		

EMPLOYMENT	DATE	ACTIVITIES ACCOMPLISHED
_____ Volunteer work		
_____ Summer employment		
_____ Other		
_____ Not applicable		

POSTSECONDARY EDUCATION AND TRAINING

_____ Community college or university
(no support needed)

_____ Community college or university
(support needed)

_____ Technical/trade school
(no support needed)

_____ Technical/trade school
(support needed)

_____ Adult education classes

_____ Other

_____ Not applicable

RESIDENTIAL

_____ Parents or relatives

_____ Intermediate care facility

_____ Community residence

_____ Supervised apartment

_____ Supported apartment

_____ Independent living

_____ Foster care/family care

_____ Respite

_____ Section 8 housing

_____ Other

TRANSPORTATION	DATE	ACTIVITIES COMPLETED

Responsibilities

_____ Independent

_____ Family transportation

_____ Car pool

_____ Public transportation

_____ Specialized transportation

_____ Agency transportation

TRANSPORTATION	DATE	ACTIVITIES COMPLETED

_____ Other

_____ Not applicable

RECREATION/LEISURE

_____ Independent recreation

_____ Family supported recreation

_____ Church groups

_____ Local clubs

_____ Community parks and recreation

_____ Specialized recreation
for individuals with disabilities

_____ Other

_____ Not applicable

PERSONAL/HOME/MONEY MANAGEMENT

_____ Independent (no support needed)

_____ Citizenship skills

_____ Insurance coverage

_____ Money management

_____ Use of community resources

_____ Meal preparation

_____ Housekeeping skills

_____ Self-care

_____ Other

ADVOCACY/LEGAL

_____ Guardianship

_____ Wills/trusts

_____ Self-advocacy

_____ Client Assistance Program (CAP)

_____ Other

MEDICAL	DATE	ACTIVITIES COMPLETED

Responsibilities

_____ Medical care, daily care

_____ Intermediate care

_____ Medical services—general checkups

_____ Specialists, medical supervision

MEDICAL	DATE	ACTIVITIES COMPLETED

_____ Dental care

_____ Use of free clinics

_____ Therapy (OT/PT, Sp./Lan.)

_____ Family insurance

_____ Individual insurance

_____ Medicaid

_____ Visiting nurse/home health

_____ Aide

_____ Medication

_____ Other

SOCIAL/SEXUAL

_____ Individual counseling

_____ Group counseling/support

_____ Family planning services

_____ Other

FINANCIAL/INCOME

_____ Earned wages

_____ Unearned income (family support, gifts)

_____ SSI/SSDI

_____ Food stamps, housing subsidy

_____ Other

COMMUNICATION

_____ Braille

_____ Assistive technology

_____ Computer applications

_____ Interpreter services

_____ Other

GLOSSARY

EDUCATIONAL TERMS

ability grouping   The grouping of children based on their achievement in an area of study.

accelerated learning   An educational process that allows students to progress through the curriculum at an increased pace.

achievement   The level of a child's accomplishment on a test of knowledge or skill.

adaptive behavior   Refers to an individual's social competence and ability to cope with the demands of the environment.

adaptive physical education   A modified program of instruction implemented to meet the needs of special students.

advocate   An individual, either a parent or professional, who attempts to establish or improve services for exceptional children.

age norms   Standards based on the average performance of individuals in different age groups.

agnosia   Refers to the child's inability to recognize objects and their meaning usually resulting from damage to the brain.

amplification device   Any device that increases the volume of sound.

anecdotal record   A procedure for recording and analyzing observations of a child's behavior; an objective, narrative description.

annual goals   Yearly activities or achievements to be completed or attained by the child with disabilities that are documented on the individual educational plan.

aphasia   The inability to acquire meaningful spoken language by age 3 usually resulting from damage or disease to the brain.

articulation   The production of distinct language sounds by the vocal chords.

at risk   Usually refers to infants or children with a high potential for experiencing future medical or learning problems.

attention deficit hyperactive disorder (ADHD)   A psychiatric classification used to describe individuals who exhibit poor attention, distractibility, impulsivity, and hyperactivity.

baseline measure   The level or frequency of behavior prior to the implementation of an instructional procedure that will later be evaluated.

behavior modification   The techniques used to change behavior by applying principles of reinforcement learning.

bilingual   The ability to speak two languages.

career education   Instruction that focuses on the application of skills and content area information necessary to cope with the problems of daily life, independent living, and vocational areas of interest.

categorical resource room   An auxiliary pull-out program that offers supportive services to exceptional children with the same disability.

cognition   The understanding of information.

consultant teacher   A supportive service for children with disabilities in which the services are provided by a specialist in the classroom.

criterion-referenced tests   Tests in which the child is evaluated on his or her own performance to a set of criterion and not in comparison to others.

declassification   The process in which a child with disabilities is no longer considered in need of special education services. This requires a meeting of the CSE and can be requested by the parent, school, or child if over age 18.

deficit   A level of performance that is less than expected for a child.

desensitization   A technique used in reinforcement theory in which there is a weakening of a response, usually an emotional response.

diagnosis   Refers to the specific disorder identified as a result of some evaluation.

distractibility   Refers to difficulty in maintaining attention.

due process   Refers to the legal steps and processes outlined in educational law that protect the rights of children with disabilities.

dyscalculia   A serious learning disability in which the child has an inability to calculate, apply, solve, or identify mathematical functions.

dysfluency   Difficulty in the production of fluent speech as in the example of stuttering.

dysgraphia   A serious learning disability in which the child has an inability or loss of ability to write.

dyslexia   A severe type of learning disability in which a child's ability to read is greatly impaired.

dysorthographia   A serious learning disability that affects a child's ability to spell.

enrichment   Providing a child with extra and more sophisticated learning experiences than those normally presented in the curriculum.

exceptional children   Children whose school performance shows significant discrepancy between ability and achievement and, as a result, requires special instruction, assistance, and/or equipment.

etiology   The cause of a problem.

free and appropriate public education (FAPE)   Used in P.L. 94-142 to mean special education and related services that are provided at public expense and conform to the state requirements and to the individual's IEP.

group homes   A residential living arrangement for adults with disabilities, especially the mentally retarded, along with several supervisors without disabilities.

habilitation   An educational approach used with exceptional children that is directed toward the development of the necessary skills required for successful adulthood.

homebound instruction   A special education service in which teaching is provided by a specially trained instructor to students unable to attend school. A parent or guardian must always be present at the time of instruction. In some cases, the instruction may take place on a neutral sight and not in the home or school.

hyperactivity   Behavior that is characterized by excessive motor activity or restlessness.

impulsivity   Non-goal-oriented activity that is exhibited by individuals who lack careful thought and reflection prior to a behavior.

individualized educational plan   A written educational program that outlines current levels of performance, related services, educational goals, and modifications for a child with disabilities. This plan is developed by a team including the child's parent(s), teacher(s), and supportive staff.

inclusion   Returning children with disabilities to their home school so that they may be educated with children without disabilities in the same classroom.

interdisciplinary team   The collective efforts of individuals from a variety of disciplines in assessing the needs of a child.

intervention   Preventive, remedial, compensatory, or survival services made on behalf of an individual with disabilities.

itinerant teacher   A teacher hired by a school district to help in the education of a child with disabilities. The teacher is employed by an outside agency and may be responsible for several children in several districts.

learning disability   Refers to children with average or above average potential intelligence who are experiencing a severe discrepancy between their ability and their achievement.

least restrictive environment   Applies to the educational setting of exceptional children and the education of children with disabilities with children without disabilities whenever realistic and possible. It is the least restrictive setting in which the child with disabilities can function without difficulty.

mainstreaming   The practice of educating exceptional children in the regular classroom.

mental age   The level of intellectual functioning based on the average for children of the same chronological age. When dealing with children with severe disabilities, the mental age may be more reflective of levels of ability than the chronological age.

mental disability   Refers to a disability in which the individual's intellectual level is measured within the subaverage range and there are marked impairments in social competence.

native language   The primary language used by an individual.

noncategorical resource room   A resource room in regular school that provides services to children with all types of classified disabilities. The children with these disabilities are able to be maintained in a regular school.

norm-referenced tests   Tests used to compare a child's performance to the performance of others on the same measure.

occupational therapist   A professional who programs and/or delivers instructional activities and materials to assist children and adults with disabilities participate in useful daily activities.

paraprofessionals   A trained assistant or parent who works with a classroom teacher in the education process.

physical therapist   A professional trained to assist and help individuals with disabilities maintain and develop muscular and orthopedic capability and to make correct and useful movements.

PINS petition   A PINS petition stands for "person in need of supervision" and is a family court referral. This referral can be made by either the school or the parent and is usually made when a child under age 16 is out of control in terms of attendance, behavior, or some socially inappropriate or destructive pattern.

positive reinforcement   Any stimulus or event that occurs after a behavior has been exhibited that affects the possibility of that behavior occurring in the future.

pupil personnel team   A group of professionals from the same school who meet on a regular basis to discuss children's problems and offer suggestions or a direction for resolution.

pupils with special educational needs (PSEN)   Students defined as having math and reading achievement lower than the 23rd percentile and requiring remediation. These students are not considered disabled but are entitled to assistance to elevate their academic levels.

pupils with handicapping conditions (PHC)   Refers to any child classified as disabled by the Committee on Special Education.

related services   Services provided to children with disabilities to assist in their ability to learn and function in the least restrictive environment. Such services may include in-school counseling, speech and language services, and so on.

remediation   An educational program designed to teach children to overcome some deficit or disability through education and training.

resource room   An auxiliary service provided to children with disabilities for part of the school day. It is intended to service children's special needs so that they can be maintained within the least restrictive educational setting.

screening   The process of examining groups of children in hopes of identifying potentially high-risk children.

Section 504   Refers to Section 504 of the Rehabilitation Act of 1973 in which guarantees are provided for the civil rights of children and adults with disabilities. It also applies to the provision of services for children whose disability is not severe enough to warrant classification but who could benefit from supportive services and classroom modifications.

self-contained class   A special classroom for exceptional children usually located within a regular school building.

sheltered workshops   A transitional or long-term work environment for individuals with disabilities who cannot or who are preparing for work in a regular setting. Within this setting the individual can learn to perform meaningful, productive tasks and receive payment.

surrogate parent   A person other than the child's natural parent who has legal responsibility for the child's care and welfare.

total communication   The approach to the education of deaf students that combines oral speech, sign language, and finger spelling.

token economy   A system of reinforcing various behaviors through the delivery of tokens. These tokens can be in the form of stars, points, candy, chips, and so on.

underachiever   A term generally used in reference to a child's lack of academic achievement in school. However, it is important that the school identify the underlying causes of such underachievement since it may be a symptom of a more serious problem.

vocational rehabilitation   A program designed to help adults with disabilities obtain and hold a job.

PSYCHOLOGICAL TERMS

affective reactions   Psychotic reactions marked by extreme mood swings.

anxiety   A general uneasiness of the mind characterized by irrational fears, panic, tension, and physical symptoms including palpitations, excessive sweating, and increased pulse rate.

assessment   The process of gathering information about children in order to make educational decisions.

baseline data   An objective measure used to compare and evaluate the results obtained during some implementation of an instructional procedure.

compulsion   A persistent, repetitive act that the individual cannot consciously control.

confabulation   The act of replacing memory loss by fantasy or by some reality that is not true for the occasion.

defense mechanisms   The unconscious means by which an individual protects himself or herself against impulses or emotions that are too uncomfortable or threatening. Examples of these mechanisms follow.

>   **denial**   A defense mechanism in which the individual refuses to admit the reality of some unpleasant event, situation, or emotion.
>
>   **displacement**   The disguising of the goal or intention of a motive by substituting another in its place.
>
>   **intellectualization**   A defense mechanism in which the individual exhibits anxious or moody deliberation, usually about abstract matters.
>
>   **projection**   The disguising of a source of conflict by displacing one's own motives onto someone else.
>
>   **rationalization**   The interpretation of one's own behavior so as to conceal the motive it expresses by assigning the behavior to another motive.
>
>   **reaction formation**   A complete disguise of a motive that is expressed in a form that is directly opposite to its original intent.

repression   Refers to the psychological process involved in not permitting memories and motives to enter consciousness but that are operating at an unconscious level.

suppression   The act of consciously inhibiting an impulse, affect, or idea, as in the deliberate act of forgetting something so as not to have to think about it.

delusion   A groundless, irrational belief or thought, usually of grandeur or of persecution. It is usually a characteristic of paranoia.

depersonalization   A nonspecific syndrome in which the individual senses that he or she has lost his or her personal identity, that he or she is different, strange, or not real.

echolalia   Refers to the repetition of what other people say as if echoing them.

etiology   Refers to the cause of something.

hallucination   An imaginary visual image or auditory sensation that is regarded as a real sensory experience by the person.

magical thinking   Refers to primitive and prelogical thinking in which the child creates an outcome to meet his or her fantasy rather than the reality.

neologisms   Made-up words that only have meaning to the child or adult.

obsessions   A repetitive and persistent idea that intrudes into a person's thoughts.

panic attacks   A serious episode of anxiety in which the individual experiences a variety of symptoms including palpitations, dizziness, nausea, chest pains, trembling, fear of dying, and fear of losing control. These symptoms are not the result of any medical cause.

paranoia   A personality disorder in which the individual exhibits extreme suspiciousness of the motives of others.

phobia   An intense irrational fear, usually acquired through conditioning to an unpleasant object or event.

projective tests   Methods used by psychologists and psychiatrists to study personality dynamics through a series of structured or ambiguous stimuli.

psychosis   A serious mental disorder in which the individual has difficulty differentiating between fantasy and reality.

Rorschach test   An unstructured psychological test in which the individual is asked to project responses to a series of 10 inkblots.

school phobia   A form of separation anxiety in which the child's concerns and anxieties are centered around school issues and as a result he or she has an extreme fear about coming to school.

symptom   Refers to any sign, physical or mental, that stands for something else. Symptoms are usually generated from the tension of conflicts. The more serious the problem or conflict, the more frequent and intense the symptom.

syndrome   A group of symptoms.

Thematic Apperception Test   A structured psychological test in which the individual is asked to project his or her feelings onto a series of drawings or photos.

Wechsler Scales of Intelligence   A series of individual intelligence tests measuring global intelligence through a variety of subtests.

MEDICAL TERMS

albinism   A congenital condition marked by severe deficiency in or total lack of pigmentation.

amblyopia   A dimness of sight without any indication of change in the eye's structure.

amniocentesis   A medical procedure done during the early stages of pregnancy for the purpose of identifying certain genetic disorders in the fetus.

anomaly   Some irregularity in development or a deviation from the standard.

anoxia   A lack of oxygen.

aphasia   The inability to acquire meaningful spoken language by age 3 as a result of brain damage.

apraxia   Pertains to problems with voluntary or purposeful muscular movement with no evidence of motor impairment.

astigmatism   A visual defect resulting in blurred vision caused by uneven curvature of the cornea or lens. The condition is usually corrected by lenses.

ataxia   A form of cerebral palsy in which the individual suffers from a loss of muscle co-ordination, especially those movements relating to balance and position.

athetosis   A form of cerebral palsy characterized by involuntary, jerky, purposeless, and repetitive movements of the extremities, head, and tongue.

atrophy   The degeneration of tissue.

audiogram   A graphic representation of the results of a hearing test.

audiologist   A specialist trained in the evaluation and remediation of auditory disorders.

binocular vision   Vision using both eyes working together to perceive a single image.

blind, legally   Visual acuity measured at 20/200 in the better eye with best correction of glasses or contact lenses. Vision measured at 20/200 means the individual must be 20 feet from something to be able to see what the normal eye can see at 200 feet.

cataract   A condition of the eye in which the crystalline lens becomes cloudy or opaque. As a result, a reduction or loss of vision occurs.

catheter   A tube inserted into the body to allow for injections or withdrawal of fluids or to maintain an opening in a passageway.

cerebral palsy   Refers to an abnormal succession of human movement or motor functioning resulting from a defect, insult, or disease of the central nervous system.

conductive hearing loss   A hearing loss resulting from obstructions in the outer or middle ear or some malformations that interfere in the conduction of sound waves to the inner ear. This condition may be corrected medically or surgically.

congenital   A condition present at birth.

cretinism   A congenital condition associated with a thyroid deficiency that can result in stunted physical growth and mental retardation.

cyanosis   A lack of oxygen in the blood characterized by a blue discoloration of the skin.

cystic fibrosis   An inherited disorder affecting pancreas, salivary, mucous, and sweat glands that causes severe, long-term respiratory difficulties.

diplegia   Paralysis that affects either both arms or both legs.

Down syndrome   A medical abnormality caused by a chromosomal anomaly that often results in moderate to severe mental retardation. The child with Down syndrome will exhibit certain physical characteristics such as a large tongue, heart problems, poor muscle tone, and broad, flat bridge of the nose.

electroencephalogram (EEG)   A graphic representation of the electrical output of the brain.

encopresis   A lack of bowel control that may also have psychological causes.

endogenous   Originating from within.

enuresis   A lack of bladder control that may also have psychological causes.

exogenous   Originating from external causes.

fetal alcohol syndrome   A condition usually found in the infants of alcoholic mothers. As a result lowbirth weight, severe retardation, and cardiac, limb, and other physical defects may be present.

field of vision   The area of space visible with both eyes while looking straight ahead; measured in degrees.

glaucoma   An eye disease characterized by excessively high pressure inside the eyeball. If untreated, the condition can result in total blindness.

grand mal seizure   The most serious and severe form of an epileptic seizure in which the individual exhibits violent convulsions, loses consciousness, and becomes rigid.

hemiplegia   Paralysis involving the extremities on the same side of the body.

hemophillia   An inherited deficiency in the blood clotting factor that can result in serious internal bleeding.

hertz   A unit of sound frequency used to measure pitch.

hydrocephalus   A condition present at birth or developing soon afterwards from excess cerebrospinal fluid in the brain and results in an enlargement of the head and mental retardation. This condition is sometimes prevented by the surgical placement of a shunt, which allows for the proper drainage of the built-up fluids.

hyperactivity   Excessive physical and muscular activity characterized by extreme inattention, excessive restlessness, and mobility. The condition is usually associated with attention deficit disorder or learning disabilities.

hyperopia   Farsightedness; a condition causing difficulty with seeing near objects.

hypertonicity   Refers to heightened state of excessive tension.

hypotonicity   Refers to an inability in maintaining muscle tone or an inability in maintaining muscle tension or resistance to stretch.

insulin   A protein hormone produced by the pancreas that regulates carbohydrate metabolism.

iris   The opaque, colored portion of the eye.

juvenile diabetes   A children's disease characterized by an inadequate secretion or use of insulin resulting in excessive sugar in the blood and urine. This condition is usually controlled by diet and/or medication. However in certain cases, control may be difficult and if untreated, serious complications may arise such as visual impairments, limb amputation, coma, and death.

meningitis   An inflammation of the membranes covering the brain and spinal cord. If untreated can result in serious complications.

meningocele   A type of spina bifida in which there is protrusion of the covering of the spinal cord through an opening in the vertebrae.

microcephaly   A disorder involving the cranial cavity characterized by the development of a small head. Retardation usually occurs from the lack of space for brain development.

monoplegia   Paralysis of a single limb.

multiple sclerosis   A progressive deterioration of the protective sheath surrounding the nerves leading to a degeneration and failure of the body's central nervous system.

muscular dystrophy   A group of diseases that eventually weakens and destroys muscle tissue leading to a progressive deterioration of the body.

myopia   Nearsightedness; a condition that results in blurred vision for distant objects.

neonatal   The time usually associated with the period between the onset of labor and six weeks following birth.

neurologically impaired   Individuals who exhibit problems associated with the functioning of the central nervous system.

nystagmus   A rapid, rhythmic, and involuntary movement of the eyes. This condition may result in difficulty reading or fixating upon objects.

ocular mobility   Refers to the eye's ability to move.

opthamologist   A medical doctor trained to deal with diseases and conditions of the eye.

optic nerve   The nerve in the eye that carries impulses to the brain.

optician   A specialist trained to grind lenses according to a prescription.

optometrist   A professional trained to examine eyes for defects and prescribe corrective lenses.

organic   Factors usually associated with the central nervous system that cause a disabling condition.

ossicles   The three small bones of the ear that transmit sound waves to the eardrum. They consist of the malleus, incus, and stapes.

ostenogenesis imperfecta   Also known as "brittle bone disease," this hereditary condition affects the growth of bones and causes them to break easily.

otitis media   Middle ear infection.

otolaryngologist   A medical doctor specializing in diseases of the ear and throat.

otologist   A medical doctor specializing in the diseases of the ear.

otosclerosis   A bony growth in the middle ear that develops around the base of the stapes, impeding its movement and causing hearing loss.

paralysis   Impairment to or a loss of voluntary movement or sensation.

paraplegia   A paralysis usually involving the lower half of the body, including both legs as a result of injury or disease of the spinal cord.

perinatal   Occurring at or immediately following birth.

petit mal seizures   A mild form of epilepsy characterized by dizziness and momentary lapses of consciousness.

phenylketonuria   Referred to as PKU, this inherited metabolic disease usually results in severe retardation. However, if detected at birth, a special diet can reduce the serious complications associated with the condition.

photophobia   An extreme sensitivity of the eyes to light. This condition is common in albino children.

postnatal   Occurring after birth.

prenatal   Occurring before birth.

prosthesis   An artificial device used to replace a missing body part.

psychomotor seizure   Epileptic seizures in which the individual exhibits many automatic seizure activities of which he or she is not aware.

pupil   The opening in the middle of the iris that expands and contracts to let in light.

quadriplegia   Paralysis involving all four limbs.

retina   The back portion of the eye, containing nerve fibers that connect to the optic nerve on which the image is focused.

retinitis pigmentosa   A degenerative eye disease in which the retina gradually atrophies, causing a narrowing of the field of vision.

retrolental fibroplasia   An eye disorder resulting from excessive oxygen in incubators of premature babies.

rheumatic fever   A disease characterized by acute inflammation of the joints, fever, skin rash, nosebleeds, and abdominal pain. This disease often damages the heart by scarring its tissues and valves.

Rh incompatibility   A blood condition in which the fetus has Rh positive blood and the mother has Rh negative blood leading to a buildup of antibodies that attack the fetus. If untreated, it can result in birth defects.

rigidity cerebral palsy   A type of cerebral palsy characterized by minimal muscle elasticity and little or no stretch reflex, which creates stiffness.

rubella   Referred to as German measles, this communicable disease is usually only of concern when developed by women during the early stages of pregnancy. If contracted at that time, there is a high probability of severe disabilities of the offspring.

sclera   The tough, white outer layer of the eyeball, which protects as well as holding contents in place.

scoliosis   A weakness of the muscles that results in a serious abnormal curvature of the spine. This condition may be corrected with surgery or a brace.

semicircular canals   The three canals within the middle ear that are responsible for maintaining balance.

sensorineural hearing loss   A hearing disorder resulting from damage or dysfunction of the cochlea.

shunt   A tube that is inserted into the body to drain fluid from one part to another. This procedure is common in cases of hydrocephalus to remove excessive cerebrospinal fluid from the head and redirect it to the heart or intestines.

spasticity   A type of cerebral palsy characterized by tense, contracted muscles, resulting in muscluar incoordination.

spina bifida occulta   A type of spina bifida characterized by a protrusion of the spinal cord and membranes. This form of the condition does not always cause serious disability.

strabismus   Crossed eyes.

tremor   A type of cerebral palsy characterized by consistent, strong, uncontrolled movements.

triplegia   Paralysis of three of the body's limbs.

Usher's syndrome   An inherited combination of visual and hearing impairments.

visual acuity   Sharpness or clearness of vision.

vitreous humor   The jelly-like fluid that fills most of the interior of the eyeball.

OCCUPATIONAL THERAPY TERMS

abduction   Movement of limb outward away from body.

active movements   Movements a child does without help.

adaptive equipment   Devices used to position or to teach special skills.

associated reactions   Increase of stiffness in spastic arms and legs resulting from effort.

asymmetrical   One side of the body different from the other, unequal or dissimilar.

ataxic   No balance, jerky.

athetoid   Child with uncontrolled and continuously unwanted movements.

atrophy   Wasting of the muscles.

automatic movements   Necessary movements done without thought or effort.

balance   Not falling over, ability to keep a steady position.

bilateral motor   Refers to skill and performance in purposeful movement that requires interaction between both sides of the body in a smooth manner.

circumduction   To swing the limb away from the body to clear the foot.

clonus   Shaky movements of spastic muscle.

compensory movement   A form of movement that is atypical in relation to normal patterns of movement.

congenital   From birth.

contracture   Permanently tight muscle or joint.

coordination   Combination of muscles in movement.

crossing the midline   Refers to skill and performance in crossing the verticle midline of the body.

deformity   Body or limb fixed in abnormal position.

diplegia   Legs mostly affected.

distractible   Not able to concentrate.

equilibrium   Balance

equilibrium reactions   Automatic patterns of body movements that enable restoration and maintenance of balance against gravity.

equinus   Toe walks.

extension   Straightening of the trunk and limbs.

eye–hand coordination   Eye is used as a tool for directing the hand to perform efficiently.

facilitation   Making it possible for the child to move.

figure–ground perception   To be able to see foreground against the background.

fine motor   Small muscle movements, use of hands and fingers.

flexion   Bending of elbows, hips, knees, and so on.

fluctuating tone   Changing from one degree of tension to another (e.g., from low to high tone).

form constancy   Ability to perceive an object as possessing invariant properties such as shape, size, color, and brightness.

gait pattern   Description of walking pattern including:

> **swing to gait**   Walking with crutches or walker by moving crutches forward and swinging body up to crutches.

> **swing thru**   Walking with crutches by moving crutches forward and swinging body in front of the crutches.

genu valgus   Knocked knee.

genu varum   Bowlegged.

gross motor   Coordinated movements of all parts of the body for performance.

guarded supervision   When an individual is close to the student to provide physical support if balance is lost while sitting, standing, or walking.

guarding techniques   Techniques used to help students maintain balance including: contact guarding when a student requires hands-on contact to maintain balance.

head control   Ability to control the position of the head.

hemiplegia   One side of the body affected.

hypertonicity   Increased muscle tone.

hypotonicity   Decreased muscle tone.

inhibition   Positions and movements that stop muscle tightness.

involuntary movements   Unintended movements.

kyphosis   Increased rounding of the upper back.

lordosis   Swayback or increased curve in the back.

manual muscle test   Test of isolated muscle strength:
- normal—100%
- good—80%
- fair—50%
- poor—20%
- zero—0

mobility   Movement of a body muscle or body part or movement of the whole body from one place to another.

motivation   Making the student want to move or perform.

motor patterns   Ways in which the body and limbs work together to make movement, also known as praxis.

nystagmus   Series of automatic back-and-forth eye movements.

organization   A student's ability to organize himself or herself in approach to and performance of activities.

orthosis   Brace.

paraplegic   Paralysis of the lower half of the body with involvement of both legs.

passive   Anything that is done to the student without his or her help or cooperation.

pathological   Due to or involving abnormality.

perception　The organization of sensation from useful functioning.

perservation　Unnecessary repetition of speech or movement.

positioning　Ways of placing an individual that will help normalize postural tone and facilitate normal patterns of movement and that may involve the use of adaptive equipment.

position in space　Child's ability to understand the relationship of an object to himself or herself.

postural balance　Refers to skill and performance in developing and maintaining body posture while sitting, standing, or engaging in a activity.

praxis　Ability to think through a new task that requires movement, also known as motor planning.

pronation　Turning of the hand with palm down.

prone　Lying on the stomach.

quadraplegic　Whole body affected.

range of motion　Joint motion.

reflex　Stereotypic posture and movement that occur in relation to specific eliciting stimuli and outside of conscious control.

righting reactions　Ability to put head and body right when positions are abnormal or uncomfortable.

right/left discrimination　Refers to skill and performance in differentiating right from left and vice versa.

rigidity　Very stiff movements and postures.

rotation　Movement of the trunk, the shoulders moving opposite to the hips.

scoliosis　C or S curvature of the spine.

sensation　Feeling.

sensory-motor experience　The feeling of one's own movements.

sequencing　Concerns the ordering of visual patterns in time and space.

spasm　Sudden tightness of muscles.

spasticity　Increased muscle tone.

spatial relations　Ability to perceive the position of two or more objects in relation to oneself and to another.

stair climbing　Methods of climbing include mark stepping (ascending or descending stairs one step at a time) and alternating steps (step over step).

stereognosis　The identification of forms and nature of objects through the sense of touch.

subluxation　A partial dislocation where joint surfaces remain in contact with one another.

supination　Turning of hand with palm up.

symmetrical　Both sides equal.

tactile　Pertaining to the sense of touch of the skin.

tandem walking　Walks in a forward progression placing heel to toe.

tone　Firmness of muscles.

vestibular system　A sensory system that responds to the position of the head in relation to gravity and accelerated and decelerated movements.

visual memory　Ability to recall visual stimuli, in terms of form, detail, position, and other significant features on both a short- and long-term basis.

visual–motor integration　The ability to combine visual input with purposeful voluntary movement of the other body parts involved in the activity.

voluntary movements　Movements done with attention and with concentration.

REFERENCES

Abery, B. (1994). A conceptual framework for enhancing self-determination. In M. Hayden and B. Abery (Eds). *Challenges for a service system in transition: Ensuring quality community experiences for persons with developmental disabilities.* Baltimore: Paul H. Brookes.

Abery, B., Eggebeen, A., Rudrud, E., Arndt, K., & Tetu, L. (1994). *A guide to enhancing the self-determination of transition-age youth with disabilities.* Minneapolis: Institute of Community Integration, University of Minnesota.

Adamec, C. (1996). *How to live with a mentally ill person: A handbook of day-to-day strategies.* New York: John Wiley & Sons.

Adult Foster Care Services (2003). *Adult foster care.* Retrieved on March 30, 2003, www.state.sd.us/dhs/dd/division/adultfc.ht.

Ahern-Preslieu, D., & Lisa Glidden, L. (1994). *A curriculum guide for the development of self-determination and advocacy skills.* Middletown, CT: A. J. Pappanikou Center.

Allen, J. (1994). *Successful job search strategies for the disabled: Understanding the ADA.* New York: John Wiley.

Allen, T. E., Rawlings, B. W., & Schildroth, A. (1989). *Deaf students and the school-to-work transition.* Baltimore: Paul H. Brookes.

Alston, R. J., & McCowan, C. J. (1994, January/February/March). Aptitude assessment in African American clients: The interplay between culture and psychometrics in rehabilitation. *Journal of Rehabilitation, 60*(1), 41–46.

Alston, R. J., & Mngadi, P. S. (1992, July/August/September). A study of the APTICOM's effectiveness in assessing level of physical functioning. *Journal of Rehabilitation, 58*(3), 35–39.

American Psychiatric Association (1994). *Diagnostic and statistical manual of mental disorders (4th ed).* Washington, DC: American Psychiatric Association.

American Vocational Association. (1992). *The AVA guide to the Carl D. Perkins Vocational and Applied Technology Education Act of 1990.* Washington, DC: Author.

Anderson, W., Chitwood, S., & Hayden, D. (1990). *Negotiating the special education maze: A guide for parents and teachers* (2nd ed.). Rockville, MD: Woodbine House.

Arc. (1998). *Introduction to mental retardation* (Rev. ed.). Silver Spring, MD: Author.

ARCH National Resource Center. (1995). *ARCH national directory of crisis nurseries and respite care programs.* Chapel Hill, NC: ARCH National Resource Center.

Arsenault, C. C. (1990). *Let's get together: A handbook in support of building relationships between individuals with developmental disabilities and their community.* Boulder, CO: Development Disabilities Center.

Asen, S. (1994). *Teaching and learning with technology.* Alexandria, VA: Association for Supervision and Curriculum Development.

Asher, D. (1995). *The fool-proof job search workbook.* Berkeley, CA: Ten Speed Press.

Association for Persons in Supported Employment (2003). *APSE Ethical Guidelines For Professionals in Supported Employment.* Retrieved on March 30, 2003, www.apse.org/aboutapse.html.

AT Basics (2003). Introduction to assistive technology. Retrieved on March 30, 2003, http://atto.buffalo.edu/registered/ATBasics.php.

Aune, E., & Ness, J. (1991). *Tools for transition: Preparing students with learning disabilities for postsecondary education.* Circle Pines, MN: AGS.

Ballard, J., Ramirez, B. A., & Weintraub, B. (1987). *Special education in America: Its legal and governmental foundations.* Reston, VA: Council for Exceptional Children.

Baxter, R., & Brashear, M. (1990). *Do-it-yourself career kit: A career planning tool.* Moraga, CA: Bridgewater Press.

Bazelton Center for Mental Health Law. (1997). *SSI–Help for children with disabilities.* Washington, DC: Author.

Beatty, R. H. (1989). *The perfect cover letter.* New York: John Wiley.

Behrmann, M. (1988). *Integrating computers into the curriculum.* Boston: College-Hill Press.

Behrmann, M. (January, 1995). *Assistive technology for students with mild disabilities.* ERIC Digest, E529.

Berhmann, M., Jones, J., & Wilds, M. (1989). Technology interventions for very young children with disabilities. *Infants and Young Children, 1*(4), 66–77.

Berkell, D. E. (1989). Strategies for the vocational assessment of students with severe disabilities. In G. F. Elrod (Ed.), *Career education for special needs individuals: Learning, earning, contributing.* Columbia, SC: Division on Career Development, Council for Exceptional Children.

Berkowitz, S. (1994). *The cleft palate story: A primer for parents of children with cleft lip and palate.* Chicago: Quintessence.

Bigge, J., & Stump, C. (1999). *Curriculum, assessment, and instruction for students with disabilities.* Belmont, CA: Wadsworth.

Bishop, K. D., & Falvey, M. A. (1989). Employment skills. In M. A. Falvey (Ed.), *Community-based curriculum: Instructional strategies for students with severe handicaps* (2nd ed.). Baltimore: Paul H. Brookes.

Bloch, D. P. (1989). *How to write a winning resume.* Lincolnwood, IL: VGM Career Horizons.

Bloch, D. P. (1992). *How to have a winning job interview.* Lincolnwood, IL: VGM Career Horizons.

Bloomfield, W. M. (1989). *Career action plan.* Bloomington, IL: Meridian Education.

Bolles, R. (1996). *What color is your parachute?* Berkeley, CA: Ten Speed Press.

Braddock, D. (1987, September). National study of public spending for mental retardation and developmental disabilities. In *American Journal of Mental Deficiency, 92* (2), 121–133.

Brady, K. A. (1995). *Current efforts to promote the DI and SSI Work Incentives: A working paper.* Washington, DC: National Academy of Social Insurance.

Brett, P. (1993). *Resume writing for results.* Belmont, CA: Wadsworth.

Brinkerhoff, L., Shaw, S., & McQuire, J. (1992). *Promoting postsecondary education for students with learning disabilities.* Austin, TX: Pro-Ed Publishers.

Brolin, D. E. (1986). *Vocational assessment in public schools.* In R. Fry (Ed.), Second national forum on issues in vocational assessment. Menomonie, WI: Materials Development Center, University of Wisconsin-Stout.

Bullis, M., & Gaylord-Ross, R. (1991). *Moving on: Transitions for youth with behavioral disorders.* Reston, VA: Council for Exceptional Children.

Burke, E. (1995). *Improving the implementation of the Individuals with Disabilities Education Act: Making schools work for all of America's children.* Washington, DC: National Council on Disabilities.

Burkhart, L. (1980). *Homemade battery-powered toys and educational devices for severely handicapped children.* College Park, MD: Author.

Calderone, M. S., & Johnson, E. W. (1990). *The family book about sexuality.* New York: HarperCollins.

Calkins, C. F., & Walker, H. M. (1990). *Social competence for workers with developmental disabilities.* Baltimore: Paul H. Brookes.

Carl D. Perkins Vocational Education Act, 20 U.S. C. Sections 2331–2342.

Carney, I., Getzel, E. E., & Uhl, M. (1992). *Developing respite care services in your community: A planning guide.* Richmond, VA: The Respite Resource Project, Virginia Institute for Developmental Disabilities.

CAST (1999). *Overview of the Center for Applied Special Technology.* Retrieved on March 30, 2003, www.cast.org/.

Champagne, M., & Walker-Hirsch, L. (1988). *Circles I: Intimacy and relationships.* Santa Barbara, CA: James Stanfield.

Charlebois-Marois, C. (1985). *Everybody's technology—A sharing of ideas in augmentative communications.* Montreal: Charlescoms.

Clark, G. M., & Kolstoe, O. P. (1990). *Career development and transitional education for adolescents with disabilities.* Boston: Allyn and Bacon.

Cleft Palate Foundation. (1997). *For parents of newborn babies with cleft lip/cleft palate.* Chapel Hill, NC: Author.

Cobb, R. B., & Danahey, A. (1986). Transitional vocational assessment. *The Journal for Vocational Special Needs Education, 8*(2), 3–7, 12.

Code of Federal Regulations (C. F. R.): Title 34; Education; Parts 1 to 499, July 1986. Washington, DC: U.S. Government Printing Office.

Code of Federal Regulations, Title 34; Education, Parts 300–301, July 1993.

Collett-Klingenberg, L., & Chadsey-Rusch, J. (1990). Using a cognitive process approach to teach social skills. In F. R. Rusch (Ed.), *Research in secondary special education and transition employment.* Champaign, IL: Transition Research Institute.

Commission of Certification of Work Adjustment and Vocational Evaluation Specialists. (1987). *Standards and procedures manual for certification in vocational evaluation.* Arlington Heights, IL: Author.

Copenhaver, J. (1995). *Section 504: An educator's primer: What teachers and administrators need to know about implementing accommodations for eligible individuals with disabilities.* Logan, UT: Mountain Plains Regional Resource Center.

Council for Exceptional Children. (1991). *Federal policy on vocational education for exceptional students: Q & A guide to the Carl D. Perkins Act of 1990.* Reston, VA: Author.

Creating Option: A Resource on Financial Aid for Students with Disabilities Heath Publications (2001). Retrieved January 5, 2003, www.heath.gwu.edu/PDFs/financialaid.pdf.

Cunanan, E. S., & Maddy-Bernstein, C. (1995, January). Career guidance and counseling: Recent legislation. *Office of Special Populations' Brief, 6*(3), 1–6.

Cutler, B. C. (1993). *You, your child, and "special" education: A guide to making the system work.* Baltimore: Paul H. Brookes.

Dacey, J. S. (1986). *Adolescents today* (3rd ed.). Glenview, IL: Scott, Foresman & Company.

Davie, A. R., Hartman, R. C., & Rendino, N. (1990). *On campus with a disability: Expanding diversity at AASCU Institutions.* Washington, DC: American Association of State Colleges and Universities.

DeBoskey, D. S. (Ed.). (1996). *Coming home: A discharge manual for families of persons with a brain injury.* Houston, TX: HDI.

DeFur, S. H., & Patton, J. (1999) *Transition and school based services: Interdisciplinary perspectives for enhancing the transition process.* Austin, TX: Pro-Ed.

DePompei, R., & Cluett, B. (1998). *All about me!* Wolfeboro, NH: L&A Publishing/Training.

DePompei, R., Blosser, J., Savage, R., & Lash, M. (1998). *Special education: IEP checklist for a student with a brain injury.* Wolfeboro, NH: L&A.

DeStefano, L., Chadsey-Rusch, J., Phelps, L. A., & Szymanshi, E. (Eds.). *Transition from school to adult life: Models, linkages, and policy* (pp. 387–389). Sycamore, IL: Sycamore Publishing.

Developmental Disabilities Assistance and Bill of Rights Act, 42 U.S. C. Section 6012.

Dick, M. A. (1987). Translating vocational assessment information into transition objectives and instruction. *Career Development for Exceptional Individuals, 10,* 76–84.

Directory of college facilities and services for the disabled (3rd ed.). (1991). Phoenix, AR: Oryx Press.

Directory of facilities and services for the learning disabled (17th ed.). (1998). Novato, CA: Academic Therapy.

Downing, J. E. (1996). *Including students with severe and multiple disabilities in typical classrooms: Practical strategies for teachers.* Baltimore: Paul H. Brookes.

Duran, E. (1992). *Vocational training and employment of the moderately and severely handicapped and autistic adolescent with particular emphasis to bilingual special education.* Springfield, IL: Charles C. Thomas Publishers.

Education for All Handicapped Children Act, Public Law 94-142, 20 U.S. C. Sections 1400–1485.

Eisenson, J. (1997). *Is my child's speech normal?* (2nd ed.). Austin TX: Pro-Ed.

Elksnin, L., & Elksnin, N. (1990). Using collaborative consultation with parents to promote effective vocational programming. *Career Development for Exceptional Individuals, 13*(2), 135–142.

Elrod, F. R. (1987). Transition-related assessment: The foundation of preparation for post-secondary success. *Diagnostique, 12*(3–4), 127–130.

Everson, J. M., & Moon, M. S. (1987). Transition services for young adults with severe disabilities: Defining professional and parental roles and responsibilities. *Journal of the Association for Persons with Severe Handicaps, 12*(2), 87–95.

Falvey, M. A (Ed.). (1989). *Community-based curriculum: Instructional strategies for students with severe handicaps* (2nd ed.). Baltimore: Paul H. Brookes.

Fardig, D. B., Algozzine, R. F., Schwartz, S. E., Hensel, J. W., & Westling, D. L. (1985). Postsecondary vocational adjustment for rural, mildly handicapped students. *Exceptional Children, 52,* 115–121.

Farley, R. C., Bolton, B., & Parkerson, S. (1992, March). Effects of client involvement in assessment on vocational development. *Rehabilitation Counseling Bulletin, 35*(3), 146–153.

Farrar, D. (1991). *Federal policy on vocational education for exceptional students: Q and A guide to the Carl D. Perkins Act of 1990.* Reston, VA: Council for Exceptional Children.

Fee, R. W. (1992). The letter of intent. NICHCY-News Digest #18 (1992) *Estate planning.* Washington DC: National Information Center for Children and Youth with Disabilities.

Fee, R. W. (1992). The special needs trust. NICHCY-News Digest #18 (1992) *Estate planning.* Washington DC: National Information Center for Children and Youth with Disabilities.

Financial aid for students with disabilities. (1989). Washington, DC: HEATH Resource Center.

Finger, A. (1990). *Past due: A story of disability, pregnancy, and birth.* Seattle, WA: Seal Press.

Ford, A., Davern, L., Meyer, L., Schnorr, R., Black, J., & Dempsey, P. (1989). *The Syracuse community-referenced curriculum guide for students with moderate and severe disabilities* (pp. 63–75). Baltimore: Paul H. Brookes.

Frolik, L. (1992). Overview of estate planning issues. In NICHCY-News Digest #18 (1992) *Estate planning.* Washington DC: National Information Center for Children and Youth with Disabilities.

Fullwood, D. (1990). *Chances and choices: Making integration work.* Baltimore: Paul H. Brookes.

Gardner, N. E. S. (1986). Sexuality. In J. A. Summers (Ed.), *The right to grow up: An introduction to adults with developmental disabilities* (pp. 45–66). Baltimore: Paul H. Brookes.

Garee, B. (1996). *A place to live.* Bloomington, IL: Accent Books.

Garee, B. (1996). *An accessible home of your own.* Bloomington, IL: Accent Books.

Gerry, M. (1987). Procedural safeguards insuring that handicapped children receive a free appropriate public education. *News Digest, 7,* 1–8.

Glang, A., Singer, G. H. S., & Todis, B. (1997). *Students with acquired brain injury: The school's response.* Baltimore: Paul H. Brookes.

Goldberg, M., & Dahl, L. (1992). *Choices: A parent's view—Choices: A consumer's view.* Minneapolis: PACER Center.

Goldstein, A. P. (1988). *The prepare curriculum: Teaching prosocial competencies.* Champaign, IL: Research Press.

Goossens, C., & Crain, S. (1987). *Augmentative communication—Assessment resource.* Wauconda, IL: Don Johnston Developmental Equipment.

Griffiths, D. M., Quinsey, V. L., & Hingsburger, D. (1989). *Changing inappropriate sexual behavior.* Baltimore: Paul H. Brookes.

Groce, M. (1996) An introduction to travel training. In NICHCY-Transition Summary #9 (March, 1996). *Travel training for youth with disabilities.* Washington DC: National Information Center for Children and Youth with Disabilities.

Groce, M. (1996). A model of a travel training program In NICHCY-Transition Summary #9 (March, 1996). *Travel training for youth with disabilities.* Washington DC: National Information Center for Children and Youth with Disabilities.

Haffner, D. W. (1990, March). *Sex education 2000: A call to action.* New York: Sex Information and Education Council of the U.S.

Hakim-Elahi, E. (1982). Contraceptive of choice for disabled persons. *New York State Journal of Medicine, 82*(11), 1601–1608.

Hamaguchi, P. M. (1995). *Childhood speech, language, & listening problems: What every parent should know.* New York: John Wiley & Sons.

Harnisch, D. L., & Fisher, A. T. (1989). *Transition literature review: Educational, employment, and independent living outcomes.* Champaign, IL: Secondary Transition Intervention Effectiveness Institute.

Harris, S. (1994). *Siblings of children with autism: A guide for families.* Bethesda, MD: Woodbine House.

Harris, S. L., & Weiss, M. J. (1998). *Right from the start: Behavioral intervention for young children with autism: A guide for parents and professionals.* Bethesda, MD: Woodbine House.

Hart, C. A. (1993). *A parent's guide to autism: Answers to the most common questions.* New York: Pocket Books, Simon & Schuster Co.

Hartman, R. C. (1991). Transition in the United States: What's happening. *HEATH, 10*(3), 1, 4–6.

Hasazi, S. B., Gordon, L. R., & Roe, C. A. (1985). Factors associated with the employment status of handicapped youth exiting high school from 1975 to 1983. *Exceptional Children, 51,* 455–469.

Hatfield, A. B. (1991). *Coping with mental illness in the family: A family guide* (Rev. ed.). Arlington, VA: National Alliance for the Mentally Ill.

Hawkridge, D., Vincent, T., & Hales, G. (1985). What is new information technology? In *New Education Technology in the Education of Disabled Children and Adults* (pp. 41–52). San Diego, CA: College-Hill Press.

Heal, L. W., Haney, J. I., & Amado, A. (1988). *Integration of individuals with developmental disabilities into the community* (2nd ed.). Baltimore: Paul H. Brookes.

Heath (2001). Creating Option: A resource on financial aid for students with disabilities. Retrieved on March 30, 2003, www.heath.gwu.edu/PDFs/financial aid.pdf.

Heiser, H. (2000). 25 questions for finding the right college. Courtesy of *The Schwab Foundation for Learning.* Retrieved on March 30, 2003, www.ldresources.com/articles/finding_college.html.

Hill, J. W., & Ledman, S. M. (1990). *Integrated after-school day care: A solution for respite care needs in your community.* Richmond, VA: Virginia Institute for Developmental Disabilities, Virginia Commonwealth University, Respite Resource Project.

Hingsburger, D. (1990). *I contact: Sexuality and people with developmental disabilities.* Mountville, PA: Vida.

Hutinger, P. (1986). *ACCT curriculum.* Macomb, IL: Western Illinois University.

Ianacone, R. N. (1987). The impact potential of curriculum-based vocational assessment in our schools. In R. R. Fry (Ed.), *The issues papers: Third national forum on issues in vocational assessment.* (pp. 145–151). Menomonie, WI: Materials Development Center, University of Wisconsin-Stout.

IDEA Amendments of 1997, Sec. 602(3)(A))

IDEA P.L. 101-476, 34 C.F.R. 300.18.

Ince, S. (1987). *Genetic counseling.* White Plains, NY: March of Dimes.

Individuals with Disabilities Education Act of 1997, P.L. 105-17.

Individuals with Disabilities Education Act, Public Law 101-476, 20 U.S. C. Chapter 33, 1990.

Interstate Research Associates. (1989, December). *Improving social skills: A guide for teenagers, young adults, and parents.* McLean, VA: Author.

Interstate Research Associates. (1989, October). *Teaching social skills to elementary school-age children: A parent's guide.* McLean, VA: Author.

Izzo, M. V., & Shumate, K. (1991). *Network for effective transitions to work: A transition coordinator's handbook.* Columbus, OH: Center for Education and Training for Employment.

Jacobsen, W. (1993). *The art and science of teaching orientation and mobility to persons with visual impairments.* New York: American Foundation for the Blind.

Jandt, F. (1996). *Using the Internet and the World Wide Web in your job search.* Indianapolis: JIST Works.

Job Training Partnership Act, 29 U.S.C. 1503, Section 4(10).

Joffee, E. (1996). Teaching travel skills to persons who are blind or visually impaired. In NICHCY- Transition Summary #9 (March, 1996). *Travel training for youth with disabilities.* Washington DC: National Information Center for Children and Youth with Disabilities.

Johnson, A. A. (1994). *Shoot for the moon.* Saunderstown, RI: The Saunderstown Press.

Johnson, B. H., McGonigel, M. J., & Kauffmann, R. K. (1991). *Guidelines and recommended practices for the individualized family service plan* (2nd ed.). Bethesda, MD: Association for the Care of Children's Health.

Johnson, L. J., Pugach, M. C., & Devlin, S. (1990). Professional collaboration: TEACHING. *Exceptional Children, 22,* 9–11.

Jordan, D. (1995). *Honorable intentions: A parent's guide to educational planning for children with emotional or behavioral disorders.* Minneapolis: PACER Center.

Jordan, D. (1996). *A guidebook for parents of children with emotional or behavior disorders.* Minneapolis: PACER Center.

Judge, S. L., & Parette, H. P. (1998). *Assistive technology for young children with disabilities: A guide to family-centered services.* Cambridge, MA; Brookline Books.

Karp, N., & Ellis, G. J. (1992). *Time out for families: Epilepsy and respite care.* Landover, MD: Epilepsy Foundation of America.

Kempton, W. (1988). *Sex education for persons with disabilities that hinder learning: A teacher's guide.* Santa Barbara, CA: James Stanfield.

Kerachsky, S., & Thornton, C. (1987). Findings from the STETS transitional employment demonstration. *Exceptional Children, 53*(6), 515–521.

Kiernan, W. E., & Brinkman, L. (1985). Barriers to employment for adults with developmental disabilities. In W. E. Kiernan & J. A. Stark (Eds.), *Employment options for adults with developmental disabilities* (pp. 160–174). Logan: Utah State University Affiliated Facility.

Kimeldorf, M. (1989). *Pathways to work.* Bloomington, IL: Meridian Education Corporation.

Kimeldorf, M. (1990). *Write into a job.* Bloomington, IL: Meridian Education Corporation.

Klein, M. D., Chen, D., & Haney, M. (in press). *PLAI: Promoting learning through active interaction: A guide to early communication with young children who have multiple disabilities.* Baltimore: Paul H. Brookes.

Kniest, B. A., & Garland, C. W. (1991). *Partners: A manual for family-centered respite care.* Lightfoot, VA: Child Development Resources; Richmond, VA: Virginia Institute for Developmental Disabilities, Virginia Commonwealth University, Respite Resource Project.

Knitzer, J., & Olson, L. (1982). *Unclaimed children: The failure of public responsibility to children and adolescents in need of mental health services.* Washington, DC: Children's Defense Fund.

Koplewicz, H. S. (1996). *It's nobody's fault: New hope and help for difficult children.* New York: Random House/Times Books.

Krebs, D. (1990, December). How to get a job and keep your benefits. *TASH Newsletter,* p. 9. Mental Health Law Project. (1991). SSI: New opportunities for children with disabilities. Washington, DC: Author.

Kroll, K., & Klein, E. (1992). *Enabling romance: A guide to love, sex, and relationships for disabled people (and the people who care for them).* New York: Crown.

Lab School of Washington. (1993). *Issues of parenting children with learning disabilities (audiotape series of 12 lectures).* Washington, DC: Author.

Lahm, E., & Elting, S. (1996). Technology: Becoming and informed consumer. In *Assistive Technology.* Washington DC: National Information Center for Children and Youth with Disabilities.

Lakin, K. C., & Bruininks, R. H. (1985.) *Strategies for achieving community integration of developmentally disabled citizens.* Baltimore: Paul H. Brookes.

Lash, M. (1998). *Resource guide: Children and adolescents with brain injuries.* Wolfeboro, NH: L&A Publishing/Training.

Lash, M., Wolcott, G., & Pearson, S. (1995). *Signs and strategies for educating students with brain injuries: A practical guide for teachers and schools.* Houston, TX: HDI.

Lazzari, A., & Wilds, M. (1989). Technology in early childhood special education: Access for rural programs. *Rural Special Education Quarterly, 9*(4), 21–24.

LD Resources. *Choosing a College for Students with Learning Disabilities.* Retrieved January 5, 2003, www.ldresources.com/articles/college_choice.html.

Leach, L. N., & Harmon, A. (1990). *Annotated bibliography on transition from school to work* (vol. 5). Champaign, IL: Transition Research Institute.

Leconte, P. (1986). *Vocational assessment of special needs learners: A vocational education perspective.* Paper presented at the meeting of the American Vocational Association in Atlanta, GA.

Leconte, P., & Neubert, D. A. (1987). Vocational education for special needs students: Linking vocational assessment and support. *Diagnostique, 12,* 156–167.

Lehr, S., & Taylor, S. J. (1987). *Teaching social skills to youngsters with disabilities: A manual for parents.* Boston: Federation for Children with Special Needs and the Center for Human Policy.

Lerner, J. (1997). *Learning disabilities: Theories, diagnosis, and teaching strategies* (7th ed.). Boston: Houghton Mifflin.

Levinson, E. M. (1993). *Transdisciplinary vocational assessment: Issues in school-based programs.* Brandon, VT: Clinical Psychology Publishing Company.

Lieberman, L. (1998). *Recreation and leisure. The National Information Clearinghouse on Children Who Are Deaf-Blind.* Retrieved January 5, 2003, www.tr.wou.edu/dblink/rec-les.htm.

Lillie, D. L., & Place, P. A. (1982). *Partners: A guide to working with schools for parents of children with special instructional needs.* Glenview, IL: Scott Foresman and Company.

Lipkin, M. (1990). *The schoolsearch guide to colleges with program services for students with learning disabilities.* Belmont, MA: Schoolsearch Press.

Livneh, H., & Male, R. (1993, October/November/December). Functional limitations: A review of their characteristics and vocational impact. *Journal of Rehabilitation, 59*(4), 44–50.

Lombard, R. C. (1994, December). Vocational assessment practices: What works. *Office of Special Populations' Brief, 6*(2), 1–6.

Lombard, R. C., Larson, K. A., & Westphal, S. E. (1993). Validation of vocational assessment services for special populations in tech-prep: A model for translating the Perkins assurances into practice. *The Journal for Vocational and Special Needs Education, 16*(1), 14–22.

Luterman, D. M. (1991). *When your child is deaf: A guide for parents.* Parkton, MD: York Press.

Lutfiyya, Z. M. (April, 1991). *Personal relationships and social networks: Facilitating the participation of individuals with disabilities in community life.* Syracuse, NY: The Center on
Human Policy.

Mackenzie, L. (1997). *The complete learning disabilities directory.* Lakeville, CT: GreyHouse.

Mangrum II, C. T., & Strichart, S. S. (1992). *Peterson's guide to colleges with programs for learning disabled students.* Princeton, NJ: Peterson's Guides.

Mannix, D. (1993). *Social skills activities for special children.* West Nyack, NY: The Center for
Applied Research in Education.

March of Dimes Birth Defects Foundation. (n.d.). *Our genetic heritage.* White Plains, NY: Author.

Matson, J. L., & Ollendick, T. H. (1988). *Enhancing children's social skills: Assessment and training.* New York: Pergamon.

Maurice, C., Green, G., & Luce, S. C. (Eds.). (1996). *Behavioral intervention for young children
with autism: A manual for parents and professionals.* Austin, TX: Pro-Ed.

McClannaham, L. E., & Krantz, P. J. (1999). *Activity schedules for children with autism: Teaching independent behavior.* Bethesda, MD: Woodbine House.

McNair, J., & Rusch, F. R. (1991). Parent involvement in transition programs. *Mental Retardation, 29*(2), 93–101.

McWilliams, P. A. (1984). Where did they come from and what do they want? In *Personal
Computers and the Disabled* (pp. 35–40). Garden City, NY: Quantum Press/Doubleday.

Medwid, D. J., & Weston, D. C. (1995). *Kid-friendly parenting with deaf and hard of hearing
children: A treasury of fun activities toward better behavior.* Washington, DC: Gallaudet University Press.

Michaels, C. (Ed.). (1994). *Transition strategies for persons with learning disabilities.* San Diego,
CA: Singular Publishing Co.

Mills v. Board of Education of the District of Columbia, 348 F. Supp. 866 (D.D.C. 1972).

Mithaug, D. E., & Horiuchi, C. N. (1983). *Colorado statewide follow-up survey of special education students.* Denver, CO: Colorado Department of Education.

Mithaug, D. E., Horivchi, C. N., & Fanning, P. N. (1985). A report on the Colorado statewide
follow-up survey of special education students. *Exceptional Children, 51,* 397–404.

Moon, M. S., Inge, K. J., Wehman, P., Brooke, V., & Barcus, J. M. (1990). *Helping persons
with severe mental retardation get and keep employment: Supported employment strategies and
outcomes.* Baltimore: Paul H. Brookes.

Moon, S. (1994). *Making schools and community recreation fun for everyone.* Baltimore: Paul
H. Brookes.

Morris, G. (2000). *Psychology: An introduction.* Englewood Cliffs, NJ: Prentice Hall.

Mount, B., & Zwernik, K. (1988). *It's never too early, it's never too late.* St. Paul, MN: Resources
for Families.

Murphy, J. (1987). Transition: The roles of parents, students, and professionals. *Transition
Summary* (4).

Murphy, M. (1990). *Road map to transition for young adults with severe disabilities.* San Jose, CA:
Santa Clara County Office of Education.

Murray, T., & Küpper, L. (1990). Adult systems. In L. Küpper (Ed.), Options after high
school for youth with disabilities, *NICHCY Transition Summary #7,* 7–10.

Musselwhite, C. (1986). *Adaptive play for special needs children.* San Diego, CA: College-Hill
Press.

Myers, A. (1996) What equal access to transportation means. In NICHCY-Transition Summary #9 (March, 1996). *Travel training for youth with disabilities.* Washington DC: National Information Center for Children and Youth with Disabilities.

Myers, J., & Werner-Scott, E. (1989). *Getting skilled, getting ahead.* Princeton, NJ: Peterson's Guides.

National Center for Education in Maternal and Child Health. (1991, January). *Understanding DNA testing: A basic guide for families.* Washington, DC: Author.

National Center for Youth with Disabilities (1990, February). *Introduction to youth with disabilities: Bibliography for professionals.* Minneapolis: University of Minnesota,

National Council on Disability. (1989). *The education of students with disabilities: Where do we
stand?* Washington, DC: Author.

National Guidelines Task Force. (1991). *Guidelines for comprehensive sexuality education:
Kindergarten–12th grade.* New York: Sex Information and Education Council of the
United States.

National Information Center for Children and Youth with Disabilities (1991, September). Options after high school for youth with disabilities, *NICHCY Transition Summary #7*, 1–28.

National Information Center for Children and Youth with Disabilities (1995). General information about disabilities which qualify children and youth for special education services under the IDEA Act. *News Digest*, Washington, DC.

National League of Cities. (1999). *Community Based Services*. January 5, 2003, www.vadrs.rg/cbs/CILS.htm.

National Resource Center on Supported Living and Choice. (1999). Promoting inclusion in recreation and leisure activities: An information package. Center on Human Policy. Retrieved on January 4, 2003, http://soeweb.syr.edu/thechp/recreation.html.

NCES (2001). *Libraries and Educational Technology*. Retrieved on March 30, 2003, http://nces.ed.gov/.

Neubert, D. (1985). Use of vocational evaluation recommendations in selected public school settings. *Career Development for Exceptional Individuals, 9*, 98–105.

Neubert, D., & Foster, J. (1987). *A community-based exploration guide for learning disabled students making the transition from school to work and post-secondary education, 1–12.* Unpublished manuscript.

NICHCY-News Digest (1991). *Questions and answers about IDEA.* Washington, DC: National Information Center for Children and Youth with Disabilities (NICHCY).

NICHCY-News Digest #12 (June, 1996). *Respite care.* Washington DC: National Information Center for Children and Youth with Disabilities.

NICHCY-News Digest #13 (April, 1996). *Assistive technology.* Washington DC: National Information Center for Children and Youth with Disabilities.

NICHCY-News Digest #15 (October, 1996). *The education of children and youth with special needs: What do the laws say?* Washington DC: National Information Center for Children and Youth with Disabilities.

NICHCY-News Digest #17 (October, 1992). *Sexuality education for children and youth with disabilities.* Washington DC: National Information Center for Children and Youth with Disabilities.

NICHCY-News Digest #18 (1992). *Estate planning.* Washington DC: National Information Center for Children and Youth with Disabilities.

NICHCY-Transition Summary #6 (December, 1990). *Vocational assessment: A guide for parents and professionals.* Washington DC: National Information Center for Children and Youth with Disabilities.

NICHCY-Transition Summary #7 (September, 1994). *Options after high school.* Washington DC: National Information Center for Children and Youth with Disabilities.

NICHCY-Transition Summary #8 (March, 1993). *Transition services in the IEP.* Washington DC: National Information Center for Children and Youth with Disabilities.

NICHCY-Transition Summary #9 (March, 1996). *Travel training for youth with disabilities.* Washington DC: National Information Center for Children and Youth with Disabilities.

Nisbet, J. (1991). *Natural supports in school, at work, and in the community for people with severe disabilities.* Baltimore: Paul H. Brookes.

Norman, A. (1987). *Job path.* New York: Vera Institute of Justice.

Northern New York Post Secondary Transition Team (1998). *Student Advocacy Handbook for High School Juniors and Seniors Transitioning to College.* Retrieved on March 30, 2003, www.vesid. nysed.gov/specialed/transition/sah1.html.

O'Connell, M. (1992). *Getting connected: How to find out about groups and organizations in your neighborhoods.* Evanston, IL: Center for Urban Affairs and Policy Research, Northwestern University.

Office of Special Education and Rehabilitative Services. (1988). *Summary of existing legislation affecting persons with disabilities.* Washington, DC: Clearinghouse on Disability Information.

Ogden, P. W. (1996). *The silent garden: Raising your deaf child* (Rev. ed.). Washington, DC: Gallaudet University Press.

Orelove, F., & Sobsey, D. (1996). *Educating children with multiple disabilities: A transdisciplinary approach* (3rd ed.). Baltimore: Paul H. Brookes.

OSEP (1999). *Twenty-Third Annual Report to Congress on the Implementation of The Individuals with Disabilities Education Act.* Retrieved on March 30, 2003, www.ed.gov/offices/OSERS/OSEP.

OSEP (2003). *What's new at OSEP?* Retrieved on March 30, 2003, http://atto.buffalo.edu/registered/ATBasics/Foundation/intro/introATidea.php.

Osman, B., & Blinder, H. (1992). *No one to play with: The social side of learning disabilities.* Novato, CA: Academic Therapy Publications.

PACER Center (1993). *Begin the between: Planning for the transition from high school to adult life.* Minneapolis: PACER Center.

Parker, R. M., Szymanski, E. M., & Hanley-Maxwell, C. (1989). Ecological assessment in supported employment. *Journal of Applied Rehabilitation Counseling, 20*(3), 26–33.

Pennsylvania Association for Retarded Citizens v. Commonwealth of Pennsylvania, 334 F. Supp. 1257 (E.D. Pa. 1971), Consent Agreement.

Powell, T. H., Pancsofar, E. L., Steer, D. E., Butterworth, J., Itzkowitz, J. S., & Rainforth, B. (1991). *Supported employment: Providing integrated employment opportunities for persons with disabilities.* White Plains, NY: Longman.

Powers, M. D. (Ed.). (2000). *Children with autism: A parent's guide* (2nd ed.). Rockville, MD: Woodbine House.

Public Law 100-146, The Developmental Disabilities and Bill of Rights Act Amendments of 1987.

Public Law 100-407, Technology-Related Assistance for Individuals with Disabilities Act of 1988.

Public Law 101-127, Children with Disabilities Temporary Care Reauthorization Act of 1989.

Public Law 101-336, Americans with Disabilities Act of 1990.

Public Law 101-476, Individuals with Disabilities Education Act (IDEA).

Public Law 101-476, The Education of the Handicapped Act Amendments of 1990.

Public Law 103-230, The Developmental Disabilities Assistance and Bill of Rights Act Amendments of 1994.

Public Law 103-239, School to Work Opportunities Act of 1994.

Public Law 105-17, Individuals with Disabilities Education Act of 1997 (IDEA '97).

Public Law 105-220, The Workforce Investment Act of 1998.

Public Law 93-11, The Rehabilitation Act of 1973.

Public Law 93-380, The Family Education Rights and Privacy Act (FERPA).

Public Law 94-142, The Education of All Handicapped Children Act of 1975.

Public Law 97-300, Job Training Partnership Act.

Public Law 98-524, The Carl Perkins Vocational Education Act of 1984.

Public Law 99-372, The Handicapped Children's Protection Act of 1986.

Public Law 99-401, The Temporary Child Care for Handicapped Children and Crisis Nurseries Act of 1986.

Racino, J. A., Walker, P., O'Conner, S., & Taylor, S. J. (1993). *Housing, support and community: Choices in strategy for adults with disabilities.* Baltimore: Paul H. Brookes.

Rainforth, B., York, J., & Macdonald, C. (1997). *Collaborative teams for students with severe disabilities: Integrating therapy and educational services* (2nd ed.). Baltimore: Paul H. Brookes.

Rehabilitation Act of 1973, 29 U.S. C. Section 103(a).

Rehabilitation Act of 1973, 29 U.S. C. Section 701-794.

Report number GAO 90-125 (1990, September). *Respite care: An overview of federal, selected state, and private programs.* Washington, DC: United States General Accounting Office (US/GAO).

Research Connections (1999). *AT and IDEA.* Retrieved on March 30, 2003, www.cec.sped.org/osep/recon.html.

Rest a Bit. (1988). *Rest a bit: A training program for respite care providers for families of children with emotional problems.* Topeka, KS: Rest a Bit of Family Together, Inc.

Rettig, M. (1987). *Microcomputers in early childhood special education: Trends and issues.* Presented at the National Early Childhood Conference on Children with Special Needs, Denver, CO.

Richards, D. (1986). Sterilization: Can parents decide? *Exceptional Parent, 16*(2), 40–41.

Rodman, H., Lewis, S. H., & Griffiths, S. B. (1984). *The sexual rights of adolescents: Competence, vulnerability, and parental control.* New York: Columbia University Press.

Rothstein, L. F. (1990). *Special education law.* White Plains, NY: Longman.

Rusch, F. R. (Ed.). (1990). *Supported employment: Models, methods, and issues.* Sycamore, IL: Sycamore.

Rusch, F. R., Hughes, C., & Kohler, P. D. (1991). *Descriptive analysis of secondary school education and transition services model programs.* Champaign, IL: Secondary Transition Intervention Effectiveness Institute.

Russell, L. M., Grant, A., Joseph, S., & Fee, R. (1995). *Planning for the future.* Evanston, IL: American Publishing Company.

Sarkees, M. D., & Scott, J. L. (1986). *Vocational special needs* (2nd ed.). Homewood, IL: American Technical Publishers, Inc.

Savage, R. (1995). *An educator's manual: What educators need to know about students with TBI* (3rd ed.). Houston, TX: HDI.

Scarbourgh, D. (1992). *Helping you to understand SSDI and SSI.* Bloomington, IL: Accent Books.

Schirm, A. and Castner, L. (2000). *Reaching those in need: State food stamp participation needs.* Alexandria, VA: Mathematica Policy Research Inc.

Schirm, A., & Castner, L. (2002). *Reaching those in need: State food stamp participation rates in 1999.* Alexandria, VA: Food and Nutrition Service, U.S. Department of Agriculture.

Schiro-Geist, C. (1990). *Vocational counseling for special populations.* Springfield, IL: Charles C. Thomas Publishers.

Schlachter, G. A., & Weber, R. D. (1992). *Financial aid for the disabled and their families: 1992–1994.* Redwood City, CA: Reference Service Press.

Schleien, S. J., & Ray, M. T. (1988). *Community recreation and persons with disabilities: Strategies for integration.* Baltimore: Paul H. Brookes.

Schoenbrodt, L. (Ed.). (2001). *Children with traumatic brain injury: A parents' guide.* Bethesda, MD: Woodbine House.

Schwartz, S. (1996). *Choices in deafness: A parents' guide to communication options* (2nd ed.). Bethesda, MD: Woodbine House.

Senator Alan Cranston: *Senate Report: Cranston-Gonzales National Affordable Housing Act, 1990.* Retrieved January 5, 2003, www.vadrs.org/cbs/CILS.htm

Shapiro, J. (1993). *No pity: People with disabilities forging a new civil rights movement.* New York: Random House.

Silver, L. (1998). *The misunderstood child: Understanding and coping with your child's learning disabilities* (3rd ed.). New York: Time Books.

Simon, R. (1996). Public transportation and the ADA. In NICHCY-Transition Summary #9 (March, 1996). *Travel training for youth with disabilities.* Washington DC: National Information Center for Children and Youth with Disabilities.

Sitlington, P. L., Brolin, D. E., Clark, G. M., & Vacanti, J. M. (1985). Career/vocational assessment in the public school setting: The position of the division on career development. *Career Development for Exceptional Individuals, 8*(1), 3–6.

Skyer, R., & Skyer, G. (1986). *What do you do after high school? A nationwide guide to residential, vocational, social, and collegiate programs service the adolescent, young adult, and adult with learning disabilities.* Rockaway Park, NY: Skyer Consultation Center, Inc.

Small, W. (1996). *College for students with learning disabilities.* Retrieved on March 30, 2003, www.ilresources.com/articles/college_choice.html.

Smith, R. (1993). *Children with mental retardation: A parents' guide.* Rockville, MD: Woodbine House.

Smith, S. (1995). *No easy answers* (Rev. ed.). New York: Bantam Books.

Smith-Davis, J., & Littlejohn, W. R. (1991). Related services for school-aged children with disabilities. *NICHCY News Digest, 1*(2).

Snyder, H. (1998). *Elvin the elephant who forgets.* Wolfeboro, NH: L&A Publishing/Training.

Sowers, J., & Powers, L. (1991). *Vocational preparation and employment of students with physical and multiple disabilities.* Baltimore: Paul H. Brookes.

Stodden, A. R., Ianacone, N. R., Boone, M. R., & Bisconer, W. S. (1987). *Curriculum-based vocational assessment: A guide for addressing youth with special needs.* Honolulu, HI: Centre Publication International Education.

Sugar, M. (Ed.). (1990). *Atypical adolescence and sexuality.* New York: W. W. Norton.

Supported employment expands opportunities for persons with severe disabilities. (1989, Summer). *OSERS News in Print, II*(2), 5.

Supported Employment Parent Training Technical Assistance (SEPT/TA) Project. (1990). *A reference manual for parent training about supported employment* (Rev. ed.). Minneapolis: Pacer Center.

Tharinger, D. J. (1987). Sexual interest. In A. Thomas & J. Grimes (Eds.), *Children's needs: Psychological perspectives.* Washington, DC: National Association of School Psychologists.

The Network News Summer. (1996). *National Transition Network, Institute on Community Integration.* Minneapolis: University of Minnesota.

The Schwab Foundation for Learning. *25 Questions for Finding the Right College.* Retrieved January 5, 2003, www.ldresources.com/articles/finding_college.html.

Trainer, M. (1991). *Differences in common: Straight talk on mental retardation, Down syndrome, and life.* Rockville, MD: Woodbine House.

Transition Services: A Planning and Implementation Guide. (1994). Albany, NY: Office of Special Education Services and Office for Vocational and Educational Services.

Transportation Research Board. (1993). *Accessible transportation and mobility.* Washington, DC: TRB.

Trohanis, P. L. (1995). Progress in providing services to young children with special needs and their families: An overview to and update on implementing the Individuals with Disabilities Education Act. *NEC*TAS Notes, 7,* 1–20.

Tucker, B. P. (1997). *IDEA advocacy for children who are deaf or hard of hearing: A question and answer book for parents and professionals.* San Diego, CA: Singular.

Turnbull, H. R., Turnbull, A. P., Bronicki, G. J., Summers, J. A., & Roeder-Gordon, C. (1990). *Disability and the family: A guide to decisions for adulthood.* Baltimore: Paul H. Brookes.

Tweed, P. K., & Tweed, J. C. (1989). *Colleges that enable: A guide to support services offered to physically disabled students on 40 U.S. campuses.* Park Ave Press.

Twelfth annual report to Congress on the implementation of the Education of the Handicapped Act. Washington, DC: U.S. Government Printing Office.

U.S. Congress, Office of Technology Assessment. (1988). *Power on! New tools for teaching and learning (OTA-SET-379).* Washington, DC: U.S. Government Printing Office.

U.S. Congress, Public Law 99-506, 1986 Amendments to the Rehabilitation Act.

USDA. (2000). *Reaching those in need: State food stamp participation rates in 1999.* Alexandria, VA: Food and Nutrition Service, U.S. Department of Agriculture.

U.S. Department of Education (1993). *The pocket guide to federal help: For individuals with disabilities.* Washington, DC: Clearinghouse on Disability Information, Office of Special Education and Rehabilitative Services.

U.S. Department of Education. (1985). *Directory of resources for adults with disabilities.* Washington, DC: Division of Adult Education, Office of Vocational and Adult Education.

U.S. Dept of Education (2000). *Twenty-second annual report to congress on the implementation of the Individuals with Disabilities Education Act.* Washington, DC: Author.

U.S. Department of Education. Office of Special Education Programs. (2002). *Twenty-third annual report to congress on the implementation of the Individuals with Disabilities Education Act.* Washington, DC: U.S. Government Printing Office.

U.S. Department of Health and Human Services, Social Security Administration. (1990, July). SSI (Social Security Administration Publication Number 05-11000). Baltimore: Author. (Available from Department of Health and Human Services, SSA, Baltimore, MD 21235.)

U.S. Department of Health and Human Services. (1980). *Learning together: A guide for families with genetic disorders* (DHHS Publication No. (HSA) 80-5131). Rockville, MD: Author.

U.S. General Accounting Office. (1989). *Special education: The attorney fees provision of Public Law 99-372.* Washington, DC: Author.

Uslan, M. M., Peck, A. F., Wiener, W. R., & Stern, A. (1990). *Access to mass transit for blind and visually impaired travelers.* New York: American Foundation for the Blind.

Valenti-Hein, D., and Mueser, K. T. (1991). *The dating skills program: Teaching social-sexual skills to adults with mental retardation.* Worthington, OH: International Diagnostic Services, Inc.

Venn, J. (1994). *Assessing students with special needs* (2nd ed.). Upper Saddle River, NJ: Merrill.

Venn, J. (2000). *Assessing students with special needs* (2nd ed.). Upper Saddle River, NJ: Merrill.

Vogel, S. (1993). *College students with learning disabilities: A handbook.* Pittsburgh, PA: LDA Bookstore.

Voorhees, P. (1996). Travel training for persons with cognitive or physical disabilities. In NICHCY-Transition Summary #9 (March, 1996). *Travel training for youth with disabilities.* Washington DC: National Information Center for Children and Youth with Disabilities.

Wagner, M. (1989, March). *The transition experiences of youth with disabilities: A report from the National Longitudinal Transition Study.* Paper presented at the annual meeting of the Council for Exceptional Children, San Francisco, CA.

Walker, P. (1999). *Promoting inclusion in recreation and leisure activities: An information package.* Syracuse, NY: Center on Human Policy, Syracuse University.

Walker, P., Edinger, B., Willis, C., & Kenney, M. (1989). *Beyond the classroom: Involving students with severe disabilities in extracurricular activities.* Syracuse, NY: Center on Human Policy, Syracuse University.

Wandry, D., & Repetto, J. (1993). Transition services in the IEP. *NICHCY Transition Summary, (1),*1 28.

Ward, M. (1991). *Self-determination revisited: Going beyond expectations.* Washington, DC: National Information Center for Handicapped Children and Youth.

Ward, M. J. (1992). Introduction to secondary special education and transition issues. In F. R. Rusch (Ed.), *Research in secondary special education and transition employment.* Champaign, IL: Transition Research Institute.

Wehman, P. (1992). *Life beyond the classroom: Transition strategies for young people with disabilities.* Baltimore: Paul H. Brookes.

Wehman, P., Kregel, J., & Seyfarth, J. (1985). Transition from school to work for individuals with severe handicaps: A follow-up study. *Journal of Association for Persons with Severe Handicaps, 10,* 132–136.

Wehman, P., & Moon, M. S. (1988). *Vocational rehabilitation and supported employment.* Baltimore: Paul H. Brookes.

Wehman, P., Moon, M. S., Everson, J. M., Wood, W., & Barcus, J. M. (1988). *Transition from school to work: New challenges for youth with severe disabilities.* Baltimore: Paul H. Brookes.

Wehmeyer, M. (1992). Self-determination and the education of students with mental retardation. *Education and Training in Mental Retardation, 27,* 302–314.

Weiner, F. (1986). *No apologies.* New York: St. Martin's Press.

West, J. (1996). *Implementing the Americans with Disabilities Act.* Cambridge, MA: Blackwell Publishers.

Whitman, C., & Parnas, S. (1999). *The Siting of Group Homes for the Disabled and Children.* Washington, D.C.: National League of Cities.

Wilds, M. (1988). *The future role of technology/computers in the preschool handicapped classroom.* Paper presented at Council for Exceptional Children Annual Convention, Washington, DC.

Wilen, T. E. (1998). *Straight talk about psychiatric medications for kids.* New York: Guilford.

Wilson, N. O. (1992). *Optimizing special education: How parents can make a difference.* New York: Insight Books.

Woodward, J., & Baxter, J. (1997). The effects of an innovative approach to mathematics on academically low achieving students in inclusive settings. *Exceptional Children, 63*(3), 373–388.

Yate, J. M. (1988). *Resumes that knock'em dead.* Boston: Bob Adams, Inc.